The
Annotated
AA
Handbook
A Companion to the Big Book

Barricade Books Inc.
Fort Lee, New Jersey

Published by Barricade Books Inc.
www.barricadebooks.com

Library of Congress Cataloging-in-Publication Data

D. Frank.
    The annotated AA handbook : a companion to the Big book /by Frank D.
       p.   cm
    Includes the complete first edition text with cross refeerences to the third edition and stories from the second edition.
    ISBN 1-56980-164-9
    1. W., Bill. Alcoholics Anonymous. 2. Alcoholics-Rehabilitation-Handbooks, manuals, etc. I. W., Bill. Alcoholics Anonymous II. Title.
    HV5278.D3 1996
    362.29'286-DC20
                            95-26653
                                CIP

Manufactured in the U.S.A.

24th Printing

The Annotated AA Handbook
A Companion to the Big Book
1996 by Frank D.

Alcoholics Anonymous and A.A. are registered trademarks of
Alcoholics Anonymous World Services, Inc.

Dedication

All glory to God
My love to my wife
My thanks to my sponsor

PREFACE

No one speaks for A.A. as a whole. This volume does not purport to be an official interpretation of the Alcoholics Anonymous program. The purpose of the Applied Alcoholics Anonymous is to assist the reader in the application of the spiritual principles that are the foundation of the Twelve Steps.

The Twelve Steps are guides to a path by which one may awaken spiritually. They consist of a body of theory and technique that must be studied and practiced. Many people read *Alcoholics Anonymous* and do not realize that it is a text book that presents vital information in a way that is designed to help them progress toward a solution to their problem. This volume adds commentary on passages of the original text in order to amplify and clarify the meaning and suggests how this information may be applied to one's life.

It is suggested that the reader disregard entirely any words, ideas, interpretations and commentary that the reader may disagree with or find objectionable. We must not allow anything to stand in the way of our finding our own individual personal spiritual experience

PAGE AND SENTENCE NUMBERING:

I have used the text of *Alcoholics Anonymous* as it appeared in the first printing of the first edition released in April, 1939. Since the first edition is out of print, each sentence in this volume has been numbered so as to correspond with the page numbering of the third edition of the book *Alcoholics Anonymous*. The third edition page numbering was inserted so that this volume can be used in sponsorship and study groups where others are using the third edition.

The first sentence on every page of the Foreword, "The Doctor's Opinion" and the first 164 pages of the basic text has been numbered in the following manner: first appears the page number, followed by a colon, which is then followed by the sentence number. The tenth sentence on page twelve of the third edition would be numbered in this volume as follows:

12:10

Sentences in this volume corresponding to the first sentence on each third edition page have also been numbered as above and are in boldface type.

Subsequent sentences are each numbered but do not reflect the page number. An example follows:

[59:1]Without help it is too much for us. [2]But there is One who has all power—That One is God. [3]May you find Him now!

CROSS REFERENCES:

The cross references included in this volume are a powerful aid to understanding the concepts presented herein. The original authors of *Alcoholics Anonymous* stated the underlying principles of this program in several different ways in the hope that we could understand or relate to one way of presentation if not another. The page and sentence number (of the third edition, where the cross-reference items appear) is followed by a term describing the concepts being linked together. The linking term may or may not be included in the sentence referenced. Following this linking term are references to third edition page and sentence numbers where a concept is presented. This may occur in a similar manner or using different terms, but the underlying concept of each is reinforced or clarified by the other. Touring the book via the cross references is certain to add to a greater understanding of the spiritual principles of the A.A. program. The cross references are also listed in the back of this book prior to the individual accounts of early members of Alcoholics Anonymous. An example of the cross references follows:

xxvii:15
Baffling:
5:12-13, 6:4,
7:11, 23:9-12,
26:9, 34:15,
35:4-5, 37:9

HISTORICAL NOTES:

Historical Notes appear below the original text referenced once again by page and sentence numbers. These notes give the reader a better understanding of people, places, times and circumstances involved in the early days of A.A.

PROFILES:

Profiles of significant personalities are included so that the reader may better understand the lives of some of the contributors to the original text.

TABLES:

Tables included in the chapters relate to significant items of interest in the original text allowing the reader to gain a better understanding of the topic.

DEFINITIONS:

Definitions of words contained in the original text are defined below the text and referenced with third edition page and sentence numbers. Context has been taken into account when choosing a definition for a word.

PERSONAL STORIES:

All personal stories contained in the first edition of *Alcoholics Anonymous* are included in this volume. Second edition personal stories that were not contained in the first edition are also included. I have taken the liberty of correcting the spelling in those stories.

AUTHOR'S NOTES:

Bill W. was the primary author of the book *Alcoholics Anonymous*. As Bill wrote the chapters he would present them to the approximately 100 other members of the fellowship that was soon to become known as Alcoholics Anonymous. These early members contributed to the main body of the text and many also added their personal accounts. Throughout this volume when I refer to "the authors" I am referring to these first 100 members of Alcoholics Anonymous.

In 1939, when *Alcoholics Anonymous* was first printed, the use of "he", "him" and "his" in reference to all people and the Deity was common practice. Our culture was not as gender conscious as today. In this volume, I have tried to be as gender neutral as possible. My hope is that the reader may set aside prejudice of all types and not allow semantics, or the authors choice of words to distract, detract or obscure the underlying message.

SPECIAL FEATURES

CONTENTS

PERSONAL STORIES

CONTENTS

Who are these Alcoholics Anonymous people? What do they have to offer me? What makes them think I'm an alcoholic? Who are they to tell me what to do? What's their angle? What do they want from me? What are their motives? Are they religious fanatics or anti–booze lobbyists? How much do I have to pay them?

These are some of the questions we have when we first decide to look at what A.A. has to offer us. While we feel that perhaps we could use some help to quit drinking, we don't want to seek help from people who will look down on us, tell us what to do or try to force their beliefs on us. We especially don't want to be taken advantage of or charged a fortune.

The Forward is short and straightforward. The authors introduce themselves (xiii:1) and immediately disclose the purpose of the book (xiii:2). One reason why the authors choose to remain anonymous is explained (xiii:7-11). A description of the fellowship is given and the purpose of the fellowship is plainly stated (xiii:12-xiv:4). Readers are invited to contact the authors for help in developing a fellowship (xiv:5–8).

The beauty of the Forward is that it addresses our concerns immediately. The authors explain who they are and inform us of their intentions. The fact that these people are so straightforward is a relief. Perhaps what they're saying is worth a closer look. It's refreshing to encounter people whose motives we feel we can trust.

The Blueprint

Introduction	This book is a collaboration of the first 100 members of the Alcoholics Anonymous fellowship, currently estimated at over two million members. Their expertise on this subject is substantiated by their recoveries.
Definition of Alcoholism	This definition of alcoholism as "a seemingly hopeless state of mind and body" is not too hard to identify with.
Purpose	They tell us clearly at the beginning what this book is all about.
Hope	The authors hope we will be convinced that this description of our problem is correct.
Explanation of Format	They tell us that they are going to present the material in an anecdotal manner. The fellowship is described.
Motives	The author's motives for writing this book are explained.

FOREWORD

xiii:1We, of Alcoholics Anonymous, are more than one hundred men and women who have recovered from a seemingly hopeless state of mind and body. ²To show other alcoholics PRECISELY HOW WE HAVE RECOVERED is the main purpose of this book. ³For them, we hope these pages will prove so convincing that no further authentication will be necessary. ⁴We think this account of our experiences will help everyone to better understand the alcoholic. ⁵Many do not comprehend that the alcoholic is a very sick person. ⁶And besides, we are sure that our way of living has its advantages for all.

⁷It is important that we remain anonymous because we are too few, at present, to handle the overwhelming number of personal appeals which may result from this publication.

Definitions:
xiii:2 Precisely: accurate in every detail. Exact. Not varying in the slightest degree from the truth.

xiii:1
Hopeless:
xxiii:6, xxvii:2, xxix:6,
xxix:16, 6:15, 7:19, 10:3, 14:16, 17:1, 20:3, 26:16, 27:5, 39:3, 42:11, 43:8-9, 44:5, 92:7, 94:12, 113:22

xiii:2
Show:
14:19, 19:4, 49:13, 51:2, 67:2, 68:21, 77:10, 92:3, 95:9, 98:17, 118:10, 152:10

xiii:2
Precisely:
20:4-6, 29:1, 45:4-9, 85:22, 86:3, 143:14

xiii:6
Advantages for All:
130:10, 153:14, 159:17

---

xiii:1 This book is not merely the opinion of one person as it relates the combined experience and knowledge of more than one hundred men and women.

xiii:1 In the very first sentence, the authors identify themselves as alcoholics and define alcoholism as a seemingly hopeless state of mind and body. Using this definition, we can compare their experience to our own. Have we any hope of recovering from the state we are in?

xiii:1 One A.A. joked that they may have called the fellowship Alcoholics Anonymous because we are no longer so conspicuous.

xiii:2 Rather than tell us what it is that we should do, the authors promise to show us how they have recovered.

Perhaps we can adopt their method of recovery. They promise they will be precise. The authors were careful when writing this book to choose the exact words to convey the idea they intended.

xiii:2 The purpose of showing us how the authors recovered is so that we may be helped by their experience. We can trust their motives.

xiii:3 Do we need to prove true what the authors say by trying yet one more time to control our drinking or can we be convinced by comparing ourselves with them?

xiii:6 Even if we are not alcoholic perhaps the authors can suggest a way of living that is more successful than the way we are living now.

FOREWORD xiii:8

xiii:9
Work:
xxiv:14,
14:18-23,
15:1, 15:7-
10, 19:2-6,
75:20, 89:1,
96:4, 102:6,
119:7

xiii:9
Avocation:
19:2-6

xiv:1
Required:
xxvii:3, 12:15,
13:22, 14:19-
20, 25:4,
50:16, 60:16,
72:5, 93:6,
94:15, 98:11,
143:9

xiv:2
Honest:
5:18, 25:13,
28:7, 57:11,
58:9, 70:8,
73:5, 96:1-8,
114:7, 147:3,
159:5, 161:11,
120:5

xiii:8Being mostly business or professional folk we could not well carry on our occupations in such an event. 9We would like it understood that our alcoholic work is an avocation.

10When writing or speaking publicly about alcoholism, we urge each of our Fellowship to omit his personal name, designating himself instead as "A Member of Alcoholics Anonymous."

11Very earnestly we ask the press also, to observe this request, for otherwise we shall be greatly handicapped.

12We are not an organization in the conventional sense of the word. xiv:1There are no fees nor dues whatsoever. 2The only requirement for membership is an honest desire to stop drinking. 3We are not allied with any particular faith, sect or denomination, nor do we oppose anyone. 4We simply wish to be helpful to those who are afflicted.

xiii:8 If established business and professional people can be alcoholic perhaps we could be also.

xiii:10 No one speaks for A.A. as a whole. This prevents well intentioned individuals from inadvertently damaging the reputation of A.A.

xiv:2 Individuals are the only ones who can determine if their desire is honest or not. Though an honest desire is all that is required for membership there are specific things we must do to recover.

xiv:3 The authors are not allied with anyone else so there are no other organizations pulling the strings. They are not reformers or anti-alcohol activists. They will accept us as we are and are not trying to force their beliefs onto us.

xiv:4 They do not want our money. They do not require that we adopt any particular religious or political beliefs. They aren't going to tell us what to do, but only show us what they have done. We can trust their motives. If we want to quit drinking, we can join them.

xiv:5We shall be interested to hear from those who are getting results from this book, particularly from those who have commenced work with other alcoholics. 6We should like to be helpful to such cases.

xiv:4
Wish:
xiii:3, 18:6,
29:5-6, 43:4,
44:2, 71:1,
89:19, 108:2,
153:10,
162:10,
163:1,

7Inquiry by scientific, medical, and religious societies will be welcomed. (The Alcoholic Foundation, Church Street Annex Post Box *658*, New York City.)*

Alcoholics Anonymous.

* A.A's current address is: Alcoholics Anonymous, P.O. Box 459, Grand Central Station, New York, NY 10163, U.S.A.

HISTORICAL NOTE

vii:12-viii:4 The A.A. preamble was adapted from this paragraph by Tom Y., the *Grapevine's* first editor. This first appeared in the June, 1947, *Grapevine*. Questions as to who was to determine what an "honest desire" was led the 1958 General Service Conference to decide to remove the word "honest". Later, the General Service Board, at it's mid-summer meeting, ratified the decision and at that time the words "AA has no dues or fees" was changed to "There are no dues or fees for A.A. Membership." A.A.'s third tradition allows that "the only requirement for A.A. membership is a desire to stop drinking."

THE DOCTOR'S OPINION

What is the cause of my drinking? When I begin drinking I never intend for it to get so out of control. When I sober up I vow that I'll never do it again but the day always comes when I drink again. What is wrong with me? Am I supposed to take the advice of a bunch of drunks? What does the medical community think of their program of recovery?

William Silkworth, M.D., a non-alcoholic, gives us his opinion of the soundness of the program of recovery outlined in this book. He also explains his theory of why alcoholics are unable to control their drinking. The doctor's description of alcoholism shows clearly the dire physical condition of the alcoholic. This illustration begins to explain why the alcoholic is seemingly beyond help.

Dr. Silkworth was the medical director, specializing in the treatment of alcoholics and drug addicts, at the Charles B. Towns Hospital located in New York. What better credentials could a person have to review this program of recovery? Dr. Silkworth's appraisal of A.A.'s program (xxvi:7) shows his great appreciation for it's effectiveness. He recounts instances of alcoholics, whom he doubted could ever recover, being restored to health by the application of the principles set forth in this volume. (xxiii:6-11, xxv:7-11, xxix:3-xxx:3)

Dr. Silkworth's theory is that the craving an alcoholic experiences after consumption of alcohol is the manifestation of an allergy (xxvi:1). This seems to make sense in light of our experience. The doctor's description of the physical symptoms of alcoholism helps us to diagnose ourselves (xxvi:8-xxvii:2, xxvi:15-xxviii:1). The doctor continues to describe the symptoms of alcoholism and the different types of alcoholics (xxviii:3-18). Dr. Silkworth plainly states that the general opinion among physicians is that chronic alcoholics are doomed (xviii:20). The doctor finishes on a hopeful note describing how two early A.A. members, though seemingly hopeless, discovered and applied the solution offered in this book (xxix:1-xxx:3).

Dr. Silkworth's advice is for us to read the book through. His hope is that we will accept the solution offered herein (xxx:4).

The Blueprint

Introduction	We can trust the opinion of a physician with qualifications such as these.
First Letter	The doctor's appraisal of the program suggested in this book lends authority to what the authors have to say.
Summary of the doctor's letters	Alcoholism is a three fold malady that affects us mentally, physically and spiritually.
Second Letter	Alcoholism is diagnosable, it has symptoms that can be recognized. It is progressive, it only gets worse never better. It cannot be cured. There is a solution, the adoption of the principles contained in this book will result in recovery.

THE DOCTOR'S OPINION

^{xxiii:1}We of Alcoholics Anonymous believe that the reader will be interested in the medical estimate of the plan of recovery described in this book. ²Convincing testimony must surely come from medical men who have had experience with the sufferings of our members and have witnessed our return to health. ³A well known doctor, chief physician at a nationally prominent hospital specializing in alcoholic and drug addiction, gave Alcoholics Anonymous this letter:

   ⁴To Whom It May Concern:

   ⁵I have specialized in the treatment of alcoholism for many years.

   ⁶About four years ago I attended a patient who, though he had been a competent business man of good earning capacity, was an alcoholic of a type I had come to regard as hopeless.

   ⁷In the course of his third treatment he acquired certain ideas concerning a possible means of recovery. ⁸As part of his rehabilitation he commenced to present his conceptions to other alcoholics, impressing upon them that they must do likewise with still others. ⁹This has become the basis of a rapidly growing fellowship of these men and their families.

xxiii:1
Plan:
xiii:2, xxix:8,
9:31, 19:13,
20:4-6, 29:1,
42:13, 45:8-
9, 58:1-2,
59:7, 72:6,
73:1, 74:15,
85:12-16,
88:6, 94:2,
96:10, 99:16,
113:4, 117:1,
126:22,
130:10,
147:1, 157:27

xxiii:2
Convincing:
xiii:3, xxx:1,
12:20, 28:6,
30:13, 49:4,
60:14, 60:16,
64:14, 71:1,
83:12

xxiii:6
Hopeless:
xiii:1, xxvii:2,
xxix:6,
xxix:16, 6:15,
7:19, 10:3,
14:16, 17:1,
20:3, 26:16,
27:5, 39:3,
42:10,43:8-9,
44:5, 92:7,
94:12,
113:22,

xxiii:6
Competent:
xiii:8, 26:1

xxiii:10
Recovered:
Title Page,
xiii:1, 17:2-3,
20:3, 29:1,
44:14, 85:14,
90:14, 96:8,
113:6,
132:20,
133:8,
146:12,

xxiv:1
Remedy:
xxix:1, 17:1-
3, 31:1,
39:19,
112:23, 144:6

xxiii:10This man and over one hundred others appear to have recovered.

11I personally know thirty of these cases who were of the type with whom other methods had failed completely. 12These facts appear to be of extreme medical importance; because of the extraordinary possibilities of rapid growth inherent in this group they may mark a new epoch in the annals of alcoholism. xxiv:1These men may well have a remedy for thousands of such situations.

2You may rely absolutely on anything they say about themselves.

3Very truly yours,

(Signed)- - - - -   M.D.

Historical Notes:
xxiii:3 Dr. Silkworth's proper title was Medical Director.
xxiii:6 Bill W. is the patient referred to.

TITLE: An opinion is just that. Our acceptance of the doctor's hypothesis is based on over 60 years of successful treatment founded on this model of alcoholism, coupled with the program of action outlined in this book.

xxiii:2-3 The authors hoped that the opinion of a physician with such appropriate experience would help convince us that their program of recovery will work for us.

xxiii:6 Though this man would be respected, he nevertheless has become a hopeless alcoholic. Alcoholism affects people of every race, creed, nationality, religion, social and economic class, moral standing, ability, intelligence and occupation.

xxiii:6-7 Bill W. was in the treatment center for the third time! There they would dry him out, nurse him back to health, explain to him the grave nature of his malady, suggest that he refrain from further drinking and send him home. After varying lengths of time, he would resume drinking and require further treatment.

xxiii:7-8 Bill gained knowledge of the nature of alcoholism from Dr. Silkworth. He was presented with the solution to his problem by his friend Ebby T. He combined these two components with a practice of carrying this solution to others.

xxiii:11 Have conventional methods, such as; warnings from friends and loved ones, promises and resolutions, treatment centers, counselors and psychiatrists, failed to help us overcome our drinking problem?

xxiv:1 The doctor recognized this program for what it is: the most successful treatment for chronic alcoholics that has ever existed. He saw that carrying this message to those who still suffered would ignite a great fire of recovery bringing this solution to alcoholics everywhere.

xxiv:4The physician who, at our request, gave us this letter, has been kind enough to enlarge upon his views in another statement which follows. 5In this statement he confirms what we who have suffered alcoholic torture must believe—that the body of the alcoholic is quite as abnormal as his mind. 6It did not satisfy us to be told that we could not control our drinking just because we were maladjusted to life, that we were in full flight from reality, or were outright mental defectives. 7These things were true to some extent, in fact, to a considerable extent with some of us. 8But we are sure that our bodies were sickened as well. 9In our belief, any picture of the alcoholic which leaves out this physical factor is incomplete.

10The doctor's theory that we have an allergy to alcohol interests us. 11As laymen, our opinion as to its soundness may, of course, mean little. 12But as ex-alcoholics, we can say that his explanation makes good sense. 13It explains many things for which we cannot otherwise account.

14Though we work out our solution on the spiritual as well as an altruistic plane, we favor hospitalization for the alcoholic

Definitions:
xxiv:10 Allergy: an abnormal reaction, an increased sensitivity.
xxiv:14 Altruistic: an action taken due to an unselfish concern for others.

xxiv:5 This "must" can be taken in two ways. (1) Our bodies are as abnormal as our minds. This is the inescapable conclusion of anyone who has experienced alcoholic addiction and the phenomenon of craving. (2) The authors might also be expressing to us that this conviction is a necessary component of our recovery.

xxiv:5-9 The doctor's theory explains why we are unable to stop drinking once we begin. We stop off after work for one drink and wind up staying till closing. We decide to have one drink to relax and end up drunk. Understanding the physical reason for this is as important as understanding the mental causes. When alcoholics drink, we develop a physical craving for alcohol compelling us to continue drinking.

xxiv:10-13 Reading this chapter helps us to take the first step in recovery from alcoholism. Admitting we are powerless over alcohol is not so difficult when the physical aspect of the illness is so clearly illustrated.

xxiv:15
Offer:
17:12-14,
25:6, 58:9,
92:19, 95:8-
10, 96:3,
97:19

xxv:2
Addiction:
xxvii:1-6,
xxviii:15,
3:24, 5:2-6,
6:7-23, 13:4,
21:3, 22:1,
22:17, 23:18,
24:1, 24:3-6,
32:2, 32:8,
39:12, 40:6,
177:8

xxv:5-6
Psychology:
xxvii:12,
xxix:19,
27:13

who is very jittery or befogged. ^xxiv:15More often than not, it is imperative that a man's brain be cleared before he is approached, as he has then a better chance of understanding and accepting what we have to offer.

^xxv:1The doctor writes:

^2The subject presented in this book seems to me to be of paramount importance to those afflicted with alcoholic addiction.

^3I say this after many years experience as Medical Director of one of the oldest hospitals in the country treating alcoholic and drug addiction.

^4There was, therefore, a sense of real satisfaction when I was asked to contribute a few words on a subject which is covered in such masterly detail in these pages.

^5We doctors have realized for a long time that some form of moral psychology was of urgent importance to alcoholics, but its application presented difficulties beyond our conception.

Historical Notes:
xxv:3 The doctor had been at Town's Hospital for approximately nine years at the time he wrote this letter.

Definitions:
xxiv:15 Imperative: mandatory
xxv:2 Paramount: First and foremost. Primary.

xxiv:14-15 The authors saw the value of medical care during withdrawal from alcohol. Application of the theories and techniques presented in this volume can best begin after we emerge from the fog of our last drunk.

xxiv:15 What this book has to offer is a simple kit of spiritual tools. These tools are offered to us rather than forced upon us.

xxv:2 What could be more important to a practicing alcoholic than the hope of a solution? We deceive ourselves about what the problem with our lives really is. We think our spouse is the problem or our children or the pressures on the job. Though we may have many troubles, the one we must address first is our alcoholism.

xxv:3 This doctor's many years of experience lends weight to his endorsement of this program of recovery.

xxv:5-6 If doctors were able to relieve us of our alcoholism, they would. If we do not respond to medical care, we may be beyond human help. Dr. Silkworth perceived that a complete change in an alcoholic's ideas and attitudes about life is what is needed for recovery. He thus concedes that medical science is not effective at bringing forth this change. The doctor further concedes that this may be beyond the realm of human ability.

xxv:6What with our ultra-modern standards, our scientific approach to everything, we are perhaps not well equipped to apply the powers of good that lie outside our synthetic knowledge.

7About four years ago one of the leading contributors to this book came under our care in this hospital and while here he acquired some ideas which he put into practical application at once.

8Later, he requested the privilege of being allowed to tell his story to other patients here and with some misgiving, we consented. 9The cases we have followed through have been most interesting, in fact, many of them are amazing. 10The unselfishness of these men as we have come to know them, the entire absence of profit motive, and their community spirit, is indeed inspiring to one who has labored long and wearily in this alcoholic field. 11They believe in themselves, and still more in the Power which pulls chronic alcoholics back from the gates of death.

12Of course an alcoholic ought to be freed from his physical craving for liquor, and this often requires a definite hospital procedure, before psychological measures can be of maximum benefit.

Definitions:
xxv:11 Chronic: 1. Habitual. 2. Physical and psychological disorders resulting from repeated and excessive use of alcohol.

xxv:7
Acquired:
xxix:8, xxx:1, 13:3-15:3, 25:8-10, 27:9-12

xxv:7
At once:
46:12, 47:10, 63:17-18, 64:1, 68:23, 84:20, 87:17, 99:8, 100:7

xxv:10
Unselfish:
xxiv:14, 14:23, 20:1, 62:2-3, 67:4, 70:14, 85:16-18, 93:15, 94:6, 97:3, 129:3, 159:12-16

xxv:11
Gates:
27:5, 30:6

xxv:12
Physical:
xxiv:9, xxvii:1, xxviii:1, xxviii:15, 22:17

xxv:12
Hospitalization:
xxiv:14, 13:4, 30:16, 91:5, 142:18, 143:1-7, 159:15, 160:5

xxv:7 Bill W. was under Dr. Silkworth's care at Town's Hospital when Ebby T. showed him this simple program of action. This together with the knowledge of the physical aspects of alcoholism and the practice of carrying the solution to others led to Bill W.'s recovery. Now that we are being presented with the solution are we willing to put the program into practical application at once?

xxv:10 For these exact reasons Alcoholics Anonymous is phenomenally successful at carrying this solution to millions of suffering alcoholics.

xxv:12 Medical science is skilled at drying drunks out. Keeping them dry is the difficulty. Quitting is not our problem, many of us are very good at quitting, having done it many, many times. Our problem is that we can't stay quit.

xxvi:1
Craving:
xxvii:1,
xxvii:15,
xxviii:1,
xxviii:15-18,
22:17

xxvi:2
Solve:
13:21, 15:4,
17:3, 25:6,
42:19, 43:6,
45:9, 52:8,
52:12, 104:6,
116:13,
117:4,
118:14,
143:14

xxvi:3
Frothy:
3:19, 90:17,
105:8

xxvi:4
Message:
17:12-14,
18:10-12,
60:1,
89:3

xxvi:1We believe, and so suggested a few years ago, that the action of alcohol on these chronic alcoholics is a manifestation of an allergy; that the phenomenon of craving is limited to this class and never occurs in the average temperate drinker. 2These allergic types can never safely use alcohol in any form at all; and once having formed the habit and found they cannot break it, once having lost their self-confidence, their reliance upon things human, their problems pile up on them and become astonishingly difficult to solve.

3Frothy emotional appeal seldom suffices. 4The message which can interest and hold these alcoholic people must have depth and weight. 5In nearly all cases, their ideals must be grounded in a power greater than themselves, if they are to re-create their lives.

Definitions:
xxvi:1 Allergy: an abnormal reaction, an increased sensitivity.
xxvi:1 Phenomenon: an observable but unexplainable fact.
xxvi:1 Temperate: moderate in indulgence.

---

xxvi:1 In 1937, Dr. Silkworth published his theory that alcoholism is the manifestation of an allergy. This allergy, which causes the phenomenon of craving, occurs only in alcoholics.

xxvi:2 Once we develop the phenomenon of craving, we can never return to non-alcoholic drinking. Any amount or type of alcohol in any of it's forms or uses, beer, wine, hard liquor, aperitifs, wine in cooking, alcohol in desserts or medications, stands to trigger the overpowering desire for more alcohol.

xxvi:2 Failing repeatedly to stop on our own destroys our self-confidence. Wives, parents, families, doctors, psychiatrists and friends all fail in their attempts to help us break the cycle of addictive drinking. We are left facing the inability of human resources to give us release. Our lives become unmanageable. We are seemingly hopeless.

xxvi:3 Everyone who loves or cares about us begins to plead with us to quit drinking. We may be angered with their meddling and ignore their pleas. We may sincerely want to quit and swear off for a time, but we always return to drinking. The authors have been where we are and offer to show us what they have done to recover. Perhaps we could listen. They propose to show us how to access a Power that will recreate our lives.

xxvi:5 We would not see the need to recreate our lives if we could just modify our behavior and were then able to manage our lives successfully once again. This is why the admission of powerlessness over alcohol—the unmanageability of our lives—is essential to our recovery.

xxvi:6If any feel that as psychiatrists directing a hospital for alcoholics we appear somewhat sentimental, let them stand with us a while on the firing line, see the tragedies, the despairing wives, the little children; let the solving of these problems become a part of their daily work, and even of their sleeping moments, and the most cynical will not wonder that we have accepted and encouraged this movement. 7We feel, after many years of experience, that we have found nothing which has contributed more to the rehabilitation of these men than the altruistic movement now growing up among them.

8Men and women drink essentially because they like the effect produced by alcohol. 9The sensation is so elusive that, while they admit it is injurious, they cannot after a time differentiate the true from the false. 10To them, their alcoholic life seems the only normal one. 11They are restless, irritable and discontented, unless they can again experience the sense of ease and comfort which comes at once by taking a few drinks—drinks which they *see* others taking with impunity.

xxvi:6
Tragedies:
xxix:5, 16:3-6, 18:3-5, 21:6, 23:17, 24:2, 123:15, 132:8

xxiv:6
Insanity:
xxvi:9, 5:7, 5:28, 6:23, 23:3, 27:3, 24:15, 33:10, 37:1-9, 37:11, 38:15, 40:10, 41:23, 42:3, 61:17, 66:12, 92:15, 101:3, 120:11, 154:17, 157:18-19

xxvi:9
True:
5:7, 30:4, 40:12, 92:12, 151:8, 155:13

xxvi:10
Normal:
25:7, 152:5

xxvi:11
Irritable:
36:4

Definitions:
xxvi:7 Altruistic: unselfish concern for others.
xxvi:11 Impunity: without punishment.

---

xxvi:7 Once again the doctor draws upon his years of experience to recommend Alcoholics Anonymous.

xxvi:8-xxvii:2 This description of alcoholism is here to help us take our first step. It describes our behavior so clearly that we can see that our own experience closely parallels that of an alcoholic. The description ends with an illustration of the baffling nature of alcoholism - that we continue to drink even when we truly desire to stop.

xxvi:9-10 After awhile we lose the ability to tell the true from the false. We go insane. Not being able to tell the true from the false is a perfect definition of insanity. Being insane, we are unable to see that our alcoholic life is abnormal to the extreme. Being insane, we believe the false to be true. We believe that we will be able to control our drinking and put our lives in order on our own. If this were the truth, then most of us would have done just that.

xxvi:11 Alcohol was our solution to our feelings of restlessness, irritability and discontent. It was a solution that produced remorse, a solution that caused even more trouble, a solution that failed.

xxvii:1After they have succumbed to the desire again, as so many do, and the phenomenon of craving develops, they pass through the well-known stages of a spree, emerging remorseful, with a firm resolution not to drink again. 2This is repeated over and over, and unless this person can experience an entire psychic change there is very little hope of his recovery.

3On the other hand—and strange as this may seem to those who do not understand—once a psychic change has occurred, the very same person who seemed doomed, who had so many problems he despaired of ever solving them, suddenly finds himself easily able to control his desire for alcohol, the only effort necessary being that required to follow a few simple rules.

4Men have cried out to me in sincere and despairing appeal: "Doctor, I cannot go on like this! 5I have everything to live for! 6I must stop, but I cannot! 7You must help me!"

Definitions:
xxvii:4 Despair: without hope.

---

xxvii:1 How many times have we started out to enjoy a few drinks and ended up drunk? We're insane to believe that "this time we will be able to control it." How many times have we vowed, while hungover, never to drink again?

xxvii:1 This return to drinking is so common among alcoholics that the authors were able to develop a theory as to why a perfectly sober individual, having a thorough understanding of the severe consequences of drinking alcohol, would drink again (34:9-12).

xxvii:1-2 This endless cycle must be broken or we will die. Much more is needed than intentions or vows to quit drinking. We must experience an entire psychic change. A complete change in the way we view the world around us and our place in it is required, if we are to gain victory over alcohol.

xxvii:1-2 Doctor Silkworth's opinion was that alcoholics are unable to drink normally and that if they are incapable of maintaining total abstinence then there is little hope for their recovery. The doctor saw that an entire psychic change was the solution to this problem, but knew of no way to bring such a change about.

xxvii:3 Do we seem doomed? The promise here is that our problem can be removed from us by following a few simple rules. What is this psychic change that will enable us to easily control our desire for alcohol? What are the rules we must follow?

xxvii:4-xxvii:7 When we realize that we can not stop, even though we honestly want to, we turn to the help of physicians, psychiatrists and counselors. If we do not respond to their treatment, we may realize that we are beyond human aid.

xxvii:8Faced with this problem, if a doctor is honest with himself, he must sometimes feel his own inadequacy. 9Although he gives all that is in him, it often is not enough. 10One feels that something more than human power is needed to produce the essential psychic change. 11Though the aggregate of recoveries resulting from psychiatric effort is considerable, we physicians must admit we have made little impression upon the problem as a whole. 12Many types do not respond to the ordinary psychological approach.

13I do not hold with those who believe that alcoholism is entirely a problem of mental control. 14I have had many men who had, for example, worked a period of months on some problem or business deal which was to be settled on a certain date, favorably to them. 15They took a drink a day or so prior to the date, and then the phenomenon of craving at once became paramount to all other interests so that the important appointment was not met. xxviii:1These men were not drinking to escape; they were drinking to overcome a craving beyond their mental control.

2There are many situations which arise out of the phenomenon of craving which cause men to make the supreme sacrifice rather than continue to fight.

xxvii:10
More:
24:15, 25:12,
44:4, 128:12

xxvii:12
Psychological:
xxv:5-6,
xxix:19,
27:13

xxvii:13
Control:
xxviii:1, 1:4,
5:24, 6:3-4,
22:11, 22:17,
24:1-6,
43:14-16

xxvii:13-xxviii:1
Defense:
6-4, 22:17,
24:1-6, 24:7-8, 33:10,
35:2, 37:7,
40:12, 41:21,
42:4, 43:14-16, 92:3-8,
157:19

xxvii:13-xxviii:1
Inappropriate:
2:9, 5:10-13,
21:13

xxvii:14
Baffling:
5:12-13, 6:4,
23:9-12,
26:9, 34:15,
35:4-5, 37:9,
40:8, 58:15,
92:1

Definitions:
xxvii:10 Essential: necessary.
xxvii:11 Aggregate: total amount of.
xxvii:15 Paramount: of primary importance

---

xxvii:13-xxviii:1 How well has mental control worked at keeping us from taking that first drink? How well does it work to control our drinking once we start?

xxvii:15-xxviii:1 When we start drinking, we may fully intend to have just a couple of drinks. Soon we are drunk and our appointments are not met. Our families usually suffer the worst of this, but eventually the problem will start affecting our work and social life.

xxvii:15-xxviii:1 We can try to identify the phenomenon of craving in our own drinking patterns. Alcoholics cannot always control how much they drink. Non-alcoholics can always control the amount of alcohol they drink.

xxviii:2 The hopelessness and self-loathing we feel when we find we can not use self-will to overcome our drinking problem leads many alcoholics to commit suicide.

xxviii:3The classification of alcoholics seems most difficult, and in much detail is outside the scope of this book. [4]There are, of course, the psychopaths who are emotionally unstable. [5]We are all familiar with this type. [6]They are always "going on the wagon for keeps." [7]They are over-remorseful and make many resolutions, but never a decision.

[8]There is the type of man who is unwilling to admit that he cannot take a drink. [9]He plans various ways of drinking. [10]He changes his brand or his environment. [11]There is the type who always believes that after being entirely free from alcohol for a period of time he can take a drink without danger. [12]There is the manic-depressive type, who is, perhaps, the least understood by his friends, and about whom a whole chapter could be written.

[13]Then there are types entirely normal in every respect except in the effect alcohol has upon them. [14]They are often able, intelligent, friendly people.

[15]All these, and many others, have one symptom in common: they cannot start drinking without developing the phenomenon of craving. [16]This phenomenon, as we have suggested, may be the manifestation of an allergy which differentiates these people, and sets them apart as a distinct entity.

[17]It has never been, by any treatment with which we are familiar, permanently eradicated. [18]The only relief we have to suggest is entire abstinence.

Definitions:
xxviii:17 Eradicated: removed completely. Removed at the roots.
xxviii:18 Abstinence: refraining from alcohol.

---

xxviii:3-xxviii:14 Though we may not fit exactly into any specific category we may see that we have some similarities with one or more of Dr. Silkworth's classification of alcoholics.

xxviii:15 How or what we drink is not important. One of the most positive ways of determining if we are alcoholic is if we ever experience the phenomenon of craving after we start to drink.

Doctor Silkworth's Classifications of Alcoholics	
xxviii:4-7	Psychopaths.
xxviii:8-10	Unwilling to admit.
xxviii:11	Believe that after a time they can drink again.
xxviii:12	Manic depressive.
xxviii:13	Entirely normal except when drinking.

xxviii:19This immediately precipitates us into a seething caldron of debate. 20Much has been written pro and con, but among physicians, the general opinion seems to be that most chronic alcoholics are doomed.

xxix:1What is the solution? 2Perhaps I can best answer this by relating an experience of two years ago.

3About one year prior to this experience a man was brought in to be treated for chronic alcoholism. 4He had but partially recovered from a gastric hemorrhage and seemed to be a case of pathological mental deterioration. 5He had lost everything worthwhile in life and was only living, one might say, to drink. 6He frankly admitted and believed that for him there was no hope. 7Following the elimination of alcohol, there was found to be no permanent brain injury. 8He accepted the plan outlined in this book.

xxviii:20
Opinion:
20:3, 26:16-17, 27:3-4, 30:16, 43:7-13

xxviii:20
Doomed:
xiii:1, xxvii:3, 24:15, 27:3-4, 43:7-8, 44:6, 73:23, 92:17

xxix:5
Worth while:
18:3-5, 38:19, 66:8

xxix:8
Accepted:
xxx:1, 12:18-19, 14:4, 42:18, 47:12, 139:4, 60:14, 145:3

Historical Notes:
xxix:3 Henry P. is the man referred to here. Henry authored the chapter "To Employers" and wrote the story "The Unbeliever".

---

xxviii:16 Non-alcoholic drinkers are always able to control how much they drink. We can ask ourselves if we are different from non-alcoholics. Do we have this allergy that results in an overpowering craving for more alcohol once we start to drink?

xxviii:17-18 Have we ever been able to stay abstinent before? If we cannot control our drinking, cannot quit completely, and there is no treatment that will make us like the non-alcoholic drinker, what hope do we have?

xxviii:20 An alcoholic who continues to drink will become chronic. Medical science has no cure and considers us doomed. We cannot drink and live and no human power, ours or our doctors, can enable us to quit. We are seemingly hopeless. Remember this book is authored by more than one hundred men and women who have recovered from this seemingly hopeless state of mind and body.

xxix:1 The good news here is that there is a solution! We are only seemingly hopeless. Where are we to place our hope if all our past experience proves to us that we are beyond human aid? We can gain hope from the experiences of those who have gone before us.

xxix:5 How far down the road to ruin has our alcoholism taken us? Are we at the gates of death? Are we deteriorating physically and mentally? Have we lost everything worthwhile in life yet? Do we see these things approaching?

xxix:6 This man took his first step. The admission to ourselves that we are beaten, that the resources we have at our disposal are not going to save us, that unless we find a solution we will die, is a necessary first step in recovery. This admission is an essential precondition to recovery. This is a vital part of the solution to our problem.

xxix:14
It Works:
xxx:2, 13:9
26:18, 56:21,
88:4, 156:6,
158:16

xxix:14
Years:
xxiii:6, xxx:2,
13:9, 32:12,
158:15-16,
162:1

xxix:16
Diagnosis:
31:10-32:2,
34:3-4,
34:16-35:1

xxix:18
Impulse:
24:3-6,
36:15-19,
41:7-10,
43:14-16

xxix:18
Willpower:
7:10, 11:9,
20:14, 22:11,
24:3-6,32:13,
33:9, 34:2,
34:12, 40:12,
42:4, 45:2-3,
76:18, 85:19-
20, 92:8,
107:19, 140:5

xxix:9One year later he called to see me, and I experienced a very strange sensation. 10I knew the man by name, and partly recognized his features, but there all resemblance ended. 11From a trembling, despairing, nervous wreck, had emerged a man brimming over with self-reliance and contentment. 12I talked with him for some time, but was not able to bring myself to feel that I had known him before. 13To me he was a stranger, and so he left me. 14More than three years have now passed with no return to alcohol.

15When I need a mental uplift, I often think of another case brought in by a physician prominent in New York City. 16The patient had made his own diagnosis, and deciding his situation hopeless, had hidden in a deserted barn determined to die. 17He was rescued by a searching party, and, in desperate condition, brought to me. 18Following his physical rehabilitation, he had a talk with me in which he frankly stated he thought the treatment a waste of effort, unless I could assure him, which no one ever had, that in the future he would have the "will power"' to resist the impulse to drink.

19His alcoholic problem was so complex, and his depression so great, that we felt his only hope would be through what we

Definitions:
xxix:18 Impulse: a sudden incitement to action, a spontaneous inclination.
Historical Notes:
xxix:15 The patient referred to is Fitz M. who authored the story, "Our Southern Friend" P. 226, He is also the man who thought he was an atheist (68:6-69:13).

xxix:16 Once again the first step in recovery is illustrated. We must make our own diagnosis of our condition. Are we alcoholic? Can we cure ourselves?

xxix:16 The authors have no intention of pronouncing us alcoholic. If we are alcoholic, perhaps we can see some similarity with ourselves in the doctor's description of alcoholism.

xxix:18 Why would we continue to believe that willpower was the answer to our drinking problem? Is willpower effective against other physical ailments? Doctor Silkworth

thought that our inability to control our drinking was the result of an allergy, an increased susceptibility to alcohol.

xxix:18 Separating the physical, mental and spiritual aspects of the alcoholic condition helps us to more clearly see what is happening. The impulse to begin drinking is a different issue from the craving that results after beginning to drink. The chapters "There is a Solution" and "More about Alcoholism" explore the impulse to begin drinking in great detail.

then called "moral psychology," and we doubted if even that would have any effect.

xxx:1However, he did become "sold" on the ideas contained in this book. [2]He has not had a drink for more than three years. [3]I see him now and then and he is as fine a specimen of manhood as one could wish to meet.

[4]I earnestly advise every alcoholic to read this book through, and though perhaps he came to scoff, he may remain to pray.

xxlx:19
Psychology:
xxv:5-6,
xxvii:12,
27:13

xxx:1
Sold:
xxix:8, 12:18-
19, 14:4,
42:18, 47:12,
139:4, 60:14,
145:3

xxx:2
Years:
xxiii:6,
xxix:14, 13:9,
32:12,
158:15-16,
162:1

3rd Edition Text Changes:
xxx:2 ". . .more than three years" a great many years

EXPERT OPINION

xxiii:6	Dr. William Silkworth,
xxviii:15-20	Dr. William Silkworth,
27:3-4	Dr. Carl Jung, Switzerland,
43:7-8	Dr. Percy Polick, Bellevue Hospital, New York,
73:23	Reference to medical opinion by Authors.

HISTORICAL NOTES

1784	Dr. Benjamin Rush, a signer of the Declaration of Independence, describes alcoholic addiction as a disease.
1849	Dr. Magnus Huss, Swedish physician, is the first to use the term "alcoholism."
1937	Dr. William Silkworth publishes his theory, "Alcoholism as the Manifestation of an Allergy" in the *Medical Record*.
1951	American Public Health Association describes alcoholism as illness.
1957	American Medical Association declares alcoholism to be a "highly complex illness."

---

xxx:1 If we can't cure ourselves, are we willing to examine the solution presented in these pages? Are we looking for a solution? Where else do we have to turn? Becoming "sold" is one way of expressing that the man made a decision to put this program of action to work in his life.

xxx:1 In this case, like the earlier one, the man admitted his powerlessness over alcohol and made the decision to accept and practice the program of action outlined in this book.

xxx:4 Are we willing to follow the doctor's advice? Are we finished with our attempts to control our drinking? Are we here to criticize and find the dissimilarities, or are we ready to accept this program of recovery with it's proven record of success?

PROFILE OF
WILLIAM DUNCAN SILKWORTH M.D.
1879-1951

We begin to wonder why it is that we cannot control our drinking. We believe ourselves weak willed or morally deficient. Dr. Silkworth saw alcoholism as an illness, a manifestation of an allergy. The doctor's opinion gives us a rational basis from which to begin our examination of the problem of alcoholism. Our own experience validates his view of the physical aspects of alcoholism. When we begin to drink we develop a craving for more alcohol that is beyond our ability to control. Dr. Silkworth treated Bill W. for alcoholism the second, third and fourth times he was admitted to Town's Hospital in New York. Dr. Silkworth explained to Bill the grave nature of his affliction. This information helped Bill to admit his powerlessness over alcohol so that he was open to the solution for alcoholism suggested to him by his high school friend Ebby T.

Following Bill's spiritual awakening, Dr. Silkworth allowed Bill to share his experience with alcoholic patients at Town's Hospital. Bill was having no success in passing on his life saving experience when the doctor suggested that he, "Stop preaching at them and give them the hard medical facts first." Bill followed this advice when he had his first meeting with Dr. Bob. Bill told Dr. Bob of what he had learned from Dr. Silkworth of the hopelessness of his own alcoholic condition.

Dr. Silkworth, a graduate of Princeton University, obtained his medical degree from New York University-Bellevue Medical School, he specialized in neurology. He treated 40,000 alcoholics during his career spending his last years at Knickerbocker Hospital in New York working with his nurse Teddy.

Dr. Esther Richards of Johns Hopkins Hospital in Baltimore suggested to Bill W. that an introduction by a specialist in the field of alcoholism would be a benefit to the book. Nine days later Dr. Silkworth wrote the first letter of endorsement for this program of recovery that appears in this book.

Just three months after the book *Alcoholics Anonymous* was printed Dr. Silkworth published the first medical paper on A.A.: "A New Approach to Psychotherapy In Chronic Alcoholism" in *Journal-Lancet* in July of 1939.

Dr. Silkworth lent A.A. money to get started and spoke in favor of the fledgling society at meetings with potential financial backers. Dr. Silkworth was a great friend to A.A. throughout the remainder of his life.

Chapter One

BILL'S STORY

What does the story of a man in the 1930's have to do with me? I'm nothing like this fellow and his situation is different than mine. How will reading about Bill's experiences help me?

Bill's Story illustrates the progression of alcoholism in a person's life. Bill's story is actually our story, to see this all we have to do is take a closer look. Initially we have fun and are exhilarated when we drink,(1:3, 3:12-16) however, it begins to take a progressively more important role in our life (3:17). We adjust our activities to allow for more drinking (3:21-25). Although we can see our drinking is beginning to interfere with our lives we feel that we are still in control (5:7). The trouble our drinking causes gets worse and we start taking actions in an attempt to regain control (5:8), we move from place to place (6:25), promise to ourselves and others that we will quit or cut down (5:19-21), we switch drinks or brands, and try swearing off drinking time and time again with the utmost sincerity (5:15-21, 5:30-6:6). When we repeatedly fail despite our best efforts our hope of recovery is destroyed (7:22-8:11). Bill, in his story, tells us how it was for him, how he found the solution and what his life was like after applying the solution.

Bill's alcoholism progressed much the same as it does for all alcoholics. What happened for Bill is that an old friend approached him with a solution to the drinking problem (9:31). It was hard for Bill to accept the solution at first as his prejudices hindered him (10:18-19). However, he saw that even though his old friend had once been just as powerless over alcohol as himself, he had obviously recovered (11:8-12:2). His friend suggested a new way of looking at the spiritual solution that answered all Bill's objections. His friend suggested, "Why don't you choose your own conception of God?" (12:10) Bill became willing to believe that a Power greater than himself could restore him to sanity (12:20-21). The application of the principles presented in this book produced in Bill a spiritual awakening (13:5-14:8). He next describes how he began to carry this solution to other alcoholics (14:19-20). Bill ends his story with a message of hope for all of us suffering from alcoholism—there is a solution. ,

All of the personal stories in this book are an attempt to help us identify with the authors. Hopefully, after reading Bill's Story we can say to ourselves "I'm very much like Bill. My alcohol use has followed a similar pattern. I have also tried many ways to control my drinking with similar results. Perhaps the program of action that Bill followed will work for me also."

The Blueprint

Beginnings	Like us, Bill's family admonitions and the warnings he received were ignored. Like us, Bill believed that good intentions and high potential were enough to ensure a happy useful life.
Progression	It works for different people for different lengths of time. In alcoholics it always becomes the focus of our lives and at some point we cross the line into chronic alcoholism.
Attempts at Control	We try everything at our disposal to control our drinking and to manage our lives, all for naught. Slowly or quickly things get worse. We try harder and harder until we fall so low that we are beyond human aid.
Alcoholic Destruction	We are seemingly hopeless. Faced with deteriorating health and mind we are living only to drink and at this rate we won't last long. Astonishingly we still cling to the insane belief that we can control our drinking.
The Solution	When we admit, to our innermost selves, that human resources have failed to solve our problem, we become willing to try this solution that has worked for millions of people.

Chapter One
BILL'S STORY

1:4
Control:
(Mental)
xxvii:13,
xxviii:1, 5:24,
6:3-4, 22:11,
22:17, 24:1-
6, 43:14-16

1:6
Lonely:
154:11
64:14, 71:1,
83:12

1:9
Moved:
10:8, 12:24-
27, 46:6

1:1War fever ran high in the New England town to which we new, young officers from Plattsburg were assigned, and we were flattered when the first citizens took us to their homes, making us feel heroic. 2Here was love, applause, war; moments sublime with intervals hilarious. 3I was part of life at last, and in the midst of the excitement I discovered liquor. 4I forgot the strong warnings and the prejudices of my people concerning drink. 5In time we sailed for "Over There." 6I was very lonely and again turned to alcohol.

7We landed in England. 8I visited Winchester Cathedral. 9Much moved, I wandered outside. 10My attention was caught by a doggerel on an old tombstone:

¹¹"Here lies a Hampshire Grenadier
Who caught his death
Drinking cold small beer.
¹²A good soldier is ne'er forgot
Whether he dieth by musket
    Or by pot."
13Ominous warning—which I failed to heed.

1:13
Obstinacy:
2:19, 39:1,
47:17, 140:5

REPLACE THE FOLLOWING WITH A DRAWING OF THE THETCHER TOMB

Here sleeps in peace a Hampshire Grenadier,
Who caught his death by drinking cold small Beer,
Soldiers be wise from his untimely fall
And when ye're hot drink Strong or none at all.
An honest soldier never is forgot
Whether he die by musket or by Pot.

Tombstone of Thomas Thetcher, 1738-1764

1:4 Forgetting the warnings we receive both from others and from our experience with drinking is a common problem of alcoholics. We suffer from the vanity of thinking we know better than others.

1:6 Turning to alcohol is an unsuccessful method of combating loneliness, although most of us have used this at one time or another. The pain of loneliness is intensified by fear of doing what needs to be done. When lonely, we need to reach out to others and seek companionship or to look for another who might need our company. These are successful methods of dealing with loneliness. Anesthetizing the pain of loneliness with alcohol is a sign of problem drinking.

1:13 The "ominous warning" in this doggerel is that alcohol is every bit as lethal as a bullet. Examples of ominous warnings that some of us have failed to heed may be the death of people we know in alcohol related accidents or the abject misery we observe in the lives of those who are addicted to alcohol. Are we so unique that these things could not possibly happen to us?

1:14Twenty-two, and a veteran of foreign wars, I went home at last. 15I fancied myself a leader, for had not the men of my battery given me a special token of appreciation? 16My talent for leadership, I imagined, would place me at the head of vast enterprises which I would manage with utmost assurance.

2:1I took a night law course, and obtained employment as investigator for a surety company. 2The drive for success was on. 3I'd prove to the world I was important. 4My work took me about Wall Street and little by little I became interested in the market. 5Many people lost money—but some became very rich. 6Why not I? 7I studied economics and business as well as law. 8Potential alcoholic that I was, I nearly failed my law course. 9At one of the finals I was too drunk to think or write. 10Though my drinking was not yet continuous, it disturbed my wife. 11We had long talks when I would still her forebodings by telling her that men of genius conceived their best projects when drunk; that the most majestic constructions of philosophic thought were so derived.

1:15-16 Do we believe that our personal potential and talents place us outside of harm's way? We never set out to be alcoholics. We never planned on our lives becoming so full of misery. What good are potential, talent and good intentions in preventing alcoholism? How well did they work in bringing about a happy useful life for us?

1:16 Big dreams and big plans are a common characteristic of alcoholics. Many of us lack a clear understanding of who and what we really are. We seem to be unable to accurately gauge our capabilities and limitations. Our lack of humility leads us to frustration. Now we find that the development of humility is a remedy to our problems.

2:2-3 Bill shows the unmanageability of our lives. We are unaware of the forces driving us (62:4). We believe that life run on self-will

can be a success (60:16). It does not occur to us that our view of life may be flawed (61:17) or what the results will be of a life run on self-will (37:17 12&12). We are blind to our need for more than human power (45:3). As we find this Power, our reliance on achievement, possessions and position as the basis of our self-worth, will be replaced with a sense of real usefulness and purpose.

2:3 Does what other people think of us make us important or give us greater worth? Our own attempts at making ourselves feel important fail. Our worth as humans comes from God, not our possessions or position. Believing that we have no worth other than our abilities, possessions or position, makes us feel that we must prove to others how important we are. Our judging of the worth of others by these criteria is equally shallow, misguided, hurtful and harmful.

2:12By the time I had completed the course, I knew the law was not for me. 13The inviting maelstrom of Wall Street had me in its grip. 14Business and financial leaders were my heroes. 15Out of this alloy of drink and speculation, I commenced to forge the weapon that one day would turn in its flight like a boomerang and all but cut me to ribbons. 16Living modestly, my wife and I saved $ 1,000. 17It went into certain securities then cheap and rather unpopular. 18I rightly imagined that they would some day have a great rise. 19I failed to persuade my broker friends to send me out looking over factories and managements, but my wife and I decided to go anyway. 20I had developed a theory that most people lost money in stocks through ignorance of markets. 21I discovered many more reasons later on.

22We gave up our positions and off we roared on a motorcycle, the sidecar stuffed with tent, blankets, change of clothes, and three huge volumes of a financial reference service. 3:1Our friends thought a lunacy commission should be appointed. 2Perhaps they were right. 3I had had some success at speculation, so we had a little money, but we once worked on a farm for a month to avoid drawing on our small capital. 4That was the last honest manual labor on my part for many a day. 5We covered the whole eastern United States in a year. 6At the end of it, my reports to Wall Street procured me a position there and the use of a large expense account. 7The exercise of an option brought in more money, leaving us with a profit of several thousand dollars for that year.

2:19
Obstinacy:
1:13, 39:1,
47:17, 140:5

3:4
Honesty:
58:5, 73:5,
145:3,
146:18, 83:16

2:10-11 The people around us may notice our unusual drinking habits before we recognize them ourselves. We rationalize our behavior with all manner of inane excuses.

2:14 Who are the people we try to emulate? Are they television or movie actors, or perhaps sports figures? Have we considered attempting to model our lives after people of good character, people who have devoted their lives to helping others, forsaking fortune and fame, people who make a real contribution to life?

2:19-3:2 Blinded by self-will we ignore the wise counsel of others. Obstinacy is a common trait of alcoholics.

3:3-16 For a time things go well, life works for us, and we experience little difficulty due to our drinking. Alcoholism progresses at different rates for different people, but it follows a general pattern that we can compare to our own experience.

3:19
Scenes:
xxvi:3, 90:17,
105:8

3:24
Jittery:
xxv:2, xxvii:6,
xxviii:15, 5:2-
6, 6:7-23,
13:4, 21:3,
22:1,
22:17,23:18,
24:1, 24:3-6,
32:2, 32:8,
39:12, 40:6,
177:8

[3:8]For the next few years fortune threw money and applause my way. [9]I had arrived. [10]My judgment and ideas were followed by many to the tune of paper millions. [11]The great boom of the late twenties was seething and swelling. [12]Drink was taking an important and exhilarating part in my life. [13]There was loud talk in the jazz places uptown. [14]Everyone spent in thousands and chattered in millions. [15]Scoffers could scoff and be damned. [16]I made a host of fair-weather friends.

[17]My drinking assumed more serious proportions, continuing all day and almost every night. [18]The remonstrances of my friends terminated in a row and I became a lone wolf. [19]There were many unhappy scenes in our sumptuous apartment. [20]There had been no real infidelity, for loyalty to my wife, helped at times by extreme drunkenness, kept me out of those scrapes.

[21]In 1929 I contracted golf fever. [22]We went at once to the country, my wife to applaud while I started out to overtake Waiter Hagen. [23]Liquor caught up with me much faster than I came up behind Waiter. [24]I began to be jittery in the morning.

3:12 Drinking begins to become a central part of an alcoholic's life. We tend to favor activities that facilitate drinking while avoiding those that do not. We may stop associating with those who do not drink as we do. Soon we may wind up drinking alone.

3:12-16 Drinking with others is fun. We thought everyone was drinking as much as we were. The truth is that we were probably putting in more shifts at the bar than others, but we did not miss them as there was always a new group to drink with. We met many people who were fun to drink with and we thought they were our friends. But, when we have trouble where are they? Drinking proves not to be a stable basis for lasting friendship.

3:17-18 Our drinking always gets worse over time, never better. When people protest that we are drinking too much, we look for new friends who will not interfere with our drinking. We eventually wind up with people whom we used to look down upon or feel sorry for and whom we would never have considered associating with in the beginning.

3:19 Our drinking begins to cause serious trouble at home. Our family members react to our drinking. Our judgment is clouded and our behavior erratic. While we are drunk we say and do things we later regret. Our hangovers cause interference with our family life and we are restless and irritable until we can drink again.

3:24 Drinking may begin to affect us physically. We may experience tremors, weight loss, liver damage or nutritional deficits. Some people begin to fail more slowly than others, but drinking will eventually ruin anyone's health who abuses it.

3:25Golf permitted drinking every day and every night. 4:1It was fun to carom around the exclusive course which had inspired such awe in me as a lad. 2I acquired the impeccable coat of tan one sees upon the well-to-do. 3The local banker watched me whirl fat checks in and out of his till with amused skepticism.

4Abruptly in October 1929 hell broke loose on the New York stock exchange. 5After one of those days of inferno, I wobbled from a hotel bar to a brokerage office. 6It was eight o'clock—five hours after the market closed. 7The ticker still clattered. 8I was staring at an inch of the tape which bore the inscription XYZ-32. 9It had been 52 that morning. 10I was finished and so were many friends. 11The papers reported men jumping to death from the towers of High Finance. 12That disgusted me. 13I would not jump. 14I went back to the bar. 15My friends had dropped several million since ten o'clock so what? 16Tomorrow was another day. 17As I drank, the old fierce determination to win came back.

18Next morning I telephoned a friend in Montreal. 19He had plenty of money left and thought 20I had better go to Canada. 21By the following spring we were living in our accustomed style. 22I felt like Napoleon returning from Elba. No St. Helena for me! 23But drinking caught up with me again and my generous friend had to let me go. 24This time we stayed broke.

4:17
Drive:
2:2, 45:3,
61:17, 62:4,

Historical Note:
4:8 XYZ = Penick and Ford, a corn products company.
4:18 Friend = Dick Johnson with Greenshields and Company a brokerage house.

3:21-25 We begin to adjust our activities to those that permit drinking. We lose interest in all other activities. We are impatient with any activity that does not allow drinking and wish it to end so that once again, we can drink.

4:3 How does having large amounts of money work at controlling alcoholism? We think we are successful at life if we have many possessions. Why doesn't having these things fix us or make us happy? Why do we think that satisfaction of our desires will lead to fulfillment in life?

4:23 Has drinking cost us jobs like it did Bill? Some of us have lost many jobs due to our drinking, while others have never lost anything. We ask for help only when we admit we are beaten. Different people recognize that alcohol has them defeated at different stages of the illness. Unfortunately, many of us have been slow to see the truth.

4:28
Home:
18:1-5,
82:14-19,
104:5-150:3

5:2-6
Necessity:
xxv:2,xxvii:6,
xxviii:15,
3:24, 6:7-23,
13:4, 21:3,
22:1,
22:17,23:18,
24:1, 24:3-6,
32:2, 32:8,
39:12, 40:6,
177:8

5:5
Endlessly:
xxvii:2, 6:22,
23:2, 26:8,
34:2, 43:6,
48:7, 151:9

5:7
Thought:
xxvi:9, 30:4,
40:12, 92:12,
151:8, 155:13

5:7
Insanity:
xxiv:6, xxvi:9,
5:28, 6:23,
23:3, 27:3,

5:8
Worse:
30:14

4:25We went to live with my wife's parents. 26I found a job; then lost it as the result of a brawl with a taxi driver. 27Mercifully, no one could guess that I was to have no real employment for five years, or hardly draw a sober breath. 28My wife began to work in a department store, coming home exhausted to find me drunk. 5:1I became an unwelcome hanger-on at brokerage places.

2Liquor ceased to be a luxury; it became a necessity. 3"Bathtub" gin, two bottles a day, and often three, got to be routine. 4Sometimes a small deal would net a few hundred dollars, and I would pay my bills at the bars and delicatessens. 5This went on endlessly, and I began to waken very early in the morning shaking violently. 6A tumbler full of gin followed by half a dozen bottles of beer would be required if I were to eat any breakfast. 7Nevertheless, I still thought I could control the situation, and there were periods of sobriety which renewed my wife's hope.

8Gradually things got worse. 9The house was taken over by the mortgage holder, my mother-in-law died, my wife and father-in-law became ill.

4:25-27 Unable to take care of ourselves, we become dependent upon others. We are able to manage our own lives for shorter and shorter periods of time.

4:27 We are not the only ones harmed by our alcoholism, our loved ones also begin to suffer.

5:2 At some point in our drinking we cross the line into alcoholism. We develop a mental obsession causing us to desire alcohol above all else. When this is present with the phenomenon of craving we are in a seemingly hopeless situation.

5:5 The shakes are a symptom of withdrawal from alcohol. Drinking to stop the shakes merely worsens our condition. The severity

of our withdrawal symptoms progresses along with our alcoholism. Medical supervision is advisable if you are experiencing withdrawal symptoms. Withdrawal from alcohol addiction can be life threatening.

5:7 We think that we will be able to quit when we want to. The truth is that alcohol affects our thinking. We think we are in control even when repeated attempts to moderate or quit drinking have failed. Believing that we are in control in the face of repeated proof that we are not is a sign of insanity.

5:8 Alcoholism is progressive. If we continue drinking, we only get worse. We can never return to the days when drinking was fun and under our control.

⁵⁺¹⁰Then I got a promising business opportunity. ¹¹Stocks were at the low point of 1932, and I had somehow formed a group to buy. ¹²I was to share generously in the profits. ¹³Then I went on a prodigious bender, and that chance vanished.

¹⁴I woke up. ¹⁵This had to be stopped. ¹⁶I saw I could not take so much as one drink. ¹⁷I was through forever. ¹⁸Before then, I had written lots of sweet promises, but my wife happily observed that this time I meant business. ¹⁹And so I did.

²⁰Shortly afterward I came home drunk. ²¹There had been no fight. ²²Where had been my high resolve? ²³I simply didn't know. ²⁴It hadn't even come to mind. ²⁵Someone had pushed a drink my way, and I had taken it. ²⁶Was I crazy? ²⁷ I began to wonder, for such an appalling lack of perspective seemed near being just that.

²⁸Renewing my resolve, I tried again. ²⁹Some time passed, and confidence began to be replaced by cocksureness. ⁶⁺¹I could laugh at the gin mills. ²Now I had what it takes! ³One day I walked into a cafe to telephone. ⁴In no time I was beating on the bar asking myself how it happened. ⁵As the whiskey rose to my head I told myself I would manage better next time, but I might as well get good and drunk then. ⁶And I did.

⁷The remorse, horror and hopelessness of the next morning are unforgettable. ⁸The courage to do battle was not there. ⁹My brain raced uncontrollably and there was a terrible sense of

5:12-13
Baffling:
xxvii:14, 6:4,
23:9-12, 26:9,
34:15, 35:4-5,
37:9, 40:8,
58:15, 92:1

5:14-24
Resolutions:
xxvii:1, xxviii:7,
5:30-6:4, 7:10,
32:11-33:2,
34:8, 38:5,
39:17, 107:11

5:18
Honest:
xiv:2, 25:13,
28:7, 57:11,
58:9, 70:8,
73:5, 96:1-8,
114:7, 147:3,
159:5, 161:11,
120:5

5:21
Fought:
41:20, 66:4,
84:24, 85:4,
103:11-12

6:7
Remorseful:
xxvii:1, xxviii:7,
37:9, 66:3,
86:12, 106:19,
109:18

6:7-23
Addiction:
xxv:2, xxvii:6,
xxviii:15, 3:24,
5:2-6, 13:4,
21:3, 22:1,
22:17, 23:18,
24:1, 24:3-6,
32:2, 32:8,
39:12, 40:6,
177:8

Historical Note:
5:18 Bill penned many promises to stop drinking in his family bible. (See P. 86 'Pass It ON')

5:13 It seems that we are unable to refrain from drinking no matter how much we want to, need to or ought to. We begin to drink when things are going well. We begin to drink when things are going poorly. Sometimes we begin to drink for no reason at all. Once we begin, the phenomenon of craving causes us to lose control of the amount we drink.

5:14-19 Sometimes in a moment of clarity or a period of remorse we realize that we cannot control our liquor consumption once we begin drinking. The first resource we may attempt to use is our own will-power. We resolve to quit drinking.

5:20-6:7 Finding that resolve is ineffective in overcoming a drinking problem we, of course, try it again even harder. We are under the delusion that our own internal strength is the only power that we have to draw upon. After repeatedly failing to prevent our drinking, we begin to doubt that we will ever recover. We begin to lose hope.

impending calamity. 6:10I hardly dared cross the street, lest I collapse and be run down by an early morning truck, for it was scarcely daylight. 11An all night place supplied me with a dozen glasses of ale. 12My writhing nerves were stilled at last. 13A morning paper told me the market had gone to hell again. 14Well, so had I. 15The market would recover, but I wouldn't. 16That was a hard thought. 17Should I kill myself? 18No—not now. 19Then a mental fog settled down. 20Gin would fix that. 21So two bottles, and—oblivion.

22The mind and body are marvelous mechanisms, for mine endured this agony two more years. 23Sometimes I stole from my wife's slender purse when the morning terror and madness were on me. 24Again I swayed dizzily before an open window, or the medicine cabinet where there was poison, cursing myself for a weakling. 25There were flights from city to country and back, as my wife and I sought escape. 26Then came the night when the physical and mental torture was so hellish I feared I would burst through my window, sash and all. 27Somehow I managed to drag my mattress to a lower floor, lest I suddenly leap. 28A doctor came with a heavy sedative. 7:1Next day found me drinking both gin and sedative. 2This combination soon landed me on the rocks. 3People feared for my sanity. 4So did I. 5I could eat little or nothing when drinking, and I was forty pounds under weight.

6:6 Bill, willpower having failed him twice now, insanely believes that it will be more effective "next time." It is not until we cease to rely exclusively upon our own willpower and turn to a Power greater than ourselves that we find the strength to quit once and for all.

6:8-13 This paragraph describes withdrawal from alcoholic addiction: remorse, horror, hopelessness, brain racing, a sense of impending doom and writhing nerves that can only be stilled by more alcohol. The cycle of alcoholic drinking turns into a downward spiral.

6:14-22 We are seemingly hopeless. If our most sincere desire and firmest resolve can-not keep us from drinking, what hope have we? The authors show that they too were once in this state.

6:25 We do things for alcohol that we never would have imagined ourselves capable of. Harshly judging ourselves weak of character and morally deficient, we may think of suicide.

6:27 Geographical cures are one of the many things we try to escape the temptation to drink. The problem is that no matter where we go, there we are. Even if temporarily successful, we eventually return to drinking. We can not see a way out.

7:6My brother-in-law is a physician, and through his kindness and that of my mother I was placed in a nationally-known hospital for the mental and physical rehabilitation of alcoholics. 7Under the so-called belladonna treatment my brain cleared. 8Hydrotherapy and mild exercise helped much. 9Best of all, I met a kind doctor who explained that though certainly selfish and foolish, I had been seriously ill, bodily and mentally.

10It relieved me somewhat to learn that in alcoholics the will is amazingly weakened when it comes to combating liquor, though it often remains strong in other respects. 11My incredible behavior in the face of a desperate desire to stop was explained. 12Understanding myself now, I fared forth in high hope. 13For three or four months the goose hung high. 14I went to town regularly and even made a little money. 15Surely this was the answer—self-knowledge.

16But it was not, for the frightful day came when I drank

7:10
Willpower:
xxix:18, 11:9,
20:14, 22:11,
24:3-6,32:13,
33:9, 34:2,
34:12, 40:12,
42:4, 45:2-3,
76:18, 85:19-
20, 92:8,
107:19, 140:5

7:11
Baffling:
xxvii:14,
5:12-13, 6:4,
23:9-12,
26:9, 34:15,
35:4-5, 37:9,
40:8, 58:15,
92:1

7:15
Self-knowl-
edge:
26:7, 36:22,
38:18, 39:3,
40:2-6, 42:4

8:9-11
Admitted:
xxviii:8,
xxix:6, 11:12,
13:7, 30:1,
30:7-8, 42:8-
9, 59:8

Historical Note:
7:6 Bill's brother-in-law was Dr. Leonard V. Strong Jr., who also introduced Bill to Willard Richardson an associate of John D. Rockefeller. Dr. Strong also became a non-alcoholic trustee of Alcoholics Anonymous.
7:6 Bill entered the Charles B. Towns Hospital, of which Dr. William Silkworth was the Medical Director.
7:7 The belladonna treatment was used to decrease an alcoholic's craving for alcohol during detoxification.

7:1 Combining drugs with alcohol accelerates our downward spiral. It is a very dangerous thing to do. Our thinking becomes even more clouded and we may lose our grasp on reality.

7:5 We are too sick to eat when we are not drinking. We are too busy pursuing another drink to eat when we are not sick and once we begin to drink we are not interested in food. We become malnourished and other physical problems begin to set in.

7:9-10 It is relieving to know that lack of character and poor morals are not the only reason for our excessive drinking. The phenomenon of craving seems to be the result of an increased physical sensitivity to alcohol. Dr. Silkworth suggested that this may

be a symptom of an allergy. The obsession for drink that crowds out all other thoughts is an illness of the mind.

7:11 If we continue to drink in the face of a desperate desire to stop, it is very likely that we are alcoholic. This is a telltale sign of alcoholism. The author's analysis of the problem seems to make sense in the light of our own experience.

7:15 Knowledge of the problem does not equal a solution. This is why alcoholics seem hopeless. We return to drink knowing full well we can not control it. We return to drink even when we have compelling reasons not to. We return to drink when we sincerely desire not to. Self-knowledge is just one more human resource we attempt to draw on in our battle for control.

7:19
Hopeless:
xiii:1, xxiii:6,
xxvii:2,
xxix:6,
xxix:16, 6:15,
10:3, 14:16,
17:1, 20:3,
26:16, 27:5,
39:3,
42:10,43:8-9,
44:5, 92:7,
94:12, 113:22

7:21
Alternatives:
8:15, 25:12,
44:6-10

8:7
Self-pity:
15:6, 61:14,
62:1, 84:2,
86:16, 88:1

8:9-11
Step One:
10:3, 11:12-
16, 13:7,
30:7-8, 59:8

once more. [7:17]The curve of my declining moral and bodily health fell off like a ski-jump. [18]After a time I returned to the hospital. [19]This was the finish, the curtain, it seemed to me. [20]My weary and despairing wife was informed that it would all end with heart failure during delirium tremens, or I would develop a wet brain, perhaps within a year. [21]She would soon have to give me over to the undertaker or the asylum

[22]They did not need to tell me. [23]I knew, and almost welcomed the idea. [24]It was a devastating blow to my pride. [8:1]I, who had thought so well of myself and my abilities, of my capacity to surmount obstacles, was cornered at last. [2]Now I was to plunge into the dark, joining that endless procession of sots who had gone on before. [3]I thought of my poor wife. [4]There had been much happiness after all. [5]What would I not give to make amends. [6]But that was over now. [7]No words can tell of the loneliness and despair I found in that bitter morass of self-pity. [8]Quicksand stretched around me in all directions. [9]I had met my match. [10]I had been overwhelmed. [11]Alcohol was my master.

Historical Note:
8:20 Delirium tremens result from excessive alcohol use and are characterized by violent restlessness, trembling and terrifying visual hallucinations.
8:20 Dementia resulting from excessive alcohol use characterized by severe personality change and loss of intellectual capacity.

7:16 Bill tells how well his attempt at control worked for him. We sometimes believe that if we only knew what it was that caused us to drink then we would be able to stop. Self-knowledge seldom works. We go to psychologists, psychiatrists and counselors. We analyze our childhoods and marriages. Now the authors of this book tell us why we can not control our drinking. We pursue drink because of a mental obsession and then while drinking we experience a craving for more that is beyond our ability to control. However, knowing this will not keep us sober.

7:20-21 Bill's alternatives are few: insanity or death. When we can not stop drinking and we can not continue as we have been, what alternatives do we have?

7:24-8:1 We feel hopeless when we exhaust all our options, when we have tried every resource at our disposal and nothing has worked to control our drinking let alone enable us to stop. Self-will and other human resources are marvelously effective for certain things but are pitifully inadequate when faced with alcoholism.

8:1-8 The hopelessness we feel can level our pride, removing a barrier to our recovery. This hopelessness can produce in us a willingness to accept the solution offered to us by the authors. The first step of this solution is the admission that we are powerless over alcohol—that our lives are unmanageable.

8:12Trembling, I stepped from the hospital a broken man.
13Fear sobered me for a bit. 14Then came the insidious insanity of that first drink, and on Armistice Day 1934, I was off
again. 15Everyone became resigned to the certainty that I
would have to be shut up somewhere, or would stumble
along to a miserable end. 16How dark it is before the dawn!
17In reality that was the beginning of my last debauch. 18I was
soon to be catapulted into what I like to call the fourth
dimension of existence. 19I was to know happiness, peace,
and usefulness, in a way of life that is incredibly more wonderful as time passes.

20Near the end of that bleak November, I sat drinking in
my kitchen. 21With a certain satisfaction I reflected there was
enough gin concealed about the house to carry me through
that night and the next day. 22My wife was at work. 23I wondered whether I dared hide a full bottle of gin near the head
of our bed. 24I would need it before daylight.

8:13
Fear:
24:3-9, 26:7-
9, 40:2-
41:21,
43:14-16,
154:15-17

8:14
Insidious:
154:17, 22:9,
23:2, 23:9,
24:6, 35:2,
37:6, 40:10,
41:20, 43:14-
16

8:15
Alternatives:
7:21, 25:12,
44:6-10

8:18
Catapulted:
11:13, 16:11,
25:7, 43:1-2,
55:2, 63:18,
100:6

8:21
Concealed:
22:1

Definitions:
8:14 Insidious: beginning inconspicuously but with grave consequences.

8:9-11 Bill, by admitting to himself his powerlessness, takes his first step. Perhaps we
feel as hopeless as Bill. Are we able to control our drinking once we start? Are we
unable to quit drinking despite our sincere
desire to do so? How have the things we
have tried to overcome drinking worked for
us? Can we admit that alcohol is more powerful than we are? If we can, then we have
taken the first step toward recovery.

8:12-14 More is required to recover from
alcoholism than the first step. The fear of the
certain consequences of drinking may keep
us sober for varying lengths of time. Many of
us never want to forget how horrible the last
days of our drinking were, but reliance on our
memories to keep us sober rarely works for
long. The proof of this is that we continue to
drink long after we realize the damage drinking has caused in our lives and to our health.

8:14 The inability to stop based solely on our
knowledge of the consequences is described

many times in this book. The authors
describe this as the insidious insanity of the
first drink (24:3-9, 26:7-9, 40:2-41:23, 43:14-
16, 154:17).

8:18-19 The image of being catapulted is one
of no return. Once the rope is cut we are on
our way. We cannot imagine the life we will
find. Until we experience it, we believe that
this way of life is unavailable to us.

8:19 We learn this new way of life by practicing the program of action outlined in this book.
The results of the way we are living now should
make us willing to change. The authors'
promise of happiness, peace and usefulness
are in stark contrast with our alcoholic life.

8:20-24 Our thinking becomes focused on the
source of our next drink. The secreting away of
alcohol and fear of losing our supply are common symptoms of alcoholism although not all
alcoholics do this. Those who are not alcoholic
never exhibit these behaviors.

⁸:²⁵My musing was interrupted by the telephone. ²⁶The cheery voice of an old school friend asked if he might come over. ⁹:¹*He was sober.* ²It was years since I could remember his coming to New York in that condition. ³I was amazed. ⁴Rumor had it that he had been committed for alcoholic insanity. ⁵I wondered how he had escaped. ⁶Of course he would have dinner, and then I could drink openly with him. ⁷Unmindful of his welfare, I thought only of recapturing the spirit of other days. ⁸There was that time we had chartered an airplane to complete a jag! ⁹His coming was an oasis in this dreary desert of futility. ¹⁰The very thing—an oasis! ¹¹Drinkers are like that.

¹²The door opened and he stood there, fresh-skinned and glowing. ¹³There was something about his eyes. ¹⁴He was inexplicably different. ¹⁵What had happened?

¹⁶I pushed a drink across the table. ¹⁷He refused it. ¹⁸Disappointed but curious, I wondered what had got into the fellow. ¹⁹He wasn't himself.

²⁰ "Come, what's all this about?" ²¹I queried.

²²He looked straight at me. ²³Simply, but smilingly, he said, "I've got religion."

²⁴I was aghast. ²⁵So that was it—last summer an alcoholic crackpot; now, I suspected, a little cracked about religion. ²⁶He had that starry-eyed look. ²⁷Yes, the old boy was on fire all right. ²⁸But bless his heart, let him rant! ²⁹Besides, my gin would last longer than his preaching.

³⁰But he did no ranting. ³¹In a matter of fact way he told how two men had appeared in court, persuading the judge to suspend his commitment. ³²They had told of a simple religious

Historical Note:
8:31 The two men were Rowland H. and Cebra G. Both men were members of the New York Oxford Group. Rowland is mentiond again in this book as a patient of Dr. Carl Jung (26:1-28:1) . The basic ideas found in the Twelve Steps of A.A. came from the Oxford Group, a Christian fellowship.

9:6-11 We wish that we could return to the days when drinking was fun, but alcoholism is a progressive illness. Once we enter into alcoholism we can never return to normal drinking.

9:22 Being presented with a spiritual solution

to our problem, we do not know what to think. Many of us have had prejudices against these ideas. However, the proof that it works is right before us. Millions of alcoholics have recovered by using the simple spiritual concepts presented in this book.

idea and a practical program of action. [9:33]That was two months ago and the result was self evident. [34]It worked!

[35]He had come to pass his experience along to me—if I cared to have it. [10:1]I was shocked, but interested. [2]Certainly I was interested. [3]I had to be, for I was hopeless.

[4]He talked for hours. [5]Childhood memories rose before me. [6]I could almost hear the sound of the preacher's voice as I sat, on still Sundays, way over there on the hillside; there was that proffered temperance pledge I never signed; my grandfather's good natured contempt of some church folk and their doings; his insistence that the spheres really had their music; but his denial of the preacher's right to tell him how he must listen; his fearlessness as he spoke of these things just before he died; these recollections welled up from the past. [7]They made me swallow hard.

[8]That war-time day in old Winchester Cathedral came back again. [9]I had always believed in a power greater than myself. [10]I had often pondered these things. [11]I was not an atheist. [12]Few people really are, for that means blind faith in the strange proposition that this universe originated in a cipher and aimlessly rushes nowhere. [13]My intellectual heroes, the

10:3
Step One:
8:9-11,
11:12-16,
13:7, 30:7-8,
59:8

10:3
Hopeless:
xiii:1, xxiii:6,
xxvii:2,
xxix:6,
xxix:16, 6:15,
7:19, 14:16,
17:1, 20:3,
26:16, 27:5,
39:3,
42:10,43:8-9,
44:5, 92:7,
94:12, 113:22

10:8
Winchester:
1:9, 12:24-
27, 46:6

10:11-12
Nowhere:
49:4-6,
54:19, 55:18

Definition:
10:12 Originated in a cipher: originated out of nothing.

9:29-34 Though the book lays out a spiritual path to recovery, no preaching or proselytizing is done. No one tells us what we must believe, but simply how to develop a belief of our own. The program of action enables us to develop our own experience so that we may begin to rely on it working for us.

9:34 This is a voluntary program. The authors tell us what worked for them. We can take it or leave it. Should we decide to take their suggestion, there are many recovered alcoholics in A.A. who will be willing to show us what they have done.

10:1-3 For many of us the willingness to begin this program was produced by our realization of the hopelessness of our situation.

We had nowhere else to turn. The program was presented to us by people for whom it had worked. Nothing else has worked for us so we grab hold of these principles as we do for life itself.

10:4-7 We may have already made our judgment of religion and spirituality. Talk of spiritual matters may arouse these prejudices in us. How important are our preconceived notions of religion when we are faced with alcoholic destruction?

10:8 Most of us can remember times when we were able to draw comfort and strength by calling upon God. Perhaps we can recall times of awe over the vastness and beauty of creation.

11:5
Doubted:
45:16-46:4,
7:3, 49:6,
112, 56:11

chemists, the astronomers, even the evolutionists, suggested vast laws and forces at work. 10:14Despite contrary indications, I had little doubt that a mighty purpose and rhythm underlay all. 15How could there be so much of precise and immutable law, and no intelligence? 16I simply had to believe in a Spirit of the Universe, who knew neither time nor limitation. 17But that was as far as I had gone.

18With ministers, and the world's religions, I parted right there. 19When they talked of a God personal to me, who was love, superhuman strength and direction, I became irritated and my mind snapped shut against such a theory.

11:1To Christ I conceded the certainty of a great man, not too closely followed by those who claimed Him. 2His moral teaching—most excellent. 3For myself, I had adopted those parts which seemed convenient and not too difficult; the rest I disregarded.

4The wars which had been fought, the burnings and chicanery that religious dispute had facilitated, made me sick. 5I honestly doubted whether, on balance, the religions of mankind had done any good. 6Judging from what I had seen in Europe and since, the power of God in human affairs was negligible, the Brotherhood of Man a grim jest. 7If there was a Devil, he seemed the Boss Universal, and he certainly had me.

10:9-17 We may have developed a conception of God. We may have rejected the God idea altogether. Are we atheists who deny the existence of God? Are we agnostic and have no direct experience with God working in our lives? What do we think? What do we know?

10:18-20 Prejudice and close-mindedness are our most substantial barriers to developing experience with a Power greater than ourselves. When we become irritated and our minds snap shut at the mention of spiritual concepts, we are condemning ourselves to ignorance and quite possibly an alcoholic death.

11:1 Our judgments of other peoples' religious practice do nothing to advance our own. Perhaps they are doing the best they can to live a spiritually-based life. We strive for spiritual progress to improve our own behavior as best we can.

11:3 We all wish to be moral and upright as long as it does not inconvenience us or interfere with our pursuit of satisfaction. How has picking and choosing which moral principles we are willing to follow worked for us so far? How has obstinately refusing to follow time-honored principles served us?

11:4-7 The authors do not ask us to join any religion, they suggest that we may awaken spiritually through our own direct experience. All we need to do is quit debating the existence of God and seek to establish contact with God, as we understand God.

11:8But my friend sat before me, and he made the point-blank declaration that God had done for him what he could not do for himself. 9His human will had failed. 10Doctors had pronounced him incurable. 11Society was about to lock him up. 12Like myself, he had admitted complete defeat. 13Then he had, in effect, been raised from the dead, suddenly taken from the scrap heap to a level of life better than the best he had ever known!

14Had this power originated in him? 15Obviously it had not. 16There had been no more power in him than there was in me at that minute; and this was none at all.

17That floored me. 18It began to look as though religious people were right after all. 19Here was something at work in a human heart which had done the impossible. 20My ideas about miracles were drastically revised right then. 21Never mind the musty past; here sat a miracle directly across the kitchen table. 22He shouted great tidings.

23I saw that my friend was much more than inwardly reorganized. 12:01He was on a different footing. 2His roots grasped a new soil.

11:8
Ourselves:
25:10, 45:5, 50:11, 70:23, 84:8, 100:6, 102:18

11:12
Admitted:
xxviii:8, xxix:6, 8:9-11, 13:7, 30:1, 30:7-8, 42:8-9, 59:8

11:13
Catapulted:
8:18, 16:11, 25:7, 43:1-2, 55:2, 63:18, 100:6

11:16
Powerless:
24:3, 34:11, 45:2-4, 46:12, 50:15, 59:2, 59:8, 60:12, 62:13, 63:6, 118:19

11:19
Heart:
55:11, 55:20, 143:8

11:21
Miracle:
25:1, 27:8, 50:11, 55:7, 57:4, 85:3, 124:14, 128:12, 133:15

11:8 The authors make similar declarations that God has enabled them to escape the seemingly hopeless condition of mind and body that is alcoholism. Attendance at any A.A. meeting will provide similar testimony. Perhaps you know of someone who has found release from alcoholism through the application of spiritual principles.

11:8-11 Bill's friend describes how he was seemingly hopeless prior to adopting this way of life. Human resources had failed to help him stop drinking. His own willpower and the help of physicians had been so ineffective that he came near to being committed for alcoholic insanity. His admission of powerlessness persuaded him to look outside of human aid for help. He plainly states that he received the help he needed.

11:14-23 The seeming hopelessness of alcoholism has been recognized for thousands of years. Prior to the advent of Alcoholics Anonymous most of those afflicted with alcoholism lost their minds or died. For over 60 years, millions of alcoholics have found relief through the application of the spiritual principles described in this book. This vast amount of experience is one very good reason for us to stop arguing and explore for ourselves this new way of life.

11:23 What is required to overcome alcoholism is more than just a moderation of outward behaviors, but a total reorganization of the character of the alcoholic. Doctor Silkworth called it an entire psychic change (xxvii:2). Doctor Jung and Alcoholics Anonymous call it a spiritual experience (25:8-10, 27:9-12, 60:1, Appendix II).

12:9-19
Step Two:
13:7, 47:9,
53:8-10, 59:9

12:10
Conception:
27:12, 45:18-
19, 46:10-11,
47:1, 47:7,
49:12, 50:6,
56:11, 86:11,
93:4-5

12:12
Intellectual:
16:10, 27:16,
44:14, 49:7,
62:12, 83:7-
8, 77:10

12:12
Shivered:
151:11

12:15
Beginning:
19:3, 25:10,
35:17, 46:9,
47:4, 47:16,
63:17, 68:23,
71:2, 84:14,
85:24,
158:10, 163:1

12:17
Arch:
47:11, 54:12,
56:19, 62:21,
63:4, 75:19-
23, 97:3,
123:11

12:3Despite the living example of my friend there remained in me the vestiges of my old prejudice. 4The word God still aroused a certain antipathy. 5When the thought was expressed that there might be a God personal to me this feeling was intensified. 6I didn't like the idea. 7I could go for such conceptions as Creative Intelligence, Universal Mind or Spirit of Nature but I resisted the thought of a Czar of the Heavens however loving His sway might be. 8I have since talked with scores of men who felt the same way.

9My friend suggested what then seemed a novel idea. 10He said, *"Why don't you choose your own conception of God?"*

11That statement hit me hard. 12It melted the icy intellectual mountain in whose shadow I had lived and shivered many years. 13I stood in the sunlight at last.

14*It was only a matter of being willing to believe in a power greater than myself.* 15*Nothing more was required of me to make my beginning.* 16I saw that growth could start from that point. 17Upon a foundation of complete willingness I might build what I saw in my friend. 18Would I have it? 19Of course I would!

12:3-8 The authors capitalize all conceptions of God used throughout the book. Perhaps if we are not comfortable with the word God we can substitute one of the other conceptions found in this book or choose one of our own. We must try to be open minded lest prejudice and misunderstanding block us off from the Power we need so badly. Intolerance of or belligerence towards spiritual principles are the only things that can defeat us in our quest (Appendix II).

12:9-10 This concept addresses all prejudices we may have. We may choose our own conception of God. We need not argue any more. What other people believe and what other people do does not matter at all. This removes the barrier to our own spiritual awakening that Bill describes as an "icy intellectual mountain." We may proceed from our own starting point without carrying the baggage of our past experience or other peoples'

religions. We can start fresh and establish our own relationship with this Power.

12:11-13 The melting of our own "icy intellectual mountains" allows us to move away from an intellectual conception of our Higher Power to direct conscious contact with this Power. The authors are not asking "blind faith" of us. They are not saying "believe this and you will be all right." They are merely asking us to try this new way of living, which begins with a willingness to look in a spiritual direction and see for ourselves if it works or not.

12:12 An intellectual understanding of spiritual matters does not equal the vital spiritual experience we require to overcome alcoholism. Our very best thinking got us where we are now. We seek direct personal experience with our Higher Power through working the twelve steps.

¹²:²⁰Thus was I convinced that God is concerned with us humans when we want Him enough. ²¹At long last I saw, I felt, I believed. ²²Scales of pride and prejudice fell from my eyes. ²³A new world came into view.

²⁴The real significance of my experience in the Cathedral burst upon me. ²⁵For a brief moment, I had needed and wanted God. ²⁶There had been a humble willingness to have Him with me—and He came. ²⁷But soon the sense of His Presence had been blotted out by worldly clamors, mostly those within myself. ¹³:¹And so it had been ever since. How blind I had been.

³At the hospital I was separated from alcohol for the last time. ⁴Treatment seemed wise, for I showed signs of delirium tremens.

⁵There I humbly offered myself to God, as I then understood Him, to do with me as He would. ⁶I placed myself

12:24-27
Cathedral:
1:9, 10:8, 46:6

12:27
Blocked:
64:1, 57:12,
63:11, 76:7

12:27
Presence:
51:3, 56:13-18,
63:6, 85:21-
23,162:2

12:27
Clamors:
46:6

13:4
Hospitalization:
xxiv:14,
xxv:12, 30:16,
91:5, 142:18,
143:1-7,
159:15, 160:5

13:5
Step Three:
59:10, 63:9-12

13:6
Reservations:
33:8, 63:16

12:14-17 Bill relates how he took his second step. All that is required is a willingness to believe and that we voluntarily look for help in a spiritual direction. We can begin to build from this foundation which is a solid foundation of willingness rather than the shifting sands of self-will.

12:14-17 This Power is available to all who seek it (46:12-15), not just churchgoers, mystics or gurus. To access this Power requires no special knowledge, talents or abilities. All that is required to make a beginning is willingness.

12:18-19 If we have admitted to ourselves that we are powerless over alcohol—that our lives are unmanageable, where else do we have to turn? Resolving not to drink anymore is an attempt to exercise a power that we admitted we do not have.

12:22-23 We pridefully believe that we are able to live without the help of a Power greater than ourselves. Our pre-judgments of spiritual matters cloud our perception of the world. When we recognize pride and prejudice as blocking our recovery, we are willing to set them aside.

12:24-27 We build upon our own individual spiritual experience. Worldly distractions may overwhelm any single experience, but through working the twelve steps we develop a substantial base of experience upon which we can draw when faced with doubt or indecision.

13:3 Withdrawal from alcoholic addiction is hazardous and medical attention should be sought.

13:5-14:8 Bill learned of the physical component of alcoholism from Dr. Silkworth. He knew that when he drank he was unable to stop. All medical science could suggest to him was entire abstinence. Knowing through his own experience that it was impossible for him to remain abstinent, Bill felt that he was hopeless. Bill was presented with the solution to his alcoholism by Ebby T., an old school friend. Ebby showed Bill a program of action used by the Oxford Group. Bill describes the ideas and attitudes he adopted and the techniques he began to practice. The result was a deep and effective spiritual experience allowing Bill access to a Power sufficient to overcome his alcoholism.

13:7
Step Two :
47:9, 53:8-10

13:8
Step Four:
64:5-71:3

13:8
Step Six:
76:1-5

13:9
It Works:
xxix:14, xxx:2

13:10
Step Five:
75:7-23, 78:22

13:11-12
Step Eight:
76:11-15,
78:22

13:14
Step Nine:
76:16-84:12

13:15
Step Ten:
84:13-85:25

13:15-20
Prayer:
85:26-86:3

13:17-18
Step Eleven:
85:26-88:6

13:21
Step Twelve:
88:7-103:12

14:1
Simple:
9:32, 88:6

14:1-3
Price:
108:17, 155:7

14:2
Self-centered-
ness:
62:2-14

unreservedly under His care and direction. ⁷I admitted for the first time that of myself I was nothing; that without Him I was lost. ⁸I ruthlessly faced my sins and became willing to have my new-found Friend take them away, root and branch. ⁹I have not had a drink since.

¹⁰My school mate visited me, and I fully acquainted him with my problems and deficiencies. ¹¹We made a list of people I had hurt or toward whom I felt resentment. ¹²I expressed my entire willingness to approach these individuals, admitting my wrong. ¹³Never was I to be critical of them. ¹⁴I was to right all such matters to the utmost of my ability.

¹⁵I was to test my thinking by the new God-consciousness within. ¹⁶Common sense would thus become uncommon sense. ¹⁷I was to sit quietly when in doubt, asking only for direction and strength to meet my problems as He would have me. ¹⁸Never was I to pray for myself, except as my requests bore on my usefulness to others. ¹⁹Then only might I expect to receive. ²⁰But that would be in great measure.

²¹My friend promised when these things were done I would enter upon a new relationship with my Creator; that I would have the elements of a way of living which answered all my problems. ²²Belief in the power of God, plus enough willingness, honesty and humility to establish and maintain the new order of things, were the essential requirements.

¹⁴:¹Simple, but not easy; a price had to be paid. ²It meant destruction of self-centeredness. ³I must turn in all things to the Father of Lights who presides over us all.

Historical Note:
13:9 On December 11, 1934, Bill was 39 years old

13:21 The promise of a new relationship with our Creator gives us hope that we can make a new beginning and our old, ineffective relationship can be replaced with a wonderfully effective personal relationship with God.

13:21 The twelve steps are each an element in this new way of life. We study and practice the steps so that we may apply them with increasing skill in every area of our lives.

14:1 Something that is simple has few parts.

Our recovery requires we take but twelve steps. Just to the extent that we resist accepting these ideas and taking these actions are these steps difficult.

14:2-3 The price we pay is that thing which we hold most dear—our self-will. No longer can we center our lives, thoughts and actions on the selfish fulfillment of our desires. With God at the center of our lives we find freedom, happiness, and serenity.

¹⁴:⁴These were revolutionary and drastic proposals, but the moment I fully accepted them, the effect was electric. ⁵There was a sense of victory, followed by such a peace and serenity as I had never known. ⁶There was utter confidence. ⁷I felt lifted up, as though the great clean wind of a mountain top blew through and through. ⁸God comes to most men gradually, but His impact on me was sudden and profound.

⁹For a moment I was alarmed, and called my friend, the doctor, to ask if I were still sane. ¹⁰He listened in wonder as I talked.

¹¹Finally he shook his head saying, "Something has happened to you I don't understand. ¹²But you had better hang on to it. ¹³Anything is better than the way you were." ¹⁴The good doctor now sees many men who have such experiences. ¹⁵He knows they are real.

¹⁶While I lay in the hospital the thought came that there were thousands of hopeless alcoholics who might be glad to have what had been so freely given me. ¹⁷Perhaps I could help some of them. ¹⁸They in turn might work with others.

¹⁹My friend had emphasized the absolute necessity of demonstrating these principles in all my affairs. ²⁰Particularly was it imperative to work with others as he had worked with me. ²¹Faith without works was dead, he said. ²²And how

14:4 Reservations: 33:8, 63:16
14:4 Accepted: xxix:8, xxx:1
14:4-8 Effect: xxvii:2-3, xxvii:10, 12:1-2, 25:8-10, 27:9-12, 44:3-4, 84:25, 143:9, 158:10, 569:1
14:11 Understand: 27:10
14:18-23 Work: xiii:9, 15:1, 15:7-10, 19:2-6, 75:20, 89:1, 102:6, 119:7
14:19-20 Required: xiv:2, xxvii:3, 12:15, 13:22, 25:4, 50:16, 60:16, 72:5, 94:15, 98:11, 143:9
19:4 Demonstration: xiii:2, 14:19, 49:13, 51:2, 55:7, 68:21, 77:10, 98:12-19
14:21 Faith: 15:2, 16:10, 76:11, 88:9, 93:14-15

14:4 The steps propose a fundamental change in the way we live our lives and relate to the world. They require a complete abandonment of and turning away from the ideas and attitudes that have caused us to fail in life. They do not call for a minor modification of our behavior, but for the adoption of an entirely new way of life. If we are hesitant about embracing this new way of life, we can ask ourselves how the way we are living now is working for us.

14:16-18 Bill wanted to share the wonderful release he had experienced with other sufferers. His simple altruistic idea has grown into what A.A. is today.

14:19 Putting these principles into practice in all areas of our lives is what enables these theories and techniques to result in permanent recovery. Attempting to present this solution to others brings it to life in our own lives. The vast experience of A.A. members is that intensive work with other alcoholics will work better to keep us sober than anything else we can do (89:1).

14:20 Attempting to carry this message to other alcoholics infuses our lives with a new purpose and direction replacing our slothful indifference to our responsibilities to God and other people.

14:21 Faith without works is dead. If we do not act on our faith, it will not survive. We will be distracted by the worldly clamors and lose contact with God. Following God's guidance keeps our faith fresh, vital and alive.

14:23
Self-sacrifice:
13:18, 20:1,
62:2, 70:14,
85:16-18,
93:15, 94:6,
97:3, 159:12-
13, 164:16

15:1
Fatal:
24:15, 33:2,
62:9, 64:16,
66:7-16,
66:13, 92:14,
70:18-19,
117:19,
154:20

15:6
Resentment:
13:11, 18:5,
36:4, 62:1,
64:15-67:19,
65:5, 66:7-
13, 70:18,
84:19,
117:19, 145:9

15:6
Self-pity:
8:7, 61:14,
62:1, 84:2,
86:16, 88:1

15:8-11
Intensive:
89:1, 102:6,
119:7,
129:14,

15:12
Part:
89:7-10

appallingly true for the alcoholic! ¹⁴:²³For if an alcoholic failed to perfect and enlarge his spiritual life through work and self-sacrifice for others, he could not survive the certain trials and low spots ahead. ¹⁵:¹If he did not work, he would surely drink again, and if he drank, he would surely die. ²Then faith would be dead indeed. ³With us it is just like that.

⁴My wife and I abandoned ourselves with enthusiasm to the idea of helping other alcoholics to a solution of their problems. ⁵It was fortunate, for my old business associates remained skeptical for a year and a half, during which I found little work. ⁶I was not too well at the time, and was plagued by waves of self-pity and resentment. ⁷This sometimes nearly drove me back to drink. ⁸I soon found that when all other measures failed, work with another alcoholic would save the day. ⁹Many times I have gone to my old hospital in despair. ¹⁰On talking to a man there, I would be amazingly lifted up and set on my feet. ¹¹It is a design for living that works in rough going.

¹²We commenced to make many fast friends and a fellowship has grown up among us of which it is a wonderful thing to feel a part. ¹³The joy of living we really have, even

---

14:23-15:3 The absolute necessity of working with others, the rewards of continued recovery, and an enhanced spiritual life are explained here. This is a matter of life and death for the alcoholic, not just the receiver of the message, but for the messenger as well. It is an old A.A. slogan that you have to give it away to keep it. Many more experienced members take newer members on twelve step calls to help them find purpose and meaning for their lives in doing this work.

15:4 Abandoning ourselves to this work is like abandoning a burning ship to reach the safety of a rescue vessel. We find that working with others is an effective way to overcome self-centeredness.

15:6-11 Helping others is a successful way to deal with the emotional turmoil of early sobriety. Brooding and withdrawing into ourselves can be fatal. Working with other alcoholics reduces our self-centeredness long enough for our emotions to stabilize. Self-pity and resentment are dangerous for alcoholics. By taking the steps we soon learn how to deal successfully with these problems.

15:12 How we begin to feel a part of this fellowship is by attending A.A. meetings regularly, coming early to help set up, staying late to help clean up, making coffee for the meeting, going out to coffee after the meetings, getting a sponsor, going on twelve step calls and most importantly taking the steps ourselves. The fifth and eighth steps are particularly effective at breaking down the walls of ego that make us feel separate, unique and alone (62:8, 82:4-5 12&12).

under pressure and difficulty. 15:14I have seen one hundred families set their feet in the path that really goes somewhere; have seen the most impossible domestic situations righted; feuds and bitterness of all sorts wiped out. 15I have seen men come out of asylums and resume a vital place in the lives of their families and communities. 16Business and professional men have regained their standing. 17There is scarcely any form of trouble and misery which has not been overcome among us. 18In one western city and its environs there are eighty of us and our families. 19We meet frequently at our different homes, so that newcomers may find the fellowship they seek. 16:1At these informal gatherings one may often see from 40 to 80 persons. 2We are growing in numbers and power. 3An alcoholic in his cups is an unlovely creature. 4Our struggles with them are variously strenuous, comic, and tragic. 5One poor chap committed suicide in my home. 6He could not, or would not, see our way of life.

15:14
Path:
49:9, 58:1,
66:24, 72:2,
100:4, 116:11

15:19
Meetings
(Reason For):
160:1

15:19
Meetings
(Descriptions):
159:19-161:8

16:3-6
Tragedies:
xxxvi:6, xix:5,
18:3-5, 21:6,
23:17, 24:2,
123:15, 132:8

16:6
Way of life:
xiii:6, 8:19,
13:21, 15:10,
42:20, 68:14-
23, 79:15,
81:21, 84:14,
97:19, 99:11,
114:21, 117:13,
124:1, 130:10,
134:15,
164:13-16

Historical Note:
16:5 Bill C., a lawyer, stayed with Bill W. and his wife for nearly a year before commiting suicide in1936.

15:13 Joy is a feeling of gratefulness and closeness to God that is not dependent on outside circumstances. This is contrasted to happiness and sadness that are caused by external circumstances. Joy stays with us when good things happen and we are happy and also when bad things happen and we are sad.

15:14-18 The proof that this way of life works is right before us evidenced by millions of recoveries. As we travel this path, we will witness God at work in the lives of many people.

15:18 At the time Bill wrote his story, one thousand A.A. members in a single large city

was considered a miracle. Now, many cities have over one thousand A.A. meetings a week, each filled with recovering alcoholics who have found this solution.

15:19 Bill explains that the reason for having A.A. meetings is for newcomers to find fellowship. The fellowship of others who have found this solution is a wonderful thing to feel a part of.

16:4-12 The A.A. way of life is life at its best. It is satisfying, fulfilling, purposeful, happy, joyous and free. We see all aspects of life in A.A. and through it all we are given the opportunity to learn and grow in God's love.

16:10
Intellectual:
12:12, 27:16,
44:14, 49:7,
62:12, 83:7-
8, 77:10

16:10
Faith:
14:21, 15:2,
76:11, 88:9,
93:14-15

16:11
Utopia:
25:7

16:7There is, however, a vast amount of fun about it all. 8I suppose some would be shocked at our seeming worldliness and levity. 9But just underneath there is deadly earnestness. 10Faith has to work twenty-four hours a day in and through us, or we perish.

11Most of us feel we need look no further for Utopia. 12We have it with us right here and now. 13Each day my friends' simple talk in our kitchen multiplies itself in a widening circle of peace on earth and good will to men.

PROFILE OF
BILL W.
1895-1971

Born in Vermont, Bill was raised primarily by his maternal grandparents after his parents' divorce. Commissioned as an artillery officer in World War I, Bill developed his talent for leadership, and a taste for liquor.

After the war Bill resolved to prove to the world he was important. He pursued success on Wall Street. His drinking grew progressively more troublesome, leading to unhappy scenes at home and arguments with friends. Devastated by the 1929 stock market crash Bill worked in Canada for a time, until his drinking cost him his job.

Bill progressed through the characteristic stages of alcoholism. Bath tub gin, three or four bottles a day, brought Bill to the brink of mental and physical collapse. Realizing that his drinking was preventing him from reaching his goal of success, Bill resolved to stop altogether and found that he could not. He was baffled as to why he could not stop drinking even though he desperately wanted to. He began to be caught up in the endless cycle of drinking to relieve severe withdrawal symptoms which quickly made matters worse.

Bill checked in to the Charles B. Towns Hospital, to be treated for alcohol addiction. Here he learned of Dr. Silkworth's allergy theory that explained why his will power could not control his drinking. Bill thought that this knowledge would enable him to remain abstinate. Suffering from the common alcoholic delusion that a lengthy dry spell would enable him to control his drinking. Bill began to drink again. Further trips to the hospital and Dr. Silkworth's assessment of his condition convinced Bill that he was in a hopeless state.

In this condition Bill was visited by an old friend, Ebby T. This friend, about to be committed for alcoholic hijinks, was rescued by Rowland H. and Cebra G., members of the Oxford Group, a Christian fellowship. Rowland had been diagnosed as an incurable alcoholic by Dr. Carl Jung, the famous psychiatrist. Rowland had found that the Oxford Group offered a solution, a course of action that resulted in a spiritual awakening of sufficient force to overcome alcoholism. Rowland had given Ebby instruction in the basic principles of the Oxford Group and Ebby had contacted Bill for the purpose of sharing this with his old drinking buddy.

Bill, faced with alcoholic destruction, was willing to set aside his prejudice toward spiritual matters after Ebby suggested that he could choose his own conception of God. Bill entered the hospital and was dried out for the last time. While in the hospital Bill was visited by his friend who helped him to understand and begin to practice spiritual principles. When Bill fully accepted these principles he experienced a sudden and profound spiritual awakening. The date was December 11, 1935. Bill was 39 years old.

Bill began to associate with the Oxford Group members at Calvary Church in New York. This was headed by the Reverend Samuel Shoemaker, an Episcopal clergyman. Rev. Shoemaker and other Oxford Group members instructed Bill in the application of spiritual principles. Bill, desiring to share his experience with other alcoholics, was unsuccessful in his earliest attempts. Though Bill had not yet had success in sobering up other people he found that his attempts to help others did keep him sober! Dr. Silkworth helped Bill by suggesting that he first present the "hard medical facts" to his alcoholic prospects so that they might understand the hopelessness of their situation and then be more willing to accept the spiritual solution he had to offer.

It was with this advice in mind that Bill, six months sober, alone in Akron, Ohio on a business trip, and facing the temptation to drink, found another drunk to talk to. This drunk was Dr. Bob S., an alcoholic surgeon. Bill's candid talk with Dr. Bob about the physical allergy, mental obsession, and spiritual solution to alcoholism led shortly thereafter to Dr. Bob abandoning all reservations and adopting this way of life. Dr. Bob's sobriety date was June 10, 1935. He was 55 years old. This date is celebrated as the birthdate of Alcoholics Anonymous.

Bill stayed with Dr. Bob and his wife Anne for three months during which time Bill and Bob were successful at helping several other men to achieve sobriety. Bill returned to New York and with his wife Lois began building upon the success of his Akron experience. By 1939 nearly 100 people had adopted this way of life and the New York, Akron and Cleveland alcoholics had severed ties with the Oxford Group. Writing the book Alcoholics Anonymous these people took it's name for their fellowship.

Bill and Dr. Bob, along with the Alcoholic Foundation they helped to form, directed the growth of the fellowship. Seeing every imaginable difficulty encountered by groups around the U.S. Bill formulated a number of ideas to ensure the survival and continued growth of A.A. He proposed the fellowship adopt these ideas as traditions. At the 1950 International Convention, held in Cleveland, Ohio, the Twelve Traditions were confirmed.

Bill wrote several other books for the fellowship including: *Alcoholics Anonymous Comes Of Age, Twelve Steps And Twelve Traditions*, and *As Bill Sees It*. Bill also wrote a paper on alcoholism that was printed in the American Journal of Psychiatry. Bill spent the remainder of his life working in his office at A.A. headquarters and devoted himself to helping A.A. carry the message of recovery around the world.

Every word in the first three chapters is here to allow me to see myself in the authors' words, enabling me to say, "Yes, I am one of them too; I must have this thing." But how can joining together with a group of people who are as sick as I am be of any help to me? The cement that binds A.A.'s together is not just that they have a common problem but that they have found a common solution (17:12).

The physical symptoms detailed in "The Doctor's Opinion" together with the mental obsession described here begin to give us a more complete view of alcoholism. The authors suggest that someone exhibiting these symptoms ". . .has probably placed himself beyond human aid" (24:15). This opinion is reinforced by the pronouncement of Dr. Carl Jung that he had never seen one single case recover where that state of mind existed as it did in Roland H. who was treated by Dr. Jung for alcoholism. The only hope Dr. Jung held out for Roland was a vital spiritual awakening (27:3-12). This deep and effective spiritual awakening is exactly what the authors state is available to us through the application of their program (25:8-10). They promise to give us "clear-cut directions" showing how this awakening was produced in their lives (29:1) and to answer "specifically" (20:5), our question as to what we are to do. They claim to have no desire to convince us that there is only one way in which faith can be acquired (28:6). We are free to choose our own concept of God (12:10).

We can see that the authors have obviously encountered the same difficulties that we have. Here they say that they have discovered a solution and successfully applied it to their own lives. They are undeniably right about what the problem is. They don't mince words about the solution. They see that what is needed is more than a mere change in behavior but rather a fundamental remaking of everything that makes us who we are. The promise that they can show us how to bring about an entire reorganization of our character gives us hope that we too can recover.

The Blueprint

Alcoholics Anonymous	The members of the fellowship were once without hope of solving their problem, but they found a solution that will work for us too.
Illness	This illness takes everyone who has it to much the same places. The writers understand the problem so well because they have been there.
Solution	A personality change sufficient to overcome alcoholism is described in no uncertain terms here. The writers promise to give us clear-cut directions showing how this can be brought about in our lives.

Chapter Two
THERE IS A SOLUTION

17:1We, of ALCOHOLICS ANONYMOUS, know one hundred men who were once just as hopeless as Bill. 2All have recovered. 3They have solved the drink problem.

4We are average Americans. 5All sections of this country and many of its occupations are represented, as well as many political, economic, social, and religious backgrounds. 6We are people who normally would not mix. 7But there exists among us a fellowship, a friendliness, and an understanding which is indescribably wonderful. 8We are like the passengers of a great liner the moment after rescue from shipwreck when camaraderie, joyousness and democracy pervade the vessel from steerage to Captain's table. 9Unlike the feelings of the ship's passengers, however, our joy in escape from disaster does not subside as we go our individual ways. 10The feeling of having shared in a common peril is one element in the powerful cement which binds us. 11But that in itself would never have held us together as we are now joined.

17:Title
Solution:
xiii:2, xxix:1,
20:4-5, 25:3,
25:8-10, 27:9-
12, 29:1,
35:16, 44:3-4,
45:4-9, 52:6,
85:7-8

17:1
Hopeless:
xiii:1, xxiii:6,
xxvii:2, xxix:6,
xxix:16, 6:15,
7:19, 10:3,
14:16, 20:3,
26:16, 27:5,
39:3, 42:10,
43:8-9, 44:5,
92:7, 94:12,
113:22, tt28:7

17:2-3
Recovered:
Title Page,
xiii:1, xxiii:10,
20:3, 29:1,
44:14, 85:14,
90:14, 96:8,
113:6, 132:20,
133:8, 146:12

17:5
Affiliation:
xlv:3, 27:16,
28:12, 74:2-3,
87:13-18,
131:15-16,

17:8-14
Vessel:
161:12,
152:28

17:1 Are we just as hopeless as Bill? Have we tried everything we can think of to regain control of our drinking? Have we exhausted every human resource available to us? What real hope do we have that we will be able to recover on our own?

17:2-5 If these seemingly hopeless alcoholics have recovered, are we so different that it won't work for us? Our pride and self–pity make us feel different and unique. This solution has worked for millions of people. It will also work for us.

17:4-6 Nothing in our background, position, achievements, or social standing disqualifies us from being alcoholic.

17:10 Imagine what the results would be if, having shared our common peril, we all dis-covered separate solutions. We would go our separate ways like the survivors of a shipwreck. At meetings we disclose our stories in a general way so that new people can see themselves in us, then we tell what happened, how we found the solution, and what the results have been.

17:12-14 A.A. at one time adopted a logo. A triangle within a circle. The circle represented the entire fellowship of A.A. The foundation of the triangle represented recovery while the other two sides represented unity and service. Recovery, unity and service are the three legacies of A.A. Finding that protecting it's ownership of this symbol was becoming a distraction from A.A.'s primary purpose of carrying the message of recovery, A.A. decided to discontinue its use.

^{17:12}The tremendous fact for every one of us is that we have discovered a common solution. ¹³We have a way out on which we can absolutely agree, and upon which we can join in brotherly and harmonious action. ¹⁴This is the great news this book carries to those who suffer alcoholism.

^{18:1}An illness of this sort—and we have come to believe it an illness—involves those about us in a way no other human sickness can. ²If a person has cancer all are sorry for him and no one is angry or hurt. ³But not so with the alcoholic illness, for with it there goes annihilation of all the things worth while in life. ⁴It engulfs all whose lives touch the sufferer's. ⁵It brings misunderstanding, fierce resentment, financial insecurity, disgusted friends and employers, warped lives of blameless children, sad wives and parents—anyone can increase the list.

⁶We hope this volume will inform and comfort those who are, or who may be affected. ⁷They are many.

⁸Highly competent psychiatrists who have dealt with us found it sometimes impossible to persuade an alcoholic to discuss his situation without reserve. ⁹Strangely enough, wives, parents and intimate friends usually find us even more unapproachable than do the psychiatrist and the doctor.

¹⁰*But the ex-alcoholic who has found this solution, who is properly armed with facts about himself, can generally win the entire confidence of another alcoholic in a few hours.* ¹¹*Until such an understanding is reached, little or nothing can be accomplished.*

18:1-5 This is a picture of an alcoholic life. It helps us to understand that alcoholism is not a moral deficiency. If these symptoms are present in our lives we may be alcoholics also. These are the opposite of the promises listed on pages 83 & 84. We find relief comes as a result of working the 12 Steps.

18:8-9 One reason we may not have been candid with others in the past is because we felt that they could not understand. Worse yet, we weren't sure ourselves why it was that we continued on in the way we did. Those close to us would give us advice that we knew we could not follow, even though many times we tried. We found it almost impossible to discuss our powerlessness over alcohol with those who did not understand.

18:10-19:1 We have found this solution to be a design for living that really works. We have practical experience applying the program of action including knowledge of who and what we really are, obtained by working steps four through nine, which gives us the ability to relay our message with a depth and weight certain to establish an understanding with a fellow alcoholic.

18:12That the man who is making the approach has had the same difficulty, that he obviously knows what he is talking about, that his whole deportment shouts at the new prospect that he is a man with a real answer, that he has no attitude of holier than thou, nothing whatever except the sincere desire to be helpful; that there are no fees to pay, no axes to grind, no people to please, no lectures to be endured—these are the conditions we found most effective. 19:1After such an approach many take up their beds and walk again.

2None of us makes a sole vocation of this work, nor do we think its effectiveness would be increased if we did. 3We feel that elimination of our drinking is but a beginning. 4A much more important demonstration of our principles lies before us in our respective homes, occupations, and affairs. 5All of us spend much of our spare time in the sort of effort which we are going to describe. 6A few are fortunate enough to be so situated that they can give nearly all of their time to the work.

7If we keep on the way we are going there is little doubt that much good will result, but the surface of the problem would hardly be scratched. 8Those of us who live in large cities are overcome by the reflection that close by hundreds are dropping into oblivion every day. 9Many could recover if they had the opportunity we have enjoyed. 10How then shall we present that which has been so freely given us?

18:10
This:
17:12-14,
60:1

18:10-11
Facts:
83:23, 84:1,
89:4-5, 89:17,
91:16-19,
123:2, 124:2-
10, 132:20

18:10
Confidence:
89:5, 92:5

18:12
Shouts:
11:22, 17:14

19:2-6
Vocation:
xiii:9

19:3
Elimination:
xxix:7, 35:17,
82:19, 51:1,
63:17, 64:2,
122:14,
103:10

19:3
Beginning:
12:15, 25:10,
35:17, 46:9,
47:4, 47:16,
63:17, 68:23,
71:2, 84:14,
85:24, 158:10,
163:1

19:4
Demonstration:
xiii:2, 14:19,
49:13, 51:2,
55:7, 68:21,
77:10, 98:12-19

18:10-19:1 We are not armed with ideas about what the other person should do, but rather facts about who we are and how we have overcome our problem with the aid of a Power greater than ourselves. This is a take it or leave it program. No one is saying we have to do these things or even that we should do them, but only that others have done them and that they worked for them. We did not do this because we are better than others, but only because we had nowhere else to turn and someone who had a real solution approached us.

19:3-4 If alcohol was the cause of our problems, quitting drinking would solve them. Why doesn't it? The reason many alcoholics drink is that we think it is a solution to our problems. Once we remove our failed solution (drinking) we are left to face the underlying causes. We learn to face and successfully deal with life's problems by practicing the steps of this simple program of action.

19:9-12 This opportunity we now enjoy is the legacy of the first one hundred men and women. This gift has been freely given to us by our sponsors, and by the people in meetings, not only those who share their experience, strength and hope, but also those who set up, clean up, run the meetings, answer the phones and work at the district, area and world levels doing service of all kinds.

19:11We have concluded to publish an anonymous volume setting forth the problem as we see it. 12We shall bring to the task our combined experience and knowledge. 13This should suggest a useful program for anyone concerned with a drinking problem.

14Of necessity there will have to be discussion of matters medical, psychiatric, social, and religious. 15We are aware that these matters are, from their very nature, controversial. 16Nothing would please us so much as to write a book which would contain no basis for contention or argument. 17We shall do our utmost to achieve that ideal. 18Most of us sense that real tolerance of other people's shortcomings and viewpoints and a respect for their opinions are attitudes which make us more useful to others. 20:1Our very lives, as ex-alcoholics, depend upon our constant thought of others and how we may help meet their needs.

2You may already have asked yourself why it is that all of us became so very ill from drinking. 3Doubtless you are curious to discover how and why, in the face of expert opinion to the contrary, we have recovered from a hopeless condition of mind and body. 4If you are an alcoholic who wants to get over it, you may already be asking, "What do I have to do?"

19:10 The study of how to most effectively carry this message is the most worthwhile study we can make. To prevent this message from being diluted or misinterpreted and to carry it to as many people as possible was the reason Alcoholics Anonymous was published. The writers were not trying to become famous, but were thinking of us and how they could best meet our needs.

19:13-17 The authors do not tell us what we ought to do, but rather show us what they have done to recover. The authors leave it up to us to decide what it is that we need to do. This is not to say that A.A. is a program of suggestions, but rather it is a suggested program which if adopted as a way of life can lead an alcoholic to recovery. When they speak of medical, psychiatric, social and religious topics, we try to avoid contempt prior to investigation (387:1). We investigate first, then we decide.

20:1 The authors of this book were educated people (xiii:8). When this book was written, great care was taken in the selection of words. They knew what they were saying when they wrote it and they wrote exactly what they meant, each word was carefully chosen. Here they are stating very simply a profound truth, a truth that had been proven by trial. Our self-centeredness is fatal to us as it can block us off from God and lead us back to drinking. How can we be selfish and self-centered if we are constantly thinking of how we can be useful to others?

20:5It is the purpose of this book to answer such questions specifically. 6We shall tell you what we have done. 7Before going into a detailed discussion, it may be well to summarize some points as we see them.

8How many times people have said to us: "*I* can take it or leave it alone. 9Why can't he?" 10"Why don't you drink like a gentleman or quit?" 11"That fellow can't handle his liquor." 12"Why don't you try beer and wine?" 13"Lay off the hard stuff." 14"His will power must be weak." 15"*He* could stop if he wanted to." 16"She's such a sweet girl, I should think he'd stop for her." 17"The doctor told him that if he ever drank again it would kill him, but there he is all lit up again."

18Now these are commonplace observations on drinkers which we hear all the time. 19Back of them is a world of ignorance and misunderstanding. 20We see that these expressions refer to people whose reactions are very different from ours.

21Moderate drinkers have little trouble in giving up liquor entirely if they have good reason for it. 22They can take it or leave it alone.

23Then we have a certain type of hard drinker. 24He may have the habit badly enough to gradually impair him physically and mentally. 21:1It may cause him to die a few years before

20:4
Do:
13:21, 50:14, 60:15, 68:13, 69:9, 152:13

20:4-6
Specifically:
xiii:2 , 29:1, 45:4-9, 85:22, 86:3, 143:14, tt34:12

20:4-5
Done:
xiii:2, xxix:1, 17:Title, 25:3, 25:8-10, 27:9-12, 29:1, 35:16, 44:3-4, 45:4-9, 52:6, 85:7-8, 95:12

20:19
Misunderstand:
18:5, 42:5, 63:15, 74:5, 112:21, 140:14

20:21-21:4
Classification:
xxviii:3, 108:18-110:17

20:21
Moderate:
34:9-15, 139:8-14

20:23
Hard:
108:18-109:9, 139:8, 149:14-16

20:4 Why might we be asking, "What do I have to do?" Perhaps because we have tried everything we can think of and like Bill (17:18) and the two fellows in the Doctor's Opinion (8:2 & 8:12) have admitted defeat and are now willing to look outside ourselves for an answer.

20:5 Faced with alcoholic destruction, we become willing to follow specific and clear-cut directions on how to recover. If we possessed the answers, we would have put them into effect long ago. We can be grateful that the authors graciously show us precisely what we can do to recover.

20:5-6 We are being offered specific answers of exactly what we can do to recover from this illness. Rather than advice about what we ought to do from people who do not understand us, we are told what these people, who suffer from our common problem, did to recover. They understand our obstinate resistance to advice. Every word in this book is designed to illustrate the path to recovery that the authors followed.

20:8-11 How could they possibly understand the phenomenon of craving or the mental obsession of the alcoholic without experiencing them?

20:21-22 Am I a moderate drinker? Can I take it or leave it alone? We can diagnose our problem by asking ourselves the questions in this book.

time. $^{21:2}$If a sufficiently strong reason—ill health, falling in love, change of environment, or the warning of a doctor— becomes operative, this man can also stop or moderate, although he may find it difficult and troublesome and may even need medical attention.

^{3}But what about the real alcoholic? ^{4}He may start off as a moderate drinker; he may or may not become a continuous hard drinker; but at some stage of his drinking career he begins to lose all control of his liquor consumption, once he starts to drink.

^{5}Here is the fellow who has been puzzling you, especially in his lack of control. ^{6}He does absurd, incredible, tragic things while drinking. ^{7}He is a real Dr. Jekyll and Mr. Hyde. ^{8}He is seldom mildly intoxicated. ^{9}He is always more or less insanely drunk. ^{10}His disposition while drinking resembles his normal nature but little. ^{11}He may be one of the finest fellows in the world. ^{12}Yet let him drink for a day, and he frequently becomes disgustingly, and even dangerously anti-social. ^{13}He has a positive genius for getting tight at exactly the wrong moment, particularly when some important decision must be made or engagement kept. ^{14}He is often perfectly sensible and well balanced concerning everything except liquor, but in that respect is incredibly dishonest and selfish. ^{15}He often possesses special abilities, skills, and aptitudes, and has a promising career ahead of him. ^{16}He uses his gifts to build up a bright outlook for his family and himself, then pulls the structure down on his head by a senseless

21:3-4 Am I a real alcoholic? Can I always maintain control of my liquor consumption once I have started drinking? These last three paragraphs are here to help us decide for ourselves if we are in fact alcoholic. This definition of an alcoholic does not include any of our stereotypical thinking of what an alcoholic is. This definition does not rest on "living on skid row" or "drinking all the time". It bases its definition solely on one's ability to always control one's consumption and one's ability to stop drinking altogether if a good reason exists.

21:5-22:5 Does this depiction roughly identify us? Of course, we don't fit this description exactly. Perhaps we don't expect we will ever exhibit some of these symptoms. Though, we never expected to be exhibiting the symptoms that we are suffering from now. If some of this description is too accurate to deny that it describes us and if we are having these things happen to us, perhaps we are alcoholic also.

series of sprees. 21:17He is the fellow who goes to bed so intox-icated he ought to sleep the clock around. 18Yet early next morning he searches madly for the bottle he misplaced the night before. 22:1If he can afford it, he may have liquor con-cealed all over his house to be certain no one gets his entire supply away from him to throw down the wastepipe. 2As mat-ters grow worse, he begins to use a combination of high-powered sedative and liquor to quiet his nerves so he can go to work. 3Then comes the day when he simply cannot make it and gets drunk all over again. 4Perhaps he goes to a doc-tor who gives him morphine or some sedative with which to taper off. 5Then he begins to appear at hospitals and sanitariums.

6This is by no means a comprehensive picture of the true alcoholic, as our behavior patterns vary. 7But this description should identify him roughly.

8Why does he behave like this? 9If hundreds of experiences have shown him that one drink means another debacle with all its attendant suffering and humiliation, why is it he takes that one drink? 10Why can't he stay on the water wagon? 11What has become of the common sense and willpower that he still sometimes displays with respect to other matters?

12Perhaps there never will be a full answer to these ques-tions. 13Opinions vary considerably as to why the alcoholic reacts differently from normal people. 14We are not sure why, once a certain point is reached, little can be done for him. 15We cannot answer the riddle.

16We know that while the alcoholic keeps away from drink as he may do for months or years, he reacts much like other

22:1 Concealed: 8:21

22:1 Addiction: xxv:2, xxvii:6, xxviii:15, 3:24, 5:2-6, 6:7-23, 13:4, 21:3, 22:17,23:18, 24:1, 24:3-6, 32:2, 32:8, 39:12, 40:6, 177:8

22:2-5 Sedatives: 7:1, 177:8

22:9 Insidious: 8:14, 23:2, 23:9, 24:6, 35:2, 37:6, 40:10, 41:20, 43:14-16, 154:17

22:9 Control: xxvii:13, xxviii:1, 1:4, 5:26, 6:3-4, 22:17, 24:1-6, 43:14-16

22:11 Willpower: xxix:18, 7:10, 11:9, 20:14, 24:3-6,32:13, 33:9, 34:2, 34:12, 40:12, 42:4, 45:2-3, 76:18, 85:19-20, 92:8, 107:19, 140:5

22:14 Can Be Done: 24:15, 25:12, 44:4, 62:11-14, 92:13

22:8-11 These are not rhetorical questions. They are placed here so that we will ask them of ourselves. Our lack of an adequate answer to these questions, that ring so soundly of the truth, shines a bright light on our predicament.

22:14 Have we reached the point where little can be done for us? Have we reached the point

where there is little hope for our recovery? Having arrived at the point where there is little that can be done for us, where is it that we can turn for a solution? Admitting that we have arrived at this point is the first step in recovery.

22:16-23:1 If our experience confirms this to be true for us, then perhaps we are alcoholic and in need of a solution.

men. ²²:¹⁷We are equally positive that once he takes any alcohol whatever into his system, something happens, both in the bodily and mental sense, which makes it virtually impossible for him to stop. ²³:¹The experience of any alcoholic will abundantly confirm that.

²These observations would be academic and pointless if our friend never took the first drink thereby setting the terrible cycle in motion. ³Therefore, the main problem of the alcoholic centers in his mind, rather than in his body. ⁴If you ask him why he started on that last bender, the chances are he will offer you any one of a hundred alibis. ⁵Sometimes these excuses have a certain plausibility, but none of them really make sense in the light of the havoc an alcoholic's drinking bout creates. ⁶They sound like the philosophy of the man who, having a headache, beat himself on the head with a hammer so that he couldn't feel the ache. ⁷If you draw this fallacious reasoning to the attention of an alcoholic, he will laugh it off, or become irritated and refuse to talk.

⁸Once in a while he may tell the truth. ⁹And the truth, strange to say, is usually that he has no more idea why he took that first drink than you have. ¹⁰Some drinkers have excuses with which they are satisfied part of the time. ¹¹But in their hearts they really do not know why they do it. ¹²Once this malady has a real hold, they are a baffled lot. ¹³There is the obsession that somehow, some day, they will beat the game. ¹⁴But they often suspect they are down for the count.

23:2 The phenomenon of craving can not overcome us as long as we do not take that first drink. This phenomenon seems to be a physical result of our increased sensitivity to alcohol. The book changes focus at this point and addresses the problem of why we are unable to abstain from drinking by using our own willpower.

23:3 The author's discussion of the mental aspects of alcoholism begins here. Our allergy to alcohol, described by Dr. Silkworth, and our mental obsession depicted here combine to make our alcoholic condition appear seemingly hopeless.

23:8-13 Alcoholics are every bit as baffled by their drinking as everyone else. Who in their right mind would continue to drink knowing the awful consequences? Many alcoholics appear to be sane when not drinking. Their judgment and willpower are adequate in many areas, but not where drinking is concerned. The delusion that we will be able to control our drinking overrides our ever growing experience that we can not.

23:15How true this is, few realize. 16In a vague way their families and friends sense that these drinkers are abnormal, but everybody hopefully waits the day when the sufferer will rouse himself from his lethargy and assert his power of will.

17The tragic truth is that if the man be a real alcoholic, the happy day will seldom arrive. 18He has lost control. 24:1At a certain point in the drinking of every alcoholic, he passes into a state where the most powerful desire to stop drinking is of absolutely no avail. 2This tragic situation has already arrived in practically every case long before it is suspected.

3The fact is that most alcoholics, for reasons yet obscure, have lost the power of choice in drink. 4*Our so-called willpower becomes practically non-existent.* 5*We are unable at certain times, to bring into our consciousness with sufficient force the memory of the suffering and humiliation of even a week or a month ago.* 6*We are without defense against the first drink.*

23:17
Real:
21:3-4, 30:1,
30:11, 31:5,
33:14, 34:3-4,
35:22, 44:5,
92:7, 109:10-21

24:1
Abstinence:
xxviii:18

24:1-6
Control:
xxvii:13, xxviii:1,
1:4; 5:26, 6:3-4,
22:11, 22:17,
43:14-16

24:1-6
Defense:
xxvii:13-xxviii:1,
6-4, 22:17,
24:7-8, 33:10,
35:2, 37:7,
40:12, 41:21,
42:4, 43:14-16,
92:3-8, 157:19

24:3
Powerless:
11:16, 34:11,
45:2-4, 46:12,
50:15, 59:2,
59:8, 60:12,
62:13, 63:6,
118:19

23:13 One A.A. explained: "The difference between an impulse, a compulsion and an obsession is that an impulse is when upon seeing a can lying in the road you want to kick it, a compulsion drives you to kick the can without thinking and an obsession causes you to search all over town for cans to kick."

23:14-15 By the time we begin to suspect our drinking might just possibly be getting out of control, that perhaps drinking might be causing some of our problems, it is probably too late to stop without help.

23:16 Those around us, many times, see that our drinking is abnormal before we do. Commonly, we deny to ourselves and others that our drinking is out of control. We feel drinking gives us relief from the circumstances of our lives.

23:17-24:2 This is a definition of alcoholism we can test for ourselves. Do we sincerely desire to quit drinking entirely? Are we able to? Have we tried to quit and failed? How many times? Have we promised our families we will stop and then found ourselves unable? Have we failed to stay sober even after we made this promise to ourselves?

24:3-6 This is why good intentions, firm resolve and sincere desire are of absolutely no use in combating alcoholism. The memory of how bad it was will not keep us sober for long. Left to our own devices we will inevitably drink again.

24:6 Where are we to turn? We are powerless over alcohol. We cannot stay away from drinking. Our human resources have failed us. Once we admit these things to ourselves, we may be willing to look to a Power greater than ourselves for a solution.

[24:7]The almost certain consequences that follow taking even a glass of beer do not crowd into the mind to deter us. [8]If these thoughts occur, they are hazy, and readily supplanted with the old threadbare idea that this time we shall handle ourselves like other people. [9]There is a complete failure of the kind of defense that keeps one from putting his hand on a hot stove.

[10]The alcoholic may say to himself in the most casual way, "It won't burn me this time, so here's how!" [11]Or perhaps he doesn't think at all. [12]How often have some of us begun to drink in this nonchalant way, and after the third or fourth, pounded on the bar and said to ourselves, "For God's sake, how did I ever get started again?" [13]Only to have that thought supplanted by "Well, I'll stop with the sixth drink." [14]Or "What's the use anyhow?"

[15]When this sort of thinking is fully established in an individual with alcoholic tendencies, he has probably placed himself beyond human aid, and unless locked up, may die, or go permanently insane. [16]These stark and ugly facts have been confirmed by legions of alcoholics throughout history. [25:1]But for the grace of God, there would have been one hundred more convincing demonstrations. [2]So many want to stop, but cannot.

24:7 What are the almost certain consequences of taking a drink? Will this be the start of another spree? Will our spouse leave us? Will we lose our job? Will we be thrown in jail?

24:8 Things become threadbare by overuse. We try so many times to drink like other people one would think we would eventually learn that it is never going to happen.

24:9 This description of the alcoholic mind explains why we are unable to stop drinking no matter how much we ought to, need to, or want to. If our thinking was like a non-alcoholic person, we would have stopped drinking the second we saw the trouble it was causing us. Our inability to stop is explained by the fact that we suffer from a form of insanity. We need only look at all the suc-cessful recoveries in A.A. to know that God can restore us to sanity.

24:15 Being beyond human aid leaves us little choice but to seek a spiritual solution to our problem. The truth is that most of us have few if any options left to us when we are presented with this program of recovery. We turned to this proven program only because we had exhausted all other avenues. If we feel as hopeless as did the authors, then perhaps we are ready to set aside our reluctance and give this method an honest try.

25:3 There is a solution! We are only seemingly hopeless. We have a program of action that has restored millions of alcoholics to happy useful lives.

25:3 *There is a solution.* ⁴Almost none of us liked the self-searching, the leveling of our pride, the confession of short-comings which the process requires for its successful consummation. ⁵But we saw that it really worked in others, and we had come to believe in the hopelessness and futility of life as we had been living it. ⁶When, therefore, we were approached by those in whom the problem had been solved, there was nothing left for us but to pick up the simple kit of spiritual tools laid at our feet. ⁷We have found much of heaven and we have been rocketed into a fourth dimension of existence, of which we had not even dreamed.

⁸The great fact is just this, and nothing less: that we have had deep and effective spiritual experiences, which have revolutionized our whole attitude toward life, toward our fellows, and toward God's universe. ⁹The central fact of our lives today is the absolute certainty that our Creator has entered into our hearts and lives in a way which is indeed miraculous. ¹⁰He has commenced to accomplish those things for us which we could never do by ourselves.

25:3 Solution: xiii:2, xxix:1, 17:Title, 20:4-5, 25:8-10, 27:9-12, 44:3-4, 52:6, 85:7-8

25:4 Requires: xiv:1, xxvii:3, 12:15, 13:22, 14:19-20, 50:16, 60:16, 94:15, 143:9

25:6 Tools: 95:8

25:8-10 Experience: xxvii:2, xxvii:3, xxvii:10, 12:1-2, 14:4-8, 27:9-12, 44:3-4, 84:25, 143:9, 158:10

25:8-10 Fact: 11:22, 17:12, 51:3, 55:11, 119:18, 130:3, 161:3, 164:12

25:10 Ourselves: 11:8, 45:5, 50:11, 70:23, 84:8, 100:6, 102:18

25:4 This program works. We may apply it to our lives if we choose to. Should we desire to give the A.A. program a try, this paragraph lists a few of the requirements for success.

25:5-6 Here are millions of people who say that this new way of life is better than anything they have ever tried. If we really are powerless over alcohol, if our lives really are unmanageable, if we really are beyond human aid, what then do we have to lose? This solution is being offered to us, not forced upon us. We can pick up these tools and begin to use them to reconstruct our shattered lives.

25:6 The people who are presenting this solution to us are not reformers or proselytizers. They are alcoholics like ourselves. Their alcoholic problem has been solved and they are willing to show us what they have done.

25:7 When we throw that switch there is no turning back. Our destination is a life of purpose, meaning, usefulness, joyousness and freedom. A life that is comprised of these things certainly seems like another dimension to those of us who have only known the misery, pointlessness and bondage of a life based on self-will.

25:8-10 This is the authors' description of a spiritual awakening. These are the results of the abandonment of one's life to the care of God and the willingness to seek and follow God's guidance in all things. So much is available to us when we are willing to pay the price which is the destruction of our self-centeredness.

25:8-10 We are promised a spiritual awakening as a result of these steps. What is described here is not a mere modification of behavior, but a reconstruction of the fundamental nature of those who experience this awakening. This awakening may come suddenly or slowly, but is inevitable if we follow the path of those who have gone before us.

25:11
Half mea-
sures:
58:14, 59:4,
98:18-19,
164:13

25:12
Turning Point:
53:8-10, 59:5

25:12
Alternatives:
7:21, 8:15,
44:6-10

25:13
Honest:
xiv:2, 5:18,
28:7, 57:11,
58:9, 70:8,
73:5, 96:1-8,
114:7, 147:3,
159:5,
161:11, 120:5

26:1
Rowland H.:
9:30

26:7
Relapse:
31:2, 30:12,
35:1, 120:6,
125:2, 147:2

26:7
Self-knowl-
edge:
7:15, 36:22,
38:18, 39:3,
40:2-6, 42:4

26:9
Baffling:
xxvii:14, 5:12-
13, 6:4, 23:9-
12, 34:15,
35:4-5, 37:9,
40:8, 58:15, 92:1

[25:11]If you are as seriously alcoholic as we were, we believe there is no middle-of-the-road solution. [12]We were in a position where life was becoming impossible, and if we had passed into the region from which there is no return through human aid, we had but two alternatives: one was to go on to the bitter end, blotting out the consciousness of our intolerable situation as best we could; and the other, to accept spiritual help. [13]This we did because we honestly wanted to, and were willing to make the effort.

[26:1]A certain American business man had ability, good sense, and high character. [2]For years he had floundered from one sanitarium to another. [3]He had consulted the best known American psychiatrists. [4]Then he had gone to Europe, placing himself in the care of a celebrated physician who prescribed for him. [5]Though experience had made him skeptical, he finished his treatment with unusual confidence. [6]His physical and mental condition were unusually good. [7]Above all, he believed he had acquired such a profound knowledge of the inner workings of his mind and its hidden springs, that relapse was unthinkable. [8]Nevertheless, he was drunk in a short time. [9]More baffling still, he could give himself no satisfactory explanation for his fall.

Historical Note:
26:1 Rowland H. found the spiritual solution for alcoholism in the Oxford Group, a christian fellowship. He helped Ebby T. find this solution and Ebby, in turn, brought this message to Bill W.
26:4 Dr. Carl Jung treated Rowland H.

25:10 We have been unable to overcome drinking. We have been unable to live up to our own ideals and values. The authors and millions of A.A.s around the world say that reliance upon a Power greater than themselves has begun to solve these problems in their lives. The program of action presented in this book shows us how to begin to access this Power.

25:11 Are we as seriously alcoholic as the authors were? Are we in a seemingly hopeless state of mind and body? Are we unable to control our drinking once we begin? Are we unable to stop drinking altogether? Do we sincerely desire to stop drinking and find that we are unable? Do we exhibit the signs of alcoholic thinking? Have we reached the point where we despair of ever recovering? Are we beyond human aid?

25:11-13 If we have reached the point where we are beyond human aid, where else do we have to turn? Our families, spouses, friends and doctors are all powerless to help us and we can't stop drinking on our own. If we are finally willing, we can quit the futile battle and accept spiritual help.

^{26:10}So he returned to this doctor, whom he admired, and asked him point-blank why he could not recover. ¹¹He wished above all things to regain self-control. ¹²He seemed quite rational and well-balanced with respect to other problems. ¹³Yet he had no control whatever over alcohol. ¹⁴Why was this?

¹⁵He begged the doctor to tell him the whole truth, and he got it. ¹⁶In the doctor's judgment he was utterly hopeless; he could never regain his position in society and he would have to place himself under lock and key, or hire a bodyguard if he expected to live long. ¹⁷That was a great physician's opinion.

¹⁸But this man still lives, and is a free man. ¹⁹He does not need a bodyguard, nor is he confined. ²⁰He can go anywhere on this earth where other free men may go without disaster, provided he remains willing to maintain a certain simple attitude.

^{27:1}Some of our alcoholic readers may think they can do without spiritual help. ²Let us tell you the rest of the conversation our friend had with his doctor.

³The doctor said: "You have the mind of a chronic alcoholic. ⁴I have never seen one single case recover, where that state of mind existed to the extent that it does in you." ⁵Our friend felt as though the gates of hell had closed on him with a clang.

⁶He said to the doctor, "*Is* there no exception?"

⁷"Yes," replied the doctor, "there is. ⁸Exceptions to cases

26:16
Hopeless:
xiii:1, xxiii:6,
xxvii:2, xxix:6,
xxix:16, 6:15,
7:19, 10:3,
14:16, 17:1,
20:3, 27:5,
39:3,
42:10,43:8-9,
44:5, 92:7,
94:12, 113:22,
tt28:7

26:16-17
Doctor:
xxviii:20, 20:3,
27:3-4, 30:16,
43:7-13

26:18
Free:
xxix:14, xxx:2,
13:9, 56:21,
88:4, 156:6,
158:16

26:20
Attitude:
25:8, 27:12,
50:13, 55:16,
63:1, 72:2,
84:5, 86:1,
99:13 143:9,
150:2

27:3-4
Thinking:
(Alcoholic)
24:15, 33:10,
35:1-2, 36:17,
37:1-4, 41:23,
42:10, 101:3,
140:10, 157:19

27:3-4
Doomed:
xiii:1, xxvii:3,
xxviii:20, 24:15,
43:7-8, 44:6,
73:23, 92:17

26:1-7 Many believe our alcoholism to be a psychiatric problem and do not recognize the physical aspect. We mistakenly believe that self-knowledge will solve our problem. We seek out counselors, psychologists and psychiatrists hoping to find an answer. When self-knowledge fails, we begin to lose our self-confidence.

26:16-17 Once again we see that many physicians agree that chronic alcoholics are doomed (xxviii:20).

26:20 This simple attitude is described earlier in this chapter (25:8-10). Our spiritual fitness requires maintenance and our willingness is a result of our admission of powerlessness. The moment we think that we have power over alcohol and that we can manage our own lives we cease to be willing to accept spiritual help.

27:3-4 To have an alcoholic mind (24:3-15) is a seemingly hopeless condition. No human power appears able to restructure a person's thinking to the necessary degree. This subtle form of insanity is why we cannot permanently abstain from drinking no matter how great our need or desire.

such as yours have been occurring since early times. [27:9]Here and there, once in a while, alcoholics have had what are called vital spiritual experiences. [10]To me these occurrences are phenomena. [11]They appear to be in the nature of huge emotional displacements and rearrangements. [12]Ideas, emotions, and attitudes which were once the guiding forces of the lives of these men are suddenly east to one side, and a completely new set of conceptions and motives begin to dominate them. [13]In fact, I have been trying to produce some such emotional rearrangement within you. [14]With many individuals the methods which I employed are successful, but I have never been successful with an alcoholic of your description."

[15]Upon hearing this, our friend was somewhat relieved, for he reflected that, after all, he was a good church member. [16]This hope, however, was destroyed by the doctor's telling him that his religious convictions were very good, but that in his case they did not spell the necessary vital spiritual experience. [28:1]Here was the terrible dilemma in which our friend found himself when he had the extraordinary experience, which as we have already told you, made him a free man.

[2]We, in our turn, sought the same escape, with all the desperation of drowning men. [3]What seemed at first a flimsy reed, has proved to be the loving and powerful hand of God. [4]A new life has been given us or, if you prefer, "a design for

---

27:9-12 What the great physician describes here is a change sufficient to overcome alcoholism. When Dr. Jung uses words such as "huge" he is not describing a slight change of attitude but an entire 180 degree turn away from our failed way of viewing and reacting to life. The things in us that have caused our failure have to be utterly abandoned and a entirely new way of life adopted. The more firmly we cling to our old ways the more slowly this revolutionary change will take place in our lives.

27:16 If our current religious convictions were working, we would not be in the condition we

are now in. We need to develop a new relationship with our Creator, one of far more depth and weight than we have ever had. The program outlined in this book has been successful at producing just such a life-sustaining spiritual awakening for millions of alcoholics.

28:1 Here is the terrible dilemma that we face. We can continue hoping that this time it will work for us or we can abandon ideas and attitudes we have held for a lifetime and adopt this completely new way of living. The choice is entirely ours.

living" that really works.

28:5The distinguished American psychologist, William James, in his book *Varieties of Religious Experience,* indicates a multitude of ways in which men have discovered God. 6We have no desire to convince anyone that there is only one way by which faith can be acquired. 7If what we have learned, and felt, and seen, means anything at all, it means that all of *us,* whatever our race, creed, or color, are the children of a living Creator with whom we may form a relationship upon simple and understandable terms as soon as we are willing and honest enough to try. 8Those having religious affiliations will find here nothing disturbing to their beliefs or ceremonies. 9There *is* no friction among *us* over such matters.

10We think it no concern of ours what religious bodies our members identify themselves with as individuals. 11This should be an entirely personal affair which each one decides for himself in the light of past associations, or his present choice. 12Not all of us have joined religious bodies, but most of us favor such memberships.

13In the following chapter, there appears an explanation of alcoholism as we understand it, then a chapter addressed to the agnostic. 14Many who once were in this class are now

28:5-12 Religion: xiv:7, 9:23, 9:32, 11:18, 17:5, 19:14, 27:16, 43:12, 49:9, 56:8, 74:3, 77:5-7, 87:14-18, 89:17-18, 93:16, 128:4-10, 131:15-16, 132:1

28:6 Only One Way: 95:19, 144:3, 164:5

28:7 Simple: xxvii:3, 9:32, 14:1, 25:6, 26:20, 46:12, 47:11, 50:14-16, 52:8, 57:5, 58:2, 62:21, 88:6, 130:9

28:9 Tolerance: 19:18, 67:2, 67:10, 70:21, 83:6, 84:23, 103:2, 118:9, 125:5, 135:14

28:12 Affiliation: (Religious) xiv:3, 17:5, 27:16, 74:2-3, 87:13-18, 131:15-16

28:2 Our admission of powerlessness makes us willing to try this way that has worked for so many others. If we are not willing, perhaps it is because we still have some faith that somehow we will win out over alcoholism through our own efforts.

28:3 The authors are not asking us to have blind faith, but merely that we give this program an honest try. Our own experience will provide proof that this Power is available to us. All we need to do to begin this new way of life is to follow the path that has been blazed by those who have gone before us.

28:5-7 No one is trying to force their beliefs on us. The authors promise to show us what they have done to recover. If we care to follow their suggestions, then we are promised the same results that they received. Though this may not be the only way, it is a path to a faith that works.

28:8-12 People of many beliefs, creeds and religions the world over have recovered from alcoholism by using this program of action.

28:14 Agnostics are those with no direct experience with God working in their lives. Many of us fall into this category. The spiritual program of action produces direct experience so that we may have a spiritual awakening about which there will be no doubt. To begin, all we need is a willingness to try.

among our members; surprisingly enough, we find such convictions no great obstacle to a spiritual experience.

29:1Further on, clear-cut directions are given showing how we recovered. 2These are followed by more than a score of personal experiences.

3Each individual, in the personal stories, describes in his own language, and from his own point of view the way he established his relationship with God. 4These give a fair cross section of our membership and a clear-cut idea of what has actually happened in their lives.

5We hope no one will consider these self-revealing accounts in bad taste. 6Our hope is that many alcoholic men and women, desperately in need, will see these pages, and we believe that it is only by fully disclosing ourselves and our problems that they will be persuaded to say, "Yes, I am one of them too; I must have this thing."

29:1 Many of us hear that there are no musts in A. A. and that there is no right or wrong way to work the steps. Hearing this we may wrongly assume that there is nothing we must do and mistakenly fear that there is nothing we can do to recover. If we knew what to do, we would have done it a long time ago. The promise of clear-cut directions is the promise that there actually is something we can do.

29:3-6 The personal stories are told to illustrate how the authors began to awaken spiritually. To see how people, who obviously suffered from the same problem that we now face, recovered will help us to see that we can also recover.

29:6 The author's hope is that we will be able to decide for ourselves if we are alcoholic or not and, if we are, that we might follow their path to recovery.

"I don't know. I see that I am quite a bit like these people, but if I can just quit drinking for awhile I'll be OK. Maybe if I only drank beer I wouldn't get into so much trouble. I see what the symptoms of alcoholism are and though I exhibit some of them I am not yet willing to accept that I am an alcoholic. I feel that I am different than the authors and that I do not need to adopt such an approach to solve my drinking problem."

The authors, being just like us, anticipate our reluctance to admit our alcoholism. The short term laying off from drinking that we hope will serve as a solution is shown to be wishful thinking. One by one our objections are addressed by the example of the authors' own experience. We are allowed to make our own diagnosis of our condition.

The authors describe our greatest obstacle and share the fact that the admission to ourselves that we are alcoholic is the first step in our recovery (30:7-8). The progressive nature of alcoholism is presented (30:10-14, 30:16). Some of our attempts at controlling our drinking are outlined (31:11). Two methods of determining if we are truly alcoholic are proposed (31:10-14, 34:3-4). The authors show that even long periods of abstinence will not restore our ability to control our drinking. If we admit we are unable to drink moderately, then the question is how to quit altogether (34:9). The baffling nature of alcoholism, our inability to quit entirely even when we sincerely desire to do so, is described (34:12-15). The mental states that precede the first drink are illustrated and we are shown the undeniable insanity of resuming drinking after having determined not to do so and having a full knowledge of the consequences (35:6-37:9). The seeming hopelessness of our situation, being presented to us in this way, leads us to the inescapable conclusion that left to our own resources we are certain to return to drinking (43:15-16).

We are presented with a clear picture of the alcoholic problem. Our hope of recovering on our own is dashed as we discover the truth of our situation. There is nowhere else we can turn to find relief but to a Power greater than ourselves.

The Blueprint

The First Step In Recovery	Clear-cut directions for taking our first step are given here.
The Nature of Alcoholism	The symptoms of alcoholism are detailed and our hope of regaining control of our drinking is smashed.
Efforts to Control Our Drinking	Various methods that we have employed in failed attempts to gain control of our drinking are examined.
We May Diagnose Ourselves	Are we alcoholic or are we not? Methods for self-diagnosis are presented. The symptoms are reiterated and the lack of prerequisites for alcoholism is shown.
Insanity of the First Drink	Examples illustrating the baffling nature of alcoholism are given. Our lack of mental defense from the first drink is plainly shown.
Hopelessness	The authors help us to recognize the hopelessness of our situation so that we may move out of hopelessness and on to recovery.

30:1
Unwilling:
xxviii:8, 39:14-
40:1, 44:9,
58:2, 110:4

30:1
Real:
21:3-4, 23:17,
24:1, 30:11,
31:5, 33:14,
34:3-4, 35:22,
44:5, 92:7,
109:10-21

30:4,
Obsession:
23:13,151:8,
155:9

30:6
Gates:
xxv:11, 27:5

Chapter Three
MORE ABOUT ALCOHOLISM

30:1Most of us have been unwilling to admit we were real alcoholics. 2No person likes to think he is bodily and mentally different from his fellows. 3Therefore, it is not surprising that our drinking careers have been characterized by countless vain attempts to prove we could drink like other people. 4The idea that somehow, someday he will control and enjoy his liquor drinking is the great obsession of every abnormal drinker. 5The persistence of this illusion is astonishing. 6Many pursue it into the gates of insanity or death.

30:1-2 When the authors use the term "most of us," they mean that it is very likely that we suffer from the same lack of willingness that they did. To help us diagnose our own alcoholism, they define it as being bodily and mentally different from our fellows. Though this is perhaps an unpleasant admission, we have to agree that in the light of our past experience this is true.

30:3-5 "Therefore" means we accept what has come before. Our unwillingness to admit our alcoholism leads us to try countless times to control our drinking. We become obsessed with the idea that this time our drinking will not get out of control, that we will enjoy our drinking as we did early in our drinking careers. Usually, if we control our drinking we do not enjoy it and if we drink enough to enjoy it, we lose control. The illusion that we have power over alcohol and that we can control it remains with us long after it is evident to everyone around us that we can not.

30:7We learned that we had to fully concede to our inner-most selves that we were alcoholics. 8This is the first step in recovery. 9The delusion that we are like other people, or presently may be, has to be smashed.

10We alcoholics are men and women who have lost the ability to control our drinking. 11We know that no real alco-holic ever recovered control. 12All of us felt at times that we were regaining control, but such intervals—usually brief—were inevitably followed by still less control, which led in time to pitiful and incomprehensible demoralization. 13We are convinced to a man that alcoholics of our type are in the grip of a progressive illness. 14Over any considerable period we get worse, never better.

30:7-8
Step One:
8:9-11,10:3,
11:12-16, 13:7,
59:8

30:9
Delusion:
32:13, 40:11,
61:17, 62:4,
154:13, 155:13

30:10
Alcoholism:
xiiii:1,18:3-5,
21:3-4, 32:17,
44:3, 73:6-17,
149:14

31:2
Relapse:
26:7, 30:12,
35:1, 120:6,
125:2, 147:2

30:14
Worse:
5:8

Definition:
30:7 Concede: to admit as true. The opposite is to deny or refuse.

30:7 There are several ways we learn that we must admit powerlessness over alcohol. We learn by reading the book up to this point and by the example of the authors as well as mil-lions of recovered alcoholics. Sometimes we learn by our own mistakes. Repeated failed attempts to control our drinking brings us to the point where we have to admit to our-selves that we are powerless over alcohol.

30:7 To fully concede is to admit that we are alcoholic. Any reservations we have must be set aside. This is not merely complying with the precepts of this program so as to avoid the negative results of drinking, but a com-plete and total surrender to the fact that we can not drink any alcohol at all and we never will be able to drink alcohol normally.

30:7 Who are we to admit our alcoholism to —our group, the police, our spouse? We are to make our admission to ourselves. No one else matters. We must speak to our hearts when making this admission.

30:7-8 These are the directions on how to take our first step. The authors' promise was that they would show us precisely and specif-ically what they have done to recover and supply us with clear-cut directions. The direc-tions are that we must admit we are, in fact, alcoholic and that we make this admission to

ourselves. From the moment we make this admission, we can begin to recover.

30:9 Every word in the book up to this point has been to help smash our delusion. The third sentence of the book explains the authors hope that we can be convinced we are bodily and mentally different from our fel-lows by reading this book. If we are not con-vinced by these pages, we may have to continue in our current ways until our own experience allows us to see the truth of what the authors say.

30:10 This is a definition of alcoholism with which we may be able to identify. We can look at our drinking history and see if at some point we lost the ability to control of our drinking. This is a sign that we may be a real alcoholic.

30:10-14 Alcoholism is diagnosable. In A.A. we determine for ourselves if we are alco-holic. Alcoholism is primary—it is the cause of our problems not the result of them. Alcoholism is progressive—gradually we get worse. Alcoholism is chronic—we usually have this illness for a long time before we try to do anything about it. Alcoholism is fatal—if not arrested it will inevitably lead to our deaths. Alcoholism is treatable—the A.A. pro-gram has over 60 years of success.

30:15We are like men who have lost their legs; they never grow new ones. 16Neither does there appear to be any kind of treatment which will make alcoholics of our kind like other men. 31:1We have tried every imaginable remedy. 2In some instances there has been brief recovery, followed always by still worse relapse. 3Physicians who are familiar with alcoholism agree there is no such thing as making a normal drinker out of an alcoholic. 4Science may one day accomplish this, but it evidently hasn't done so yet.

5Despite all we can say, many who are real alcoholics are not going to believe they are in that class. 6By every form of self-deception and experimentation, they will try to prove themselves exceptions to the rule, therefore non-alcoholic. 7If anyone, who is showing inability to control his drinking, can do the right-about-face and drink like a gentleman, our hats are off to him. 8Heaven knows, we have tried hard enough and long enough to drink like other people!

9Here are some of the methods we have tried: drinking beer only, limiting the number of drinks, never drinking alone, never drinking in the morning, drinking only at home, never having it in the house, never drinking during business hours, drinking only at parties, switching from scotch to brandy, drinking only natural wines, agreeing to

---

30:12 Our inability to control our drinking destroys our confidence in ourselves and in all human aid. We despair of ever recovering. Prior to our understanding of the physical and mental aspects of this disease we thought ourselves weaklings. Now we understand that will power is of very little use against alcoholism. Our hope of recovery rests in finding a Power greater than ourselves.

30:13 We suffer from an illness, a state of unsound physical and mental health. This illness, just like many other illnesses, can not be conquered by will power. Only a spiritual awakening can bring about the profound changes needed for us to recover.

31:1-9 How many of these methods of controlling our drinking have we tried? How many

of our own methods have we tried? How did they work? For how long did they work? People who are not alcoholic do not devise methods to control their drinking. People who are not alcoholic can always control the amount they drink. This is a good test to determine if we are alcoholic.

31:7-8 The authors are not abolitionists or reformers, they are merely people who have faced the same problem we face and have tried the same sort of things we have tried to control their drinking.

31:10 In A.A. we diagnose ourselves. Are we alcoholic or not? Does our drinking fit the pattern described? Do we need to further authenticate what is written in this book?

resign if ever drunk on the job, taking a trip, not taking a trip, swearing off forever (with and without a solemn oath), taking more physical exercise, reading inspirational books, going to health farms and sanitariums, accepting voluntary commitment to asylums—we could increase the list ad infinitum.

^{31:10}We do not like to brand any individual as an alcoholic, but you can quickly diagnose yourself. ¹¹Step over to the nearest barroom and try some controlled drinking. ¹²Try to drink and stop abruptly. ¹³Try it more than once. ^{32:1}It will not take long for you to decide, if you are honest with yourself about it. ²It may be worth a bad case of jitters if you get a full knowledge of your condition.

³Though there is no way of proving it, we believe that early in our drinking careers most of us could have stopped drinking. ⁴But the difficulty is that few alcoholics have enough desire to stop while there is yet time. ⁵We have heard of a few instances where people, who showed definite signs of alcoholism, were able to stop for a long period because of an overpowering desire to do so. ⁶Here is one.

⁷A man of thirty was doing a great deal of spree drinking. ⁸He was very nervous in the morning after these bouts and quieted himself with more liquor. ⁹He was ambitious to succeed

---

31:10-32:2
Diagnosis:
xxix:16, 34:3-4,
34:16-35:1

31:10-32:2
Stop:
xiv:2, xxvii:6,
7:10-11, 19:3,
20:8-20, 20:21-
21:2, 22:17,
23:17, 25:2,
32:16-33:2,
33:8-11, 33:15,
34:9-15, 39:2-4,
109:24, 110:5

32:1
Monesty: (Self)
13:22, 47:3,
55:15, 58:2,
63:17, 64:12,
65:7, 67:19,
73:5, 73:22,
73:24, 83:15

32:2
Jitters:
xxv:2, xxvii:6,
xxviii:15, 3:24,
5:2-6, 6:7-23,
13:4, 21:3,
22:1, 22:17,
23:18, 24:1,
24:3-6, 32:8,
39:12, 40:6,
177:8

31:10 In A.A. we diagnose ourselves. Are we alcoholic or not? Does our drinking fit the pattern described? Do we need to further authenticate what is written in this book?

31:12-32:2 This advice is to help us admit our powerlessness. If we admit to ourselves that we are powerless over alcohol then we will do what it takes to find a Power greater than ourselves. If we still believe we have some power over alcohol then we may waste our time attempting to adopt some new code of morals or a better philosophy of life in the insane belief that our newest plan will work even when all our other plans have failed.

31:12-32:2 This is one way to find out if we are alcoholic once and for all. If we are not alcoholic then we should be able to control our drinking or quit altogether. If our experi-

ment at controlled drinking fails it should smash the delusion that we have some power over alcohol.

32:2 A full knowledge of our condition is a humbling thing. We are powerless over alcohol. Left to human resources we are unable to control our destructive drinking. With nowhere else to go we can turn to a Power we may not have even thought was available to us. Until we have a humble understanding of our inability to help ourselves we are resistant to turn to this Power.

32:3-33: To help smash the delusion that we are like other people is the purpose of this illustration. If we are alcoholic, over time we get worse, never better. The ability to control our drinking never returns, no matter how long we abstain from drinking.

32:11-33:2
Resolutions:
xxvii:1, xxviii:7,
5:14-24, 5:30-
6:4, 7:10, 34:8,
38:5, 39:17,
107:11

32:12
Long:
xxiii:6, xxix:14,
xxx:2, 13:9,
158:15-16,
162:1

32:13
Delusion:
30:9 ,40:11,
61:17, 62:4,
154:13, 155:13

32:16-33:2
Stop:
xlv:2, xxvii:6
7:10-11, 19:3,
20:8-20, 20:21-
21:2, 22:17,
23:17, 25:2,
31:10-32:2,
33:8-11, 33:15,
34:9-15, 39:2-4,
109:24, 110:5,
122:14

32:17
Resources:
(Human)
38:8, 45:3,
50:15, 61:3-6

33:6
Cure:
xxviii:17,30:15-
16, 85:14

33:8
Reservations:
13:6, 14:4,
32:11, 50:16,
63:16, 155:11

in business, but saw that he would get nowhere if he drank at all. ³²:¹⁰Once he started, he had no control whatever. ¹¹He made up his mind that until he had been successful in business and had retired, he would not touch another drop. ¹²An exceptional man, he remained bone dry for twenty-five years, and retired at the age of fifty-five, after a successful and happy business career. ¹³Then he fell victim to a belief which practically every alcoholic has—that his long period of sobriety and self-discipline had qualified him to drink as other men. ¹⁴Out came his carpet slippers and a bottle. ¹⁵In two months he was in a hospital, puzzled and humiliated. ¹⁶He tried to regulate his drinking for a while, making several trips to the hospital meantime. ¹⁷Then, gathering all his forces, he attempted to stop altogether and found he could not. ¹⁸Every means of solving his problem which money could buy was at his disposal. ³³:¹Every attempt failed. ²Though a robust man at retirement, he went to pieces quickly, and was dead within four years.

³This case contains a powerful lesson. ⁴Most of us have believed that if we remained sober for a long stretch, we could thereafter drink normally. ⁵But here is a man who at fifty-five years found he was just where he had left off at thirty. ⁶We have seen the truth demonstrated again and again: "Once an alcoholic, always an alcoholic." ⁷Commencing to drink after a period of sobriety, we are in a short time as bad as ever. ⁸If we are planning to stop drinking, there must be no reservation of any kind, nor any lurking notion that someday we will be immune to alcohol.

32:7-8 Spree drinking, nervousness and drinking in the morning to calm our nerves are signs of alcoholism. We can compare the progression of our own drinking to this fellow. Are we showing signs of alcoholism?

32:9 This man possessed high ambitions and common sense but was still alcoholic. Do we think that our good intentions will protect us from alcoholism? How about will power and firm resolve? This fellow's reliance on resolve kept him sober for 25 years, but then failed him.

32:13 Do we have this belief? Will we also fall victim to it? How have past periods of abstinence worked to restore our ability to control our drinking?

32:18 After self-discipline repeatedly fails to work, we begin to lose confidence in ourselves and seek help from others. When the help of our families, spouses, friends and doctors all fail we are left seemingly hopeless. Unless we can find something greater than human power, we may be doomed as this fellow was.

^{33:9}Young people may be encouraged by this man's experience to think that they can stop, as he did, on their own willpower. ¹⁰We doubt if many of them can do it, because none will really want to stop, and hardly one of them, because of the peculiar mental twist already acquired, will find he can win out. ¹¹Several of our crowd, men of thirty-five or less, had been drinking only a few years, but they found themselves as helpless as those who had been drinking twenty years.

¹²To be gravely affected, one does not necessarily have to drink a long time, nor take the quantities some of us have. ¹³This is particularly true of women. ¹⁴Potential feminine alcoholics often turn into the real thing and are gone beyond recall in a few years. ¹⁵Certain drinkers, who would be greatly insulted if called alcoholics, are astonished at their inability to stop. ¹⁶We, who are familiar with the symptoms, see large numbers of potential alcoholics among young people everywhere. ^{34:1}But try and get them to see it!

33:9
Willpower:
xxix:18, 7:10,
11:9, 20:14,
22:11, 24:3-6,
32:13, 34:2,
34:12, 40:12,
42:4, 45:2-3,
76:18, 85:19-
20, 92:8,
107:19, 140:5

33:10
Mental Twist:
xxvii:13-xxviii:1,
6-4, 22:17,
24:1-6, 24:7-8,
35:2, 37:7,
40:12, 41:21,
42:4, 43:14-16,
92:3-8, 157:19

33:14
Real:
(Alcoholic)
21:3-4, 23:17,
24:1, 30:1,
30:11, 31:5,
34:3-4, 35:22,
44:5, 92:7,
109:10-21

33:8 To stop drinking permanently requires the abandonment of all reservations.
Some of us have fallen prey to the idea that we will quit drinking until the current crisis we are facing passes, then we can begin again. Perhaps a judge has threatened us with fines or imprisonment. Or maybe our spouse is ready to leave us. We quit drinking for the length of the sentence or until our spouse cools off. We may attend A.A. meetings. When the crisis has passed, we stop going to meetings and resume our drinking. This is compliance rather than surrender. Compliance will only keep us sober for as long as the threat of unfavorable consequences hangs over our head.

33:8 A.A. is an entirely voluntary program. We can take it or leave it. Should we decide to take it, there are certain things that the authors found they must do to gain permanent success. They found that their reservations about quitting for good and delusions that time would restore their control over alcohol had to be abandoned.

33:9-11 Many of us feel we are under control and can quit drinking when we want to. This may be true in the earliest stages of alcoholism. Unfortunately, we could not foresee that when the consequences of drinking got bad enough to warrant quitting, the alcohol would have warped our minds producing an overwhelming desire to continue regardless of the consequences. Through our alcoholic haze we may see that the consequences of drinking are becoming more severe but invariably we will attribute the resulting problems to other causes.

33:12 The earlier we are able to spot the symptoms of alcoholism in ourselves the sooner we can move toward recovery. We need not continue drinking ourselves to death in ignorance believing ourselves weak or immoral. We can now see that we are physically and mentally affected by this illness, admit our powerlessness and seek a Power sufficient to solve our problem.

^{34:2}As we look back, we feel we had gone on drinking many years beyond the point where we could quit on our willpower. ³If anyone questions whether he has entered this dangerous area, let him try leaving liquor alone for one year. ⁴If he is a real alcoholic and very far advanced, there is scant chance of success. ⁵In the early days of our drinking we occasionally remained sober for a year or more, becoming serious drinkers again later. ⁶Though you may be able to stop for a considerable period, you may yet be a potential alcoholic. ⁷We think few, to whom this book will appeal, can stay dry anything like a year. ⁸Some will be drunk the day after making their resolutions; most of them within a few weeks.

⁹For those who are unable to drink moderately the question is how to stop altogether. ¹⁰We are assuming, of course, that the reader desires to stop. ¹¹Whether such a person can quit upon a non-spiritual basis depends upon the extent to which he has already lost the power to choose whether he will drink or not. ¹²Many of us felt that we had plenty of character. ¹³There was a tremendous urge to cease forever. ¹⁴Yet we found it impossible. ¹⁵This is the baffling feature of alcoholism as we know it—this utter inability to leave it alone, no matter how

---

33:15 Nobody likes to be called an alcoholic because of the negative images associated with the term. The insult we feel at this label is due to our lack of humility. We have a lack of understanding of who and what we really are. If we are alcoholic, the sooner we are able to diagnose ourselves, by comparing our drinking to that of the authors, the sooner we can admit that we are powerless over alcohol and begin to recover.

33:16 Now, thanks to the authors, we are familiar with the symptoms of alcoholism: the inability to control the amount we drink once we begin and the inability to stop drinking entirely despite our most urgent need or most sincere desire.

34:2-8 If drinking is causing us trouble, why don't we try this test? If we are successful, we probably are not alcoholic. If we can't do it after a sincere effort, we are probably alcoholic. Go ahead, give it your best shot. We hope you will be successful. If you are not, A.A. will be there, ready to show you what we have done to recover.

34:8 Once again the ineffectiveness of using resolve to overcome alcoholism is made clear. How have our resolutions not to drink as much or at all worked in the past? What makes us think that this time our resolve will work any better?

34:9-15 When reviewing our drinking history, we can ask ourselves if we are able to drink moderately? If we are unable to drink moderately, we can ask ourselves if we desire to stop drinking altogether? If we desire to stop, we can ask ourselves if we can do it on our own? How has our desire to stop drinking worked in the past? If a sincere desire or great need to stop drinking is insufficient, we may be unable to quit on a non-spiritual basis.

great the necessity or the wish.

^{34:16}How then shall we help our readers determine, to their own satisfaction, whether they are one of us? ¹⁷The experiment of quitting for a period of time will be helpful, but we think we can render an even greater service to alcoholic sufferers, and perhaps to the medical fraternity. ^{35:1}So we shall describe some of the mental states that precede a relapse into drinking, for obviously this is the crux of the problem.

²What sort of thinking dominates an alcoholic who repeats time after time the desperate experiment of the first drink? ³Friends, who have reasoned with him after a spree which has brought him to the point of divorce or bankruptcy, are mystified when he walks directly into a saloon. ⁴Why does he? ⁵Of what is he thinking?

⁶Our first example is a friend we shall call Jim. ⁷This man has a charming wife and family. ⁸He inherited a lucrative

34:16-35:1
Diagnosis:
xxix:16, 31:10-
32:2, 34:3-4

35:1
Relapse:
26:7, 30:12,
31:2,120:6,
125:2, 147:2

35:1-2
Mental States:
24:15, 27:3-4,
33:10, 36:17,
37:1-4, 41:23,
42:10, 101:3,
140:10, 157:19

35:1
Crux:
23:3, 43:14-16

35:2
Insidious:
(Insanity of the
first drink)
8:14, 22:9,
23:2, 23:9,
24:6, 37:6,
40:10, 41:20

34:15 Are we baffled by our inability to quit drinking entirely? The most dire necessity and most sincere desire are not sufficient to keep us away from that first drink. Even when we can plainly see that the first drink will lead to another spree, we always succumb to our overpowering desire for alcohol. What hope is there for us? Where can we find the power to resist our compulsion to drink?

34:16 The many definitions of alcoholism, descriptions of the symptoms, and the personal accounts illustrating the progression of this illness, are included in the first chapters of this book to help us determine if we are alcoholic or not.

34:16 This chapter focuses on the mental component of alcoholism. We have seen the physical symptoms clearly illustrated. Now, the authors address the mental symptoms in the hope that we may see whether we possess an alcoholic mind.

35:1 We would not have to worry about our inability to control the amount we drink if we never took that first drink. The real problem is our inability to avoid taking that first drink. If we have decided to quit drinking, it is likely that we have tried many of the same meth-

ods as the authors. Our decisions to quit never seemed to work. We tried self-will, self-knowledge, firm resolve, renewing our resolve, moving to another area, doctors, psychiatrists, counselors, but nothing we tried worked for very long. Always, we returned to drinking.

35:2 We call this alcoholic thinking. Once this type of thinking takes hold of an alcoholic's mind very little can be done to help the alcoholic to recover. It appears to be a type of insanity in that repeated demonstrations of the inability to control consumption of alcohol fails to prevent further futile attempts. We repeat our same mistakes and insanely expect different results.

35:2 The desperate experiment of the first drink results in our failure to control our drinking once again. So what do we do? We try the same experiment again and expect different results.

35:6-12 Again the authors show that family, money, courage, achievement, talent, personality, and intelligence are no insurance against alcoholism. Over and over we are shown that alcoholism affects all types of people. No one is immune.

automobile agency. [35:9]He had a commendable world war record. [10]He is a good salesman. [11]Everybody likes him. [12]He *is* an intelligent man, normal so far as we can see, except for a nervous disposition. [13]He did no drinking until he was thirty-five. [14]In a few years he became so violent when intoxicated that he had to be committed. [15]On leaving the asylum, he came into contact with us.

[16]We told him what we knew of alcoholism and the answer we had found. [17]He made a beginning. [18]His family was reassembled, and he began to work as a salesman for the business he had lost through drinking. [19]All went well for a time, but he failed to enlarge his spiritual life. [20]To his consternation, he found himself drunk half a dozen times in rapid succession. [21]On each of these occasions we worked with him, reviewing carefully what had happened. [22]He agreed he was a real alcoholic and in serious condition. [23]He knew he faced another trip to the asylum if he kept on. [24]Moreover, he could lose his family for whom he had deep affection.

[36:1]Yet he got drunk again. [2]We asked him to tell us exactly how it happened. [3]This is his story: "I came to work on Tuesday morning. [4]I remember I felt irritated that I had to be a salesman for a concern I once owned. [5]I had a few words with the boss, but nothing serious. [6]Then I decided to drive into the country and see one of my prospects for a car. [7]On the way I felt hungry so I stopped at a roadside place where they have a bar. [8]I had no intention of drinking. [9]I just thought I would get

---

35:16 Here the authors present the solution to Jim in the same way that they present it to us. They show us what they have done.

35:17-20 Jim made a beginning—he stopped drinking. This is only the beginning of the solution that the authors have found. A person who is powerless over alcohol must find a Power greater than themselves to maintain permanent sobriety. Left to our own resources we will drink again.

35:22-36:1 Knowledge of our alcoholism and of the disagreeable consequences resulting

from our drinking is insufficient to prevent us from drinking again. Reading of the experiences of others and reviewing our own drinking histories shows us that this is true.

36:4 The authors suggest that resentment destroys more alcoholics than anything else. This re-feeling of past pains, the accompanying replaying of past events, and planning of future revenge block us from the Power we need to maintain our sobriety. In the Fourth Step, we learn a successful method of dealing with resentment that frees us from our anger.

a sandwich. 36:10I also had the notion that I might find a customer for a car at this place, which was familiar, for I had been going to it for years. 11I had eaten there many times during the months I was sober. 12I sat down at a table and ordered a sandwich and a glass of milk. 13Still no thought of drinking. 14I ordered another sandwich and decided to have another glass of milk.

15"Suddenly the thought crossed my mind that if I were to put an ounce of whiskey in my milk, it couldn't hurt me on a full stomach. 16*I ordered a whiskey and poured it into the milk.* 17*I vaguely sensed I was not being any too smart, but felt reassured, as I was taking the whiskey on a full stomach.* 18The experiment went so well that I ordered another whiskey and poured it into more milk. 19That didn't seem to bother me so I tried another."

20Thus started one more journey to the asylum for Jim. 21Here was the threat of commitment, the loss of family and position, to say nothing of that intense mental and physical suffering which drinking always caused him. 22*He had much knowledge about himself as an alcoholic.* 23*Yet all reasons for not drinking were easily pushed aside in favor of the foolish idea he could take whiskey if only he mixed it with milk?*

37:1Whatever the precise definition of the word may be, we call this plain insanity. 2How can such a lack of proportion, of the ability to think straight, be called anything else?

36:15-19
Impulse:
Xxix:18, 24:3-6, 41:7-10, 43:14-16

36:17
Alcoholic Mind:
24:15, 27:3-4, 33:10, 35:1-2, 37:1-4, 41:23, 42:10, 101:3, 140:10, 157:19

36:22
Self-knowl-edge:
7:15, 26:7, 38:18, 39:3, 40:2-6, 42:4

37:1-4
Thinking:
24:15, 27:3-4, 33:10, 35:1-2, 36:17, 41:23, 42:10, 101:3, 140:10, 157:19

37:1-9
Insanity:
xxiv:6, xxvi:9, 5:7, 5:28, 6:23, 23:3, 27:3, 24:15, 33:10, 37:11, 38:15, 40:10, 41:23, 42:3, 61:17, 66:12, 92:15, 101:3, 120:11, 154:17, 157:18-19

36:8 When our best intentions and the certain consequences of taking even one drink do not stop us from taking that first drink, we must admit our powerlessness over alcohol. To remain sober we must find a Power greater than ourselves.

36:15 Alcoholic insanity leads us to believe that it would be OK for us to have a drink despite the fact that our own experience proves this to be false. People who are insane do not realize it at the time. We act on our false beliefs and take that first drink setting in motion the physical craving for more alcohol that compels us to continue drinking.

36:22 Our very best thinking will not prevent us from drinking. It never has before, why would it begin to work now?

37:1-2 Here is a definition of insanity that perhaps we can identify with. We seem to lack the ability to properly evaluate the risks compared to the benefits of drinking. We somehow fail to connect our drinking with its almost certain consequences. A straight line of thinking might lead us to conclude that when we take that first drink we begin an uncontrollable spree. The worst part is that even if we are able to connect the cause with the result, at certain times we are unable to effectively use this knowledge.

37:3You may think this an extreme case. 4To us it is not far-fetched, for this kind of thinking has been characteristic of every single one of us. 5We have sometimes reflected more than Jim did upon the consequences. 6But there was always the curious mental phenomenon, that parallel with our sound reasoning there inevitably ran some insanely trivial excuse for taking the first drink. 7Our sound reasoning failed to hold us in check. 8The insane idea won out. 9Next day we would ask ourselves, in all earnestness and sincerity, how it could have happened.

10In some circumstances we have gone out deliberately to get drunk, feeling ourselves justified by nervousness, anger, worry, depression, jealousy or the like. 11But even in this type of beginning we are obliged to admit that our justification for a spree was insanely insufficient in the light of what always happened. 12We now see that when we began to drink deliberately, instead of casually, there was little serious or effective thought during the period of premeditation of what the terrific consequences might be.

13Our behavior is as absurd and incomprehensible with respect to the first drink as that of an individual with a passion, say, for jaywalking. 14He gets a thrill out of skipping in front of fast-moving vehicles. 15He enjoys himself a few years in

---

37:3-12 One of the hallmarks of alcoholics is that we go to extremes. We don't just get a little nervous, angry, worried, depressed or jealous. We take these emotions to extreme levels.

37:3-9 This insanity is one of the hallmarks of alcoholism. The authors try to illustrate this type of thinking by showing us examples. Who in their right mind would drink again knowing full well that they are unable to control it once they start? What sane person would drink knowing full well that the consequences will be terrible? An alcoholic will drink in both these circumstances. This is why we consider alcoholics insane. The second step in recovery is to come to believe that a Power greater than ourselves can restore us to sanity. The authors have

found through their experience that by the time we get to Step Ten that sanity will have returned (84:25).

37:7-8 Our sound reasoning fails to keep us in check because the insanity of alcoholism is more powerful than our best thinking. Our very best thinking will not prevent us from drinking. Only someone who is insane would believe that a method that has repeatedly failed to stop their return to drinking would somehow begin to work if only it were tried again.

37:13-16 The authors illustrate the absurdity of our thinking by being absurd. Look closely at how the story of the jaywalker parallels the progression of alcoholism.

spite of friendly warnings. ³⁷:¹⁶Up to this point you would label him as a foolish chap having queer ideas of fun. ³⁸:¹Luck then deserts him and he is slightly injured several times in succession. ²You would expect him, if he were normal, to cut it out. ³Presently he is hit again and this time has a fractured skull. ⁴Within a week after leaving the hospital a fast-moving trolley car breaks his arm. ⁵He tells you he has decided to stop jaywalking for good, but in a few weeks he breaks both legs.

⁶On through the years this conduct continues, accompanied by his continual promises to be careful or to keep off the streets altogether. ⁷Finally, he can no longer work, his wife gets a divorce, he is held up to ridicule. ⁸He tries every known means to get the jaywalking idea out of his head. ⁹He shuts himself up in an asylum, hoping to mend his ways. ¹⁰But the day he comes out he races in front of a fire engine, which breaks his back. ¹¹Such a man would be crazy, wouldn't he?

¹²You may think our illustration is too ridiculous. ¹³But is it? ¹⁴We, who have been through the wringer, have to admit if we substituted alcoholism for jaywalking, the illustration would fit us exactly. ¹⁵However intelligent we may have been in other respects, where alcohol has been involved, we have been strangely insane. ¹⁶It's strong language—but isn't it true?

¹⁷Some of you are thinking: "Yes, what you tell us is true, but it doesn't fully apply. ¹⁸We admit we have some of these symptoms, but we have not gone to the extremes you fellows did, nor are we likely to, for we understand ourselves so well after what you have told us that such things cannot happen again. ¹⁹We have not lost everything in life through drinking and we certainly do not intend to. ³⁹:¹Thanks for the information."

²That may be true of certain non-alcoholic people who, though drinking foolishly and heavily at the present time, are

---

38:5
Resolutions:
Xxvii:1, xxviii:7,
5:14-24, 5:30-
6:4, 7:10,
32:11-33:2,
34:8, 39:17,
107:11

38:6
Promises:
5:18, 177:9

38:8
Resources:
(Human)
32:17, 45:3,
50:15, 61:3-6

38:15
Insanity:
xxiv:6, xxvi:9,
5:7, 5:28, 6:23,
23:3, 27:3,
24:15, 33:10,
37:1-9, 37:11,
40:10, 41:23,
42:3, 61:17,
66:12, 92:15,
101:3, 120:11,
154:17, 157:18-
19

38:18
Self-knowl-
edge:
7:15, 26:7,
36:22, 39:3,
40:2-6, 42:4

38:18
Symptoms: (Of
alcoholism)
xlii:1, 18:3-5,
33:16, 40:1,
52:6

38:19
Worthwhile:
xxix:5, 18:3-5,
66:8

38:19
Intentions: (and
attributes)
1:15-2:6,
35:6-13, 36:8,
39:6-11

39:1
Obstinacy:
1:13, 2:19,
47:17, 140:5

38:17-39:1 If we are experiencing some of these symptoms, it is likely only a matter of time before alcoholism takes us to the extremes that the authors experienced. Once again, self-knowledge will not keep us sober and neither will our good intentions. The information we are receiving is intended to illustrate our powerlessness, not to give us the illusion of power.

able to stop or moderate, because their brains and bodies have not been damaged as ours were. ³⁹:³But the actual or potential alcoholic, with hardly an exception, will be absolutely unable to stop drinking on the basis of self-knowledge. ⁴This is a point we wish to emphasize and re-emphasize, to smash home upon our alcoholic readers as it has been revealed to us out of bitter experience. ⁵Let us take another illustration.

⁶Fred is partner in a well known accounting firm. ⁷His income is good, he has a fine home, is happily married and the father of promising children of college age. ⁸He is so attractive a personality that he makes friends with everyone. ⁹If ever there was a successful business man, it is Fred. ¹⁰To all appearance he is a stable, well balanced individual. ¹¹Yet, he is alcoholic. ¹²We first saw Fred about a year ago in a hospital where he had gone to recover from a bad case of jitters. ¹³It was his first experience of this kind, and he was much ashamed of it. ¹⁴Far from admitting he was an alcoholic, he told himself he came to the hospital to rest his nerves. ¹⁵The doctor intimated strongly that he might be worse than he realized. ¹⁶For a few days he was depressed about his condition. ¹⁷He made up his mind to quit drinking altogether. ¹⁸It never occurred to him that perhaps he could not do

---

39:7 Fred had everything going for him including position, money, material possessions, happiness, marriage, children, personality, success and stability. These things will not protect us from becoming alcoholic.

39:12 The jitters or shakes are a sign of withdrawal from alcohol.

39:13 We feel ashamed of ourselves when we lose control of our drinking. This shows a lack of humility—the understanding that we are powerless over alcohol.

39:16-40:8 Being unwilling to acknowledge and admit our powerlessness over alcohol keeps us from acting on the truth that we

need a Power greater than ourselves to keep us from drinking.

39:18 Our character (i.e., the ability to follow through on our decisions) is affected by alcoholism. When we see we are losing control, our self-confidence is shaken. If we cannot accept our inability to control our drinking, we may try to make excuses or cover it up. It is intolerable to us that our willpower, our primary human resource, is inadequate in this area. Many of us who felt that the position we had achieved in life somehow granted us immunity were surprised when alcohol became our master. Lofty position never saved anyone from alcoholism.

so, in spite of his character and standing. [39:19]Fred would not believe himself an alcoholic, much less accept a spiritual remedy for his problem. [20]We told him what we knew about alcoholism. [40:1]He was interested and conceded that he had some of the symptoms, but he was a long way from admitting that he could do nothing about it himself. [2]He was positive that this humiliating experience, plus the knowledge he had acquired, would keep him sober the rest of his life. [3]Self-knowledge would fix it.

[4]We heard no more of Fred for a while. [5]One day we were told that he was back in the hospital. [6]This time he was quite shaky. [7]He soon indicated he was anxious to see us. [8]The story he told is most instructive for here was a chap absolutely convinced he had to stop drinking, who had no excuse for drinking, who exhibited splendid judgment and determination in all his other concerns, yet was flat on his back nevertheless.

[9]Let him tell you about it: "I was much impressed with what you fellows said about alcoholism, but I frankly did not believe it would be possible for me to drink again. [10]I somewhat appreciated your ideas about the subtle insanity which precedes the first drink, but I was confident it could not happen to me after what I had learned. [11]I reasoned I was not so far advanced as most of you fellows, that I had been usually successful in licking my other personal problems, that I would therefore be successful where you men failed. [12]I felt I had every right to be self-confident, that it would be only a matter

39:19
Remedy:
xxiv:1, xxix:1,
17:1-3, 31:1,
112:23, 144:6

40:1
Symptoms:
xiii:1, 18:3-5,
33:16, 38:18,
52:6

40:2-41:21
Humiliating:
8:13, 24:3-9,
26:7-9, 43:14

40:2-6
Self-knowledge:
7:15, 26:7,
36:22, 38:18,
39:3, 42:4

40:6
Addiction:
22:17,23:18,
24:1-6, 32:2,
32:8, 39:12

40:8
Baffling:
xxvii:15, 5:12-
13, 6:4, 7:11,
23:9-12, 26:9,
34:15, 35:4-5,
37:9, 58:15,
92:1

40:10
Subtle:
8:14, 22:9,
23:2, 23:9,
24:6, 35:2,
37:6, 41:20,
43:14-16,
154:17

40:11
Delusion:
30:9, 32:13,
61:17, 62:4,
154:13, 155:13

39:19 Why would anyone who refused to acknowledge their alcoholism turn to a spiritual solution? Our admission of powerlessness makes us willing to look for a spiritual solution to our problems.

40:2-3 Painful memories, fear of humiliation and self-knowledge will not deter an alcoholic from drinking. Eventually the time will come when these memories, fears and knowledge will not be strong enough to overcome the desire to drink.

40:9-41:22 The insidious insanity of the first drink is a subtle insanity. It is not that we are suddenly struck stark raving mad, that comes later, but this insanity waits quietly and patiently in ambush for us. When our guard is down, it rears its powerful head. Seemingly, out of the blue, we get the idea that a drink or two would be a good thing. We remember the pleasure of drinking and forget about the overwhelming craving for alcohol. The memory of the pain and anguish that drinking causes is somehow subdued to the point that our insane desire for alcohol overpowers our sane resolve not to drink.

40:12
Willpower:
xxix:18,7:10,
11:9, 20:14,
22:11, 24:3-
6,32:13, 33:9,
34:2, 34:12,
42:4, 45:2-3,
76:18, 85:19-
20, 92:8,
107:19, 140:5

40:12
Keep on Guard:
xxvii:13-xxviii:1,
6:4, 22:17,
24:1-6, 24:7-8,
33:10, 35:2,
37:7, 41:21,
42:4, 43:14-16,
92:3-8, 157:19

41:7-10
Impulse:
xxix:18, 24:3-6,
36:15-19,
43:14-16

41:20
Fought:
5:21, 66:4,
84:24, 85:4,
103:11-12

41:20
First Drink:
(Insidious
Insanity of)
8:14, 22:9,
23:2, 23:9,
24:6, 35:2,
37:6, 40:10,
43:14-16,
154:17

41:21
Thought:
xxvii:13-xxviii:1,
6:4, 22:17,
24:1-6, 24:7-8,
33:10, 35:2,
37:7, 40:12,
42:4, 43:14-16,
92:3-8, 157:19

41:23
Alcoholic Mind:
24:15, 27:3-4,
33:10, 35:1-2,
36:17, 37:1-4,
42:10, 101:3,
140:10, 157:19

of exercising my willpower and keeping on guard.

40:13"In this frame of mind, I went about my business and for a time all was well. 14I had no trouble refusing drinks, and began to wonder if I had not been making too hard work of a simple matter. 15One day I went to Washington to present some accounting evidence to a government bureau. 41:1I had been out of town before during this particular dry spell, so there was nothing new about that. 2Physically, I felt fine. 3Neither did I have any pressing problems or worries. 4My business came off well, I was pleased and knew my partners would be too. 5It was the end of a perfect day, not a cloud on the horizon.

6"I went to my hotel and leisurely dressed for dinner. 7As I crossed the threshold of the dining room, the thought came to mind it would be nice to have a couple of cocktails with dinner. 8That was all. 9Nothing more. 10I ordered a cocktail and my meal. 11Then I ordered another cocktail. 12After dinner I decided to take a walk. 13When I returned to the hotel it struck me a highball would be fine before going to bed, so I stepped into the bar and had one. 14I remember having several more that night and plenty next morning. 15I have a shadowy recollection of being in an airplane bound for New York, of finding a friendly taxicab driver at the landing field instead of my wife. 16The driver escorted me about for several days. 17I know little of where I went, or what I said and did. 18Then came the hospital with unbearable mental and physical suffering.

19"As soon as I regained my ability to think, I went carefully over that evening in Washington. 20Not only had I been off guard, I had made no fight whatever against that first drink. 21This time I had not thought of the consequences at all.

22"I had commenced to drink as carelessly as though the cocktails were ginger ale. 23I now remembered what my alcoholic friends had told me, how they prophesied that if I had an alcoholic mind, the time and place would come—I would drink again. 42:1They had said that though I did raise a defense, it would one day give way before some trivial reason for having a drink. ⁴²:²Well, just that did happen and more, for what I had learned of alcoholism did not occur to me at all. ³I knew from that moment that I had an alcoholic mind. ⁴I saw that willpower and self-knowledge would not help in those strange mental blank spots. ⁵I had never been able to understand people who said that a problem had them hopelessly defeated. ⁶I knew then. ⁷It was a crushing blow.

⁸"Two of the members of Alcoholics Anonymous came to see me. ⁹They grinned, which I didn't like so much, and then asked me if I thought myself alcoholic and if I were really licked this time. ¹⁰I had to concede both propositions. ¹¹They piled on me heaps of evidence to the effect that an alcoholic mentality, such as I had exhibited in Washington, was a hopeless condition. ¹²They cited cases out of their own experience by the dozen. ¹³This process snuffed out the last flicker of conviction that I could do the job myself.

¹⁴"Then they outlined the spiritual answer and program of action which a hundred of them had followed successfully. ¹⁵Though I had been only a nominal churchman, their

42:3
Alcoholic Mind:
24:15, 27:3-4, 33:10, 35:1-2, 36:17, 37:1-4, 42:10, 101:3

42:4
Self-knowledge:
7:15, 26:7, 36:22, 38:18, 39:3, 40:2-6

42:4
Defense:
xxvii:13-xxviii:1, 6:4, 22:17, 24:1-6, 24:7-8, 33:10

42:5
Understand:
18:5, 20:19, 63:15, 74:5, 112:21, 140:14

42:9-10
Admitted:
xxviii:8, xxix:6 8:9-11, 11:12, 13:7, 30:1, 30:7-8, 59:8

42:14
More:
xiii:1, xxiii:10, 19:12, 51:3

42:3 Our inability to permanently resist the temptation to drink is the proof that we have an alcoholic mind. Despite the consequences and despite a sincere desire to stay away from drinking, the person with an alcoholic mind will eventually return to drinking.

42:4-7 The hopelessness we feel when we realize that willpower and self-knowledge can not keep us sober is a result of our mistaken belief that these are the only resources available to us. We are attempting to use the wrong tools to accomplish our goal of staying sober. Willpower and self-knowledge are effective when applied in the appropriate circumstances. The authors hope that we will be willing to set aside willpower and self-knowledge and pick up the simple kit of spiritual tools that are explained in this book. These tools have proven to be wonderfully effective at overcoming alcoholism.

42:8-19 First we are shown that we truly are hopeless without divine help. We are then presented with the solution, a program of action that allows us to awaken spiritually and begin a new way of life.

42: 8-19 The first chapters in this book present the evidence that we are hopeless apart from divine help. We are then presented with the solution—a program of action that allows us to awaken spiritually and to a new, successful way of life.

42:11 What power is there that can fundamentally change the way a person thinks? This is a seemingly impossible task. We need far more than a change of behavior to recover from alcoholism. We must experience what Dr. Silkworth called an entire psychic change (xxvii:2).

42:10-13 This is Fred's first step! The early members called this feeling of utter hopelessness deflation at depth. This admission of powerlessness can produce in us a willingness to proceed with this program of action.

proposals were not, intellectually, hard to swallow. 42:16But the program of action, though entirely sensible, was pretty drastic. 17It meant I would have to throw several lifelong conceptions out of the window. 18That was not easy. 19But the moment I made up my mind to go through with the process, I had the curious feeling that my alcoholic condition was relieved, as in fact it proved to be.

20"Quite as important was the discovery that spiritual principles would solve all my problems. 21I have since been brought into a way of living infinitely more satisfying and, I hope, more useful than the life I lived before. 43:1My old manner of life was by no means a bad one, but I would not exchange its best moments for the worst I have now. 2I would not go back to it even if I could."

3Fred's story speaks for itself. 4We hope it strikes home to thousands like him. 5He had felt only the first nip of the wringer. 6Most alcoholics have to be pretty badly mangled before they really commence to solve their problems.

42:17 Some of the conceptions that we have to abandon are that: our education, achievements, possessions or position preclude us from being alcoholic; we can control our drinking once we start; we can stay away from drinking through willpower and self-knowledge; we can continue doing the same thing over and over and somehow get different results; and the help of God is unavailable to us.

42:18 This is not an easy thing to do, but the hopelessness of our current situation makes us willing to try this program of action that has worked for so many people.

42:19 This decision is the third step in the program of action. Many people report that when they made this decision they found that the obsession to drink was removed from them.

42:20-21 Stopping drinking is only the beginning of this new way of life. The attempt to apply these principles in all our affairs is a new focus for us. We find that this path is far more satisfying and successful than the road to ruin we are on now.

43:4 The hope of the authors is that we may see ourselves in Fred's story. If we are unable to stay away from alcohol when we sincerely want to, then we may be alcoholics of the hopeless variety. Have we tried will power and failed? Have we placed our faith in self-knowledge only to fail again?

43:6 We hang on to our threadbare ideas until the holes in our logic become so large that our glaring failure can no longer be hidden. Thinking we have only our own resources to hold on to we still are reluctant to let go. Usually, we must be beaten over and over again before we concede defeat. It is just this concession of defeat that is needed for us to move toward recovery. Without this admission of powerlessness, we usually continue to try to recover under our own power. The admission of powerlessness is the bedrock upon which the foundation of complete willingness lays.

43:7Many doctors and psychiatrists agree with our conclu- sions. 8One of these men, staff member of a world renowned hospital, recently made this statement to some of us: "What you say about the general hopelessness of the average alco- holic's plight is, in my opinion, correct. 9As to two of you men, whose stories I have heard, there is no doubt in my mind that you were 100% hopeless, apart from Divine help. 10Had you offered yourselves as patients at this hospital, I would not have taken you, if I had been able to avoid it. 11People like you are too heartbreaking. 12Though not a reli- gious person, I have profound respect for the spiritual approach in such cases as yours. 13For most cases, there is virtually no other solution."

14Once more: the alcoholic at certain times has no effective mental defense against the first drink. 15Except in a few rare cases, neither he nor any other human being can provide such a defense. 16His defense must come from a higher Power.

43:7-8
Doomed:
xlii:1, xxvii:3
xxviii:20, 24:15,
27:3-4, 44:6,
73:23, 92:17

43:7-13
Doctors:
xxviii:20, 20:3,
26:16-17, 27:3-
4, 30:16

43:8-9
Hopeless:
xlii:1, xxiii:6,
xxvii:2, xxix:6,
xxix:16, 6:15,
7:19, 10:3,
14:16, 17:1,
20:3, 26:16,
27:5, 39:3,
42:10, 44:5,
92:7, 94:12,
113:22

43:14-16
Defense:
xxvii:13-xxviii:1,
6-4, 22:17,
24:1-6, 24:7-8,
33:10, 35:2,
37:7, 40:12,
41:21, 42:4,
92:3-8, 157:19

Historical Notes:
43:8 Doctor Percy Polick a psychiatrist, at Bellevue Hospital in New York.

43:7-13 This book quotes the opinion of sev- eral medical professionals who plainly state that they consider alcoholics hopeless. More importantly, the authors recount their own experience with trying human measures to overcome their alcoholism. They repeatedly illustrate how willpower and self-knowledge are not capable of winning out over this pow- erful illness. Do our own drinking histories and attempts to control our drinking parallel theirs? Have we exhausted the resources available to us in our own characters, the help of friends and loved ones and the medical community? Where do we place our hope of finding the power to stop drinking and recover from alcoholism?

43:14-16 If drinking produces in us a crav- ing beyond our ability to control and we are unable to refrain from drinking despite our knowledge of the adverse consequences and our most firm resolve not to, then apart from divine help, we are most certainly defenseless.

43:14-16 Our best thinking offers no insur- ance against relapse. Human power cannot overcome either the phenomenon of craving or alcoholic insanity. When we admit that we are powerless over alcohol, we have nowhere else to turn but to a Higher Power.

I'm not going for this God stuff. How could there possibly be a God when there are so many starving people and wars where everybody says God is on their side. What about those sanctimonious church goers who judge me for my sins and then commit their own. I am not going to accept damnation and hell fire from some old man with a white beard sitting in the clouds. What about all those preachers who talk about heaven and then live like hell?

First, no one is telling us that we have to believe in anything. If we do not care for the conception of God suggested by other people we need not even consider it. Most of us have had our objections to the idea of God. When we look at them in the light of alcoholic destruction we see that they are insignificant and that our prejudices only serve to block us off from the Power we need to recover.

We Agnostics begins by defining alcoholism (44:3) and presenting the basic premise of this book, that alcoholism is an illness which only a spiritual experience can conquer (44:4). Alcoholics are sometimes resistant to accept such a solution so we are presented with alternatives (44:6). Why our moral codes and firmly held philosophies are not sufficient to overcome alcoholism is explained clearly (45:1-4). Access to a Power greater than ourselves is the solution to our powerlessness and a promise is made to show us exactly how to find this Power (45:4-9). Our many objections to accepting this solution are addressed.

It is suggested that we lay aside our prejudices and that willingness is all we need to begin to get results (46:9). The directions for Step Two are given in the form of a simple question (47:9). We are cautioned to abandon attitudes that handicap us. All we have to do is acknowledge the existence of this Power and we can begin to use it (46:12). This Power is within the reach of everyone. To begin, all we have to do is to set aside our prejudices and take an honest look at the God idea (47:3). Sound reasons for believing are enumerated (48-52). The efficacy of self-sufficiency is discussed (52:9-10). A reasonable and practical description of faith is given and our choice is laid before us (53:8-10).

We agnostics have no direct experience accessing a Power greater than ourselves. This chapter masterfully addresses our objections and gives us practical reasons why we should try this way of life. Instructions on how to make a beginning are also provided.

The Blueprint

Basic Premise   In order to recover from alcoholism we must awaken spiritually.

Lack of Power   We as humans do not possess the power to overcome alcoholism.

Objections   Our prejudice towards spirituality stands in the way of our recovery.

Step Two   Willingness to believe in a Power greater than ourselves is all that is
                 required for us to make our beginning.

Reasons to   Faith is shown to be practical, logical and effective.
Believe

How to Begin   Clear-cut directions are given showing how to begin to awaken spiritually.

Chapter Four
WE AGNOSTICS

44:1In the preceding chapters, you have learned something of alcoholism. 2We hope we have made clear the distinction between the alcoholic and the non-alcoholic. 3If, when you honestly want to, you find you cannot quit entirely, or if, when drinking, you have little control over the amount you take, you are probably alcoholic. 4If that be the case, you may be suffering from an illness which only a spiritual experience will conquer.

44:3
Alcoholism:
xiii:1, xxviii:3-
18,18:3-5
20:8-20, 21:5-
22:7, 24:1

44:3-4
Experience:
xxvii:2, xxvii:3,
xxvii:10, 12:1-2,
14:4-8, 25:8-10,
27:9-12, 84:25,
143:9, 158:10,
569:1

44:4
Basic Premise:
xxvii:2, 27:9,
43:14-16

Title: The title of this chapter is not "Those Agnostics" but rather "We Agnostics." We, who have no direct personal experience of God working in our lives are agnostics.

44:2-3 Every word up to this point is to help us determine whether we are alcoholic or not. We have examined the doctor's opinion which is that we suffer from an allergy to alcohol that results in a physical craving that is beyond our control. We have been shown the classic progression of alcoholism in Bill's story. We have seen that alcoholic insanity condemns us to drink despite the need or desire to abstain. Now the authors sum up

the description of alcoholism in one sentence.

44:4 The authors use the word "may" to allow us to decide for ourselves if this is true. To determine if this is true for us, we need to examine our drinking in the light of the information contained in the previous chapters.

44:4 This is the basic premise of the Alcoholics Anonymous program. If we have reached the point where human aid is of no avail we have nowhere to turn but to a spiritual solution to our problem. A.A. is not a self-help program. If we were able to help ourselves we would not need A.A.

44:5
Real:
21:3-4, 23:17,
24:1, 30:1,
30:11, 31:5,
33:14, 34:3-4,
35:22, 92:7,
109:10-21

44:6
Doomed:
xiii:1, xxvii:3,
xxviii:20, 24:15,
27:3-4, 43:7-8,
73:23, 92:17

44:6-10
Alternatives:
7:2,18:15,
25:12

44:9
Unwilling:
xxviii:8
30:1, 39:14-
40:1, 58:2,
110:4

44:14
Intellectual:
12:12
16:10, 27:16,
49:7, 62:12,
83:7-8, 77:10

⁴⁴:⁵To one who feels he is an atheist or agnostic such an experience seems impossible, but to continue as he is means disaster especially if he is an alcoholic of the hopeless variety. ⁶To be doomed to an alcoholic death or to live on a spiritual basis—not always easy alternatives to face.

⁷But it isn't so difficult. ⁸About half our fellowship were of exactly that type. ⁹At first some of us tried to avoid the issue, hoping against hope we were not true alcoholics. ¹⁰But after a while we had to face the fact that we must find a spiritual basis of life—or else. ¹¹Perhaps it is going to be that way with you. ¹²But cheer up, something like fifty of us thought we were atheists or agnostics. ¹³Our experience shows that you need not be disconcerted.

¹⁴If a mere code of morals, or a better philosophy of life were sufficient to overcome alcoholism, many of us would have recovered long ago. ⁴⁵:¹But we found that such codes and philosophies did not save us, no matter how much we tried. ²We could wish to be moral, we could wish to be

---

44:5-6 Tangible assistance from a Power greater than ourselves seems unavailable to those of us who are without hope. This help seems out of our reach and only available to monks, priests and gurus. Faced with alcoholic destruction we become willing to attempt to access this Power that the authors declare has solved their problem.

44:9 To be a true alcoholic means that to recover we have to abandon our old ways of thinking and methods of dealing with life. Many of us hold tightly to the idea that our lives based on self can be successful if only we try hard enough. We resist, sometimes for years, beginning to rebuild our lives on a spiritual foundation.

44:9-10 Many of us try for years to avoid the spiritual solution hoping that mere fellowship with sober people will help us recover. Sooner or later we realize that our lives run on self-will are unsuccessful and we begin to seek a solution. Some of us unfortunately return to our old solution and begin once again to

drink. Others of us discover a true solution in the spiritually based way of life suggested in this book.

44:9-10 Alcoholism destroys all things worthwhile in our lives leaving only feelings of worthlessness, hopelessness and guilt. Association with sober people in A.A cannot bring about a personality change sufficient to overcome alcoholism. The power capable of restoring meaning and purpose to our lives can be found only by adopting a spiritual way of life.

44:14 To recover we need to experience an entire psychic change (xxvii:2). We must abandon the ideas and attitudes that currently shape our lives and adopt entirely new ones (27:11-12). Our selfishness and self-centeredness are obstacles to gaining this new life (62:2-14). We as humans lack the power to remake our character to the extent necessary. Only God can replace the foundations and motivations for our actions and emotions.

philosophically comforted, in fact, we could will these things with all our might, but the needed power wasn't there. ⁴⁵:³Our human resources, as marshalled by the will, were not sufficient; they failed utterly.

⁴Lack of power, that was our dilemma. ⁵We had to find a power by which we could live, and it had to be *A Power Greater Than Ourselves*. ⁶Obviously. ⁷But where and how were we to find this Power?

⁸Well, that's exactly what this book is about. ⁹Its main object is to enable you to find a Power greater than yourself, which will solve your problem. ¹⁰That means we have written a book which we believe to be spiritual as well as moral. ¹¹And it means, of course, that we are going to talk about God. ¹²Here difficulty arises with agnostics. ¹³Many times we talk to a new man and watch his hope rise as we discuss his alcoholic problems and explain our fellowship. ¹⁴But his face falls when we speak of spiritual matters, especially when we mention God, for we have re-opened a subject which our man thought he had neatly evaded or entirely ignored.

¹⁵We know how he feels. ¹⁶We have shared his honest doubt and prejudice. ¹⁷Some of us have been violently anti-religious.

45:2-4
Powerless:
11:16, 24:3, 34:11, 46:12, 50:15, 59:2, 59:8, 60:12, 62:13, 63:6

45:3
Resources:
32:17, 38:8, 50:15, 61:3-6

45:4-9
Exactly:
xiii:2, 20:4-6, 29:1, 85:22, 86:3, 143:14

45:5
Ourselves:
11:8, 25:10, 50:11, 70:23, 84:8, 100:6, 102:18

45:9
Solve:
xxvi:2, 13:21, 15:4, 17:3, 25:6, 42:19, 43:6, 52:8, 52:12, 104:6, 116:13, 117:4

45:14
Evaded:
53:8, 53:12

45:16-46:4,
Prejudice:
11:4, 47:3, 49:6, 51:12, 56:11

45:3 In Bill's Story we saw how human resources failed to conquer alcoholism. Good intentions, high abilities, firm resolve, renewal of resolve, sincere promises, self-knowledge, fear, family, friends, and medical science are incapable of producing the total reorganization of a person's psyche that is necessary for recovery from alcoholism.

45:8 We lack the power to recover from alcoholism and must find a way to establish a relationship with a Power capable of helping us. This book suggests theories that we may adopt to replace our current failed ideas about life. Each of the 12 Steps contain techniques that we may practice. Practicing these techniques allows us to build a body of experience proving that God is working in our life. We thus develop faith—a reliance upon this new way of life.

45:8-9 In the forward the authors explain that the main purpose of this book is to show us precisely what they have done to recover (xiii:2). They promise to answer our questions about what we have to do specifically (20:5) by telling us what they did and by giving us clear-cut directions (29:1). The main object of this book is to show us how we can find a Power greater than ourselves.

45:10 The term spiritual concerns the attempt to awaken to the existence of God. Moral refers to the guiding principles by which we live.

45:15 The authors can speak to us of our doubt and prejudice from their own experience. In their personal stories the authors describe the barriers they found to their spiritual awakenings. We can draw upon their experience and overcome some of these barriers to our own recovery.

45:18-19
Conception:
12:10, 27:12,
46:10-11, 47:1,
47:7, 49:12,
50:6, 56:11,
86:11, 93:4-5

45:21
Dependent:
52:8, 68:10-14,
80:13, 85:15,
87:5, 98:9,
99:21, 100:1,
164:3

46:6
Clamors:
12:27

46:6
Moved:
1:9, 10:8,
12:24-27

46:9
Beginning:
12:15, 19:3,
25:10, 35:17,
47:4, 47:16,
63:17, 68:23,
71:2, 84:14,
85:24, 158:10

⁴⁵:¹⁸To others, the word "God" brought up a particular idea of Him with which someone had tried to impress them during childhood. ¹⁹Perhaps we rejected this particular conception because it seemed inadequate. ²⁰With that rejection we imagined we had abandoned the God idea entirely. ²¹We were bothered with the thought that faith and dependence upon a Power beyond ourselves was somewhat weak, even cowardly. ⁴⁶:¹We looked upon this world of warring individuals, warring theological systems, and inexplicable calamity, with deep skepticism. ²We looked askance at many individuals who claimed to be godly. ³How could a Supreme Being have anything to do with it all? ⁴And who could comprehend a Supreme Being anyhow? ⁵Yet, in other moments, we found ourselves thinking, when enchanted by a starlit night, "Who, then, made all this?" ⁶There was a feeling of awe and wonder, but it was fleeting and soon lost.

⁷Yes, we of agnostic temperament have had these thoughts and experiences. ⁸Let us make haste to reassure you. ⁹We

Definitions:
46:2 Askance: with suspicion, mistrust or disapproval.

45:15-46:2 Faced with alcoholic destruction we must not let our past experience, ideas and attitudes prevent us from finding the Power we need to live. What harm could come to us from abandoning these attitudes? Must we cling to our failed views until we die? Are we willing to set these ideas aside long enough to give the development of spiritual experience an honest try?

45:17 We are not being asked to adopt a religion. The authors are merely saying this is what worked for them, we may try it if we please. The purpose of this book is to enable us to develop our own experience with a spiritual way of life and to find a Power by which we can live. It does not matter what religious people or any other people believe or what they do. All that matters is what we ourselves believe. This program of action can help us build our faith based upon our own personal experience.

45:18 When other peoples' conceptions of God did not work for us we mistakenly concluded that God was unavailable. The pur-

pose of this program of action is to develop or expand our own conception of God. Through the application of spiritual principles in our lives we awaken to a conscious awareness of the existence of God.

45:21 Having adopted the view that we have only our own resources to draw upon we attempt to use self-will to bring about happiness. We believe that the satisfaction of our desires is the sole purpose for living. Weakness results from having only human resources to draw upon. Cowardliness is being afraid to let go of that which we cling to most dearly—our self-will. Faith is not a crutch for the cowardly and weak but a source of strength and power that enables us to exceed our own capabilities.

46:1-2 It is ironic that we who have failed to live up to our own ideals should judge so harshly the failure of other individuals and institutions to meet these standards. We must set aside our judgment of others if we are to develop our own experience with our Higher Power.

found that as soon as we were able to lay aside prejudice and express even a willingness to believe in a Power greater than ourselves, we commenced to get results, even though it was impossible for any of us to fully define or comprehend that Power, which is God.

46:10-11
Conception:
12:10, 27:12,
45:18-19, 47:1,
47:7, 49:12,
50:6, 56:11,
86:11, 93:4-5

46:10-11
Simple:
47:11-16

46:12
As Soon As:
47:10,
63:17-18,
68:23, 100:7

46:10Much to our relief, we discovered we did not need to consider another's conception of God. 11Our own conception, however inadequate, was sufficient to make the approach and to effect a contact with Him. 12As soon as we admitted the

ATTITUDES THAT HINDER OUR PROGRESS

45:17	Anti-religious,
45:19-20	Rejection of inadequate childhood conception and abandonment of God,
45:21	The thought that faith was somewhat weak, even cowardly,
46:1	Warring individuals, warring theological systems, inexplicable calamity,
46:2	Judgment of individuals claiming to be godly,
46:3	How could a supreme being have anything to do with it at all?,
46:4	Incomprehensibility of God,
46:10	Distraction by other's conception of God,
47:3	Prejudice against spiritual terms,
47:12	Assumption that we must accept many things on faith,
47:17	Obstinacy, sensitiveness, and unreasoning prejudice,
48:1	Antagonism towards reference to spiritual things,
49:4	Our perverse streak,
49:7-8	The vain idea that our intelligence is the beginning and end of all,
49:13	Cynically dissecting spiritual beliefs and practices,
50:1	Using peoples shortcomings as a basis of wholesale condemnation,
50:2	We talked of intolerance when we were intolerant ourselves,
50:4	We never gave the spiritual side of life a fair hearing,
51:12	We are biased and unreasonable about the realm of the spirit,
52:12	We stick to the idea that self-sufficiency would solve our problems,
53:18	We lean too heavily on reason for our support,
54:3	We had been abjectly faithful to the God of Reason,
54:7	We worship people, sentiment, things, money and ourselves,
55:6	Obscured by calamity, pomp, by worship of other things,
56:2	Rebellion at religious education,
56:7	Idea that God has never done anything for us.

46:9 We agnostics are reluctant to subscribe to any spiritual philosophy because of the unfathomable nature of God. Adopting a willingness to act as if there is a God coupled with the application of certain principles will produce spiritual experience even for agnostics.

46:9 The directions are clear-cut: lay aside prejudice and express a willingness to believe in a Power greater than ourselves. The promise is given: we will begin to get results.

46:12
Power:
50:15, 63:6,
85:22

46:12
Provided:
17:10, 50:14,
101:2-4

46:12
Simple:
xxvii:3, 9:32,
14:1, 25:6,
26:20, 28:7,
47:11, 50:14-
16, 52:8, 57:5,
58:2, 62:21,
88:6, 130:9

46:12-15
Seek:
55:9-17, 57:11,
60:13

47:3
Prejudice:
11:4, 45:16-
46:4, 49:6,
51:12, 56:11

47:4
Conscious:
51:3, 55:17,
56:18, 59:18,
63:6, 85:23,
87:2, 130:3

47:9
Step Two:
12:9-19, 13:7,
53:8-10, 59:9

possible existence of a Creative Intelligence, A Spirit of the Universe underlying the totality of things, we began to be possessed of a new sense of power and direction, provided we took other simple steps. 46:13We found that God does not make too hard terms with those who seek Him. 14To us, the Realm of Spirit is broad, roomy, all inclusive; never exclusive or forbidding, to those who earnestly seek. 15It is open, we believe, to all men.

47:1When, therefore, we speak to you of God, we mean your own conception of God. 2This applies, too, to other spiritual expressions which you find in this book. 3Do not let any prejudice you may have against spiritual terms deter you from honestly asking yourself what they mean to you. 4At the start, this is all we needed to commence spiritual growth, to effect our first conscious relation with God as we understood Him. 5Afterward, we found ourselves accepting many things which then seemed entirely out of reach. 6That is growth, but if we wished to grow, we had to begin somewhere. 7So we used our own conception, however limited it was.

8We needed to ask ourselves but one short question. 9"*Do I now believe, or am I even willing to believe, that there is a Power greater than myself?*" 10As soon as a man can say that he

---

46:12 The specific instruction is to "admit the possible existence" of God. The promise is that we will be able to access the infinite power of God and find a new purpose for living. The prerequisite is to continue along this path.

46:13-15 This Power is available to us and is not reserved only for others. To make a beginning willingness is all that is required. To seek God in earnest by practicing the rest of the 12 Steps will produce the same awakening in us that it has in the millions of alcoholics who have gone before us.

47:3-4 Prejudice is opinion formed prior to a reasoned examination. A.A. suggests that we examine this way of life for ourselves and then decide whether it is the best way for us. Here we are given a direction to follow should we desire to begin. This direction is clear-cut and suggests that we may begin by examin-

ing, in the light of our own experience, what it is that we believe. This examination makes us consciously aware of our beliefs and gives us a starting place.

47:9 This is the second step. If we have admitted that we are alcoholic then we clearly see that we must find a Power greater than ourselves. To move towards recovery, from our seemingly hopeless state of mind and body, we need to ask ourselves this question.

47:10 If our answer is no we need to examine whether we truly believe that we are alcoholic and powerless over alcohol—that our lives are unmanageable. If we have the power to overcome our drinking problem then we have no need to seek help from a Power greater than ourselves. If we have, after an honest examination of our situation, no hope does believe, or is willing to believe, we emphatically assure him that he is on his way. ^{47:11}It has been repeatedly proven among us that upon this simple cornerstone a wonderfully effective spiritual structure can be built.

¹²That was great news to us, for we had assumed we could not make use of spiritual principles unless we accepted many things on faith which seemed difficult to believe. ¹³When people presented us with spiritual approaches, how frequently did we all say: "I wish I had what that man has. ¹⁴I'm sure it would work if I could only believe as he believes. ¹⁵But I cannot accept as surely true the many articles of faith which are so plain to him." ¹⁶So it was comforting to learn that we could commence at a simpler level.

¹⁷Besides a seeming inability to accept much on faith, we often found ourselves handicapped by obstinacy, sensitiveness, and unreasoning prejudice. ^{48:1}Many of us have been so touchy that even casual reference to spiritual things made us bristle with antagonism. ²This sort of thinking had to be abandoned. ³Though some of us resisted, we found no great difficulty in casting aside such feelings. ⁴Faced with alcoholic destruction, we soon became as open minded on spiritual matters as we had

47:11
Cornerstone:
12:17, 54:12,
56:19, 62:21,
63:4, 75:19-23,
97:3, 123:11

47:12
Great News:
17:14, 158:21

47:11-16
Simpler Level:
46:10-11

47:12
Accepted:
xxix:8, xxx:1
12:18-19, 14:4,
42:18, 139:4,
60:14, 145:3

47:17,
Obstinacy:
1:13, 2:19,
39:1, 140:5

47:17-48:1
Touchy:
125:10

48:4
Faced:
23:5, 57:6

---

of being able to recover through human efforts then where else are we to turn? Are we unable to grasp the hope offered us by the authors and the millions of alcoholics who have recovered through this method?

47:11 The cornerstone determines the trueness of a structure, whether it is plumb, level and square. This willingness to believe is essential to the new structure of our lives. It is a guiding principle, a solid base for our future decisions and actions. Willingness, coupled with honesty and open-mindedness is essential and indispensable to our recovery.

47:12-16 Blind faith is not a requirement. The authors are saying try this and see if it works for you too. By taking the steps we build personal experience upon which we base our belief. We practice new ways of looking at situations and new methods to access Power

beyond our own to solve problems that, in the past, we believed impossible. Over and over we see for ourselves that this way of life works. We learn to rely upon the principles contained in the steps and in the power of God. Thus, we develop an undeniably effective relationship with God. The key to this new way of life is a simple willingness to believe.

47:17-48:1 The authors know us well. This description of us is all too true and shows us some of the attitudes that weigh us down and slow our spiritual progress. Our stubborn resistance to accepting a spiritual solution creates problems in many areas of our lives. Our quickness to argue over spiritual or religious matters prevents us from seeing the truth. Our opinions formed prior to investigating the spiritual way of life keep us in the darkness of ignorance.

48:7
Tedious:
Xxvii:2, 5:5,
6:22, 23:2,
26:8, 34:2,
43:6, 151:9

48:16
Assumption:
xxiv:12, 7:11

tried to be on other questions. [48:5]In this respect alcohol was a great persuader. [6]It finally beat us into a state of reasonableness. [7]Sometimes this was a tedious process; we hope no one will be prejudiced as long as some of us were.

[8]The reader may still ask why he should believe in a Power greater than himself. [9]We think there are good reasons. [10]Let us have a look at some of them. [11]The practical individual of today is a stickler for facts and results. [12]Nevertheless, the twentieth century readily accepts theories of all kinds, provided they are firmly grounded in fact. [13]We have numerous theories, for example, about electricity. [14]Everybody believes them without a murmur of doubt. [15]Why this ready acceptance? [16]Simply because it is impossible to explain what we see, feel, direct, and use, without a reasonable assumption as a starting point.

[17]Everybody nowadays, believes in scores of assumptions for which there is good evidence, but no perfect visual proof. [18]And does not science demonstrate that visual proof is the

Definitions:
48:7 Tedious: long and tiresome, painfully slow.

48:2-7 Here is a specific and clear-cut direction to abandon this type of thinking. How have these attitudes been working for us? They are a ball and chain pulling us to the bottom of an ocean of despair. Casting aside these ideas allows us to reach the surface and breathe the fresh air of recovery. Our opinions and attitudes we hold so dearly matter little when we finally admit that we are powerless over alcohol and will likely die unless we abandon them.

48:4-7 We turn to God out of necessity rather than any type of moral or spiritual superiority. This necessity adds to the earnestness of our search and our gratefulness at finding a solution. How badly beaten must we be before we are willing to set aside our prejudice?

48:5-6 Are we to the point where we are willing to listen to reason? Will we set aside our preconceived ideas about spirituality long enough to examine the possible benefits of this way of life? Will we stubbornly hold on to our old ideas and reject the experience of mil-

lions of others?

48:11-16 The reasonable assumption to start from is that there is a Power greater than ourselves that can restore us to sanity. Without this beginning it is unlikely that we would continue with the rest of the steps. When we falter with the following steps we can return to this point and use our belief as a motivation to continue.

48:12 Doctor Silkworth observed that alcoholics at some point lose their ability to control their drinking. He formed the theory that, as a result of an allergy, alcoholics develop an irresistible craving for alcohol. This, coupled with the delusion that we can still control our drinking in the face of conclusive evidence that we cannot, is a form of insanity should convince us that we are powerlessness over alcohol. Likewise a willingness to accept the idea that a Power greater than ourselves can restore us to sanity can help us decide to continue with this program of recovery.

weakest proof? [48:19]It is being constantly revealed, as mankind studies the material world, that outward appearances are not inward reality at all. [20]To illustrate:

[21]The prosaic steel girder is a mass of electrons whirling

48:21
Electrons:
54:19-20

Definitions:
48:21 Prosaic: commonplace.

REASONS TO BELIEVE

44:4	You may be suffering from an illness which only a spiritual experience will conquer,
47:11	It has been repeatedly proven among us that upon this simple cornerstone a wonderfully effective spiritual structure can be built,
48:16	Reasonable assumption as a starting point,
49:11	People of faith have a logical idea of what life is all about,
49:12	We used to have no reasonable conception whatever,
49:13	Spiritually minded persons demonstrate a degree of stability, happiness and usefulness which we should have sought ourselves,
50:9-12	These men and women have gained access to and believe in a Power Greater than themselves,
50:13-51:3	One hundred people saying that the consciousness of the Presence of God is the most important fact of their lives, presents a powerful reason why one should have faith,
52:8-10	Our ideas did not work. But the God idea did,
52:13	Others show us that God-sufficiency worked with them,
53:7	The authors think it is reasonable, and more sane and logical to believe than not to believe,
53:8-10	We have to face the proposition that either God is or God isn't,
54:4	Faith had been involved all along,
54:15	In one form or another we had been living by faith and little else,
55:4	We had seen spiritual release,
55:7	For faith in a Power greater than ourselves, and miraculous demonstrations of that power in human lives are facts as old as man himself,
55:8	We finally saw that faith in some kind of God was a part of our makeup,
55:11	We found the Great Reality deep down within us,
55:20	His change of heart was dramatic, convincing and moving,
56:8	Is it possible that all the religious people I have known are wrong?,
56:11	Who are you to say there is no God?,
56:21	His alcoholic problem was taken away,
57:3	God had restored his sanity,
57:4-5	What is this but a miracle of healing? Yet it's elements are simple,
57:6	Circumstances made him willing to believe,
57:8	Even so has God restored us all to our right minds,
57:11	But he has come to all who have honestly sought him,
57:12	When we drew near to Him He disclosed Himself to us.

49:4-6
Nowhere:
10:11-12,
54:19, 55:18

49:6
Prejudice:
11:4, 45:16-
46:4, 47:3,
51:12, 56:11

49:7
Intellectual:
12:12, 16:10,
27:16, 44:14,
62:12, 83:7-8,
77:10

49:9,
Path:
15:13, 58:1,
66:24, 72:2,
100:4, 116:11

49:9
Religion:
xiv:7, 9:22,
9:32, 11:18,
17:5, 19:14,
27:16, 28:5-12,
43:12, 56:8,
74:3, 77:5-7,
87:14-18,
89:17-18,
93:16, 128:4-
10, 131:15-16,
132:1

49:12
Conception:
12:10, 27:12,
45:18-19,
46:10-11, 47:1,
47:7, 50:6,
56:11, 86:11,
93:4-5

around each other at incredible speed. ⁴⁹:¹These tiny bodies are governed by precise laws, and these laws hold true throughout the material world. ²Science tells us so. ³We have no reason to doubt it. ⁴When, however, the perfectly logical assumption is suggested that underneath the material world and life as we see it, there is an All Powerful, Guiding, Creative Intelligence, right there our perverse streak comes to the surface and we laboriously set out to convince ourselves it isn't so. ⁵We read wordy books and indulge in windy arguments, thinking we believe this universe needs no God to explain it. ⁶Were our contentions true, it would follow that life originated out of nothing, means nothing, and proceeds nowhere.

⁷Instead of regarding ourselves as intelligent agents, spearheads of God's ever advancing Creation, we agnostics and atheists chose to believe that our human intelligence was the last word, the alpha and the omega, the beginning and end of all. ⁸Rather vain of us, wasn't it?

⁹We, who have traveled this dubious path, beg you to lay aside prejudice, even against organized religion. ¹⁰We have learned that whatever the human frailties of various faiths may be, those faiths have given purpose and direction to millions. ¹¹People of faith have a logical idea of what life is all about.

¹²Actually, we used to have no reasonable conception whatever.

Definitions:
49:4 Perverse: determined to go counter to what is expected or desired.
49:9 Dubious: of doubtful value.

49:4 We can ask ourselves "how is it working for us?" Are we going to hold on to our old ideas until they kill us? Can't we set aside our arguments long enough to give a spiritually based way of life an honest appraisal?

49:9 The authors, whose drinking patterns were so similar to ours, state that they have also had these objections to leading a spiritually based way of life. The very strong terms in which this suggestion is made shows how important this is to our recovery. Our prejudices will block our progress.

49:10 People, rather than God, have caused the problems with religions. There is a sufficient amount of food on this planet. There are only human reasons why some people starve. People judge others. People cause the wars and fighting. People like us. While blaming others we ignore our own responsibility for the troubles of the world. Decisions and actions based on selfishness and self-centeredness have caused many of the problems we face both as members of the human race and as individuals.

49:11-12 Our conception of what life is about may be based on the flawed idea that the satisfaction of our desires is the route to happiness. Having never examined the basis for our lives until now we have in the past blamed our unhappiness on others for interfering with our pursuit of happiness.

49:13We used to amuse ourselves by cynically dissecting spiritual beliefs and practices when we might have observed that many spiritually-minded persons of all races, colors, and creeds were demonstrating a degree of stability, happiness and usefulness which we should have sought ourselves.

50:1Instead, we looked at the human defects of these people, and sometimes used their shortcomings as a basis of wholesale condemnation. 2We talked of intolerance, while we were intolerant ourselves. 3We missed the reality and the beauty of the forest because we were diverted by the ugliness of some of its trees. 4We never gave the spiritual side of life a fair hearing.

5In our personal stories you will find wide variation in the way each teller approaches and conceives of the Power which is greater than himself. 6Whether we agree with a particular approach or conception seems to make little difference. 7Experience has taught that these are matters about which, for our purpose, we need not be worried. 8They are questions for each individual to settle for himself. 9On one proposition, however, these men and women are strikingly agreed. 10Everyone of them has gained access to, and believes in, a Power greater than himself. 11This Power has in each case

49:13
Observed:
52:8-10,
87:19-20

49:13
Demonstrating:
xiii:2, 14:19,
19:4, 51:2,
55:7, 68:21,
77:10, 98:12-19

50:1
Condemnation:
11:4, 45:16-
46:4, 47:3 ,
49:6, 51:12,
56:11

50:5
Stories:
29:3, 58:8,
60:10

50:8
Individual:
(Decide)
103:1, 132:7

50:9-11
Agree:
17:13

50:11
Miracle:
11:21, 25:1,
27:8, , 55:7,
57:4, 85:3,
124:14, 128:12,
133:15

50:11
Ourselves:
11:8, 25:10,
45:5, 70:23,
84:8, 100:6,
102:18

Definitions:
49:13 Cynically: looking past the appearance of good will, searching to find a rotten core of self-interest.

Historical Note:
50:12 The statesman referred to was Alfred E. Smith, four time Governor of New York , and in 1928, the first Roman Catholic Presidential candidate.

49:13-50:4 If we are so competent to judge the lives, activities and beliefs of others why is our own life in such a state of disorder? Our prejudice towards spirituality and religion does nothing for us and only prevents us from seeing that faith helps people live happier and more useful lives. Acting upon our misguided ideas and attitudes has stripped our lives of purpose and meaning. Setting aside these ideas that have failed us will allow us to begin on the path to true happiness and usefulness.

50:5-8 The purpose of the personal stories in the back of the book is to help us find a concept of and a way to make contact with a Power greater than ourselves. We ignore the differences and look for ways that we are sim-

ilar with the authors. If we find a concept we can agree with we are free to adopt it. Should we find no concept with which we can abide, we are free to believe what we will. Being powerless over alcohol we are betting our lives on the concept we choose, so deep thought on this subject is needed. We may begin to build our new lives upon our own concept whatever that may be.

50:9-11 The basis for the A.A. program is that we learn to access a Power greater than ourselves to solve our problems. This is the purpose of the 12 Steps. This simple program of action worked for the authors and has worked for millions of alcoholics the world over.

accomplished the miraculous, the humanly impossible. ¹²As a celebrated American statesman puts it, "Let's look at the record."

⁵⁰:¹³Here are one hundred men and women, worldly indeed. ¹⁴They flatly declare that since they have come to believe in a Power greater than themselves, to take a certain attitude toward that Power, and to do certain simple things, there has been a revolutionary change in their way of living and thinking. ¹⁵In the face of collapse and despair, in the face of the total failure of their human resources, they found that a new Power, peace, happiness, and sense of direction flowed into them. ¹⁶This happened soon after they wholeheartedly met a few simple requirements. ¹⁷Once confused and baffled by the seeming futility of existence, they will show the underlying reasons why they were making heavy going of life. ⁵¹:¹Leaving aside the drink question, they tell why living was so unsatisfactory. ²They will show how the change came over them. ³When one hundred people are able to say that the consciousness of The Presence of God is today the most important fact of their lives, they present a powerful reason why one should have faith.

Historical Note:
50:13 "one hundred" changed to thousands in third edition.

OBJECTIONS ADDRESSED

50:13-51:1 This paragraph offers us a wonderful promise that power, peace, happiness and sense of direction will replace our current helplessness, anxiety, despair and feelings of uselessness. For this program to work for us we may do the things that the authors show us they did: "come to believe," "take a certain attitude toward God," "do certain simple things," and "meet a few simple require-ments." We are certain to succeed if we follow the path laid out by those who have gone before us.

50:13 That thousands of people have recovered using this spiritual program of action is a convincing reason to believe that faith in a Power greater than ourselves is a practical and effective method of overcoming alcoholism.

51:4This world of ours has made more material progress in the last century than in all the milleniums which went before. 5Almost everyone knows the reason. 6Students of ancient history tell us that the intellect of men in those days was equal to the best of today. 7Yet in ancient times material progress was painfully slow. 8The spirit of modern scientific inquiry, research and invention was almost unknown. 9In the realm of the material, men's minds were lettered by superstition, tradition, and all sorts of fixed ideas. 10The contemporaries of Columbus thought a round earth preposterous. 11Others like them came near putting Galileo to death for his astronomical heresies.

12We asked ourselves this: are not some of us just as biased and unreasonable about the realm of the spirit as were the ancients about the realm of the material? 13Even in the present century, American newspapers were afraid to print an account of the Wright Brothers first successful flight at Kittyhawk. 14Had not all efforts at flight failed before? 15Did not Professor Langley's absurd flying machine go to the bottom of the Potomac river? 16Was it not true that the best mathematical minds had proved man could never fly? 17Had not people said God had reserved this privilege to the birds? 52:1Only thirty years later the conquest of the air was almost an old story and airplane travel was in full swing.

2But in most fields our generation has witnessed complete liberation of our thinking. 3Show any longshoreman a Sunday supplement describing a proposal to explore the moon by means of a rocket and he will say, "I bet they do it—maybe not so long either." 4Is not our age characterized by the ease with

51:3 Presence: 12:27, 56:13-18, 63:6, 85:21-23,162:2

51:3 Fact: 11:22, 17:12, 25:8-10, 55:11, 119:18, 130:3, 161:3, 164:12

51:3 One Hundred: xiii:1, xxiii:10, 19:12, 42:14,

51:3 Conscious: 47:4, 55:17, 56:18, 59:18, 63:6, 85:23, 87:2, 130:3

51:12 Biased: 11:4, 45:16-46:4, 47:3, 49:6, 56:11

52:4 Old Ideas: 27:12, 42:17, 52:9-10, 58:14

52:6 Alcoholism: xiii:1, xxviii:3-18, 18:3-5, 20:8-20, 21:5-22:7, 24:1, 30:10, 37:13-38:14, 44:3, 56:5, 109:10-22, 149:14

Historical Note:
51:15 Samuel Langley (1834-1906), U.S. pioneer in aeronautics. In 1896 launched the first successful pilotless power driven heavier-than-air craft which flew 1/2 mile over the Potomac river near Washington, D.C. Later a larger version crashed into the river and sank.

51:3 Perhaps right now the most important fact in our lives is our inability to quit drinking and the overwhelming troubles both physical, mental and spiritual that our drinking and current way of life have caused. The promise is that peace, happiness, and sense of direction will come as a result of working the 12 Steps.

51:12 Once again it is pointed out that judgment of spirituality prior to investigation is unreasonable. All that is suggested is that we be willing to explore this new way of life and come to our own conclusions based on our experience rather than our biases.

52:6
Bedevilments:
18:3-5,
82:14-18

52:6
Solution:
xiii:2, xxix:1,
17:Title, 20:4-5,
25:3, 25:8-10,
27:9-12, 29:1,
35:16, 44:3-4,
45:4-9, 85:7-8,
95:12

52:6
Symptoms:
xiii:1, 18:3-5,
33:16, 38:18,
40:1

52:8
Reliance:
20:1, 45:21,
68:10, 68:14,
80:13, 85:15,
87:5, 98:9,
99:21, 100:1,
164:3

which we throw away the theory or gadget which does not work for something new which does?

⁵²:⁵We had to ask ourselves why we shouldn't apply to our human problems this same readiness to change the point of view. ⁶We were having trouble with personal relationships, we couldn't control our emotional natures, we were a prey to misery and depression, we couldn't make a living, we had a feeling of uselessness, we were full of fear, we were unhappy, we couldn't seem to be of real help to other people—was not a basic solution of these bedevilments more important than whether we should see newsreels of lunar flight? ⁷Of course it was.

⁸When we saw others solve their problems by simple reliance upon the Spirit of this universe, we had to stop doubting the power of God. ⁹Our ideas did not work. ¹⁰But the God idea did.

Definitions:
52:6 Bedevilment: things that torment us, such as doubts, distractions and worries.

52:4 Now that we see that there is a better way to live we can discard our old ideas for new ideas that work.

52:6 This is a list of some of the symptoms of alcoholism. If merely quitting drinking were the solution to our problem these bedevilments would disappear when we sobered up. A fundamental reorganization of the way we relate to the world is needed if these problems are to be solved. This program offers us the chance to develop through experience a faith that works in solving these problems. Problems that we despaired of ever solving will fall away as we begin the practice of the spiritual principles presented in this book.

52:6 This paragraph offers criteria to measure our progress in this program. If we are still beset by problems such as these perhaps we have not developed sufficient spiritual experience to draw upon so that they may be solved. Problems such as these are a clear indication of the unmanageability of our lives.

52:8 Our reliance on God is a result of an accumulation of experience. We gain experience by calling upon this Power to solve our problems. We learn for ourselves that this works. Just as we learn for ourselves that the way we have been trying to address our problems has failed. Seeing this way of life work for others gives us the willingness to try to apply these principles in our own lives.

52:8 This is a very practical approach to solving our problems. Seeing that this way of life works for others can give us the willingness to try to apply these principles to our own lives. Once we are willing and make the decision to try to build a relationship with God we are given techniques that when practiced repeatedly produce a body of successful spiritual experiences the result of which allows us to develop a faith that works.

52:9-10 How is the way we have been trying to address our problems working for us? What makes us believe that if only we apply our failed ideas even harder that they will ever work? The truth is that the way we have been living will never work. Here are a vast number of people for whom the idea of God is working. All we need is to be willing to give it a try. If it works we can keep doing it and if does not work we are free to try something else.

52:11The Wright Brothers' almost childish faith that they could build a machine which would fly was the mainspring of their accomplishment. 12Without that, nothing could have happened. 13We agnostics and atheists were sticking to the idea that self-sufficiency would solve our problems. 14When others showed us that "God-sufficiency" worked with them, we began to feel like those who had insisted the Wrights would never fly.

53:1Logic is great stuff. 2We liked it. 3We still like it. 4It is not by chance we were given the power to reason, to examine the evidence of our senses, and to draw conclusions. 5That is one of man's magnificent attributes. 6We agnostically inclined would not feel satisfied with a proposal which does not lend itself to reasonable approach and interpretation. 7Hence we are at pains to tell why we think our present faith is reasonable, why we think it more sane and logical to believe than not to believe, why we say our former thinking was soft and mushy when we threw up our hands in doubt and said, "We don't know."

8When we became alcoholics, crushed by a self-imposed crisis we could not postpone or evade, we had to fearlessly face the proposition that either God is everything or else He is nothing. 9God either is, or He isn't. 10What was our choice to be?

53:8 Evaded: 45:14, 53:12

53:8 When: 60:14, 63:13, 63:18, 64:1, 74:13, 76:1, 76:6, 76:11, 76:16-18, 84:14-16, 84:20-21, 86:4, 86:14, 90:1, 94:18, 98:4, 158:8

53:8-10 Step Two: 12:9-19, 13:7, 47:9, 59:9

53:1-7 The only way to know if this way of life will work for us is to give it a try. If it works we can continue. If it does not work we can try something else. It would clearly be insane to keep doing what we have been doing hoping that somehow it will begin to work after having failed so many times before. The only logical choice is to try something different, something that many other people say works for them.

53:8 The self-imposed crisis is the failure of our current way of life. Where are we to turn for help? We have arrived at the point where only a Power greater than ourselves can help us. If we continue on the way we are going we are doomed. We are forced under the lash of alcoholism to turn to God. Here we must decide if we are willing to seek God's help.

53:8-10 Our answer to this question will be the foundation from which we base our future decisions and actions. If we decide there is no God then we will act as if we are on our own and have only our own resources to draw upon. If on the other hand we decide that there is a God then we will adopt attitudes and take actions to access this Power that can solve our problems.

53:8-10 A decision to act as if there is a God will give us the opportunity to develop first hand experience with spiritually based life. When we are confronted with a choice of which way to turn we can draw upon our foundation of willingness to help us determine which course to take. Having a firm base for our decisions helps us to do the right thing in all situations.

53:8-10
Turning Point:
25:12, 59:5

53:13
Shore of Faith:
56:17

53:18
Reason:
12:12, 16:10,
27:16, 44:14,
49:7, 62:12,
83:7-8, 77:10

⁵³:¹¹Arrived at this point, we were squarely confronted with the question of faith. ¹²We couldn't duck the issue. ¹³Some of us had already walked far over the Bridge of Reason toward the desired shore of faith. ¹⁴The outlines and the promise of the New Land had brought lustre to tired eyes and fresh courage to flagging spirits. ¹⁵Friendly hands had stretched out in welcome. ¹⁶We were grateful that Reason had brought us so far. ¹⁷But somehow, we couldn't quite step ashore. ¹⁸Perhaps we had been leaning too heavily on Reason that last mile and we did not like to lose our support.

¹⁹That was natural, but let us think a little more closely. ²⁰Without knowing it, had we not been brought to where we stood by a certain kind of faith? ²¹For did we not believe in our own reasoning? ⁵⁴:¹Did we not have confidence in our ability to think? ²What was that but a sort of faith? ³Yes, we had been faithful, abjectly faithful to the God of Reason. ⁴So, in one way or another, we discovered that faith had been involved all the time!

⁵We found, too, that we had been worshippers. ⁶What a state of mental goose-flesh that used to bring on! ⁷Had we not variously worshipped people, sentiment, things, money, and ourselves? ⁸And then, with a better motive, had we not

Definitions:
54:3 Abjectly: shamelessly servile.
54:5 Worship: to pay reverent homage to that considered sacred.
54:7 Sentiment: feeling or emotion.

53:18-54:4 Many of us exalt reason to the level of a God. We come to rely upon Reason, seemingly our only resource, to solve our problems. We base our decisions and actions upon our ability to reason out the correct course in each situation. We still do this, but now we have a guiding principle upon which to base our reasoning. The principle of the existence of a Higher Power.

54:5-15 Our ideas, attitudes and actions shape our lives. We model our behavior after those people we feel are most successful in achieving what we want for ourselves. We used to think that achievement and possessions would bring us happiness and satisfaction. We suggest that satisfaction,

fulfillment and joy are to be found by leading a life based upon reliance upon God.

54:5-15 We have built our lives on the faulty foundation of self-will. When this way of life fails to bring us satisfaction we seek a solution to the feeling that our lives have no purpose or meaning. We think if only we had more money, then things would be all right. If only we had a spouse or a different spouse, then things would be all right. If only we had a job, or a different job, then things would be all right. Seeing these things as a solution we pursue them with all our will. When these things fail to satisfy us it adds to the feeling of life's meaninglessness.

worshipfully beheld the sunset, the sea, or a flower? 54:9Who
of us had not loved something or somebody? 10How much
did these feelings, these loves, these worships, have to do
with pure reason? 11Little or nothing, we saw at last. 12Were
not these things the tissue out of which our lives were constructed? 13Did not these feelings, after all, determine the
course of our existence? 14It was impossible to say we had no
capacity for faith, or love, or worship. 15In one form or
another we had been living by faith and little else.

54:12
Constructed:
12:17, 47:11,
56:19, 62:21,
63:4, 75:19-23,
97:3, 123:11

DIRECTIONS FOR MAKING A BEGINNING

44:10	We had to face the fact that we must find a spiritual basis for life—or else.
46:9	We found that as soon as we were able to lay aside our prejudice and express even a willingness to believe in a Power greater than ourselves, we commence to get results.
46:12	As soon as we admitted the possible existence of a Creative Intelligence, A Spirit of the Universe underlying the totality of things, we began to be possessed of a new sense of power and direction, provided we took other simple steps.
47:3	Do not let any prejudice you may have against spiritual terms deter you from honestly asking yourself what they mean to you.
47:8-9 ing	We needed to ask ourselves but one short question, "Do I now believe or am I even will- to believe in a Power greater than myself?"
48:2	This sort of thinking had to be abandoned.
48:4	Faced with alcoholic destruction we soon became as open minded on spiritual matters as we had tried to be on other questions.
49:9	. . . lay aside prejudice, even against organized religion.
50:16	This happened soon after they wholeheartedly met a few simple requirements,
51:12	We asked ourselves this: are not some of us just as biased and unreasonable about the realm of the spirit as were the ancients about the realm of the material?
52:5	We had to ask ourselves why we shouldn't apply to our human problems this same readiness to change our point of view,
52:8	. . . we had to stop doubting the power of God.
53:8-10	. . . we had to fearlessly face the proposition that God is either everything or else He is nothing. God either is, or He isn't. What was our choice to be?
55:11-12	We found the Great Reality deep down within us. In the last analysis it is only there that He may be found.
55:15-17	. . . sweep away prejudice . . . think honestly . . . search diligently within yourself. . . . join us on the Broad Highway. With this attitude you cannot fail. The consciousness of your belief is sure to come to you.
57:11-12	. . .He has come to all who have honestly sought him. When we drew near to Him He dis- closed Himself to us!

⁵⁴:¹⁶Imagine life without faith! ¹⁷Were nothing left but pure reason, it wouldn't be life. ¹⁸But we believed in life—of course we did. ¹⁹We could not prove life in the sense that you can prove a straight line is the shortest distance between two points: yet, there it was. ²⁰Could we still say the whole thing was nothing but a mass of electrons, created out of nothing, meaning nothing, whirling on to a destiny of nothingness? ²¹Of course we couldn't. ²²The electrons themselves seemed more intelligent than that. ²³At least, so the chemist said.

²⁴Hence, we saw that reason isn't everything. ²⁵Neither is reason, as most of us use it, entirely dependable though it emanates from our best minds. ⁵⁵:¹What about people who proved that man could never fly?

²Yet we had been seeing another kind of flight, a spiritual liberation from this world, people who rose above their problems. ³They said God made these things possible, and we only smiled. ⁴We had seen spiritual release, but liked to tell ourselves it wasn't true.

⁵Actually we were fooling ourselves, for deep down in every man, woman, and child, is the fundamental idea of God. ⁶It may be obscured by calamity, by pomp, by worship of other things, but in some form or other it is there. ⁷For faith in a Power greater than ourselves, and miraculous demonstrations of that power in human lives, are facts as old as man himself.

⁸We finally saw that faith in some kind of God was a part of our make-up, just as much as the feeling we have for a friend. ⁹Sometimes we had to search fearlessly, but He was there. ¹⁰He was as much a fact as we were. ¹¹We found the Great Reality deep down within us. ¹²In the last analysis

---

55:2-4 Millions of alcoholics restored to happy useful lives by adopting a spiritual basis for their lives are a very good reason for us to give this way of life a try.

55:6 Have we let calamity such as wars, famine, misery and hardship, the ceremony of religions, the pride of people and the pursuit of material satisfactions block us off from God? Can we see past these things to establish a relationship with God?

55:11 If we are having difficulty establishing conscious contact with God here is the place to focus our search and some directions on what to do: search fearlessly, search diligently and think honestly. The promise that we cannot fail and that the consciousness of our belief will come to us gives us gives us hope that is founded in the experience of millions of recovered alcoholics.

it is only there that He may be found. [55:13]It was so with us.

[14]We can only clear the ground a bit. [15]If our testimony helps sweep away prejudice, enables you to think honestly, encourages you to search diligently within yourself, then if you wish you can join us on the Broad Highway. [16]With this attitude you cannot fail. [17]The consciousness of your belief is sure to come to you.

[18]In this book you will read the experience of a man who thought he was an atheist. [19]His story is so interesting that some of it should be told now. [20]His change of heart was dramatic, convincing, and moving.

[56:1]Our friend was a minister's son. [2]He attended church school, where he became rebellious at what he thought an overdose of religious education. [3]For years thereafter he was dogged by trouble and frustration. [4]Business failure, insanity, fatal illness, suicide—these calamities in his immediate family embittered and depressed him. [5]Post-war disillusionment, ever more serious alcoholism, impending mental and physical collapse, brought him to the point of self-destruction.

[6]One night, when confined in a hospital, he was approached by an alcoholic who had known a spiritual experience. [7]Our friend's gorge rose as he bitterly cried out: "If there is a God, He certainly hasn't done anything for me." [8]But later, alone in his room, he asked himself this question: "Is it possible that all the religious people I have known are wrong?" [9]While

55:15
Honestly:
13:22, 32:1,
47:3, 58:2,
63:17, 64:12,
65:7, 67:19,
73:5, 73:22,
73:24, 83:15

55:16
Attitude:
25:8, 26:20,
27:12, 50:13,
63:1, 72:2,
84:5, 86:1,
99:13 143:9

55:16
Fail:
14:23, 15:7,
35:19, 58:1,
60:6, 72:13-16,
78:6, 78:19,
89:2, 93:18

55:17
Conscious:
47:4, 51:3,
56:18, 59:18,
63:6, 85:23,
87:2, 130:3

55:20
Heart:
11:19, 55:11,
143:8

56:7
Self-centered-
ness:
14:2, 61:21,
62:2-14,
116:14, 124:1

56:8
Religion:
xiv:7, 9:23,
9:32, 11:18,
17:5, 19:14,
27:16, 28:5-12,
43:12, 49:9,
74:3, 77:5-7

Definition:
55:15 Diligently: attentive and persistent

55:15 One A.A. joked that it is good that the Highway is Broad, as that means the gutter is farther away.

56:2-5 Here is the story of many of our lives. Rather than adopting a spiritual life we experience the results of a life based on self-will, trouble and frustration. Restricted to our own resources by our faulty perception we are unable to meet life's challenges. Alcoholism strips our lives of purpose and meaning, we become sick physically and mentally and seek escape.

56:7 Here is an example of self-centeredness. We think only of what God and other people can do for us. This is a defect in perception that brings only frustration and unhappiness when things do not go our way. Trying to place God at the center of our lives and seeking ways to further God's will is a way of life that brings happiness, freedom and joy.

56:8 We can ask ourselves this same question. We can also ask if the millions of alcoholics who say that they have been restored to happy useful lives by practicing these principles could be wrong?

pondering the answer he felt as though he lived in hell. ⁵⁶:¹⁰Then, like a thunderbolt, a great thought came. ¹¹It crowded out all else:

"WHO ARE YOU TO SAY THERE IS NO GOD?"

¹²This man recounts that he tumbled out of bed to his knees. ¹³In a few seconds he was overwhelmed by a conviction of the Presence of God. ¹⁴It poured over and through him with the certainty and majesty of a great tide at flood. ¹⁵The barriers he had built through the years were swept away. ¹⁶He stood in the Presence of Infinite Power and Love. ¹⁷He had stepped from bridge to shore. ¹⁸For the first time, he lived in conscious companionship with his Creator.

¹⁹Thus was our friend's cornerstone fixed in place. ²⁰No later vicissitude has shaken it. ²¹His alcoholic problem was taken away. ²²That very night three years ago it disappeared. ⁵⁷:¹Save for a few brief moments of temptation the thought of drink has never returned; and at such times a great revulsion has risen up in him. ²Seemingly he could not drink even if he would. ³God had restored his sanity.

⁴What is this but a miracle of healing? ⁵Yet its elements are simple. ⁶Circumstances made him willing to believe. ⁷He humbly offered himself to his Maker—then he knew.

⁸Even so has God restored us all to our right minds. ⁹To this man, the revelation was sudden. ¹⁰Some of us grow into it more slowly. ¹¹But He has come to all who have honestly sought Him.

¹²When we drew near to Him He disclosed Himself to us!

Definitions:
56:20: Vicissitude: change of circumstances.

56:17-18 Stepping from the Bridge of Reason to the solid ground of faith is the beginning of our relationship with God. The extent of our willingness to believe determines how completely we are able to adopt this new way of life.

56:21-57:3 The result of our willingness to believe and a way of life based upon that belief is the removal of our alcoholic problem and a restoration to sanity. What better reason could there be for us to believe in a Power greater than ourselves?

57:6 This miracle of healing is not reserved for those of saintly demeanor but is available to we who have become willing to believe out of necessity.

57:12 This is a direction for finding God. If we do what we must to clear away what is blocking us we are certain to be successful.

The problem is clearly stated—we are alcoholic—our lives are unmanageable. We understand the severity of the problem which is that no human power could relieve our alcoholism. Faced with alcoholic destruction we have become willing to look in the direction of spiritual help. We have compared our own experience with that of the authors and see the truth. Alcoholism has annihilated all things worthwhile in life or is in the process of doing so. All of our efforts to overcome this illness have failed. Convinced we do not possess the power to stop drinking, we are willing to go to any lengths to recover. We ask those who have recovered "What do we have to do?"

In the forward the authors promised that they would show us precisely how they had recovered (xiii:2). Following this, they said they would tell us specifically what we can do (20:4-5) and also that they would give us clear-cut directions how to do it (29:1). In "How It Works" the authors present us with their program of recovery. Step by step they show us what they have done (59:8-60:1). The directions for Step One are on page 30:7. The directions for Step Two are on page 47:8-9. The directions for Steps Three and Four are given in "How it Works."

In Step Three we are shown that the difficulties we experience in life are the result of a life based on self-will (60:16-63:7). We are shown the reason we have been unable to live up to our own philosophical and moral convictions and are asked to make a decision to begin a new way of life (63:8-12). True to the authors' promise of providing clear-cut directions this new way of life begins with techniques for taking a fearless moral inventory of ourselves (63:18-64:3). As we begin the process of accessing this Power we find that there are aspects of our character that prevent us from receiving the help we need. To discover just exactly what these things in us are that block us from establishing a new relationship with God is the purpose of the fourth step.

A.A. is a suggested program, not a program of suggestions. We can take it or leave it, but the authors warn us that taken half way this program will avail us nothing. If we are willing to let go of all our old ideas and ask for God's protection and care with complete abandon, we are ready to begin.

Having conceded to our innermost selves that we are powerless over alcohol—that our lives are unmanageable, we find ourselves faced with the reality that we need help from a Power greater than ourselves if we are to survive. We come to believe, as the authors have told us, that this power is available to us. Thus we ask God for protection and care.

The program of action is outlined (59:8-60:1). We are encouraged to make progress towards the ideals set down (60:2-9). The conceptual basis for the first two steps are reiterated (60:10-13). We are given a method to determine if we are at the third step (60:14). The results of living a life based on self-will are described (60:16-64:3).

The root of our troubles is disclosed (62:2-9). The severity of, and solution to our troubles is laid out (62:11-14). Why and how to find this solution is related (62:15-21). The benefits of applying this solution are promised (63:1-7). The directions for beginning the Third Step are given (63:8-13). The proper time to begin our Fourth Step, the attitude to adopt while working on it and the reasons this step is necessary is spelled out (63:18-64:3). The similarity between a business inventory and our moral inventory is shown (64:4-12). The directions for the first three columns of the Fourth Step resentment list are found (64:13- 65:7). A pause in which to view the people we have been mad at in a new way is suggested (65:8-67:10) The instructions for the Fourth column of our resentment list are given (67:11-19). A method by which we may examine and begin to outgrow our fears is suggested (67:20-68:23). Our sex problems may be addressed by applying the program of action detailed (68:24-70:22). The chapter is summarized (70:17-23). The authors' hopes are related (71:1-3).

The Blueprint

Introduction — The authors introduce the program of action.

The Twelve Steps — The Twelve Steps are summarized into one sentence statements. We may adopt these suggestions if we choose.

The A, B, C's — If we have accepted these three propositions, we have taken the first two steps towards recovery and are ready for step three.

Step Three — The root of our troubles is disclosed, and a new attitude towards God is suggested along with a prayer that is the beginning of our new way of relating to and relying on our Higher Power.

Step Four Resentment List — We identify our resentments, who what and why we have been angered. Next we learn a new way of dealing with them through forgiveness and reliance upon God.

Step Four Fears List — Our fears are brought out into the light and we learn that reliance upon God is a successful way to outgrow them.

Step Four Sex List — We examine our sex relations learning to turn to God to mold our ideals and help us live up to them. We find that by seeking we are given the guidance we need on how to make amends in each situation.

Chapter Five
HOW IT WORKS

58:1
Fail:
14:23, 35:19,

58:1
Thoroughly:
65:7, 70:17

58:1
Path:
15:13, 66:24,
72:2, 100:4

58:2
Unwilling:
xxviii:8, 30:1

58:2
Self Honesty:
13:22, 32:1

58:5
Rigorous
Honesty:
3:4, 73:24

58:9
Decided:
42:19, 59:10,
60:14, 62:18,
64:1, 71:2,
79:5, 96:12

58:9
It:
76:19, 79:5

58:9
Offer:
17:12-14, 25:6

⁵⁸:¹Rarely have we seen a person fail who has thoroughly followed our path. ²Those who do not recover are people who cannot or will not completely give themselves to this simple program, usually men and women who are constitutionally incapable of being honest with themselves. ³There are such unfortunates. ⁴They are not at fault; they seem to have been born that way. ⁵They are naturally incapable of grasping and developing a manner of living which demands rigorous honesty. ⁶Their chances are less than average. ⁷There are those, too, who suffer from grave emotional and mental disorders, but many of them do recover if they have the capacity to be honest.

⁸Our stories disclose in a general way what we used to be like, what happened, and what we are like now. ⁹If you have decided you want what we have and are willing to go to any length to get it—then you are ready to take certain steps.

¹⁰At some of these we balked. ¹¹We thought we could find

58:1 The authors, as well as many others who have gone before us, have laid down a path for us to follow. We have stumbled blindly through life with no reasonable conception of life's meaning. By following this new path, we find a way of life that goes somewhere.

58:2-5 The unfortunate people referred to here are us. These are clear warnings that unless we can find the willingness to give this program an honest try we will not recover.

58:5 We grasp this program as the drowning grasp a life preserver. We develop this way of life by practicing the 12 Steps in all areas of our lives.

58:8 The study of how best to carry the message of this book is a very rewarding pursuit. Here are directions on how to present our experience, strength and hope. Too detailed of an accounting would accentuate the differences between individuals rather than the similarities of the progression of alcoholism

in one's life. We who have recovered explain to the new person that we have experienced the same baffling symptoms. This helps them see that we know what we are talking about so when we speak of the solution we found the new person can see how to apply this solution for themselves. Telling of these results gives the new person hope that this way of life will also work for them.

58:9 What do these people have that we would want? What is it that we need to be willing to go to any lengths to get? The "it" they are referring to is a spiritual awakening (79:5), the result of which is victory over alcohol (76:19).

58:10 This seems a polite way of saying that we balk at all of these steps. We refuse to admit our powerlessness over alcohol until it becomes undeniable even to us. We are unwilling to believe in the power of God until we see we have nowhere else to turn. We hang onto our self-will until misery makes us let go. We resist an inventory of ourselves out of fear

58:14
Ideas: (Old)
27:12, 42:17,
52:4, 52:9-10

58:15
Baffling:
xxvii:15, 5:12-
13, 6:4, 7:11,
23:9-12, 26:9,
34:15, 35:4-5

59:4
Half measures:
25:11, 164:13

59:5
Turning Point:
25:12, 53:8-10

59:7
Suggest:
xxviii:18, 12:9,
19:13, 86:3,
92:4, 94:13,
104:4, 142:18,
143:14, 144:2,
144:10, 153:10,
164:5

an easier, softer way. 58:12But we could not. 13With all the earnestness at our command, we beg of you to be fearless and thorough from the very start. 14Some of us have tried to hold on to our old ideas and the result was nil until we let go absolutely.

15Remember that we deal with alcohol—cunning, baffling, powerful! 59:1Without help it is too much for us. 2But there is One who has all power—That One is God. 3May you find Him now!

4Half measures availed us nothing. 5We stood at the turning point. 6We asked His protection and care with complete abandon.

7Here are the steps we took, which are suggested as a Program of Recovery:

---

and pride. We hang on to our secrets until the weight of them nearly drags us down. We are unwilling to let go of the worst aspects of our characters until we clearly see that they are the cause of our failure in life. Still, we doubt the power of God and think we should work to overcome our defects rather than let God remove them.

58:11-12 What could be harder than stumbling through the dark as we have been? A well-trodden path, illuminated by the light of God, stretches out before us. We can be encouraged that even the difficult parts lead us closer to our destination. Those who have traveled this path before us assure us that they have tried every conceivable alternate route and have found this to be the surest way.

58:14 As we progress through the steps, we see how our ideas and attitudes have caused us trouble. In the first step, we must let go of the idea that someday we will be able to control and enjoy our drinking. In the second step, we must let go of our prejudice toward spiritual principles. As we continue, we let go of all those things in us that block us off from God.

58:14 Partially adopting this way of life, picking those aspects of it that we find convenient and not too difficult, will not produce the desired result. A mere change of behavior does not equal the entire psychic change

necessary to overcome alcoholism.

59:1 This is the foundation of the first and second steps: we are powerless over alcohol and help is available by turning to a Power greater than ourselves.

59:4 Once again the authors state that nothing short of a complete abandonment of our old way of life is required. Half measures do not yield half results. This is an all or nothing proposition (53:9-10). We can hold on to our old ideas and continue to suffer or we can cast them away and adopt a completely new set of ideas and attitudes. God makes this possible. Our old lives, based on the notion of self-sufficiency, did not work. To begin this new life, all we need to do is voluntarily ask for God's help.

59:7 This is a suggested program, not a program of suggestions. We can adopt this way of life if we want or reject it if we feel we know a better way. Adopting some parts of this program and ignoring or evading other parts is unlikely to allow us to experience an entire psychic change. This is not a mere code of morals or a better philosophy of life. This is a program of action which if practiced in whole will bring about a vital spiritual awakening that will remake our fundamental natures in a way that is indeed miraculous.

59:8 1. We admitted we were powerless over alcohol—that our lives had become unmanageable.

9 2. Came to believe that a Power greater than ourselves could restore us to sanity.

10 3. Made a decision to turn our will and our lives over to the care of God *as we understood Him.*

11 4. Made a searching and fearless moral inventory of ourselves.

12 5. Admitted to God, to ourselves, and to another human being the exact nature of our wrongs.

13 6. Were entirely ready to have God remove all these defects of character.

14 7. Humbly asked Him to remove our shortcomings.

15 8. Made a list of all persons we had harmed, and became willing to make amends to them all.

16 9. Made direct amends to such people wherever possible, except when to do so would injure them or others.

17 10. Continued to take personal inventory and when we were wrong promptly admitted it.

18 11. Sought through prayer and meditation to improve our conscious contact with God *as we understood Him* praying only for knowledge of His will for us and the power to carry that out.

60:1 12. Having had a spiritual experience as the result of these steps, we tried to carry this message to alcoholics, and to practice these principles in all our affairs.

59:8
Step One:
8:9-11, 10:3,
11:12-16, 13:7,
30:7-8
155:6

59:9
Step Two:
12:9-19, 47:9,
53:8-10, 55:8

59:10
Step Three:
13:5, 60:14,
63:9-12, 158:8

59:11
Step Four:
13:8, 13:11,
25:4,
64:5-71:3

59:12
Step Five:
13:10, 25:4,
72:13, 75:7-23,
78:22

59:13
Step Six:
13:8, 76:1-5

59:14
Step Seven:
76:6-10

59:15
Step Eight:
13:11-12,
76:11-15,
78:22,

59:16
Step Nine:
13:14, 69:21,
76:16-84:12,
156:1-6

59:17
Step Ten:
13:15, 84:13-
85:25,
86:4-13

59:18
Step Eleven:
13:17-18,
85:26-88:6,
164:8

60:1
Step Twelve:
13:21, 19:10
88:7-103:12,
164:16

^{60:2}Many of us exclaimed, "What an order! ³I can't go through with it." ⁴Do not be discouraged. ⁵No one among us has been able to maintain anything like perfect adherence to these principles. ⁶We are not saints. ⁷The point is, that we are willing to grow along spiritual lines. ⁸The principles we have set down are guides to progress. ⁹We claim spiritual progress rather than spiritual perfection.

¹⁰Our description of the alcoholic, the chapter to the agnostic, and our personal adventures before and after make clear three pertinent ideas:

¹¹(a) That we were alcoholic and could not manage our own lives.

¹²(b) That probably no human power could have relieved our alcoholism.

¹³(c) That God could and would if sought.

¹⁴Being convinced, we were at step three, which is that we decided to turn our will and our life over to God as we understood Him. ¹⁵Just what do we mean by that, and just what do we do?

¹⁶The first requirement was that we be convinced that any life run on self-will could hardly be a success. ¹⁷On that basis

59:8-60:1 Here the program of action is laid out for us to examine. If we have taken the first two steps toward recovery, we can now decide whether we want to continue. To go on as we have been, or to accept a way of life based on the conscious awareness of the existence of God, what is our choice to be?

60:2-9 Awakening spiritually does not stop us from being human. At times we willfully disregard the will of our Higher Power. We try to apply these principles in every area of our lives, but being human we sometimes fall short. The benefits of trying to lead a spiritually based life are so great that we return to the path as soon as we recognize the errors of our ways. As we progress spiritually, the time we spend in the darkness of self-will lessens and the time we spend in the Sunlight of the Spirit lengthens.

60:10 We have seen the symptoms of alcoholism presented very clearly: the development of a physical craving for more once we begin to drink and a subtle form of insanity that prevents the almost certain consequences of drinking from keeping us from taking the first drink.

60:14 We are not at the third step unless we are convinced of propositions A, B and C above. We can ask ourselves, if we agree absolutely with these three ideas. If we are not convinced, we should re-read the book to this point. It is unlikely that we will be willing to do what is necessary to recover if we are not convinced.

60:15 The authors said earlier that they would tell us specifically what they had done to recover. If we have decided to adopt the methods that were successful for them, we must meet a few simple requirements.

we are almost always in collision with something or some-body, even though our motives are good.

60:17
Motives:
27:12, 70:7,
86:16-18,
102:18,
126:11-12

60:18Most people try to live by self-propulsion. 19Each person is like an actor who wants to run the whole show; is forever trying to arrange the lights, the ballet, the scenery and the rest of the players in his own way. 20If his arrangements would only stay put, if only people would do as he wishes, the show would be great. 61:1Everybody, including himself, would be pleased. 2Life would be wonderful. 3In trying to make these arrangements our actor may sometimes be quite virtuous. 4He may be kind, considerate, patient, generous; even modest and self-sacrificing. 5On the other hand, he may be mean, egotistical, selfish and dishonest. 6But, as with most humans, he is more likely to have varied traits.

60:18-62:14
Self-seeking:
61:16, 62:4,
66:4, 67:13,
84:4, 86:16,
88:3, 122:8-13

61:3-6
Resources:
32:17, 38:8,
45:3, 50:15

61:14
Self-pity:
8:7, 15:6, 62:1,
84:2, 86:16,
88:1

61:13
Resentment:
13:11, 15:6,
18:5, 36:4,
62:1, 64:15-
67:19, 65:5,
66:7-13, 70:18,
84:19, 86:5,
117:19, 145:9

7What usually happens? 8The show doesn't come off very well. 9He begins to think life doesn't treat him right. 10He decides to exert himself some more. 11He becomes, on the next occasion, still more demanding or gracious, as the case may be. 12Still the play does not suit him. 13Admitting he may be somewhat at fault, he is sure that other people are more to blame. 14He becomes angry, indignant, self-pitying. 15What is his basic trouble? 16Is he not really a self-seeker even when

---

60:16 How has the way we have been living working for us? Are we not prey to misery, depression, resentment and remorse? These things are caused by the failed basis of our lives, the basis of self-will. We have lived as though the satisfaction of our instinctual desires for sex, society and security will bring us happiness and fulfillment.

60:16 When we hear that "there are no musts in A.A.," many of us are relieved and think that this means we will not have to do anything to recover. But when we hear that "there is no right or wrong way to work this program," we who have admitted powerlessness over alcohol are fearful that there is nothing we can do to recover. This is a suggested program; we do not have to follow it if we do not want to. But if we do wish to follow this

path there are things we must do and requirements we must meet. Should we decide to do the things that the authors did, we can expect the same results—recovery from alcoholism.

61:3-6 We have developed many of our personality traits because we believed that by applying them we would get our way in life. These traits are some of the human resources we have at our disposal. They are seemingly effective in many circumstances. We feel successful when we get our way.

61:7 How are these techniques for living working for us? We believe that these techniques are all we have and when our self-seeking behavior does not work we try even harder to manipulate the situation to suit us.

trying to be kind? [61:17]Is he not a victim of the delusion that he can wrest satisfaction and happiness out of this world if he only manages well? [18]Is it not evident to all the rest of the players that these are the things he wants? [19]And do not his actions make each of them wish to retaliate, snatching all they can get out of the show? [20]Is he not, even in his best moments, a producer of confusion rather than harmony?

[21]Our actor is self-centered—ego-centric, as people like to call it nowadays. [22]He is like the retired business man who lolls in the Florida sunshine in the winter complaining of the sad state of the nation; the minister who sighs over the sins of the twentieth century; politicians and reformers who are sure all would be Utopia if the rest of the world would only behave; the outlaw safe cracker who thinks society has wronged him; and the alcoholic who has lost all and is locked up. [62:1]Whatever their protestations, are not most of us concerned with ourselves, our resentments, or our self-pity?

[2]Selfishness-self-centeredness! [3]That, we think, is the root of our troubles. [4]Driven by a hundred forms of fear, self-delusion, self-seeking, and self-pity, we step on the toes of our fellows and they retaliate. [5]Sometimes they hurt us, seemingly, without provocation, but we invariably find that at some time in the past we have made decisions based on self, which later

Definitions:
61:17 Delusion: a false belief held despite invalidating evidence.

61:15 The foundation from which we currently base our ideas, attitudes, decisions, and actions is that the satisfaction of our instinctual desires for sex, security and society will lead to happiness and fulfillment. Once we recognize that because we have constructed our lives on this faulty foundation we can never be truly successful, we can begin to structure our lives upon a new stable foundation. Our admission of powerlessness is the solid bedrock (tt21:10) upon which we set a foundation of complete willingness and begin to build our new lives (12:17).

62:2 Acting in our own legitimate self-interest is not selfishness. Selfishness is a lack of concern for the welfare of others.

62:2 If alcohol were the cause of our troubles, they would go away when we stop drinking. What this program addresses is the root cause of our troubles in life. Our selfishness causes us to ignore our responsibilities to others. We pursue the satiation of our desires and disregard the effect our actions may have on others.

62:4-5 The reasons we feel and behave as we do are not always readily apparent. The ability to recognize why we react as we do is one of the benefits of the fourth step. We examine in detail and learn ways to remove the aspects of our characters that block us off from God and prevent us from leading a successful life.

placed us in a position to be hurt.

62:6So our troubles, we think, are basically of our own making. 7They arise out of ourselves, and the alcoholic is an extreme example of self-will run riot, though he usually doesn't think so. 8Above everything, we alcoholics must be rid of this selfishness. 9We must, or it kills us! 10God makes that possible. 11And there often seems no way of entirely getting rid of self without Him. 12Many of us had moral and philosophical convictions galore, but we could not live up to them even though we would have liked to. 13Neither could we reduce our self-centeredness much by wishing or trying on our own power. 14We had to have God's help.

15This is the how and why of it. 16First of all, we had to quit playing God. 17It didn't work. 18Next, we decided that hereafter in this drama of life, God was going to be our Director. 19He is the Principal, we are His agent. 20He is the Father, and we are His children. 21Most good ideas are simple and this concept was the keystone of the new and triumphant arch through which we passed to freedom.

Definitions:
62:21 Keystone: something upon which associated things depend.

62:6 Everyone has problems in life and alcoholics are no different (tt114:1-15). However, leading the selfish, self-centered life of an alcoholic makes for especially hard going (52:6). Restricted by the belief that we have only our own human resources to draw upon, we fail to solve our problems. Our troubles multiply and appear impossible to solve (xxvi:2). The purpose of this book is to enable us to find a Power that will solve our problems (45:8-9).

62:7 One of the hallmarks of alcoholic insanity is the certainty that our thinking is sound and that everyone else is the cause of our problems. Taking the steps of this program brings us toward the restoration of sanity. The first requirement is that we must discard the idea that we can be successful by selfishly applying our will to any situation.

62:8 We can find the willingness to abandon our old way of life by admitting that if we do not we may die. The misery we are going through now will only get worse as long as we continue to live our lives based on selfishness and self-centeredness. The authors show us the way out of the seemingly inescapable trap we are in.

62:12-20 The reason we cannot live up to our own ideals is that we lack the needed power. God has the power to remake our lives and this book shows us how to find this Power. If we could change ourselves to be the kind of people we want to be, we would have done so a long time ago. Most of us have tried a number of methods to bring about just such a change with little or no effect. The authors, who are like us in this respect, report that they have found a way that works. They promised that they would show us precisely what they have done (xiii:2) and that they would answer our questions specifically (20:5), giving us clear-cut directions (29:1). They keep their promise by telling us how to find God and why we need to follow their directions.

62:9
Fatal:
15:1, 24:15, 33:2, 64:16, 66:7-16, 66:13, 92:14, 70:18-19, 117:19

62:11-14
God's Help:
22:14, 24:15, 25:12, 44:4

62:12
Philosophical:
12:12, 16:10, 27:16, 44:14, 49:7, 83:7-8

62:13
On Our Own:
11:16, 24:3, 34:11, 45:2-4, 46:12, 50:15, 59:2, 59:8

62:18,
Decision:
xxviii:7, 42:19, 58:9, 59:10, 60:14, 64:1, 71:2, 79:5, 95:15

62:21
Arch:
12:17, 47:11, 54:12, 56:19, 63:4, 75:19-23, 97:3, 123:11

⁶³:¹When we sincerely took such a position, all sorts of remarkable things followed. ²We had a new Employer. ³Being all powerful, He provided what we needed, if we kept close to Him and performed His work well. ⁴Established on such a footing we became less and less interested in ourselves, our little plans and designs. ⁵More and more we became interested in seeing what we could contribute to life. ⁶As we felt new power flow in, as we enjoyed peace of mind, as we discovered we could face life successfully, as we became conscious of His presence, we began to lose our fear of today, tomorrow, or the hereafter. ⁷We were reborn.

62:21 We gain victory over alcohol by finding freedom from the tyranny of selfishness.

62:21-63:3 The keystone holds all the other pieces of our arch in place. It is the concept upon which all the other concepts presented in this program depend. Currently, we determine our course by deciding which actions are most likely to bring about the satisfaction of our instinctual desires for sex, society and security. The authors are suggesting that the only successful guiding principle is to seek to fulfill God's will rather than our own.

62:21-63:3 We are given several concepts of God in the hope that we will be able to adopt one that will work for us. Prejudices towards religious terms and spiritual concepts can only hinder our progress. We choose a conception of God that we can accept and begin to work at expanding it.

63:1 The position we take is one that is God-centered rather than self-centered. This is the position we must assume to have God begin to work in our lives. This is the beginning of our new life and the end of our agnosticism. Reliance upon God comes as a result of our direct personal experience with this Power solving problems for us that we could never solve on our own.

63:3 We may be confused about what it is that we need. We thought that if we satisfied our desires we would be happy. We thought that if only we could get our way we would be

happy. As we awaken spiritually, we find that the inner joy that comes from conscious contact with our Higher Power stays with us through happy times and sad times and is truly all we need.

63:5 Our attention, thoughts and actions when focused upon ourselves result in misery. Turning our attention to how we may be of use to others results in freedom from self and a sense of purpose and usefulness. This new way of life begins with the decision to redirect ourselves in this manner.

63:6 Moving ourselves from the center of our lives creates a vacuum that God rushes in to fill. We find power available to us that we formerly did not possess. The redirection of our thinking and reliance upon God gives us a peace and serenity that supplies the relief that we formerly sought through self-will.

63:9-12 Prayer is a method of establishing contact with God. People who pray find that it works. To make a beginning all we need to do is try. The next steps work to clear away the things in us that block us off from God. We learn to ask God through prayer to save us from our resentments (67:5), outgrow our fears (68:22), mold our ideals (69:18), and remove our defects of character (76:7). The following steps serve to make us capable of following the direction of our Higher Power (77:4). The final steps help us to broaden and deepen our relationship with God.

^{63:8}We were now at step three. ⁹Many of us said to our Maker, *as we understood Him:* "God, I offer myself to Thee—to build with me and to do with me as Thou wilt. ¹⁰Relieve me of the bondage of self, that I may better do Thy will. ¹¹Take away my difficulties, that victory over them may bear witness to those I would help of Thy Power, Thy Love, and Thy Way of life. ¹²May I do Thy will always!" ¹³We thought well before taking this step making sure we were ready; that we could at last abandon ourselves utterly to Him.

¹⁴We found it very desirable to take this spiritual step with an understanding person, such as our wife, best friend, or spiritual adviser. ¹⁵But it is better to meet God alone than with one who might misunderstand. ¹⁶The wording was, of course, quite optional so long as we expressed the idea, voicing it without reservation. ¹⁷This was only a beginning, though if honestly and humbly made, an effect, sometimes a very great one, was felt at once.

¹⁸Next we launched out on a course of vigorous action, the first step of which is a personal housecleaning, which many of us had never attempted. ^{64:1}Though our decision was a vital and crucial step, it could have little permanent effect unless at once followed by a strenuous effort to face, and to be rid of, the things in Ourselves which had been blocking us. ²Our liquor was but a symptom. ³So we had to get down to causes and conditions.

63:9-12
Step Three:
13:5, 59:10,
60:14, 158:8

63:11
Take Away:
12:27, 57:12,
64:1, 76:7

63:15
Misunderstand:
18:5, 20:19,
42:5, 74:5,
112:21, 140:14

63:16
Reservation:
13:6, 14:4,
32:11, 33:8,
50:16, 155:11

63:17-18
At once:
xxv:7, 46:12,
47:10, 64:1,
68:23, 84:20,
87:17, 99:8,
100:7

63:18
Next:
53:8, 60:14,
63:13, 64:1,
74:13, 76:1,
76:6, 76:11,
76:16-18,
84:14-16,
84:20-21, 86:4,
86:14, 90:1,
94:18, 98:4,
158:8

63:18
Attempted:
25:4

63:9-12 This is the third step prayer. All of the subsequent steps depend upon the decision made in this step.

63:13 To abandon something is to give up all claim to it. Once we have decided to turn our will and our lives over to God, we give up all claim to reject how God intends to direct our lives.

63:15 It is important that we take this step with someone who understands alcoholics. Those who do not understand the desperate nature of the dilemma we find ourselves in may think this too drastic a step and attempt to change our plan (74:15). We who must find

a Power greater than ourselves must not be deterred from following this path by those who do not understand.

63:17 This is the beginning of our new way of life. To the extent that we are able to surrender our will to God do we feel the results of our decision.

63:18-64:1 This is precise, specific and clear-cut direction for when to begin our fourth step. We follow our third step decision "at once" with our fourth step. Procrastination will leave us blocked from the Power we need.

64:1
Decision:
Xxviii:7, 42:19,
58:9, 59:10,
60:14, 62:18,
71:2, 79:5,
95:15, 96:12

64:1
Blocked:
12:27, 57:12,
63:11, 76:7

64:2
But a
Symptom:
xxix:7 19:3,
35:17, 82:19,
51:1, 63:17,
122:14, 103:10

64:5-71:3
Step Four:
13:8, 13:11,
59:11

64:4Therefore, we started upon a personal inventory. 5*This was step four.* 6A business which takes no regular inventory usually goes broke. 7Taking a commercial inventory is a fact-finding and a fact-facing process. 8It is an effort to discover the truth about the stock-in-trade. 9One object is to disclose damaged or unsalable goods, to get rid of them promptly and without regret. 10If the owner of the business is to be successful, he cannot fool himself about values.

11We did exactly the same thing with our lives. 12We took stock honestly. 13First, we searched out the flaws in our make-up which caused our failure. 14Being convinced that self, manifested in various ways, was what had defeated us, we considered its common manifestations.

64:1 Our third step decision is vital (life giving, crucial and necessary). We are unlikely to continue this program if we have not taken the third step.

64:1 How many times have we made decisions and then found ourselves unable to carry out our decisions? The emotions that caused us to make our decision fades or our circumstances change and we lose the motivation for action. Our third step decision is just the beginning. The authors promise us permanent effect from our decision if we work hard at the following steps.

64:1 Our fourth step is a method of identifying and admitting the truth about the makeup of our character. What exactly is it in ourselves that blocks us off from God? If we are to access this Power, we must place ourselves in the position to have these defects removed. Our fourth step, followed by the subsequent steps, accomplishes this.

64:2-3 Our drinking and the unmanageability of our lives are symptoms of the fundamental defects of our character. If our problems in life were caused by drinking, then they would go away once we stopped drinking. The improvement in our lives resulting from abstinence is likely a temporary respite if we fail to address the things in us that block us off from our Higher Power.

64:4 The fourth step is a technique by which we identify the aspects of our characters that block us off from God. During our fourth step, we learn methods of accessing the power of God to accomplish things that we have been unable to accomplish for ourselves.

64:10 We have fooled ourselves about the value of the principles by which we now live. Many of us tell lies hoping to make ourselves more attractive to other people. Rather than helping to build close relationships with these people our lies separate us from them. We developed many of our methods of relating to others as tools to get us what we wanted. Here is our opportunity to evaluate the way we live, think and act.

64:13 The examination of our character is a daunting task. The authors suggest where we should begin. We must not be distracted by trying to soothe our damaged egos, build our self esteem or develop pride. A healthy self-respect will come as a result of this work along with humility that produces self-worth based on fact rather than delusion or misplaced ideals. Recognition of who and what we really are, coupled with an effort to seek and do God's will, fills our lives with value and meaning replacing our prideful self-loathing and self-pity.

^{64:15}Resentment is the "number one" offender. ¹⁶It destroys more alcoholics than anything else. ¹⁷From it stem all forms of spiritual disease, for we have been not only mentally and physically ill, we have been spiritually sick. ¹⁸When the spiritual malady is overcome, we straighten out mentally and physically. ¹⁹In dealing with resentments, we set them on paper. ²⁰We listed people, institutions or principles with whom we were angry. ²¹We asked ourselves why we were angry. ²²In most cases it was found that our self-esteem, our pocketbooks, our ambitions, our personal relationships (including sex), were hurt or threatened. ^{65:1}So we were sore. ²We were "burned up."

64:15-67:19
Resentment:
13:11, 15:6,
18:5, 36:4,
62:1, 65:5,
66:7-13, 70:18,
84:19, 86:5,

64:16
Fatal:
15:1, 24:15,
33:2, 62:9

64:18
Straighten Out:
98:1, 98:7-8,
127:10, 135:15

64:19-20
On Paper:
65:3, 67:11,
67:17-18, 68:3,
69:15, 70:17-
22, 76:13

Definition:
64:15 Resentment: to re-feel an injury or insult.

64:15 To hold a resentment is to re-feel the anger of a past event. Sometimes we will replay an argument in our minds. A conversation in which we felt we were slighted is replayed over and over and we imagine what we should have said in return. Perhaps we plan what we will say the next time we encounter the offending person.

64:17 The physical illness we suffer is our allergy to alcohol. The mental illness is our inability to stop drinking entirely. Our spiritual illness is our selfishness and self-centeredness. The solution to our problem comes when we overcome this spiritual malady.

64:19-20 The fourth step is simple, but the lack of willingness to follow directions is a common trait of alcoholics. Rather than tell us what we should do, the authors show us what they have done: "In dealing with resentments we set them on paper." If we desire the same results as the authors, we must be willing to follow their example. The first instruction for the fourth step is that we are to write our resentments down on paper.

64:19-20 The format for the resentment list of our fourth step is a four column table. The first three columns are illustrated in paragraph 65:5 and the fourth column is explained on 67:11-19.

64:20 To begin our fourth step all we need to do is write the name of someone at whom we

have been angry or resentful. This is simple. We have all been angry at someone at one time or another. It is likely that we are currently holding grudges against several people. Perhaps we could start by listing our family members. Many of us harbor resentment at institutions such as the court systems, schools, our workplaces and of societal institutions such as marriage. The authors suggest that we also list these. Guiding principles we feel have been imposed upon us are another source of resentment and should be included in our list. We write down all those people, institutions or principles that readily come to mind. As we progress we add to this list any further resentments that we can recall.

64:21-22 The directions for the second column are simple; we write down why we were angry. As we develop insight, we will see that our interpretation of events is not always accurate. Many of us have found it helpful to list the facts and write only what actually happened rather than our interpretation. As an example we could write, "My spouse told me to slow down." This is what actually happened. An example of how we might interpret the events is as an attack upon our competency as a driver and an attempt by our spouse to control our actions. Our interpretation of the event should be saved for the third column, where we describe what in us was affected by the event.

65:3
Write:
64:19-20,
67:11, 67:17-
18, 68:3, 69:15,
70:17-22, 76:13

65:5
Resentment:
13:11, 15:6,
18:5, 36:4,
62:1, 64:15-
67:19, 66:7-13,
70:18, 84:19,
86:5, 117:19,
145:9

65:7
Thoroughly:
58:1, 58:13,
68:2, 70:17

65:7
Honesty: (Self)
13:22, 32:1,
47:3, 55:15,
58:2, 63:17,
64:12, 67:19,
73:5, 73:22,
73:24, 83:15

65:8
Finished:
72:5, 73:2,
76:10, 84:18,
99:16

65:3On our grudge list we set opposite each name our injuries. 4Was it our self-esteem, our security, our ambitions, our personal, or sex relations, which had been interfered with? 5We were usually as definite as this example:

I'm resentful at:	The Cause	Affects my:
Mr. Brown	His attention to my wife.	Sex relations. Self-esteem (fear)
	Told my wife of my mistress.	Sex relations. Self-esteem (fear)
	Brown may get my job at the office.	Security. Self-esteem (fear)
Mrs. Jones	She's a nut—she snubbed me. She commited her husband for drinking. He's my friend. She's a gossip.	Personal relationship. Self-esteem (fear)

65:3-4 We begin the third column of our resentment list by examining exactly how we are affected by the events in the second column. The authors give us a list of areas likely to be affected. It may help to write one sentence for each area that is affected and elaborate a bit on each one. This examination helps us sort out why we are mad and enables us to develop insight. We begin to see why we feel and react the way that we do.

65:5 The first three columns of our resentment list are illustrated. There is a fourth column that is not shown. That column is described later in the chapter. The three columns that we see here are roughly what our three columns will look like if we follow the direction of the authors. We have found a legal pad (8 1/2" x 14") of paper works nicely when turned on its side so that it is longer than it is tall. Leave plenty of room for the fourth column.

65:6 Many of us have found it useful to begin with resentments that have lost some of their impact on us through the passage of time. When we are in the heat of a resentment we may hold on too strongly to our interpretations of events and our justifications for our feelings and actions. We practice on less immediate resentments and in this way gain the insight to accurately analyze our most current and significant resentments. If we feel an immediate need to address a current and troubling resentment, we should by all means proceed.

65:7 It does not matter how eloquent we are or if our spelling is correct, all that matters is thoroughness and honesty. If we have not included all we need to, then we have not been thorough. If we have not told the truth, if we have embellished upon or left out important details, then we have not been honest. It does not matter what format we use as long as we are able to see the truth about ourselves.

65:7 One of A.A.'s greatest strengths is that there is no dogma. How we do this does not matter. If we want to do it differently, we are free to. As long as we look at the areas suggested, we will obtain the same results as the authors.

I'm resentful at:	The Cause	Affects my:	
My employer	Unreasonable-Unjust - Overbearing - Threatens to fire me for drinking and padding my expense account.	Self-esteem (fear) Security.	**66:3** Remorseful: xxvii:1, xxviii:7, 6:7, 37:9, 86:12, 106:19, 109:18
			66:4 Fought: 5:21, 41:20, 84:24, 85:4, 103:11-12
My wife	Misunderstands and nags. Likes Brown. Wants house put in her name.	Pride-Personal and sex relations- - Security (fear)	**66:4** Self-seeking: 60:18-62:14, 61:16, 62:4, 67:13, 84:4, 86:16, 88:3, 122:8-13

66:7-13
Resentment:
13:11, 15:6,
18:5, 36:4,
62:1, 64:15-
67:19, 65:5,
70:18, 84:19,
86:5, 117:19,
145:9

65:6We went back through our lives. 7Nothing counted but thoroughness and honesty. 8When we were finished we considered it carefully. 9The first thing apparent was that this world and its people were often quite wrong. 66:1To conclude that others were wrong was as far as most of us ever got. 2The usual outcome was that people continued to wrong us and we stayed sore. 3Sometimes it was remorse and then we were sore at ourselves. 4But the more we fought and tried to have our way, the worse matters got. 5As in war, the victor only *seemed* to win. 6Our moments of triumph were short-lived.

66:7-16
Fatal:
15:1, 24:15,
33:2, 62:9,
64:16, 66:13,
92:14, 70:18-
19, 117:19,
154:20

66:8
Squander:
88:3

66:8
Worthwhile:
xxix:5, 18:3-5,
38:19

7It is plain that a life which includes deep resentment leads only to futility and unhappiness. 8To the precise extent that we permit these, do we squander the hours that might have been worth while. 9But with the alcoholic whose hope is the maintenance and growth of a spiritual experience, this business

66:8
Extent:
58:14, 59:5,
63:13, 63:16
68:13, 164:13

Definitions:
66:3 Remorse: to feel regret (re: again, morse: bite).

65:8 This "careful consideration" refers to the first three columns of our resentment list. We are going to learn a new and successful method of dealing with these resentments that incorporates asking for the help of God.

66:7-8 God speaks softly and when our minds are loud and angry we are deaf to the guidance we want and need to live. While we stew in the boiling pot of resentment, we are not free to be happy and useful to others.

66:10 "Our very lives depend upon our constant thought of others and how we may meet their needs" (20:1). While our minds are spinning resentments and weaving plots of revenge, we are blocked off from other people and God.

of resentment is infinitely grave. 66:10We found that it is fatal. 11For when harboring such feelings we shut ourselves off from the sunlight of the Spirit. 12The insanity of alcohol returns and we drink again. 13And with us, to drink is to die.

14If we were to live, we had to be free of anger. 15The grouch and the brainstorm were not for us. 16They may be the dubious luxury of normal men, but for alcoholics these things are poison.

17We turned back to the list, for it held the key to the future. 18We were prepared to look at it from an entirely different angle. 19We began to see that the world and its people really dominated *us*. 20In that state, the wrong-doing of others, fancied or real, had power to actually kill. 21How could we escape? 22We saw that these resentments must be mastered, but how? 23We could not wish them away any more than alcohol.

24This was our course: we realized that the people who wronged us were perhaps spiritually sick. 67:1Though we did not

Definitions:
66:14 Free: not bound by. Out from under the control of.
66:15 Grouch: a person who sulks.
66:15 Brainstorm: a sudden violent attack of mental disturbance.

66:12-13 This is a good reason to abandon our old ways of dealing with resentment. A resentment that occupies our mind and hearts leaves no room for our Higher Power to enter into our lives. Without this Power we are defenseless against the first drink.

66:14 To be free of something is to be out from under its control. We are not suggesting that we must be without anger. However, it is essential that we be in control of this powerful emotion and not the other way around. Our Creator gave us the ability to be angry so that we could protect ourselves, not so that our anger could harm us and those we love.

66:18 We become prepared to abandon our old ways by seeing for ourselves, through our fourth step, that our way does not work. If we do not learn new ways of dealing with life, our lives will remain miserable even after we stop drinking. We did not quit drinking to remain miserable, we quit so that we could find peace and happiness.

66:19 By allowing the actions of others to

determine what we think and feel, we lose control of our own lives. Like an occupying army, resentment takes our lives hostage.

66:22-23 The authors, once again, show us what they have done. The way we have been dealing with resentments has allowed them to accumulate to the point where they threaten our very lives. We turn to spiritual help to conquer our resentments. By being willing to look at those who have harmed us in a new way and asking God to help, we learn a successful way of dealing with resentment. Repeatedly seeing for ourselves that this aspect of a spiritually-based life works, enables us to rely ever more fully upon God to solve our problems.

66:24-67:1 A shift in perception is suggested. We judge ourselves by our intentions while others judge us by our actions. We, being spiritually ill, are unable to live up to our own ideals. Even though we have good intentions, we harm others by trying to get what we want. Perhaps those who harm us are like their symptoms and the way these disturbed us, they, like ourselves were sick, too. ⁶⁷:²We asked God to help us show them the same tolerance, pity, and patience that we would cheerfully grant a sick friend. ³When a person offended we said to ourselves, "This is a sick man. ⁴How can I be helpful to him? ⁵God save me from being angry. ⁶Thy will be done."

⁷We avoid retaliation or argument. ⁸We wouldn't treat sick people that way. ⁹If we do, we destroy our chance of being helpful. ¹⁰We cannot be helpful to all people, but at least God will show us how to take a kindly and tolerant view of each and every one.

¹¹Referring to our list again. ¹²Putting out of our minds the wrongs others had done, we resolutely looked for our own mistakes. ¹³Where had we been selfish, dishonest, self-seeking and frightened? ¹⁴Though a situation had not been entirely our fault, we tried to disregard the other person involved entirely. ¹⁵Where were we to blame? ¹⁶The inventory was ours, not the other man's. ¹⁷When we saw our faults we listed them. ¹⁸We placed them before us in black and white. ¹⁹We admitted our wrongs honestly and were willing to set these matters straight.

67:2
Show:
xiii:2, 14:19, 19:4, 49:13, 51:2, 68:21, 77:10, 92:3, 95:9, 98:17, 118:10, 152:10

67:2
Tolerance:
19:18, 28:9, 67:10, 70:21, 83:6, 84:23, 103:2, 118:9, 125:5, 135:14

67:7
Criticize:
13:13, 67:14, 77:18, 78:1, 98:16-19

67:11
Write:
64:19-20, 65:3, 67:17-18, 68:3, 69:15, 70:17-22, 76:13

67:13
Self-seeking:
61:16, 60:18-62:14, 62:4, 66:4, 84:4, 86:16, 88:3, 122:8-13

well-intentioned but spiritually ill also. If we can see their harmful actions as symptoms of this illness rather than an attack upon us as individuals, we can give them the understanding and forgiveness that we desire for ourselves.

67:2-6 This prayer is a method of accessing Divine Power to accomplish what we are unable to do for ourselves. We decide to change our minds and we ask God to change our hearts. By repeatedly trying to practice this spiritual principle, we live our way into a new way of thinking.

67:11-19 We use this pause between the third and fourth columns of our resentment list to access a Power greater than ourselves. Now, having accessed this Power to remove from us the anger that blocks us from seeing our part in these situations, we begin to take our own inventory. Just as in their directions

for the third column, the authors offer us several areas of our character to explore in the fourth column of our resentment list. Writing a sentence describing how these characteristics apply in each situation is helpful in showing us the varying manifestations of each defect. Knowing precisely what each of these terms means is important if we are to see clearly how they affect our lives and the lives of those we come into contact with. These terms are a good starting point in the examination of our moral makeup. There are many other character defects that we may learn to identify in ourselves and thus position ourselves for their removal.

67:17-18 The authors intend for us to include this written roster of character defects in our fourth step. Having left most of our page blank after the first three columns were finished, we have plenty of room to include this list.

FOURTH STEP RESENTMENT LIST

I'm Resentful At:	The Cause:	Affects My:	Where Have I Been :	
		Self-esteem:	Selfish:	
		Security:	Dishonest:	
		Ambitions:	Self-seeking:	
		Personal Relations:	Frightened:	
		Sex Relations:		

^{67:20}Notice that the word "fear" is bracketed alongside the difficulties with Mr. Brown, Mrs. Jones, the employer, and the wife. ²¹This short word somehow touches about every aspect of our lives. ²²It was an evil and corroding thread; the fabric of our existence was shot through with it. ²³It set in motion trains of circumstances which brought us misfortune we felt we didn't deserve. ²⁴But did not we, ourselves, set the ball rolling? ²⁵Sometimes we think fear ought to be classed with stealing. ^{68:1}It seems to cause more trouble.

²We reviewed our fears thoroughly. ³We put them on paper, even though we had no resentment in connection with them. ⁴We asked ourselves why we had them. ⁵Wasn't it because self-reliance failed us? ⁶Self-reliance was good as far as it went, but it didn't go far enough. ⁷Some of us once had great self-confidence, but it didn't fully solve the fear problem, or any other. ⁸When it made us cocky, it was worse.

67:20-24
Threadbare:
24:8

67:23-24
Retaliate:
62:4-5

68:2
Thoroughly:
58:13, 65:7,
70:17

68:3
Write:
64:19-20,65:3,
67:11, 67:17-
18, 69:15,
70:17-22, 76:13

Definitions:
67:20 Fear: a faith that something bad is going to happen.

67:19 Once we honestly admit our wrongs to ourselves and see clearly the harm these shortcomings cause us, we can be willing to renounce our resentments and go about correcting the mistakes we have made.

67:20 Fear is a faith that something bad is going to happen. The authors show us where to note the fears that we identify. In our next fourth step list, we examine the fears that we have noted here and learn a successful method of outgrowing these fears.

67:21 Unexamined fears unconsciously control our actions. When, in many situations we act upon our faith that something bad is going to happen, we place ourselves in the position to be hurt.

68:2-23 The clear-cut directions for the fears list of our fourth step are given here. Clearly, we are to write this list down. We add to the fears we identified in our resentment list any other fears that we may have. The first column contains a description of our fear, e.g.,

"I am afraid of being alone." The second column contains the reason we have this fear and the third column contains the solution to our fear. The authors suggest a reason for our fears, which is a reliance upon our human resources rather than God.

We who have no experience with God working in our lives believe that our own human resources are the only power to which we have access. Our fear comes from the knowledge that our own power is often not enough. Some of our fears are instinctual, such as the fear of falling that we have from the time we are born. We learn some fears from experience. We experience a negative result and we have faith that we will always experience that same result. We may ask someone for help and be rejected, so we fear we will be rejected again. Fears such as this govern our actions. Some fears serve to keep us out of danger but when we are controlled by unreasonable fears we are not always free to act in our own best interests. This is a method of applying reason and the Power of God to our fears.

68:13
Do:
13:21, 20:4,
50:14, 60:15,
69:9, 152:13

68:13
Extent:
58:14, 59:5,
63:13, 63:16,
66:8, 164:13

68:14
Dependent:
20:1, 45:21,
52:8, 68:10,
80:13, 85:15,
87:5, 98:9,
99:21, 100:1,
164:3

68:21
Demonstration:
xiii:2, 14:19,
19:4, 49:13,
51:2, 55:7,
77:10, 98:12-19

⁶⁸:⁹Perhaps there is a better way—we think so. ¹⁰For we are now on a different basis; the basis of trusting and relying upon God. ¹¹We trust infinite God rather than our finite selves. ¹²We are in the world to play the role He assigns. ¹³Just to the extent that we do as we think He would have us, and humbly rely on Him, does He enable us to match calamity with serenity.

¹⁴We never apologize to anyone for depending upon our Creator. ¹⁵We can laugh at those who think spirituality the way of weakness. ¹⁶Paradoxically, it is the way of strength. ¹⁷The verdict of the ages is that faith means courage. ¹⁸All men of faith have courage. ¹⁹They trust their God. ²⁰We never apologize for God. ²¹Instead we let Him demonstrate, through us, what He can do. ²²We ask Him to remove our fear and direct our attention to what He would have us be. ²³At once, we commence to outgrow fear.

Defininitions:
68:18 Paradoxically: apparently contradictory, i.e., dependence upon God equals freedom and strength.

68:2 We look at our fears again. Many of the fears that control us are unreasonable. We have never applied reason to them. We adopted many of the ideas behind our fears prior to becoming mature adults. This is our chance to re-evaluate our fears when we are sober adults.

68:3 By listing the fears that we have, we develop the ability to identify the forces within us that drive us to act the way we do. Many of our less desirable reactions to life are the result of fears. We may treat our spouse badly because we fear they may leave us. We may avoid other people because we fear they may not like us. We may steal because we fear we may not be able to make it on our own. None of these methods of coping with life are entirely successful. By listing our fears, examining them in the light of our new way of life, and seeking help from God, we place ourselves in the position to begin to outgrow them.

68:8 Using bravado to cover up our fear and denying that we have it is one of the signs of fear causing us to act in foolish ways.

68:10-12 We adopted this new basis for our lives by making our third step decision.

This is a good example of exactly how to put our decision into action. Our old way was to rely solely on our own inner resources and coping skills we had developed over time. We either avoided the source of our fear or we denied having it and acted in an unsuccessful way to overcome it. Our new way to deal with our fear is to identify it, examine it and ask God to remove it. This way works. As we try it repeatedly on all our fears, we see for ourselves that it does work and we come to rely upon it.

68:13 The key word here is "do." Seeking to do God's will as we gain a thorough understanding of who and what we really are will produce in us the humility necessary to receive God's grace. We see that our problems are of our own making, that we are the source of the calamity in our lives. God gives us the strength to meet life's difficulties when we are humble enough to ask for it.

68:18-21 Knowing that God will give us the strength to meet any of life's challenges gives us courage. When we relied solely on our own power, fear of failure would sometimes prevent us from even trying. When we are seeking to do God's will, we know even what seems

FOURTH STEP FEARS LIST

I'm Fearful of: At:	Why Do I Have This Fear:	A Better Way:

123

HOW IT WORKS 68:24

69:9
Do:
13:21, 20:4,
50:14, 60:15,
68:13, 152:13

⁶⁸:²⁴Now about sex. ²⁵Many of us needed an overhauling there. ²⁶But above all, we tried to be sensible on this question. ²⁷It's so easy to get way off the track. ²⁸Here we find human opinions running to extremes—absurd extremes, perhaps. ²⁹One set of voices cry that sex is a lust of our lower nature, a base necessity of procreation. ⁶⁹:¹Then we have the voices who cry for sex and more sex; who bewail the institution of marriage; who think that most of the troubles of the race are traceable to sex causes. ²They think we do not have enough of it, or that it isn't the right kind. ³They see its significance everywhere. ⁴One school would allow man no flavor for his fare and the other would have us all on a straight pepper diet. ⁵We want to stay out of this controversy. ⁶We do not want to be the arbiter of anyone's sex conduct. ⁷We all have sex problems. ⁸We'd hardly be human if we didn't. ⁹What can we do about them?

to be failure will turn out for the best. We can learn and grow rather than have our self-esteem destroyed by our failures.

68:22 This prayer is the key to overcoming our fears. Turning to God for help is the guiding principle of our new way of life. This prayer asking God to remove our fear is an important part of our new way of life. Rather than be driven by worrying about what we may lose or fail to gain for ourselves, we ask God to help shape our lives.

68:23 Our fears, based on self, no longer fit in our new lives. As we change the focus of what we desire in life from the satisfaction of our instinctual drives to a life based upon seeking God's will our fears seem to disappear. By relying upon our Higher Power, we find that our needs are met and that our wants change. Our self-centered fears of losing what we have and of not getting what we want lose their power over us.

68:24-70:16 The third area we focus on in our fourth step is sex. We continue the columnar format we learned in the resentment list . The direction to write this down is clear (69:15). The authors suggest the aspects of our sex lives we should concentrate on (69:10-14).

We begin to practice spiritual principles in this area of our lives by asking for God's help (69:18).

68:26 How we best ensure sound judgment in the area of relationships with others is by following the authors' suggestions to avoid hysterical thinking or advice (70:2), seek the calm rational counsel of others (69:26), seek the guidance of God (69:18) and in the end let God be our judge (69:26).

69:5-6 The authors do not speak to us from a moral hilltop. They do not assume to be empowered to judge us. This attitude can enable us to be useful to others when they come to us for advice. Regardless of our own beliefs in this matter, the spiritual solution is available to us to solve any problems we may have.

69:9 This book gives us specific answers to our question about what we can do regarding our sex problems. The authors give us clear-cut directions on how to solve the sex problems in our lives by showing us precisely what they have done. If we are willing, we can follow the authors' example and find out how to solve our sex problems by accessing the power of God.

69:10We reviewed our own conduct over the years past. 69:15
Write:
64:19-20,
65:3, 67:11,
67:17-18, 68:3,
70:17-22, 76:13 11Where had we been selfish, dishonest, or inconsiderate? 12Whom had we hurt? 13Did we unjustifiably arouse jealousy, suspicion or bitterness? 14Where were we at fault, what should we have done instead? 15We got this all down on paper and looked at it.

69:18,
Prayer:
xxx4,13:15-20,
59:18, 63:9-12,
67:5, 68:22,
69:22, 70:12,
75:17, 76:5,
76:6-9, 76:18,
79:5, 82:5,
83:6, 84:20,
85:26-86:3,
86:13-21,
87:6-20, 164:8

16In this way we tried to shape a sane and sound ideal for our future sex life. 17We subjected each relation to this test— was it selfish or not? 18We asked God to mold our ideals and help us to live up to them. 19We remembered always that our sex

---

69:10 Once again, we search our past and re-examine each of our relationships. In doing so we recognize behaviors that we repeat, causing all of our relationships to end the same way. When laid out before us in black and white it is easier for us to determine if the way we have been living is working for us or not.

69:11 Our selfish and self-centered basis for life also affects our sex lives and relationships. We lie to and manipulate others to get our way. We disregard the best interests and well being of others. We cause great harm physically, mentally and spiritually to those we come in contact with.

69:12 We hurt those we have relationships with and also those around them in a widening ripple effect. The parents, siblings, children, future sex partners and spouses of those with whom we have had relationships may all feel the effects of the harm we have caused through our sex conduct.

69:13 We list each such instance where we feel our conduct has awakened these feelings in others. These feelings may arouse a desire to retaliate that is very hard to break free of and has destroyed many relationships.

69:14 Our new outlook upon life allows us to stop blaming others and to see where we

were at fault. The shortcomings listed in this paragraph are just a starting point. The more precise we can be when identifying our defects, the better we will be at recognizing them when they appear. We have many defects of character that may be listed. (See index of character defects located later in this book.)

69:14 Our new outlook upon life opens our eyes to see what we should have done in our relationships. We see the result of our being driven by our own selfish goals and what would have been best for each person involved. In this way we can begin to form guiding principles for our future conduct.

69:18 By making this prayer, we get to experience for ourselves the guidance and power of God. We abandon our old way of living and thinking. The new basis for our lives is to rely upon God. If we were able to live up to our ideals on our own, we probably would have. The prayer suggested here brings the power of God to bear upon our relationships and sex lives. This is a practical method and as we experience its effectiveness we develop faith that it will continue to work if we practice it.

69:19 As alcoholics, we may tend toward extremes. We are seeking balance in our lives. The two views cited here are extremes and should be avoided.

70:2
Advice:
xxx:4, 73:21,
90:4, 96:11,
106:18

70:3
Stumble:
60:4-5, 99:7

70:7
Motives:
27:12, 60:17,
86:16-18,
102:18, 126:11-
12

70:8
Forgive:
66:24-67:6,
70:21, 76:21,
77:17, 79:18,
86:13

70:8
Honest:
xiv:2 , 5:18,
25:13, 28:7,
57:11, 58:9,
73:5, 96:1-8,
114:7, 147:3,
159:5, 161:11,
120:5

powers were God-given, and therefore good, neither to be used lightly or selfishly nor to be despised and loathed.

⁶⁹:²⁰Whatever our ideal turns out to be, we must be willing to grow toward it. ²¹We must be willing to make amends where we have done harm, provided that we do not bring about still more harm in so doing. ²²In other words, we treat sex as we would any other problem. ²³In meditation, we ask God what we should do about each specific matter. ²⁴The right answer will come, if we want it.

²⁵God alone can judge our sex situation. ²⁶Counsel with persons is often desirable, but we let God be the final judge. ⁷⁰:¹We realize that some people are as fanatical about sex as others are loose. ²We avoid hysterical thinking or advice.

³Suppose we fall short of the chosen ideal and stumble? ⁴Does this mean we are going to get drunk? ⁵Some people tell us so. ⁶But this is only a half-truth. ⁷It depends on us and our motives. ⁸If we are sorry for what we have done, and have the honest desire to let God take us to better things, we believe we will be forgiven and will have learned our lesson. ⁹If we are not sorry, and our conduct continues to harm others, we are quite sure to drink. ¹⁰We are not theorizing. ¹¹These are facts out of our experience.

¹²To sum up about sex: we earnestly pray for the right

69:20-24 We are learning how to deal successfully with life's problems. The self-examination and reliance upon God's help that we practice in the fourth step, coupled with the actions suggested in the subsequent steps of this program, result in our being able to overcome difficulties that used to baffle us. This is a way of life that works.

70:3-11 If we remain the same selfish, self-centered people we are now, we are certain to drink again. It is only by the total refocusing of our motives in life, as a result of our spiritual awakening, that we are delivered from the gates of death. Indifference to the welfare of others is evidence that we are basing our decisions on selfishness. Our sobriety and our very lives depend upon our consciously seeking to act in the best interest of others (20:1).

To begin this new way of life, we ask God daily to direct our thinking and eliminate self-seeking motives (86:16).

70:8 When we forgive someone we give of ourselves prior to receiving anything from the other person. We may have mistakenly believed we would have to be a "good" person before we could receive help from God. God gives us the power we need to live up to our ideals as soon as we are humble enough to ask.

70:12-22 The solution to our problems lies in our being willing to seek God's help. The fourth step helps us to identify exactly what the problem is. Without this self-examination we may be confused as to what is the real problem. We have defects in our characters,

FOURTH STEP SEX CONDUCT LIST

Where Was I :	Whom Did I Hurt:	Where Was I At Fault? What Should I Have Done Instead?	Solution:
Selfish:			
Dishonest:			
Inconsiderate:			
Where did I arouse:			
Jealosy:			
Suspicion:			
Bitterness:			

70:14
Unselfish:
xxiv:14, xxv:10,
14:23, 20:1,
62:2-3, 67:4,
85:16-18,
93:15, 94:6,
97:3, 129:3,
159:12-16

70:17
Thorough:
58:1, 58:13,
65:7, 68:2,

70:17-22
Write:
64:19-20, 65:3,
67:11, 67:17-
18, 68:3, 69:15,
76:13

70:18
Resentment:
13:11, 15:6,
18:5, 36:4,
62:1, 64:15-
67:19, 65:5,
66:7-13, 84:19,
86:5, 117:19,
145:9

70:21
Tolerance:
19:18, 28:9,
67:2, 67:10,
83:6, 84:23,
103:2, 118:9,
125:5, 135:14

70:23
Ourselves:
11:8, 25:10,
45:5, 50:11,
84:8, 100:6,
102:18

ideal, for guidance in each questionable situation, for sanity, and for the strength to do the right thing. 70:13If sex is very troublesome, we throw ourselves the harder into helping others. 14We think of their needs and work for them. 15This takes us out of ourselves. 16It quiets the imperious urge, when to yield would mean heartache.

17If we have been thorough about our personal inventory, we have written down a lot. 18We have listed and analyzed our resentments. 19We have begun to comprehend their futility and their fatality. 20We have commenced to see their terrible destructiveness. 21We have begun to learn tolerance, patience and good will toward all men, even our enemies, for we look on them as sick people. 22We have listed the people we have hurt by our conduct, and were willing to straighten out the past if we could.

23In this book you read again and again that faith did for us what we could not do for ourselves. 71:1We hope you are convinced now that God can remove whatever self-will has blocked you off from Him. 2If you have already made a decision, and an inventory of your grosser handicaps, you have made a good beginning. 3That being so you have swallowed and digested some big chunks of truth about yourself.

mistaken ideas and attitudes about the source of happiness and satisfaction. By seeing the un-successful and even harmful results of our acting on our old beliefs, we become willing to continue to learn the new way of life suggested in this book.

71:1-3 The way that we become convinced of the ability of God to change our lives is by doing the things suggested in this program. When we experience for ourselves that this works to solve our problems, we acquire faith —a reliance upon the power of God. It is our old ideas and attitudes about life, the symptoms of which are our defects of character, that stand in the way of our access to God. By swallowing and digesting big chunks of

truth about ourselves, we are nourished and can grow.

71:3 We do not do our fourth step merely to gain self-knowledge. Self-knowledge will not solve our alcoholic problem (39:3). Our writing helps to clear away self-justification which allows us to honestly appraise our character. When combined with attempts to establish a relationship with God, it produces spiritual experience, experiences of God working in our lives. We may build upon this as we continue in this new way of life. Our purpose is to discover the obstacles in ourselves so that the grace of God can enter us and expel the obsession that compels us to drink.

Chapter Six
INTO ACTION

We have admitted to ourselves that we are powerless over alcohol—that our lives are unmanageable. We are coming to believe that a Power greater than ourselves can restore us to sanity. We have made the decision to turn our will and our lives over to the care of the God of our understanding. We have made a searching and fearless moral inventory of ourselves. Where do we go from here?

Into Action gives us the instructions for the next seven steps. This chapter begins by describing how the authors chose someone to discuss their inventory with (72:1-75:1). By following their example, we take Step Five (72:4-17). By being thorough and honest in our attempts at working the first five steps we become ready to let God remove our defects of character (75:16-76:4). By humbly asking God to remove our shortcomings, we take Step Seven (76:6-9). As a result of having begun the practice of the first eight steps we become willing to make amends to those we have harmed (76:13-15). We take our list of those we have harmed and proceed to make these right (76:16). The benefit of beginning this way of life is a complete transformation of our ideas and attitudes (83:21-84:12). Continuing to take personal inventory enables us to see where we are wrong, allowing us to promptly admit it (84:13-85:25). Having been restored to sanity by this process, we strive to broaden and deepen our relationship with God (85:26-88:6).

The authors have shown us what they have done to recover from alcoholism and in doing so have given us specific instruction and clear-cut directions illustrating what we can do to solve our own problem. We have been presented with a body of theory and technique that must be studied and practiced if we are to master and apply these principles to our own lives.

The Blueprint

Step Five	This vital step will break down the barriers between ourselves, our fellows and our Higher Power.
Steps Six, Seven and Eight	By working the prior steps we become ready to abandon the aspects of our character that interfere with our usefulness to God. We turn to God to remove our defects and begin our attempt to clean up the wreckage of our past.
Step Nine	A practical method of making amends to those we have harmed frees us from the chains that bind us to our past.
Step Ten	We continue to practice the techniques we have learned by working the prior steps.
Step Eleven	We are given methods by which we may expand our contact with our Higher Power.

72:2
Attitude:
25:8, 26:20,
27:12, 50:13,
55:16, 63:1,
84:5, 86:1,
99:13 143:9,
150:2

72:2
Trying:
77:4, 85:11

72:2
Path:
15:14, 49:9,
58:1, 66:24,
100:4, 116:11

72:5
Required:
xiv:1, xxvii:3,
12:15, 13:22,
14:19-20, 25:4,
50:16, 60:16,
93:6, 94:15,
98:11, 143:9

72:5
Completed:
65:8, 73:2,
76:10, 84:18,
99:16

72:6
Program:
xiii:2, xxiii:1,
xxix:8, 9:32,
19:13, 20:4-6,
29:1, 42:14,
45:8-9, 58:1-2,
59:7, 73:1

Chapter Six

INTO ACTION

^{72:1}Having made our personal inventory, what shall we do about it? ²We have been trying to get a new attitude, a new relationship with our Creator, and to discover the obstacles in our path. ³We have admitted certain defects; we have ascertained in a rough way what the trouble is; we have put our finger on the weak items in our personal inventory. ⁴Now these are about to be cast out. ⁵This requires action on our part, which, when completed, will mean that we have admitted to God, to ourselves, and to another human being, the exact nature of our defects. ⁶This brings us to *the fifth step* in the Program of Recovery mentioned in the preceding chapter.

⁷This is perhaps difficult—especially discussing our defects with another person. ⁸We think we have done well enough in admitting these things to ourselves. ⁹There is doubt about that. ¹⁰In actual practice, we usually find a solitary self-appraisal insufficient. ¹¹Many of us thought it necessary to go much further. ¹²We will be more reconciled to discussing ourselves with another person when we see good reasons why we should

---

72:1 There is no way that we can proceed until after we have made our inventory.

72:2 To view those who harm us as spiritually ill, to see that the reason for our fears is that we believe we have only ourselves to rely upon and to realize that our selfishness is the cause of our sex problems, is to encompass the new attitude we have been attempting to develop. In each fourth step list we have been given suggestions for prayer. To deal with our resentments we pray to be released from the control that our anger has on us (67:5). To out grow our fear we ask God to remove our fears and direct our attention to what God would have us be (68:22). To address our sex problems we ask God to mold our ideals and give us the strength to live up to them (69:18) as well as to show us what we should do about each matter (69:23). These practical prayers are the beginning of our new relationship with God.

72:4-5 This is not a self-help program. This is a method by which we may gain access to God's help. God removes those defects of character that we have admitted block our usefulness to God and our fellows. We must willingly participate in this process if we are to realize its benefits. By taking the Fifth Step, we place ourselves in the best position to receive God's help.

72:7 "This is perhaps difficult" seems humorous, as much an understatement as "At some of these we balked" (58:10). The authors know us well.

72:12-16 This is a practical program. We do it because it works. The experience of millions of recovered alcoholics is impossible to deny. If we fail to follow our third step decision with these actions, it likely will have no permanent effect (64:1). If we cannot establish a relationship with a Power greater than ourselves, we may not recover from alcoholism (44:3-4).

do so. $^{72:13}$The best reason first: if we skip this vital step, we may not overcome drinking. ^{14}Time after time newcomers have tried to keep to themselves certain facts about their lives. ^{15}Trying to avoid this humbling experience, they have turned to easier methods. ^{16}Almost invariably they got drunk. $^{73:1}$Having persevered with the rest of the program, they wondered why they fell. ^{2}We think the reason is that they never completed their house cleaning. ^{3}They took inventory all right, but hung on to some of the worst items in stock. ^{4}They only *thought* they had lost their egoism and fear; they only *thought* they had humbled themselves. ^{5}But they had not learned enough of humility, fearlessness and honesty, in the sense we find it necessary, until they told someone else *all* their life story.

^{6}More than most people, the alcoholic leads a double life. ^{7}He is very much the actor. ^{8}To the outer world he presents his stage character. ^{9}This *is* the one he likes his fellows to see. ^{10}He wants to enjoy a certain reputation, but knows in his heart he doesn't deserve it.

^{11}The inconsistency is made worse by the things he does on

72:13-16
Not Overcome:
14:23, 15:7,
35:19, 55:16,
58:1, 60:6,
78:6, 78:19,
89:2, 93:18

73:2
Finished:
65:8, 72:5,
76:10, 84:18,
99:16

73:5
Honest: (Means
Business)
Xiv:2, 5:18,
25:13, 28:7,
57:11, 58:9,
70:8, 96:1-8,
114:7, 147:3,
159:5, 161:11,
120:5

73:5
Honesty: (Self)
13:22, 32:1,
47:3, 55:15,
58:2, 63:17,
64:12, 65:7,
67:19, 73:22,
73:24, 83:15

73:5
Honesty:
(Rigorous)
3:4, 58:5,
145:3, 146:18,
83:16

72:15 This step is humbling. It produces an understanding of who and what we really are and is the first step toward becoming who we might be. This humility removes the need for the barriers we build to protect ourselves from other people. We can not be humiliated in areas where we are humble. If we are seven feet tall no amount of talk about our being too short would disturb us. However, if we have not admitted to ourselves that we are taller than average then comments about our height will offend us. If we develop humility then our self-esteem becomes unshakable.

73:1 This explains why we need to take all of the steps in order. As we work the following steps our understanding of the previous ones broadens and deepens. Picking and choosing which steps we prefer to take produces little or no results. This is a suggested program not a program of suggestions. Each subsequent step depends and builds upon our experience with each of the earlier steps. Few who have not admitted powerlessness

will be willing to abandon their old way of life and adopt a new one. Few who are unwilling to believe in a Power greater than themselves will decide to turn their will and life over to the care of God. Why do a moral inventory if we are not seeking to be rid of those aspects of ourselves that block us from God? What admission can we make to God, ourselves and another person if we have not developed the insight to recognize the real problem? We need to take all the steps to successfully overcome alcoholism.

73:2-5 The authors are being polite and trying to avoid making judgments of us. Let us not fool ourselves into believing that they are referring to someone else. Cross out the word "they" in every sentence and replace it with "I". We need to learn the benefits of this way of life first hand. We need to have our own individual spiritual experiences. Practicing the fifth step enables us to directly experience this spiritually based way of life and to reap it's benefits.

his sprees. ⁷³:¹²Coming to his senses, he is revolted at certain episodes he vaguely remembers. ¹³These memories are a nightmare. ¹⁴He trembles to think someone might have observed him. ¹⁵As fast as he can, he pushes these memories far inside himself. ¹⁶He hopes they will never see the light of day. ¹⁷He is under constant fear and tension—that makes for more drinking.

¹⁸Psychologists are inclined to agree with us. ¹⁹We have spent thousands of dollars for examinations. ²⁰We know but few instances where we have given these doctors a fair break. ²¹We have seldom told them the whole truth, nor have we followed their advice. ²²Unwilling to be honest with these sympathetic men, we were honest with no one else. ²³Small wonder many in the medical profession have a low opinion of alcoholics and their chance for recovery!

²⁴We must be entirely honest with somebody if we expect to live long or happily in this world. ⁷⁴:¹Rightly and naturally, we think well before we choose the person or persons with whom to take this intimate and confidential step. ²Those of us belonging to a religious denomination which requires confession, must, and of course, will want to go to the properly appointed authority whose duty it is to receive it. ³Though we have no religious connection, we may still do well to talk with someone ordained by an established religion. ⁴We often find such a person quick to see and understand our problem. ⁵Of course, we sometimes encounter people who do not understand alcoholics.

73:6-17 This is a description of an alcoholic. We can see how well we fit this description. We are egomaniacs with inferiority complexes. Our drinking causes us many embarrassments, but our egotistic outlook sets us up for humiliation and remorse even when we are sober. If drinking was the cause, we would no longer suffer this fear and tension when we quit drinking. We have much more work to do if we are to develop the degree of humility necessary to gain release from the humiliations caused by our self-centeredness.

73:21-23 We lie to those who try to help us to prevent them from interfering with our self-will. We hate to be opposed and obstinately refuse to follow advice. This is why this book is written in such soft, non-judgmental language. We would reject any advice the authors tried to give us and the truth would hurt our feelings. The authors, being alcoholics themselves, knew this and thus make no judgments and offer no advice. We are free to decide whether to follow their successful example or not.

^{74:6}If we cannot, or would rather not do this, we search our acquaintance for a close-mouthed, understanding friend. ⁷Perhaps our doctor or psychologist will be the person. ⁸It may be one of our own family, but we cannot disclose anything to our wives or our parents which will hurt them and make them unhappy. ⁹We have no right to save our own skin at another person's expense. ¹⁰Such parts of our story we tell to someone who will understand, yet be unaffected. ¹¹The rule is we must be hard on ourself, but always considerate of others.

¹²Notwithstanding the great necessity for discussing ourselves with someone, it may be one is so situated that there *is* no suitable person available. ¹³If that *is* so, this step may be postponed, only, however, if we hold ourselves in complete readiness to go through with it at the first opportunity. ¹⁴*We* say this because we are very anxious that we talk to the right person. ¹⁵It *is* important *that* he be able to keep a confidence; that he fully understand and approve what we are driving at; that he will not try to change our plan. ^{75:1}But we must not use this as a mere excuse to postpone.

²When we decide who is to hear our story, we waste no time. ³We have a written inventory, and we are prepared for a

---

74:5 This is a good reason to choose a sponsor. Someone who has taken the steps can show us what they have done. Someone "armed with facts about themselves" can be very helpful to us as we seek the truth about ourselves. Our sponsor will understand our need to be absolutely honest.

74:8-11 This is one of the only rules in this book. Do we have such a lack of concern for the well-being of others that we would try to gain relief for ourselves at their expense? We are attempting to gain freedom from selfishness.

74:12-14 The right person will understand the spiritual necessity of discussing our shortcomings with them. We gain humility through this step. Our ego, our conscious separation from God and our fellows, is decreased by admitting our faults to others. Admitting our wrongs and taking the steps to make matters right eliminates the guilt we feel. When a matter has been righted, the pangs of remorse we now feel are replaced with spiritual experience from which we may draw strength. Our worst failings, when coupled with humility, become the tools God uses to help others.

75:1 We grow accustomed to the prison of secrets we have built for ourselves. We fear replacing the cruel but familiar tyrant of self-will with the, as yet unknown, guidance of God. We procrastinate because we are prideful and wish others to believe in the false character we present. Admitting to God, to ourselves, and another person who we really are and what our actual motivations have been allows us to be free to live this new way of life.

75:7-23
Step Five:
13:10, 59:12,
78:22

75:17
Prayer:
xxx:4, 13:15-
20, 59:18, 63:9-
12, 67:5, 68:22,
69:18, 69:22,
70:12, 76:5,
76:6-9, 76:18,
79:5, 82:5,
83:6, 84:20,
85:26-86:3,
86:13, 86:16,
86:21, 87:6-11,
87:14-18,
87:19-20, 164:8

long talk. [75:4]We explain to our partner what we are about to do, and why we have to do it. [5]He should realize that we are engaged upon a life-and-death errand. [6]Most people approached in this way will be glad to help; they will be honored by our confidence.

[7]We pocket our pride and go to it, illuminating every twist of character, every dark cranny of the past. [8]Once we have taken this step, withholding nothing, we are delighted. [9]We can look the world in the eye. [10]We can be alone at perfect peace and ease. [11]Our fears fall from us. [12]We begin to feel the nearness of our Creator. [13]We may have had certain spiritual beliefs, but now we begin to have a spiritual experience. [14]The feeling that the drink problem has disappeared will often come strongly. [15]We feel we are on the Broad Highway, walking hand in hand with the Spirit of the Universe.

[16]Returning home we find a place where we can be quiet for an hour, carefully reviewing what we have done. [17]We thank God from the bottom of our heart that we know Him better. [18]Taking this book down from our shelf we turn to the

---

75:4 We are about to admit to another person the exact nature of our wrongs. We are going to discuss our deepest motives, exactly what it is in us that makes us act the way we do. We will discuss our selfishness, our self-seeking actions, our dishonesty and fears. The reason we reveal our innermost selves is that we must if we are to gain lasting sobriety. We are attempting to learn a way of life based on humility, fearlessness and honesty. We are willing to discuss our shortcomings because our very lives depend upon our beginning the practice of this step.

75:8-15 This list of promises, which are the results of taking our Fifth Step, make it all worthwhile. This is a very practical program. It works! If we did not realize results from adopting these practices we would abandon them. One benefit is that humility replaces humiliation. Instead of the pain of humiliation that we fear exposing of our secrets will bring, we gain the peace of forgiveness. We are able to forgive ourselves for being human and full of faults. We can see the path ahead that

leads us to the type of life we have always wished we could live.

75:13 Experience is the best teacher. We gain experience by repeated practice of the techniques explained in each of the 12 Steps. This is our own personal experience gained through direct application of spiritual principles to solve our problems. As we progress, we develop faith that God will give us the help we need.

75:16-23 These are specific instructions for preparing for the sixth step. We become entirely ready to have God remove our defects of character by taking the five previous steps. Our admission of powerlessness over alcohol and unmanageability of our lives turns us necessarily to a Power greater than ourselves. Making the decision to turn our lives over to the care of God sends us on the quest to face and be rid of the things in us that block us off from God. By identifying our failings and admitting them to God, ourselves and another human being, we become entirely ready to have God remove them.

page which contains the twelve steps. 75:19Carefully reading the first five proposals we ask if we have omitted anything, for we are building an arch through which we shall walk a free man at last. 20Is our work solid so far? 21Are the stones properly in place? 22Have we skimped on the cement put into the foundation? 23Have we tried to make mortar without sand?

76:1If we can answer to our satisfaction, we then look at *step six*. 2We have emphasized willingness as being indispensable. 3Are we now ready to let God remove from us all the things which we have admitted are objectionable? 4Can He now take them all—every one? 5Should we still cling to something we will not let go, we ask God to help us be willing.

6When ready, we say something like this: "My Creator, I am now willing that you should have all of me, good and bad. 7I pray that you now remove from me every single defect of character which stands in the way of my usefulness to you and my fellows. 8Grant me strength, as I go out from here, to do your bidding. 9Amen." 10We have then completed *Step Seven*.

75:19-23
Arch:
12:17, 47:11,
54:12, 56:19,
62:21, 63:4,
97:3, 123:11

75:20
Work:
xiii:9, xxiv:14,
14:18-23, 15:1,
15:7-10, 19:2-6,
89:1, 96:4

76:1
When: (To take
the steps)
53:8, 60:14,
63:13, 63:18,
64:1, 74:13,
76:6, 76:11,
76:16-18,
84:14-16,
84:20-21, 86:4,
86:14, 90:1

76:1-5
Step Six:
13:8, 59:13

76:6-10
Step Seven:
59:14

76:7
Blocked:
12:27, 64:1,
57:12, 63:11

75:17 The admission of our defects brings us closer to God. When we draw close, God is revealed to us (57:12). The instruction for this prayer is simple. The expression of our gratitude to God places us in the proper frame of mind to continue with the next steps.

75:19 An arch is a stable and strong structure capable of withstanding pressure and strain. The component pieces of an arch work together to support themselves, thus each component part of the arch is necessary. (See diagram to identify each component). The omission of any part of the arch will cause the whole structure to fall.

76:2-5 These are the directions for Step Six. They are simple and straightforward. Are we willing to abandon our selfish self-centered way of life and adopt fully a life guided by God? We have discovered many character flaws. Have we admitted that these things are the truth? Are we willing to let go of our old ideas, attitudes and actions? Are we willing to adopt this new outlook on life? Are we willing to pray for willingness in those areas at

which we balk? If we are willing, we will continue to the Seventh Step.

76:6-9 The Seventh Step prayer is an expression of humility. We are acknowledging our need to have God's help in overcoming our defects of character. We have analyzed our character and admitted to God, ourselves and another person, what it is in us that blocks us off from God. By doing this, we become ready to have God remove our defects of character.

76:6-9 This is not a self-help program. If we were able to live up to our ideals, we would have done so. We are powerless to bring about the total rearrangement of our ideas, emotions and attitudes that is necessary if we are to live this new way of life. We adopt, as a new guiding principle for our lives, the search to find and do God's will. We place ourselves in the position to receive God's help by making a conscious decision to abandon our old idea that the application of self-will would produce happiness and satisfaction.

76:11-15
Step Eight:
13:11-12,
59:15, 78:22

76:13
List:
64:19-20, 65:3,
67:11, 67:17-
18, 68:3, 69:15,
70:17-22

76:16-84:12
Step Nine:
13:14, 59:16

76:19
Victory:
58:9, 79:5

76:11Now we need more action without which we find that "Faith without works is dead." 12Lets look at *steps eight and nine.* 13We have a list of all persons we have harmed and to whom we are willing to make amends. 14We made it when we took inventory. 15We subjected ourselves to a drastic self-appraisal. 16Now we go out to our fellows and repair the damage done in the past. 17We attempt to sweep away the debris which has accumulated out of our effort to live on self-will and run the show ourselves. 18If we haven't the will to do this, we ask until it comes. 19Remember it was agreed at the beginning *we would go to any lengths for victory over alcohol.*

Definitions:
76:13 Amend: to change for the better.

76:6 By allowing God to make use of all aspects of our characters, our strengths and our weaknesses, we more completely abandon self-seeking and self-centeredness.

76:7 We allow God to determine which aspects of our character are most useful. What we perceive as a weakness may make us more approachable to others. What we perceive as a strength may diminish our usefulness. We let God decide.

76:8 If we were able to do God's will we would. By practicing the principles of this program we learn how to access this Power greater than ourselves. One of the techniques we use is to ask for help in prayer.

76:8 We do not seek God's help to accomplish our self-seeking objectives. The new focus of our lives is to find and do God's will for us. Our seeking will result in our finding God's will for us. God's power is available to us for the asking, with it we will be able to overcome the temptation to act in self-seeking ways.

76:10 The steps are not magic tricks that fix us at first try, but rather techniques for living life successfully.

76:11 True faith will result in works and works will keep our faith alive. For our faith to be life giving we must act upon it. By acting upon our faith we acquire spiritual experience. Faith is not an intellectual exercise, we must re-establish our lives upon a spiritual basis if we are to live. Being guided by the principle of love of God and love of our fellows, our actions bring our faith to life.

76:13-15 These are the directions for the eighth step. We use the names from our fourth step lists, however, we may need to include others. We may want to examine our relationships with any additional people we add to our list in the ways we have learned in the fourth step. We have become willing to make amends to these people as we now can clearly see the harm we have caused.

76:14 The commentary on the book entitled: "*Twelve Steps and Twelve Traditions*" contains detailed instructions for a thorough examination of harms done to others. That text suggests we analyze our actions and motives as a way of determining exactly which of our character traits are the source of the harms we cause others.

76:15 Our appraisal is of ourselves, not the other person.

76:13-15 We falsely believe that by avoiding our responsibility to right our wrongs we have escaped punishment for them. When we think of many of the people we have harmed, we feel the cringe of guilt and hope never to see them again. This self-imposed punishment is far worse than the humiliation or judgment

76:20Probably there are still some misgivings. 21As we look over the list of business acquaintances and friends we have hurt, we may feel diffident about going to some of them on a spiritual basis. 22Let us be reassured. 23To some people we need not, and probably should not emphasize the spiritual feature on our first approach. 77:1We might prejudice them. 2At the moment we are trying to put our lives in order. 3But this is not an end in itself. 4Our real purpose is to fit ourselves to be of maximum service to God and the people about us. 5It is seldom wise to approach an individual, who still smarts from our injustice to him, and announce that we have gone religious. 6In the prize ring, this would be called leading with the chin. 7Why lay ourselves open to being branded fanatics or religious bores? 8We may kill a future opportunity to carry a beneficial message. 9But our man is sure to be impressed with a sincere desire to set right the wrong. 10He is going to be more interested in a demonstration of good will than in our talk of

77:4
Purpose:
72:2, 85:11

77:4
Fit:
85:11-15,
100:18, 101:3

77:4
Service:
8:19, 13:18,
19:18, 20:1,
42:21, 49:13,
52:6, 76:7,
84:2, 86:12,
89:17, 102:16,
130:7, 132:1,
132:17, 153:3,
158:17

77:10
Demonstration:
xiii:2, 14:19,
19:4, 49:13,
51:2, 55:7,
68:21, 98:12-19

77:10
Intellectual:
12:12, 16:10,
27:16, 44:14,
49:7, 62:12,
83:7-8

from others we fear we will receive when we admit our mistakes. The replacement of our fear with the feeling of release brought about by our amends is proof positive that this spiritual way of life works. This is spiritual experience that we can draw upon when faced with fear and doubt of what to do when we are in conflict with others.

76:17 The debris caused by our misapplication of self-will blocks us from God, hinders our progress, and chains us to the past. We must clear up these matters to be free to live our new lives. Not dealing with the harms we cause in a timely manner allows them to build up. This piling up of neglected responsibilities makes the load we carry in life unbearable. In the Eighth Step we learn how to right our wrongs and in the Tenth Step we learn how to prevent them from beginning to pile up again.

76:18 Asking in prayer for the willingness to face up to our past will work if we do it. Remember, we are no longer operating solely on our own limited power and courage, but we now have access to the limitless power of God. God can do for us what we are unable to do for ourselves.

76:19 "If you have decided you want what we have and are willing to go to any length to get it—then you are ready to take certain steps" (58:9). Victory over alcohol and a spiritual experience (79:5) are the "it" we are willing to go to any length to get. Step Nine is one "length" we must go to if we are to realize these goals.

77:4 We have decided to abandon self-seeking as our path in life. We are not seeking the satisfaction of our desires, but rather to find our place in God's plan. We practice these principles and thus expand our capabilities. By the repeated practice of making amends, we expand our personal experience with a spiritually based way of life. We develop skill through repetition. We learn how to be useful to God and other people by trying. We prove to ourselves that this way of life works.

77:5 Specific and clear-cut direction for the Ninth Step begins here. We should study these instructions carefully prior to beginning our amends so that we may avoid making matters worse. We can gain from the experience of those who have already begun the practice of making amends.

77:17
Forgive:
66:24-67:6,
70:8, 70:21,
76:21, 79:18,
86:13

77:18
Criticize:
13:13, 67:7,
67:14, 78:1,
98:16-19

78:1
Not Discussed:
13:13, 67:7,
67:14, 77:18,
98:16-19

spiritual discoveries.

[11]We don't use this as an excuse for shying away from the subject of God. [12]When it will serve any good purpose, we are willing to announce our convictions with tact and common sense. [13]The question of how to approach the man we hated will arise. [14]It may be he has done us more harm than we have done him and, though we may have acquired a better attitude toward him, we are still not too keen about admitting our faults. [15]Nevertheless, with a person we dislike, we take the bit in our teeth. [16]It is harder to go to an enemy than to a friend, but we find it much more beneficial to us. [17]We go to him in a helpful and forgiving spirit, confessing our former ill feeling and expressing our regret.

[18]Under no condition do we criticize such a person or argue. [19]Simply we tell him that we will never get over drinking until we have done our utmost to straighten out the past. [20]We are there to sweep off our side of the street, realizing that nothing worth while can be accomplished until we do so, never trying to tell him what he should do. [78:1]His faults are not discussed. [2]We stick to our own. [3]If our manner is calm, frank, and open, we will be gratified with the result.

77:10 "The spiritual life is not a theory. We have to live it" (83:7-8). When we demonstrate our willingness to admit our wrongs, ask forgiveness for them and (if appropriate) to repay, we make a powerful statement about the benefits of a spiritually based life. Our actions speak far more powerfully and persuasively than our words.

77:12 We look to serve rather than to gain by our actions. When our motives for announcing our convictions are to be helpful to another person rather than to bolster our own confidence in our new way of life, we are applying our tradition of attraction rather than promotion. When we seek to give rather than take, our message will have a depth, weight and power unavailable to us when our motives are self-seeking.

77:15 We take these steps voluntarily.

This act of surrender frees us of the bondage of pride. The effect of making amends for our wrongs is that the chains that bind us to our old way of living are broken. Their control over us is removed. We are set free to become the people we most wish to be.

77:16 It is easier to lift a small weight, but only by lifting a heavy weight do we grow. It did not take much spiritual effort to stop drinking when we saw that it was killing us. It takes a great deal more effort to develop the humility required to fully recover from alcoholism.

77:18-78:3 These are specific instructions for us to follow. If we want the promised results we must follow the example of those who have gone before us. Our focus must be on giving not taking. We are not doing this to extract confessions of wrong doing from those we have harmed. If they wish to their

78:4In nine cases out of ten the unexpected happens.
5Sometimes the man we are calling upon admits his own fault; so feuds of years' standing melt away in an hour. 6Rarely do we fail to make satisfactory progress. 7Our former enemies sometimes praise what we are doing and wish us well. 8Occasionally, they will offer assistance. 9It should not matter, however, if someone does throw us out of his office. 10We have made our demonstration, done our part. 11It's water over the dam.

12Most alcoholics owe money. 13We do not dodge our creditors. 14Telling them what we are trying to do, we make no bones about our drinking; they usually know it anyway, whether we think so or not. 15Nor are we afraid of disclosing our alcoholism on the theory it may cause financial harm. 16Approached in this way, the most ruthless creditor will sometimes surprise us. 17Arranging the best deal we can we let these people know we are sorry. 18Our drinking has made us slow to pay. 19We must lose our fear of creditors no matter how far we have to go, for we are liable to drink if we are afraid to face them. 20Perhaps we have committed a criminal offense which might land us in jail if known to the authorities. 21We may be short in our accounts and unable to make good. 22We have already admitted this in confidence to another person, but we are sure we would be imprisoned or lose our job if it were known. 23Maybe it's only a petty offense such as padding the expense account. 24Most of us have done that sort of thing. 79:1Maybe we are divorced, and have remarried but haven't kept up the alimony to number one. 2She is indignant about it, and

78:6 Fail: 14:23, 15:7, 35:19, 55:16, 58:1, 60:6, 72:13-16, 78:19, 89:2, 93:18

78:22 Step Five: 13:10, 59:12, 75:7-23

78:22 Step Eight: 13:11-12, 59:15, 76:11-15

own wrongdoing we let them, but we should not attempt to manipulate them into doing this.

78:24 Most of us, sharing common character defects, bring similar types of trouble into our lives. Greed causes us to steal in large or small amounts, envy causes us to slander or gossip, sloth causes us to neglect our responsibilities, wrath causes us to lose control, gluttony causes us to seek more pleasures than are good for us, pride causes us to put up false fronts and lust causes us to damage our relationships. These defects, present in various degrees, have the power to control us until we admit to ourselves, to God and to another person, that they exist and ask God to remove them. Being free from the control of these shortcomings, we then take the actions described in the Ninth Step to bring our new found faith to life.

has a warrant out for our arrest. 79:3That's a common form of trouble too.

4Although these reparations take innumerable forms, there are some general principles which we find guiding. 5Reminding ourselves that we have decided to go to any lengths to find a spiritual experience, we ask that we be given strength and direction to do the right thing, no matter what the personal consequences may be. 6We may lose our position or reputation, or face jail, but are willing. 7We have to be. 8We must not shrink at anything.

9Usually, however, other people are involved. 10Therefore, we are not to be the hasty and foolish martyr who would needlessly sacrifice others to save himself from the alcoholic pit. 11A man we know had remarried. 12Because of resentment and drinking, he had not paid alimony to his first wife. 13She was furious. 14She went to court and got an order for his arrest. 15He had commenced our way of life, had secured a position, and was getting his head above water. 16It would have been impressive heroics if he had walked up to the Judge and said, "Here I am."

17We thought he ought to be willing to do that if necessary, but if he were in jail, he could provide nothing for either family. 18We suggested he write his first wife admitting his faults and

79:5 Though we may not have recognized it for what it was, the conscious awareness of the existence of God and the resulting change in the lives of those we know who have experienced this is what first attracted us to this way of life. The authors found that the result of taking these steps is a spiritual awakening. As we practice these steps we begin to awaken spiritually. We continue practicing these principles because we see for ourselves that it works.

79:5-7 We make direct amends to those we have harmed except when to do so would harm them or others. We sometimes hear that we are to consider ourselves as one of the "others." This is not what the book says. We have avoided making amends because we feared the consequences, thus the weight of our misdeeds builds into an unbearable

load. By facing the consequences, whatever they may be, we bring our faith in God to life. We do not make amends under our own power, but under the guidance and protection of God.

79:9-10 We must not lighten our own load while increasing the burden of others. Careful thought and consultation with others must precede each amend we make. Selfishly pursuing our own relief while disregarding the best interest of others will only compound our problems.

79:17-22 Our amends are concrete evidence to ourselves and others of the benefits of a spiritual life. Repaying money owed, asking for forgiveness for harm done others, and attempting to set our wrongs right makes us fit to be of use to God and our fellows.

asking forgiveness. 79:19He did, and also sent a small amount of money. 20He told her what he would try to do in the future. 21He said he was perfectly willing to go to jail if she insisted. 22Of course she did not, and the whole situation has long since been adjusted.

80:1Before taking drastic action which might implicate other people we secure their consent. 2If we have obtained permission, have consulted with others, asked God to help, and the drastic step is indicated we must not shrink.

3This brings to mind a story about one of our friends. 4While drinking, he accepted a sum of money from a bitterly-hated business rival, giving him no receipt for it. 5He subsequently denied having received the money and used the incident as a basis for discrediting the man. 6He thus used his own wrong-doing as a means of destroying the reputation of another. 7In fact, his rival was ruined.

8He felt he had done a wrong he could not possibly make right. 9If he opened that old affair, he was afraid it would destroy the reputation of his partner, disgrace his family and take away his means of livelihood. 10What right had he to involve those dependent upon him? 11How could he possibly make a public statement exonerating his rival?

12After consulting with his wife and partner he came to the conclusion that it was better to take those risks than to stand before his Creator guilty of such ruinous slander. 13He saw that he had to place the outcome in God's hands or he would soon start drinking again, and all would be lost anyhow. 14He attended church for the first time in many years. 15After the

80:2
Drastic:
14:4, 42:16,
58:9, 60:2,
76:15, 76:19,
79:5, 90:13,
94:15, 112:18,
142:8, 142:18,
158:8

80:13
In God's
Hands:
20:1, 45:21,
52:8, 68:10,
68:14, 85:15,
87:5, 98:9,
99:21, 100:1,
164:3

80:1-2 We are given explicit instructions on how to proceed. Consultation with others is important. They will be able to see our situation more objectively. Prayer is essential in enlisting the help of God. We are no longer living under our own direction and power. We can proceed confidently knowing our actions are well thought out and that we have a higher purpose to attend to. The knowledge that our amends will bring us closer to God can help us overcome our fear of the conse-

quences of our actions. By making amends we prove to ourselves that we can trust God.

80:3-17 The experience of others helps to bolster our courage. Repeatedly acting upon our new found faith gives us our own spiritual experience to rely upon. In this manner, we build our faith and it becomes a living part of our lives. Our new way of life is simple and practical. It works!

81:20
Rule:
74:11,79:10,
84:23, 101:10,
118:11

sermon, he quietly got up and made an explanation. [80:16]His action met widespread approval, and today he is one of the most trusted citizens of his town. [17]This all happened three years ago.

[18]The chances are that we have domestic troubles. [19]Perhaps we are mixed up with women in a fashion we wouldn't care to have advertised. [81:1]We doubt if, in this respect, alcoholics are fundamentally much worse than other people. [2]But drinking does complicate sex relations in the home. [3]After a few years with an alcoholic, a wife gets worn out, resentful, and uncommunicative. [4]How could she be anything else? [5]The husband begins to feel lonely, sorry for himself. [6]He commences to look around in the night clubs, or their equivalent, for something besides liquor. [7]Perhaps he is having a secret and exciting affair with "the girl who understands." [8]In fairness we must say that she may understand, but what are we going to do about a thing like that? [9]A man so involved often feels very remorseful at times, especially if he is married to a loyal and courageous girl who has literally gone through hell for him.

[10]Whatever the situation, we usually have to do something about it. [11]If we are sure our wife does not know, should we tell her? [12]Not always, we think. [13]If she knows in a general way that we have been wild, should we tell her in detail? [14]Undoubtedly we should admit our fault. [15]She may insist on knowing all the particulars. [16]She will want to know who the woman is and where she is. [17]We feel we ought to say to her that we have no right to involve another person. [18]We are sorry for what we have done, and God willing, it shall not be repeated. [19]More than that we cannot do; we have no right to go further. [20]Though there may be justifiable exceptions, and though we wish to lay down no rule of any sort, we have often

81:10-20 Suggestions for dealing with trouble at home are given. We will have examined our sex lives in Step Four. We have asked God to help mold our ideals. Straightening out our domestic situation is a primary part of our attempt to live up to our new ideals. "A mere code of morals or a better philosophy of life" will not result in our recovery. Only by living, with God's help, our new way of life can we expect to overcome the troubles we have been experiencing.

found this the best course to take.

81:21Our design for living is not a one-way street. 22It is as good for the wife as for the husband. 23If we can forget, so can she. 82:1It is better, however, that one does not needlessly name a person upon whom she can vent jealousy.

2Perhaps there are some cases where the utmost frankness is demanded. 3No outsider can appraise such an intimate situation. 4It may be both will decide that the way of good sense and loving kindness is to let by-gones be by-gones. 5Each might pray about it, having the other one's happiness uppermost in mind. 6Keep it always in sight that we deal with that most terrible human emotion—jealousy. 7Good generalship may decide that the problem be attacked on the flank, rather than risk a face-to-face combat.

8Should we have no such complication, there is plenty we should do at home. 9Sometimes we hear an alcoholic say that the only thing he needs to do is to keep sober. 10Certainly he must keep sober, for there will be no home if he doesn't. 11But he is yet a long way from making good to the wife or parents whom for years he has so shockingly treated. 12Passing all understanding is the patience mothers and wives have had with alcoholics. 13Had this not been so, many of us would have no homes today, would perhaps be dead.

14The alcoholic is like a tornado roaring his way through the lives of others. 15Hearts are broken. 16Sweet relationships are dead. 17Affections have been uprooted. 18Selfish and

81:21
Design For Living:
xiii:6, 8:19, 13:21, 15:11, 16:6, 42:21, 68:14-23, 79:15, 84:14, 97:19, 99:11, 114:21, 117:13, 124:1, 130:10, 134:15, 164:13-16, tt15:4

82:5
Prayer:
xxx4, 13:15-20, 59:18, 63:9-12, 67:5, 68:22, 69:18, 69:22, 70:12, 75:17, 76:5, 76:6-9, 76:18, 79:5, 83:6, 84:20, 85:26-86:3, 86:13, 86:16, 86:21, 87:6-11, 87:14-18, 87:19-20, 164:8

82:14-16
Tornado:
4:28,18:1-5, 104:5-150:3

82:14-18
Bedevilments:
18:3-5, 52:6,

inconsiderate habits have kept the home in turmoil. 82:19We feel a man is unthinking when he says that sobriety is enough. 20He is like the farmer who came up out of his cyclone cellar to find his home ruined. 21To his wife, he remarked, "Don't *see* anything the matter here, Ma. 22Ain't it grand the wind stopped blowin'?"

83:1Yes, there is a long period of reconstruction ahead. 2We must take the lead. 3A remorseful mumbling that we are sorry won't fill the bill at all. 4We ought to sit down with the family and frankly analyze the past as we now see it, being very careful not to criticize them. 5Their defects may be glaring, but the chances are that our own actions are partly responsible. 6So we clean house with the family, asking each morning in meditation that our Creator show us the way of patience, tolerance, kindliness and love.

7The spiritual life is not a theory. 8 *We have to live it.* 9Unless one's family expresses a desire to live upon spiritual principles we think we ought not to urge them. 10We should not talk incessantly to them about spiritual matters. 11They will change in time. 12Our behavior will convince them more than our words. 13We must remember that ten or twenty years of drunkenness would make a skeptic out of anyone.

14There may be some wrongs we can never fully right. 15We

82:14-19 Selfishness and self-centeredness are at the root of our problems (62:2). Stopping drinking, while imperative, is just the beginning (19:2). The way we think, feel, view and react to the world must change if we are to live happily (27:12). Step Nine is an important part of bringing about the needed change.

83:1-6 The instructions that the authors give us for straightening out our home lives are clear. Having examined ourselves and admitted our defects, we turn to God to have them removed. We now see the past in a different light. The truth is not obscured by the shadow of selfish self-interest. The acknowledgment of our part in family troubles will set an example for our family of a successful way to deal with difficulties.

83:6 When we turn to God for guidance, we are presented with opportunities to act in accordance with God's will. We find ourselves in situations that call for decisions. We can act in our own illusory self-interest and experience the same baleful results as we always have or we can act under the guidance of God and experience different results. As we awaken spiritually, we become better at recognizing the wonderful opportunities we are given and begin to watch for them.

83:7-8 This is not an intellectual exercise. Codes of morals and philosophies of life will not save us. If we are to live, we must establish an effective relationship with a Power greater than ourselves. We are not in need of a mere change of behavior, but a change of heart.

don't worry about them if we can honestly say to ourselves that we would right them if we could. [83:16]Some people cannot be seen—we send them an honest letter. [17]And there may be a valid reason for postponement in some cases. [18]But we don't delay if it can be avoided. [19]We should be sensible, tactful, and considerate and humble without being servile or scraping. [20]As God's people we stand on our feet; we don't crawl before anyone.

[21]If we are painstaking about this phase of our development, we will be amazed before half through. [22]We are going to know a new freedom and happiness. [23]We will not regret the past nor wish to shut the door on it. [24]We will comprehend the word serenity and know peace. [84:1]No matter how far down the scale we have gone, we will see how our experience can benefit others. [2]That feeling of uselessness and self-pity will disappear. [3]We will lose interest in selfish things and gain interest in our fellows. [4]Self-seeking will slip away. [5]Our whole attitude and

83:16 Honesty: (Rigorous) 3:4, 58:5, 73:5, 145:3, 146:18

83:23 The Past: 18:10-11, 84:1, 89:4-5, 89:17, 91:16-19, 123:2, 124:2-10, 132:20

84:2 Self-pity: 8:7, 15:6, 61:14, 62:1, 86:16, 88:1

84:4 Self-seeking: 60:18-62:14, 61:16, 62:4, 66:4, 67:13, 86:16, 88:3, 122:8-13

84:5 Attitude: 25:8, 26:20, 27:12, 50:13, 55:16, 63:1, 72:2, 86:1, 99:13 143:9,

83:21-84:12 The famous A.A. promises are brought about by the application of spiritual principles in our lives. They are not the result of merely quitting drinking and attending A.A. meetings. A spiritual awakening results in a change in the way we act and perceive the world around us. This new way of life addresses the problems of the past and prevents new problems from arising. We have a new way of dealing even with the seeming hardships and tragedies that are a part of life.

83:21 During this phase of our development, we learn the theory and techniques that make up our new way of life. By practicing repeatedly the application of these spiritual principles in every area of our lives, we build spiritual experience. Our experience enables us to rely upon God.

83:22 We begin to experience freedom from the hundreds of forms of fear, self-delusion, self-seeking, and self-pity that are the root cause of our failed outlook, attitudes, emotions and actions.

83:23 Our regrets are addressed in Steps Four through Nine. In the Steps Four and Five we reinterpret our past. In Steps Six and

Seven we position ourselves for the removal of those character defects that have caused our problems. In Steps Eight and Nine we repair the damage we have done. These steps transform our painful past into a useful spiritual tool.

83:24 The peace and serenity we experience comes as a result of conforming our will to that of God's.

84:1 Our past becomes an asset that we can use to help other people. Our past helps new people identify with us and shows them that new lives are also possible for them.

84:2 Adopting this new way of life gives us a new direction and purpose for living.

84:3-4 As we are restored to sanity, we see the rewards of selflessness greatly exceed the illusory benefits of self-seeking.

84:5 Our attitude towards life and our view of the world based on self-centered fear are changed as a result of practicing these spiritual principles. We live our way into a new way of thinking.

84:8
Could Not Do:
11:8, 25:10,
45:5, 50:11,
70:23, 100:6,
102:18

84:13-85:25
Step Ten:
13:15, 59:17

84:14
Commenced:
12:15, 19:3,
25:10, 35:17,
46:9, 47:4,
47:16, 63:17,
68:23, 71:2,
85:24, 158:10,
163:1

84:18
Lifetime:
85:15-16
99:16, 100:4

outlook upon life will change. [84:6]Fear of people and of economic insecurity will leave us. [7]We will intuitively know how to handle situations which used to baffle us. [8]We will suddenly realize that God is doing for us what we could not do for ourselves.

[9]Are these extravagant promises? [10]We think not. [11]They are being fulfilled among us—sometimes quickly, sometimes slowly. [12]They will always materialize if we work for them.

[13]This thought brings us to *step ten*, which suggests we continue to take personal inventory and continue to set right any new mistakes as we go along. [14]We vigorously commenced this way of living as we cleaned up the past. [15]We have entered the world of Spirit. [16]Our next function is to grow in understanding and effectiveness. [17]This is not an overnight matter. [18]It should continue for our life time. [19]Continue to

---

84:6 When we focus on what we can give rather than what we can take, we lose our fear that we will not get what we want. We are no longer afraid that our own resources are all that we have to draw upon. We find that conscious contact with God is all we really need to be happy in life.

84:7 We practice the application of spiritual principles as a way of addressing our problems and find the guidance of God is available to us when we seek it.

84:8 The truth is that if we could have stopped drinking, addressed our defects of character, and righted our past wrongs on our own power we would have done so long ago. By seeking in earnest, we have accessed a Power greater than ourselves. All we need to do for proof is to examine the results.

84:12 The key is that we must work to build sufficient spiritual experience so that we may draw upon it when we are challenged or tempted. These profound changes in our lives come about as the result of the repeated application of spiritual principles in all areas of our lives. It works for everyone who honestly tries.

84:13 To continue, we must first begin. We learn how to take inventory in Steps Four and

Five. We learn how to address our character defects in Steps Six and Seven. We learn how to make amends for the harm we cause in Steps Eight and Nine. We practice these techniques until we master them. Then we are at Step 10.

84:15 We enter the world of the spirit when we have cleared away all the obstacles that stand in our way. To maintain our conscious contact with our Higher Power we must continue to practice the principles of the program. Should we revert back to self-sufficiency we become separated from God.

84:16 We grow by study and practice. Bill W. adopted spiritual ideas and practices that brought about a spiritual awakening while in Town's Hospital. He reflected upon his experience so that he could transmit this experience to others. The result was the Twelve Steps of A.A. By studying this program of action and practicing the principles described in this book, we become more effective at carrying this solution to others.

84:18 The steps of this program are not magic tricks to be performed once so that they might solve all our problems. Rather, the steps are a discipline, a body of theory and technique that must be studied and practiced

watch for selfishness, dishonesty, resentment, and fear.
84:20When these crop up, we ask God at once to remove them.
21We discuss them with someone immediately and make
amends quickly if we have harmed anyone. 22Then we resolutely turn our thoughts to someone we can help. 23Love
and tolerance of others is our code.

24And we have ceased fighting anything or anyone even
alcohol. 25For by this time sanity will have returned. 26We will
seldom be interested in liquor. 27If tempted, we recoil from
it as from a hot flame. 28We react sanely and normally, and
will find that this has happened automatically. 85:1We see that
our new attitude toward liquor has been given us without
any thought or effort on our part. 2It just comes! 3That is the
miracle of it. 4We are not fighting it, neither are we avoiding
temptation. 5We feel as though we had been placed in a position of neutrality—safe and protected. 6We have not even
sworn off. 7Instead, the problem has been removed. 8It does
not exist for us. 9We are neither cocky, nor are we afraid.
10That is our experience. 11That is how we react so long as
we keep in fit spiritual condition.

12It is easy to let up on the spiritual program of action and

84:23 Tolerance: 19:18, 28:9, 67:2, 67:10, 70:21, 83:6, 103:2, 118:9, 125:5, 135:14

84:23 Code: 74:11, 79:10, 101:10, 118:11

84:24 Fighting: 5:21, 41:20, 66:4, 85:4, 103:11-12

84:24-85:11 Removed: 101:3, 120:17

84:25 Restored: 57:3, 57:8, 59:9, 101:3, 120:17,161:13

84:27 Hot: 24:9

84:27 Temptation: 57:1, 85:4, 101:6, 120:12-13, 146:19

---

if we are to be able to apply this program to our lives. We continue with the techniques we have begun to practice in the earlier steps. We continue to write our inventory. We continue to admit our shortcomings. We continue to ask God for relief from our shortcomings and we continue to make amends when we are wrong.

84:22-23 Being freed from the chains of self-ishness we are able to follow a path that leads to happiness, joy and fulfillment. Our very lives depend upon this change of moti-vation (20:1). While we are in the grip of self-ishness we are dead to the Spirit. Our work helping others brings our faith to life so that we may truly live.

84:25 As a result of these steps, the ability to differentiate the true from the false returns. We have become convinced of the truth of the ABC's (60:11-13). The truth is that we

have built our lives on a false foundation of selfishness and self-centeredness and it has caused our lives to come tumbling down around our ears. We re-found our lives based on faith in God and helpfulness to others. This new way of life brings us happiness and a sense of purpose.

85:1-11 Our spiritual malady must be over-come before we straighten out mentally and physically (64:18). The obsession to drink leaves many of us as we admit to ourselves, to God and to another person, the exact nature of our wrongs (75:14). Though all our human resources have failed to overcome our alcoholism, we find that God can and will.

85:12 Stopping drinking and finding God does not make us spiritual giants. Many of us come crawling in with our lives shattered, will-ing to do anything for a hope of escape from

85:14
Cure:,
xxviii:17,
30:15-16, 33:6

85:15
Contingent:
20:1, 45:21,
52:8, 68:10,
68:14, 80:13,
87:5, 98:9,
99:21, 100:1,
164:3

85:15-16
Reprieve:
99:16, 100:4

85:16-18
Constant:
20:1, 85:28,
87:20, 159:19,
164:7

85:22
Directions:
xiii:2, 20:4-6,
29:1, 45:8-9,
86:3, 121:1

85:22
Flow:
46:12, 50:15,
63:6

rest on our laurels. ⁵:¹³We are headed for trouble if we do, for alcohol is a subtle foe. ¹⁴We are not cured of alcoholism. ¹⁵What we really have is a daily reprieve contingent on the maintenance of our spiritual condition. ¹⁶Every day is a day when we must carry the vision of God's will into all of our activities. ¹⁷"How can I best serve Thee—Thy will (not mine) be done." ¹⁸These are thoughts which must go with us constantly. ¹⁹We can exercise our will power along this line all we wish. ²⁰It is the proper use of the will.

²¹Much has already been said about receiving strength, inspiration, and direction from Him who has all knowledge and power. ²²If we have carefully followed directions, we have begun to sense the flow of His Spirit into us. ²³To some extent we have become God-conscious. ²⁴We have begun to develop this vital sixth sense. ²⁵But we must go further and that means more action.

Definitions:
85:12 Laurels: honors won for achievement.
85:15 Reprieve: temporary respite from punishment.

alcoholic torture. Soon the pain and suffering is forgotten and our egos begin to resurface. We begin to feel a conscious separation from God. The insanity returns. We feel that we are capable of managing our own lives and God is relegated to the role of bush league pinch hitter. Yesterday's conscious contact will not keep us sober today. We must continue the practices we have learned in the steps.

85:15 Our spiritual condition is one of humility developed through our admission of powerlessness and confession of our character defects. God's help is available to us only when we are humble enough to acknowledge our need for it. Should the illusion of self-sufficiency return in sufficient strength to block us from God, our own human resources will be all we have at our disposal when confronted with temptation or uncertainty. Continuing the practices that help to humble keeps us in fit spiritual condition.

85:16-20 The realignment of our motivations, thinking and actions brings about miraculous changes in our lives. Casting aside our selfishness, we fill our thoughts and lives with the search for ways to be useful to God and our fellows. We thus gain access to the infinite power of God. The authors suggest several techniques throughout this book that we may use to direct our thinking towards God's will.

85:22 Taking what we want from this program of action and leaving the rest will not bring about the spiritual awakening that we must experience if we are to overcome alcoholism. Picking and choosing those parts that are most appealing to us will not allow us to undergo the entire psychic change that results in our restoration to sanity. The authors give clear-cut directions (29:1) for us to follow if we desire to have victory over alcohol (76:19) and find a spiritual experience (79:5).

85:22 By admitting to ourselves our need for God, confessing our shortcomings, and attempting to clean up the wreckage of our past, we open ourselves to the entry of God. The abandonment of our old ways of thinking and acting creates a cavity in us that the Spirit quickly fills.

85 26*Step eleven* suggests prayer and meditation. 27We should-n't be shy on this matter of prayer. 28Better men than we are using it constantly. 86:1It works, if we have the proper attitude and work at it. 2It would be easy to be vague about this matter. 3Yet, we believe we can make some definite and valuable suggestions.

86:1
Attitude:
25:8, 26:20,
27:12, 50:13,
55:16, 63:1,
72:2, 84:5,

86:3
Definite:
xiii:2, 20:4-6,
29:1, 45:4-9,
85:22, 143:14

SUGGESTED PRAYERS

63:9-12	Third Step prayer,
67:3-6	Fourth Step resentment prayer,
68:22	Fourth Step fear prayer,
69:18	Fourth Step ideals prayer,
69:23	Fourth Step sex relations amends prayer,
70:12	Fourth Step prayer for ideals, guidance, sanity and strength,
75:15	"We thank God from the bottom of our heart that we know Him better."
76:5	"We ask God to help us be willing."
76:6-9	The Seventh Step prayer,
76:18	"We ask until it comes."
79:5	"We ask that we be given strength and direction to do the right thing."
82:5	"Each might pray about it, having the other one's happiness uppermost in mind."
83:6	"...asking each morning that our Creator show us the way of patience, kindliness, tolerance and love."
84:20	"...we ask God at once to remove them."
86:13	"...we ask God's forgiveness and inquire what corrective measures should be taken."
86:16	"...we ask God to direct our thinking...."
86:21	"...we ask God for inspiration, an intuitive thought or a decision."
87:6-11	"...that we be shown all through the day..."
87:19-20	"...ask for the right thought or action."
164:8	"...in your morning meditation..."

85:23 We become God-conscious by the direct personal experience we develop through working the steps. We adopt new ways of viewing the world and our part in it. We practice accessing the power of God to solve our problems. In these practical ways we come to believe in the ability of this Power to restore us to sanity. We come to know from our experience that we can rely upon the help of our Higher Power.

86:1 When we admit we really do need God and can not manage our own lives, we are able to seek God with a willingness that is unavailable to us for as long as we hold on to the idea that self-sufficiency will someday result in our happiness.

[86:4]When we retire at night, we constructively review our day. [5]Were we resentful, selfish, dishonest, or afraid? [6]Do we owe an apology? [7]Have we kept something to ourselves which should be discussed with another person at once? [8]Were we kind and loving toward all? [9]What could we have done better? [10]Were we thinking of ourselves most of the time? [11]Or were we thinking of what we could do for others, of what we could pack into the stream of life? [12]But we must be careful not to drift into worry, remorse or morbid reflection, for that would diminish our usefulness to others. [13]After making our review we ask God's forgiveness and inquire what corrective measures should be taken.

[14]On awakening let us think about the twenty-four hours ahead. [15]We consider our plans for the day. [16]Before we begin, we ask God to direct our thinking, especially asking that it be divorced from self-pity, dishonest or self-seeking motives. [17]Under these conditions we can employ our mental faculties with assurance for after all God gave us brains to use. [18]Our thought life will be placed on a much higher plane when our thinking is cleared of wrong motives.

86:4 We are to constructively, rather than destructively review our day. We are attempting to learn and grow from our experiences. If we never look again at our mistakes and successes, we will not learn from them.

86:5 We learn how harmful our resentments, selfishness, dishonesty and fears are by taking our Fourth Step inventory. We should be quite skilled at recognizing these shortcomings in ourselves by now. Praying to God to save us from being angry and to remove our shortcomings worked when we took the earlier steps, so we have learned to rely on prayer to work now.

86:6 We have learned that making amends works so well at lightening the load we carry in life that we know just what to do when our mistakes cause harm to others.

86:7 Our admission of character defects dismantles the wall that separates us from others. Few techniques we have learned have been so successful at allowing the Spirit of God to flow into us as this one. Of course it will continue to work for us as long as we continue to apply this principle to our lives.

86:8-11 Having been restored to sanity, we can plainly see where our thinking is off the beam. We know now how to handle situations that used to baffle us. When we feel remorseful, we know it is due to our selfishness and self-seeking. Constant thought of others and how we might help to meet their needs is the answer we have found (20:1).

86:13 As in each of the steps, we are given clear-cut directions on how to access the power of God to make needed changes in our lives. We ask God to forgive us—to come to us first. When we fall short of perfection, we ask God for help. Thankfully this works. When we ask God for guidance to live up to our ideals, we receive the help we need.

86:19In thinking about our day we may face indecision. 20We may not be able to determine which course to take. 21Here we ask God for inspiration, an intuitive thought or a decision. 22We relax and take it easy. 23We don't struggle. 24We are often surprised how the right answers come after we have tried this a while. 87:1What used to be the hunch or the occasional inspiration gradually becomes a working part of the mind. 2Being still inexperienced and just making conscious contact with God, it is not probable that we are going to be inspired at all times. 3We might pay for this presumption in all sorts of absurd actions and ideas. 4Nevertheless we find that our thinking will, as time passes, be more and more on the plane of inspiration. 5We come to rely upon it.

6We usually conclude the period of meditation with a prayer that we be shown all through the day what our next step is to be, that we be given whatever we need to take care of such problems. 7We ask especially for freedom from self-will, and

86:19-24
Guidance:
13:17

87:2
Conscious:
47:4, 51:3,
55:17, 56:18,
59:18, 63:6,
85:23, 130:3

87:5
Rely:
20:1, 45:21,
52:8, 68:10,
68:14, 80:13,
85:15, 98:9,
99:21, 100:1,
164:3

87:6-11
Prayer:
xxx4, 13:15-20,
59:18, 63:9-12,
67:5, 68:22,
69:18, 69:22,
70:12, 75:17,
76:5, 76:6-9,
76:18, 79:5,
82:5, 83:6,
84:20, 85:26-
86:3, 86:13,
86:16, 86:21,
87:14-18,
87:19-20, 164:8

86:16 Our restoration to sanity is the result of the replacement of selfishness and self-centeredness with God consciousness. Rather than leap immediately into planning how to arrange our affairs to suit ourselves, we pray for direction from God. God's will, rather than self-seeking, is the focus of our thoughts. Should we ignore these clear-cut directions, our thinking will be self-directed. Remembering how well self-directed thinking has worked for us in the past, we can be motivated to follow this method of re-directing the focus of our thoughts.

86:16 Many people joke that A.A. will ruin one's drinking. Likewise praying for God to keep our thinking from being influenced by our defects serves to make us conscious of our motivations. We see plainly what it is that is driving our thoughts and actions and turn to God for relief.

86:19-87:1 Asking God for guidance allows God to use our lives to the greatest benefit. We are able to "relax and take it easy" because we know we can rely upon the will of God to work out for the best. Even our troubles become opportunities to demonstrate and thus deepen our faith.

87:2-5 We must be careful not to confuse rationalizations for our actions with guidance from God (103:7-8 12&12). Checking with others on the guidance we receive is a prudent practice (60:5-11 12&12). Our attempts to establish and maintain a channel of communication with God allow us to spend more and more time in conscious contact with our Creator.

87:6 Have you ever bought a new car and suddenly become aware of how many similar cars are on the road? All of the sudden you see other cars like yours several blocks away when in the past you would never have noticed them. As meditation upon God's will for us replaces self-seeking, opportunities for usefulness in ways large and small appear all around us. We begin to see the true purpose and meaning of our lives.

87:6-11 Be careful what you pray for, you just might get it. This old adage rings true. We know the baleful results of achieving our selfish ends. We decided in the third step to quit playing God and instead turned our will and our lives over to the care of God. When used properly, prayer turns us into a mighty tool to be wielded by God.

are careful to make no request for ourselves only. 87:8We may ask for ourselves, however, if others will be helped. 9We are careful never to pray for our own selfish ends. 10Many of us have wasted a lot of time doing that, and it doesn't work. 11You can easily see why.

12If circumstances warrant, we ask our wives or friends to join us in morning meditation. 13If we belong to a religious denomination which requires a definite morning devotion, we attend to that also. 14If not members of religious bodies, we sometimes select and memorize a few set prayers which emphasize the principles we have been discussing. 15There are many helpful books also. 16Suggestions about these may be obtained from one's priest, minister, or rabbi. 17Be quick to see where religious people are right. 18Make use of what they offer.

19As we go through the day, we pause when agitated or doubtful, and ask for the right thought or action. 20We constantly remind ourselves we are no longer running the show, humbly saying to ourselves many times each day "Thy will be done." 88:1We are then in much less danger of excitement, fear, anger, worry, self-pity, or foolish decisions. 2We become much more efficient. 3We do not tire so easily, for we are not burning up energy foolishly as we did when trying to arrange life to suit ourselves.

4It works-it really does.

87:13 Our practices should in no way conflict with an individual's religious observances. Many of us find a new understanding and a deeper relevance to our individual religious beliefs.

87:17 We are no longer blinded by unreasoned prejudice from seeing the spiritual truths contained in the religious beliefs and practices of others. We can benefit greatly from those who have made deep study of the nature of God.

87:19 Pausing when agitated or doubtful is a change from our old way of dealing with these situations. Rather than lashing out in a vain attempt to manipulate events to our favor, we ask God for guidance.

87:20 We may use prompts to remind us that we have decided to turn our will and our lives over to the care of God. When we pass through doorways we can say to ourselves "Thy will not mine be done." Perhaps we have a squeak in our car that we can use as a reminder. Whatever we use, the idea is to direct our thinking toward God as often as possible.

88:3 We no longer squander our thoughts upon resentment, fear and worry. A God-directed life is free of the frustration of not getting our way, free of the self-doubt of self-sufficiency, free of the results of our self-seeking decisions and actions. The tremendous relief we feel from being freed of the burden of self is wonderful.

88:5We alcoholics are undisciplined. 6So we let God discipline us in the simple way we have just outlined.

7But this is not all. 8There is action and more action. 9"Faith without works is dead." 10The next chapter is entirely devoted to step twelve.

88:6
Discipline:
66:22 ,155:15

88:6
Simple:
xxvii:3, 9:32,
14:1, 25:6,
26:20, 28:7,
46:12, 47:11,
50:14-16, 52:8,
57:5, 58:2,
62:21, 130:9

Definitions:
88:6 Discipline: a path to developing certain skills. A body of theory and technique that must be studied and practiced to be mastered.

88:5-6 The authors are not referring to punishment when they use the term "discipline." A discipline is a body of theory and technique that must be studied and practiced if we are to master it and apply it to our lives. We adopt a new foundation for our lives. Trust and reliance upon God replaces the illusion of self-sufficiency from which we had constructed our failed lives. For the rest of our lives, we repeatedly practice successful methods of dealing with life on life's terms. We improve our skills for living and cut the chains that bind us to our past. Awakened spiritually and restored to sanity we begin our lives anew.

88:9 Having discovered the greatest treasure in all the universe we cannot help but feel the need to share it with others. Knowing that the wonderful release we have found is available to all, we seek to be useful to others. True faith will show itself by the works we do and the works we do will broaden and deepen our faith. We must not only give it away to keep it, we must give it away to truly get it.

Chapter Seven
WORKING WITH OTHERS

The authors take for granted that we will be restored to sanity by the application of the principles outlined in this book. They are also certain that we will receive the same benefits from taking these steps as they received.

The result of working A.A.'s Twelve Steps is a spiritual awakening. To broaden and deepen our spirituality becomes our focus. "Faith without works is dead." The study and practice of how to carry this message can be the most worthwhile effort of our lives. Working with others is an experience we must not miss. Through a great deal of trial and error the early members worked out a method for approaching a practicing alcoholic. If we follow the instructions given here we stand the greatest chance of success.

The end of our indifference to spiritual principles allows us to see the great opportunity we have to carry the message that we have so freely been given. The ability to be truly useful and the actions we take to do this fill our lives with purpose and meaning. The promise of a fellowship growing up around us is a promise of true satisfaction in life.

The authors walk us through the initial contacts so that we may be of maximum use in helping the alcoholic to find the solution offered through the practice of the Twelve Steps. Step by step instructions are given on how to best help the family of the alcoholic. Guidance is also offered to help us arrange the initial visit and to present the solution in a way that will be most successful.

Working With Others begins by explaining the practical considerations behind the suggestion to carry the message (89:1-5). The benefits of carrying the message are detailed (89:7-10). Ways to find a prospect are suggested (89:11-13). We are cautioned to avoid arousing prejudice (89:14-19). Important considerations for qualifying the prospect & timing our approach (90:1-91:12). The importance of gaining our prospect's confidence and ways to accomplish this are illustrated (91:13-92:6). Detailed are ways to most effectively present the foundation concepts of hopelessness (92:7-18), and hope of a solution (92:18-93:7). We are again counseled to avoid arousing prejudice (93:8-94:1). Ways to present the program of action (94:2-16), and introduce the fellowship (94:18) are explained. Successful techniques for carrying the message are illustrated (95:1-96:12) such as; being helpful (96:13-98:3), avoiding enabling (98:4-11), dealing with domestic problems (98:12-100:17), and avoiding intolerance (103:2-12). The reason for all this effort is made clear: spiritual fitness protects us from drinking (100:18-103:1).

The Blueprint

Step Twelve	Carrying this message to other alcoholics protects us from drinking.
The First Visit	God gives us the ability to be useful to alcoholics. We practice proven techniques for helping alcoholics.
The Second Visit	Having had the experience ourselves we can be helpful to an alcoholic who is ready to begin practicing the Twelve Steps.

Chapter Seven
WORKING WITH OTHERS

89:1 Practical experience shows that nothing will so much insure immunity from drinking as intensive work with other alcoholics. ²It works when other activities fail. ³This is our *twelfth suggestion:* Carry this message to other alcoholics! ⁴You can help when no one else can. ⁵You can secure their confidence when others fail. ⁶Remember they are very ill.

⁷Life will take on new meaning. ⁸To watch people recover, to see them help others, to watch loneliness vanish, to see a fellowship grow up about you, to have a host of friends—this is an experience you must not miss. ⁹We know you will not want to miss it. ¹Frequent contact with newcomers and with each other is the bright spot of our lives.

89:1
Intensive:
15:8-11, 102:6,
119:7, 129:14,
156:10, 181:4

89:4-5
Assets:
18:10-11,
83:23, 84:1,
89:17, 91:16-
19, 123:2,
124:2-10,
132:20

89:5
Confidence:
18:10, 92:5

89:7-10
Fellowship:
xliii:10, xxlii:9,
15:11, 15:19,
17:7, 44:8,
45:13, 90:15,
94:18, 95:10,
96:7, 152:16,
152:21, 153:16

89:7-10
Part Of:
15:12

Definitions:
Practical: resulting from practice.

89:1 This is not a theory. It works. The vast experience of A.A. members the world over proves it to be true. If you want to recover from alcoholism nothing you can do will be of more help than working with other alcoholics. Intensive work is what is called for, not mere casual association. Working through the steps with our sponsors, studying this program with our A.A. group and helping another alcoholic to recover are all examples of intensive work with other alcoholics.

89:2 If we are having a hard time staying sober and are wondering what it is we have to do, here is clear-cut direction. Explaining the theories and ideas that are the foundation of our new lives to a newcomer will do more than anything else to help us under-

stand them for ourselves. We have to give it away to get it.

89:3 The message that this book carries to alcoholics is that there is a method by which we may recover(17:12-14). On their last visit Dr. Bob cautioned Bill W. to "Keep it simple." By this he meant that we should not dilute the message of this book with any other messages. Let us work the A.A. program and not be distracted by other influences. Let us study, practice and master this program before we delve off into other issues.

89:4 We know why we were beyond human aid. We were blinded from the truth by the illusion of self-sufficiency. We were blocked from God by our character defects. We were so

89:17
Usefulness:
8:19, 13:18,
19:18, 20:1,
42:21, 49:13,
52:6, 76:7,
77:4, 84:2,
86:12, 102:16,
130:7, 132:1,
132:17, 153:3,
158:17

89:17-18
Religion:
xiv:7, 9:23,
9:32, 11:18,
17:5, 19:14,
27:16, 28:5-12,
43:12, 49:9,
56:8, 74:3,
77:5-7, 87:14-
18, 93:16,
128:4-10

89:19
Aim:
xiii:3, xiv:4,
18:6, 29:5-6,
43:4, 44:2,
71:1, 108:2,
153:10, 162:10,
163:1

⁸⁹:¹¹Perhaps you are not acquainted with any drinkers who want to recover. ¹²You can easily find some by asking a few doctors, ministers, priests and hospitals. ¹³They will be only too glad to assist you. ¹⁴Don't start out as an evangelist or reformer. ¹⁵Unfortunately a lot of prejudice exists. ¹⁶You will be handicapped if you arouse it. ¹⁷Ministers and doctors are competent and you can learn much from them if you wish, but it happens that because of your own drinking experience you can be uniquely useful to other alcoholics. ¹⁸So cooperate; never criticize. ¹⁹To be helpful is our only aim.

⁹⁰:¹When you discover a prospect for Alcoholics Anonymous, find out all you can about him. ²If he does not want to stop drinking, don't waste time trying to persuade him. ³You may spoil a later opportunity. ⁴This advice is given for his family also. ⁵They should be patient, realizing they are dealing with a sick person.

selfish and self-centered that we could find justifications for our most bizarre behaviors. Now we have found a real solution to the problem God, can make us very effective at presenting it to alcoholics.

89:5 Our past becomes transformed by God into our greatest asset. It helps others to identify with us. We know what it is like to be in the seemingly hopeless state of mind and body that is alcoholism. We know what it is like to have our problems pile up on us to the point that we despair of a solution. We know what it is to be beyond human aid. We also know how to recover from this state. This chapter is concerned with the study of how we may most effectively carry this message to those who suffer from alcoholism (89:6). Alcoholics are spiritually, mentally and physically ill. If we just dry out nothing changes with our spiritual and mental conditions. If we try to adjust mentally our physical and spiritual states take us back into insanity. We must attack the problem in all three planes.

89:7 Replacing our slothful indifference to our spiritual responsibilities and the welfare of others with intensive work with other alcoholics brings meaning and purpose to our lives. Nothing we do will bring us more satisfaction and fulfillment than attempting to be of real service to others. Whether we are successful or not our attempt to repay this wonderful gift we have received fills our hearts with gratefulness for the opportunity to be a part of God's great plan.

8:11-19 We find few things are as rewarding as the study of how best to carry this message. The directions begin here. We should use our common sense. How would we have reacted to an evangelist or reformer? Probably we would have rejected everything they had to say as we would not have trusted their motives. We alcoholics are cynical and look very closely to find hidden motives. We should not attempt to justify our attempts to gain power or moral authority over others as trying to be helpful. If we have no other agenda than to be helpful we are certain to be much more successful as God will be able to work through us without us getting in the way.

90:2-3 This is a program for people who want it. There are unfortunately many who need to recover but do not want to. We wish to attract the prospect to our solution rather than waste our time with promotion. Timing our approach

⁹:⁶If there is any indication that he wants to stop, have a good talk with the person most interested in him, usually his wife. ⁷Get an idea of his behavior, his problems, his background, the seriousness of his condition, and his religious leanings. ⁸You need this information to put yourself in his place, to see how you would like him to approach you if the tables were turned.

⁹Usually it is wise to wait till he goes on a binge. ¹⁰The family may object to this, but unless he is in a dangerous physical condition, it is better to risk it. ¹¹Don't deal with him when he is very drunk, unless he is ugly and the family needs your help. ¹²Wait for the end of the spree, or at least for a lucid interval. ¹³Then let his family or a friend ask him if he wants to quit for good and if he would go to any extreme to do so. ¹⁴If he says yes, then his attention should be drawn to you as a person who has recovered. ¹⁵You should be described to him as one of a fellowship who, as a part of their own recovery, try to help others, and who will be glad to talk to him if he cares to see you.

¹⁶If he does not want to see you, never force yourself upon him. ¹⁷Neither should the family hysterically plead with him to do anything, nor should they tell him much about you. ¹⁸They

90:4
Advice:
xxx:4, 70:2,
73:21, 96:11,
106:18

90:13
Any Extreme:
14:4, 42:16,
58:9, 60:2,
76:15, 76:19,
79:5, 80:2,
94:15, 112:18,
142:8, 142:18,
158:8

90:14
Recovered:
Title Page,
xiii:1, xxiii:10,
17:2-3, 20:3,
29:1, 44:14,
85:14, 96:8,
113:6, 132:20,
133:8, 146:12

90:15
Fellowship:
xiii:10, xxiii:9,
15:11, 15:19,
17:7, 44:8,
45:13, 89:7-10,
94:18, 95:10,
96:7, 152:16,
152:21, 153:16,
159:7, 160:1,
161:8, 162:10,
164:4, 164:17

to reach the prospect when the desire to stop is likely to be strongest is our best plan. After a binge alcoholics many times regret their actions and truly wish they had the power to stop drinking altogether. This is the best time to approach them with the promise of a real solution. The key is that they must want to quit drinking for good.

90:9-15 Stopping drinking has to be our own idea. We alcoholics are obstinate. We resist taking directions from others. The directions here are to wait until the prospect is emerging remorseful from a spree and truly wants to quit drinking once and for all.

90:17 "Frothy emotional appeals seldom suffice" (xxvi:3). Waiting until the alcoholic comes off a binge may be the best time to suggest they seek a solution. The hopelessness of

their current state is most clear at this time. Resistance to the truth will be low at this time. If our message has depth and weight we will be most likely to gain their attention.

90:19 This book has a proven record of being able to transmit the message of recovery to alcoholics. It is laid out in such a manner as to present us with information we need in the sequence we need to understand it. First the hopelessness of our physical condition is explained. Next, a story of an alcoholic tells what it was like, what happened and what it is like now. Hope of a solution is given to us followed by a chapter that illustrates the mental state that condemns an alcoholic to continue drinking despite the ever worsening consequences. These chapters help us to take our first step towards recovery.

should wait for the end of his next drinking bout. [90:19]You might place this book where he can see it in the interval. [20]Here no specific rule can be given. [21]The family must decide these things. [91:1]But urge them not to be over-anxious, for that might spoil matters.

[2]Usually the family should not *try* to tell your story. [3]When possible, avoid meeting a man through his family. [4]Approach through a doctor or an institution is a better bet. [5]If your man needs hospitalization, he should have it, but not forcibly, unless he is violent. [6]Let the doctor if he will tell him he has something in the way of a solution.

[7]When your man is better, the doctor might suggest a visit from you. [8]Though you have talked with the family, leave them out of the first discussion. [9]Under these conditions your prospect will see he is under no pressure. [10]He will feel he can deal with you without being nagged by his family. [11]Call on him while he is still jittery. [12]He may be more receptive when depressed.

[13]See your man alone, if possible. [14]At first engage in general conversation. [15]After a while, turn the talk to some phase of drinking. [16]Tell him enough about your drinking habits, symptoms, and experiences to encourage him to speak of himself. [17]If he wishes to talk, let him do so. [18]You will thus get a better idea of how you ought to proceed. [19]If he is not communicative, give him a sketch of your drinking career up to the time you quit. [20]But say nothing, for the moment, of how that was accomplished. [21]If he is in a serious mood dwell on

---

91:3 Our resentments and secrets block us off from the ones who love us most. Sometimes we will take the advice of a stranger before that of those closest to us. This may be silly but if we recognize what works best with alcoholics we stand the best chance of being able to help.

91:11-12 The best time for approaching us is while our grand opinion of our ability to control our drinking has been freshly shattered. It is hard to defend our insane illusion of control while we are sick and shaking from withdrawal. As soon as we feel good again we forget just how badly we recently felt.

91:13-23 Specific and clear-cut instructions on how to approach an alcoholic are helpful to us. We can learn from the authors' experience and not have to learn from trial and error. Err we may, but if we are sincerely trying to be of service to those we would help we should not be hard on ourselves over our mistakes. Our own experience will reinforce the lessons of what works and what does not work.

the troubles liquor has caused you, being careful not to moralize or lecture. $^{91:22}$If his mood is light, tell him humorous stories of your escapades. ^{23}Get him to tell some of his.

^{24}When he sees you know all about the drinking game, commence to describe yourself as an alcoholic. $^{92:1}$Tell him how baffled you were, how you finally learned that you were sick. ^{2}Give him an account of the struggles you made to stop. ^{3}Show him the mental twist which leads to the first drink of a spree. ^{4}We suggest you do this as we have done it in the chapter on alcoholism. ^{5}If he is alcoholic, he will understand you at once. ^{6}He will match your mental inconsistencies with some of his own.

^{7}If you are satisfied that he is a real alcoholic, begin to dwell on the hopeless feature of the malady. ^{8}Show him, from your own experience, how the queer mental condition surrounding that first drink prevents normal functioning of the willpower. ^{9}Don't at this stage refer to this book, unless he has seen it and wishes to discuss it. ^{10}And be careful not to brand him an alcoholic. ^{11}Let him draw his own conclusion. ^{12}If he sticks to the idea that he can still control his drinking, tell him that possibly he can—if he is not too alcoholic. ^{13}But insist that if he is severely afflicted, there may be little chance he can recover by himself.

92:1
Baffling:
xxvii:15, 5:12-13, 6:4, 7:11, 23:9-12, 26:9, 34:15, 35:4-5, 37:9, 40:8, 58:15

92:3
Show:
xiii:2,14:19, 19:4, 49:13, 51:2, 67:2, 68:21,77:10, 95:9, 98:17, 118:10, 152:10

92:3-8
Mental Twist:
xxvii:13-xxviii:1, 6-4, 22:17, 24:1-6, 24:7-8, 33:10, 35:2, 37:7, 40:12, 41:21, 42:4, 43:14-16, 157:19

92:4
Suggest:
xxvii:18, 12:9, 19:13,59:7, 86:3, 94:13, 104:4, 142:18, 143:14, 144:2, 144:10, 153:10, 164:5

92:7
Real Alcoholic:
21:3-4, 23:17, 24:1, 30:1, 30:11, 31:5, 33:14, 34:3-4, 35:22, 44:5, 109:10-21

92:3 Study the chapter More About Alcoholism. The chapter begins with the directions for the first step, illustrates clearly the baffling nature of alcoholism and ends by leading us into the second step. This book is brilliantly constructed to explain to us the exact nature of the problem and then point us in the direction of the solution.

92:4-6 The physical craving for alcohol produced by drinking (xxviii:15-16) coupled with evidence of alcoholic thinking (34:15) are symptoms only alcoholics experience. If our prospect identifies with our description of the symptoms we can be confident of their alcoholism. Our job now is to help them to admit to their innermost selves that they are alcoholic—that they cannot manage their own lives.

92:6-22 Once a pickle, always a pickle. There is no return to normal drinking for a person who has begun to experience the phenomenon of craving. Examining "Bill's Story" will help prepare us to relate some of our failed attempts to overcome drinking through willpower, self knowledge, firm resolve etc. Once we acquire an alcoholic mind there is little hope of recovery through human power (24:15). Left to our own resources we undoubtedly will return to drinking.

92:23-26 The symptoms of our alcoholism are the craving we experience for more alcohol once we begin to drink and the subtle form of insanity that permits us to disregard the consequences of our drinking no matter how severe. Our inability to control our drinking and the trouble our drinking causes get

⁹²:¹⁴Continue to speak of alcoholism as a sickness, a fatal malady. ¹⁵Talk about the conditions of body and mind which accompany it. ¹⁶Keep his attention focussed mainly on your personal experience. ¹⁷Explain that many are doomed who never realize their predicament. ¹⁸Doctors are rightly loath to tell alcoholic patients the whole story unless it will serve some good purpose. ¹⁹But you may talk to him about the hopelessness of alcoholism, because you offer a solution. ²⁰You will soon have your friend admitting he has many, if not all, of the traits of the alcoholic. ²¹If his own doctor is willing to tell him that he *is* alcoholic, so much the better. ²²Even though your protege may not have entirely admitted his condition, he has become very curious to know how you got well. ⁹³:¹Let him ask you that question, if he will. ²If he does not ask, proceed with the rest of your story. ³*Tell him exactly what happened to you.* ⁴Stress the spiritual feature freely. ⁵If the man be agnostic or atheist, make it emphatic that *he does not have to agree with your conception of God.* ⁶He can choose any conception he likes, provided it makes sense to him. ⁷*The main thing is that he be willing to believe in a Power greater than himself and that he live by spiritual principles.*

⁸When dealing with such a person, you had better use everyday language to describe spiritual principles. ⁹There is no

worse and worse over time. Being in the grips of an illness we cannot control and do not understand we seek ways to justify and excuse our drinking. We blame circumstances and those around us for our drinking. We hope that no one notices our lack of control and we attempt to cover up our failures. We may begin to hide our alcohol to prevent any interruption of supply. Eventually we experience increasingly severe physical and mental problems as a direct result of our intake of alcohol. If we do not stop drinking it is probable that we will die as a result. Long before we die our lives will disintegrate into a tortuous hell. The progression of alcoholism is plain for all to see. Unfortunately those who suffer from the illness are many times the last to recognize the seemingly hopeless state they are in.

92:31-93:2 These are techniques of attraction rather than promotion. We describe our own alcoholism in hopes that our prospects will see themselves in our story. In this way we lead them into asking us about the solution. We are then on the footing of showing them what we have done rather than telling them what they should do. This method has proven to be successful.

93:2-9 We were presented with the solution in the early chapters of this book. Reviewing Bill's meeting with his boyhood friend (12:9-19) and the chapter to Agnostics will be very helpful. We can follow the authors' example of how best to present the God idea without arousing prejudice and antipathy.

use arousing any prejudice he may have against certain theological terms and conceptions, about which he may already be confused. [93:10]Don't raise such issues, no matter what your own convictions are.

[11]Your prospect may belong to a religious denomination. [12]His religious education and training may be far superior to yours. [13]In that case he is going to wonder how you can add anything to what he already knows. [14]But he will be curious to learn why his own convictions have not worked, and yours seem to work so well. [15]He may be an example of the truth that faith alone is insufficient. [16]To be vital, faith must be accompanied by self sacrifice and unselfish, constructive action. [17]Let him see that you are not there to instruct him in religion. [18]Admit that he probably knows more about it than you do, but call to his attention the fact that however deep his faith and knowledge, he could not have applied it, or he would not drink. [19]Perhaps your story will help him see where he fails to practice the very precepts he knows so well. [20]We represent no particular faith or denomination. [94:1]We are dealing only with general principles common to most denominations.

93:15-16
Faith Alone:
14:21, 15:2,
16:10, 76:11,
88:9

93:16
Selfish
Program:
13:18, 14:23,
20:1, 62:2,
70:14, 85:16-
18, 94:6, 97:3,
102:4-5, 120:1,
159:12-13,
164:16

93:16
Unselfish:
xxv:10, xxiv:14,
14:23, 20:1,
62:2-3, 67:4,
70:14, 85:16-
18, 94:6, 97:3,
129:3, 159:12-
16

93:17
Religion:
xiv:7, 9:23,
9:32, 11:18,
17:5, 19:14,
27:16, 28:5-12,
43:12, 49:9,
56:8, 74:3,
77:5-7, 87:14-
18, 89:17-18,
128:4-10,
131:15-16,
132:1

Definitions:
93:19 Precept: a rule guiding moral conduct.

93:9 We are here to be helpful, not to force our particular conception of God upon our prospect. Working the steps will allow our prospect to personally experience a conscious relationship with God. Bringing our personal conception of God into the picture only runs the risk of handicapping our prospect with prejudice. Separating our religious convictions from our A.A. fundamentals is vitally important. We must abandon our extraneous agendas if we wish to be truly useful.

93:15-16 "Faith without works is dead." For God to live in us, God must live through us. "The spiritual life is not a theory. We have to live it" (83:7-8). We must fill our hearts and minds with constant thoughts of God and helpfulness to our fellows if we desire to live at all. One certain sign of true spiritual awakening is the beginning of works by which we attempt to participate in God's great plan.

93:18 An old timer describes the difference

between belief and faith in this way: "The greatest high wire artist in all the world announces an attempt to push a wheelbarrow across the Grand Canyon on a tight rope. Being renowned as the world's best you believe that the high wire artist will make it. If you had faith you would be willing to get in the wheelbarrow."

93:18 Wisdom is being able to put our knowledge to work in our lives. It is the application of spiritual principles that allows our faith to change our lives.

94:1 Applying this program produces a conscious awareness of the existence of God. We have no need or desire to force anyone to conform to any spiritual mold of our conception. Personal religious beliefs are a private matter for the individual and should be of no concern to others. Likewise we must avoid burdening others with our own personal concept of God.

^{94:2}Outline the program of action, explaining how you made a self-appraisal, how you straightened out your past, and why you are now endeavoring to be helpful to him. ³It is important for him to realize that your attempt to pass this on to him plays a vital part in your own recovery. ⁴Actually, he may be helping you more than you are helping him. ⁵Make it plain he is under no obligation to you, that you hope only that he will try to help other alcoholics when he escapes his own difficulties. ⁶Suggest how important it is that he place the welfare of other people ahead of his own. ⁷Make it clear that he is not under pressure, that he needn't see you again, if he doesn't want to. ⁸You should not be offended if he wants to call it off, for he has helped you more than you have helped him. ⁹If your talk has been sane, quiet and full of human understanding, you have perhaps made a friend. ¹⁰Maybe you have disturbed him about the question of alcoholism. ¹¹This is all to the good. ¹²The more hopeless he feels, the better. ¹³He will be more likely to follow your suggestions.

94:2-8 The treasure we have found is beyond measure. We have to give it away if we want to keep it. Explaining this program to others allows us to gauge our own understanding of the spiritual principles of which it is comprised. We see very clearly the holes in our understanding when we are tested in this way. We also see areas where our knowledge is not being translated into action. Hypocritical exhortations for another to act in ways we ourselves are not willing to will never be helpful. By revealing to ourselves the extent of our actual application of spiritual principles great strides forward in willingness can be made. We truly do benefit from our attempts to be useful to others.

94:12 The feeling of hopelessness is a ray of truth shining through the black cloud of alcoholic destruction. We don't decide to turn our will and lives over to the care of God because we are saintly people. We turn to God as a last resort. In the grace of God we find relief we thought unavailable to us.

94:13 Complete deflation of our ego evidenced by the feeling of hopelessness is seemingly the only thing that will allow us to admit our powerlessness, set aside our prejudices and old ideas of how we are to relate to the world and decide to allow God to guide us through our lives. The more hopeless we feel at the beginning the more willing we will be. Willingness is the key that opens the door to our new life.

94:14-17 If we know ourselves well, we will be able to anticipate the suggestions our prospects will balk at. When we are new we are sometimes confused about the cause of our problems. A moral inventory followed by an admission of our faults to another person may seem as though it will not address our problems. Confusing pride with self-esteem, and humility with humiliation we think that admitting our faults to others will make us feel worse about ourselves. We may feel that if only we felt better about ourselves we would not drink so much. Our progress depends upon our willingness to abandon our old ideas and to give this new way of life an honest try. We find that the source of genuine self-esteem is humility rather than pride.

94:14Your candidate may give reasons why he need not follow all of the program. 15He may rebel at the thought of a drastic housecleaning which requires discussion with other people. 16Do not contradict such views. 17Tell him you once felt as he does, but you doubt whether you would have made much progress had you not taken action. 18On your first visit tell him about the fellowship of Alcoholics Anonymous. 19If he shows interest, lend him your copy of this book.

95:1Unless your friend wants to talk further about himself, do not wear out your welcome. 2Give him a chance to think it over. 3If you do stay, let him steer the conversation in any direction he likes. 4Sometimes a new man is anxious to proceed at once, and you may be tempted to let him do so. 5This is sometimes a mistake. 6If he has trouble later, he is likely to say you rushed him. 7You will be most successful with alcoholics if you do not exhibit any passion for crusade or reform. 8Never talk down to an alcoholic from any moral or spiritual hilltop, simply lay out the kit of spiritual tools for his inspection. 9Show him how they worked with you. 10Offer him friendship and fellowship. 11Tell him that if he wants to get well you will do anything to help. 12If he is not interested in your solution, if he expects you to act only as a banker for his financial difficulties or a nurse for his sprees, you may have to drop him until he changes his mind. 13This he may do after he gets hurt some more.

14If he is sincerely interested and wants to see you again, ask him to read this book in the interval. 15After doing that, he must decide for himself whether he wants to go on. 16He should

94:15 Required: xiv:1, xvii:3, 12:15, 13:22, 14:19-20, 25:4, 50:16, 60:16, 72:5, 93:6, 98:11, 143:9

94:18 Visit: 96:9

94:18 Fellowship: xiii:10, xxiii:9, 15:11, 15:19, 17:7, 44:8, 45:13, 89:7-10, 90:15, 95:10, 96:7, 152:16, 152:21, 153:16, 159:7, 160:1, 161:8, 162:10, 164:4, 164:17

95:8 Tools: 25:6

95:8-10 Offer: xxiv:15, 17:12-14, 25:6, 58:9, 92:19, 96:3, 97:19

95:9 Show: xiii:2, 14:19, 19:4, 49:13, 51:2, 67:2, 68:21,77:10, 92:3, 98:17, 118:10, 152:10

95:12 Enable: 96:19-97:1, 97:16, 98:6, 115:17

95:12 Solution: xiii:2, xxix:1, 17:Title, 20:4-5, 25:3, 25:8-10, 27:9-12, 29:1, 35:16, 44:3-4, 45:4-9, 52:6

95:7-8 Many of us having come crawling into A.A. on our knees, begging for help, soon forget just how sick we were when we arrived. For us to speak from a spiritual hilltop would be ironic. We have been saved by the grace of God rather than any power of our own. Humbly telling our prospect what it was like for us, what we did to recover and what life is like for us now will do more to attract our prospect to our way of life than all the promotion and preaching we could ever do.

95:10-11 Just as God comes to us when we can do nothing but take. We forgive our prospect. We give of ourselves first. Realizing that our prospect is capable only of taking we ask for nothing. We know that our prospect will discover the tremendous benefits of helping others as part of recovery from alcoholism.

95:15
Decision:
xxviii:7, 42:19,
58:9, 59:10,
60:14, 62:18,
64:1, 71:2,
79:5, 96:12

95:19
Monopoly:
28:6, 144:3,
164:5

96:1-8
Honest: (Means
Business)
xiv:2, 5:18,
25:13, 28:7,
57:11, 58:9,
70:8, 73:5,
114:7, 161:11

96:1-8
Waste of Time:
142:15-17

96:3
Offer:
xxiv:15, 17:12-
14, 25:6, 58:9,
92:19, 95:8-10,
97:19

not be pushed or prodded by you, his wife, or his friends. ⁹⁵:¹⁷If he is to find God, the desire must come from within. ¹⁸If he thinks he can do the job in some other way, or prefers some other spiritual approach, encourage him to follow his own conscience. ¹⁹We have no monopoly on God; we merely have an approach that worked with us. ²⁰But point out that we alcoholics have much in common and that you would like, in any case, to be friendly. ²¹Let it go at that.

⁹⁶:¹Do not be discouraged if your prospect does not respond at once. ²Search out another alcoholic and try again. ³You are sure to find someone desperate enough to accept with eagerness what you offer. ⁴We find it a waste of time to keep chasing a man who can not or will not work with you. ⁵If you leave such a person alone, he may soon become convinced that he cannot recover by himself. ⁶To spend too much time on

95:12 Many of us experience repeated post-spree calls from a remorseful alcoholic. Though for awhile they feel terrible and are full of contrition soon they are feeling better and see no reason to adopt such a drastic solution as the one we offer. We hear no more from them until they once again emerge from a spree. This can be a tedious process.

95:12 Many alcoholics, dry for now, fail to work the steps. They call their sponsors repeatedly with relationship, marital, work related and financial problems. They are under the mistaken impression that the temporary relief we get from talking about our problems is in some way dealing successfully with them. We only harm them by allowing them to hide from their problems by talking rather than taking the necessary action. All we can do is to remind these unfortunate souls of where the solution to all their problems lie.

95:14 Reading the book will help our prospect to understand first the dire nature of their alcoholism and second what the solution to their situation is. Ideas and techniques are presented in a way that has proved successful in carrying the message to millions of alcoholics.

95:15 Our willingness is a result of our admission of powerlessness. If we still believe that we possess the power to control our alcohol consumption, if we still believe that we can successfully manage our own lives, we will not be willing to turn our will and our lives over to God. If we are willing we will voluntarily do the things that are required to recover.

95:15 If we are pressured we may submit to the fact that we cannot drink. Submission is not surrender. Submission does not lead to recovery.

95:19 We know our way works. We have no need to discourage attempts at other methods of finding God or of recovering from alcoholism. If other ways work—more power to them. A.A. scrupulously avoids adopting any dogmatic approach to spirituality. This includes any official interpretation of how one should approach the steps. The book contains a suggested method of recovery from alcoholism. It worked for us you may try it if you care to.

96:1-6 A famous A.A. joke: A newcomer called her sponsor to ask how to deal with sex problems. Her sponsor told her to read page 69 as that is where suggestions on dealing with sex matters are in the book. Being new and still a little bit confused the young woman mistakenly began to read page 96 instead. (Read 96:1-6) any one situation is to deny some other alcoholic an opportunity to live and be happy. ⁹⁶:⁷One of our fellowship failed entirely with his first half dozen prospects. ⁸He often says that if he had continued to work on them, he might have deprived many others, who have since recovered, of their chance.

⁹Suppose now you are making your second visit to a man. ¹⁰He has read this volume and says he is prepared to go through with the twelve steps of The Program of Recovery. ¹¹Having had the experience yourself, you can give him much practical advice. ¹²Let him know you are available if he wishes to make a decision and tell his story, but do not insist upon it if he prefers to consult someone else.

¹³He may be broke and homeless. ¹⁴If he is, you might try to help him about getting a job, or give him a little financial assistance. ¹⁵But you should not deprive your family or creditors of money they should have. ¹⁶Perhaps you will want to take the man into your home for a few days. ¹⁷But be sure you use discretion. ¹⁸Be certain he will be welcomed by your family, and that he is not trying to impose upon you for money, connections, or shelter. ¹⁹Permit that and you only harm him. ²⁰You will be making it possible for him to be insincere. ⁹⁷:¹You may be aiding in his destruction, rather than his recovery.

²Never avoid these responsibilities, but be sure you are doing the right thing if you assume them. ³Helping others is the foundation stone of your recovery. ⁴A kindly act once in a while isn't enough. ⁵You have to act the Good Samaritan every day, if need be. ⁶It may mean the loss of many nights sleep,

96:7
Fellowship:
xiii:10, xxiii:9,
15:11, 15:19,
17:7, 44:8,
45:13, 89:7-10,
90:15, 94:18,
95:10, 152:16,
152:21, 153:16,
159:7, 160:1,
161:8, 162:10,
164:4, 164:17

96:8
Recovered:
Title Page,
xiii:1, xxiii:10,
17:2-3, 20:3,
29:1, 44:14,
85:14, 90:14,
113:6, 132:20,
133:8, 146:12

96:9
Visit:
94:18

96:10
Program:
xiii:2, xxiii:1,
xxix:8, 9:32,
19:13, 20:4-6,
29:1, 42:14,
45:8-9, 58:1-2,
59:7, 72:6,
73:1, 74:15,
85:12-16, 88:6,
94:2, 99:16,
113:4, 117:1,
126:22, 130:10

96:12
Decision:
xxviii:7, 42:19,
58:9, 59:10,
60:14, 62:18,
64:1, 71:2,
79:5, 95:15

96:19-97:1
Enable:
97:16, 95:12,
98:6, 115:17

97:3
Foundation:
12:17, 47:11,
54:12, 56:19,
62:21, 63:4,
75:19-23,
123:11

Definition:
97:3 Foundation Stone: stones making up the foundation of a structure.

97:1 Several times we are cautioned that our attempts at helpfulness may do more harm than good. When we allow another person to rely upon us rather than God to solve their problems we harm them. A person's faith in the spiritual life cannot be built by reliance upon human power. All of us must learn to seek God for ourselves.

97:3 Each time we help others we place another stone in the foundation of our recovery. We shore up our faith from the stormy waters of self-centeredness by selfless action. Helping others reinforces our faith by continually providing spiritual experience. Helping others is evidence of our gratefulness for the gift we have been given.

97:15-16
Enable:
95:12, 96:19-
97:1, 98:6,
115:17

97:19
Offer:
xxiv:15, 17:12-
14, 25:6, 58:9,
92:19, 95:8-10,
96:3

97:19
Way of life:
xiii:6, 8:19,
13:21, 15:11,
16:6, 42:21,
68:14-23,
79:15, 81:21
84:14, 99:11,
114:21, 117:13,
124:1, 130:10,
134:15, 164:13-
16, tt15:4

98:1
Straighten Out
Spiritually First:
64:18, 98:7-8,
127:10, 135:15

98:6
Enable:
95:12, 96:19-
97:1, 97:16,
115:17

great interference with your pleasures, interruptions to your business. ⁹⁷:⁷It may mean sharing your money and your home, counseling frantic wives and relatives, innumerable trips to police courts, sanitariums, hospitals, jails and asylums. ⁸Your telephone may jangle at any time of the day or night. ⁹Your wife may sometimes say she is neglected. ¹⁰A drunk may smash the furniture in your home, or burn a mattress. ¹¹You may have to fight with him if he is violent. ¹²Sometimes you will have to call a doctor and administer sedatives under his direction. ¹³Another time you may have to send for the police or an ambulance. ¹⁴Occasionally you will have to meet such conditions.

¹⁵We seldom allow an alcoholic to live in our homes for long at a time. ¹⁶It is not good for him, and it sometimes creates serious complications in a family.

¹⁷Though an alcoholic does not respond, there is no reason why you should neglect his family. ¹⁸You should continue to be friendly to them. ¹⁹The family should be offered your way of life. ²⁰Should they accept, and practice spiritual principles, there is a much better chance the head of the family will recover. ²¹And even though he continues to drink, the family will find life more bearable. ²²For the type of alcoholic who is able and willing to get well, little charity, in the ordinary sense of the word, is needed or wanted. ⁹⁸:¹The men who cry for money and shelter before conquering alcohol, are on the wrong track. ²Yet we do go to great extremes to provide each other with these very things, when such action is warranted. ³This may seem inconsistent, but we think it is not.

⁴It is not the matter of giving that is in question, but when and how to give. ⁵That often makes the difference between failure and success. ⁶The minute we put our work on a service plane, the alcoholic commences to rely upon our assistance

---

98:1 We are following a new path now. We seek a real solution to our problem through spiritual means. Our current state is a result of our quest for fulfillment through material satisfaction and reliance upon human resources. Reliance upon God will bring us inner strength and peace. We will find that what we truly need most in life—God's grace —is supplied to us in abundance.

rather than upon God. ⁹⁸:⁷He clamors for this or that, claiming he cannot master alcohol until his material needs are cared for. ⁸Nonsense. ⁹Some of us have taken very hard knocks to learn this truth: job or no job—wife or no wife—we simply do not stop drinking so long as we place dependence upon other people ahead of dependence on God.

¹⁰Burn the idea into the consciousness of every man that he can get well regardless of anyone. ¹¹The only condition is that he trust in God and clean house.

¹²Now, the domestic problem: There may be divorce, separation, or just strained relations. ¹³When your prospect has made such reparation as he can to his family, and has thoroughly explained to them the new principles by which he is living, he should proceed to put those principles into action at home. ¹⁴That is, if he is lucky enough to have a home. ¹⁵Though his family be at fault in many respects, he should not be concerned about that. ¹⁶He should concentrate on his own spiritual demonstration. ¹⁷Argument and fault-finding are to be avoided like leprosy. ¹⁸In many homes this is a difficult thing to do, but it must be done if any results are to be expected. ⁹⁹:¹If persisted in for a few months, the effect on a man's family is sure to be great. ²The most incompatible people discover they have a basis upon which they can meet. ³Little by little the family may see their own defects and admit them. ⁴These

98:9
Dependence:
20:1, 45:21,
52:8, 68:10,
68:14, 80:13,
85:15, 87:5,
99:21, 100:1,
164:3

98:11
Only Condition:
xiv:1, xxvii:3,
12:15, 13:22,
14:19-20, 25:4,
50:16, 60:16,
72:5, 93:6,
94:15, 143:9

98:12-19
Demonstration:
xiii:2, 14:19,
19:4, 49:13,
51:2, 55:7,
68:21, 77:10

98:16-19
Fault-finding:
13:13, 67:7,
67:14, 77:18,
78:1

98:18-19
Any Results:
25:11, 58:14,
59:4, 164:13

98:9-11 Our lives depend upon finding a Power greater than ourselves by which we may live. Our first priority must be to find this Power. Material and physical well-being can only follow our spiritual progress. If we continue to place the cart before the horse we will never get anywhere.

98:11 First we recover spiritually, then we recover mentally, physically and materially. First we rely upon God then we are given the strength to overcome our problem. Our real problem is that we have restricted our access to any power other than our own by our selfish and self-centered outlook upon life. Washed up upon the rocks of self-reliance we founder.

98:13-17 Twice in this paragraph we are shown that the spiritual life is not a theory. We have to live it. We should begin to put these new guiding principles into action in our homes. We are to demonstrate our spiritual lives not just think about them. Faith without works is dead.

99:1 The promise of great results from our new way of life requires that we avoid arguments and fault-finding for a few months. We have learned how to deal with our resentments, fears, relationship problems and the harms we cause others by working the 12 Steps. Now we must put these principles into action.

can then be discussed in an atmosphere of helpfulness and friendliness.

⁹⁹:⁵After they have seen tangible results, the family will perhaps want to go along. ⁶These things will come to pass naturally and in good time, provided, however, the alcoholic continues to demonstrate that he can be sober, considerate, and helpful, regardless of what anyone says or does. ⁷Of course, we all fall much below this standard many times. ⁸But we must try to repair the damage immediately lest we pay the penalty by a spree.

⁹If there be divorce or separation, there should be no undue haste for the couple to get together. ¹⁰The man should be sure of his recovery. ¹¹The wife should fully understand his new way of life. ¹²If their old relationship is to be resumed, it must be on a better basis, since the former did not work. ¹³This means a new attitude and spirit all around. ¹⁴Sometimes it is to the best interests of all concerned that a couple remain apart. ¹⁵Obviously, no rule can be laid down. ¹⁶Let the alcoholic continue his program day by day. ¹⁷When the time for living together has come, it will be apparent to both parties.

¹⁸Let no alcoholic say he cannot recover unless he has his family back. ¹⁹This just isn't so. ²⁰In some cases the wife will never come back for one reason or another. ²¹Remind the prospect that his recovery is not dependent upon people. ¹⁰⁰:¹It is dependent upon his relationship with God. ²We have seen men get well whose families have not returned at all. ³We have seen others slip when the family came back too soon.

99:5 Our actions speak louder than our words. We can talk about spiritual theories until we are blue in the face. Our most eloquent arguments will not be as convincing as our honest attempt at living by our new principles. This makes a powerful statement to all those who know us. We can be living proof before their eyes of the transformative power of God.

99:8 We have adopted the theory that the harm we do others hinders us in our usefulness to God and our fellows. We have learned techniques for self-examination, confession of our wrongs and methods of accessing our Higher Power. Putting these principles to work immediately helps to prevent resentment from building and overwhelming us.

99:18-100:3 Our recovery is solely dependent upon our relationship with God. We are sometimes tempted to fall back into the same old trap of trying to manipulate life to suit ourselves. This way of life can only lead to frustration and discontentment. For many of us falling into this trap leads to a return to drinking. Playing God by trying to arrange life to suit us blocks us off from the Spirit and restricts us to our own resources.

100:4Both you and the new man must walk day by day in the path of spiritual progress. 5If you persist, remarkable things will happen. 6When we look back, we realize that the things which came to us when we put ourselves in God's hands were better than anything we could have planned. 7Follow the dictates of a Higher Power and you will presently live in a new and wonderful world, no matter what your present circumstances!

8When working with a man and his family, you should take care not to participate in their quarrels. 9You may spoil your chance of being helpful if you do. 10But urge upon a man's family that he has been a very sick person and should be treated accordingly. 11You should warn against arousing resentment or jealousy. 12You should point out that his defects of character are not going to disappear over night. 13Show them that he has entered upon a period of growth. 14Ask them to remember, when they are impatient, the blessed fact of his sobriety.

15If you have been successful in solving your own domestic problems, tell the newcomer's family how that was accomplished. 16In this way you can set them on the right track without becoming critical of them. 17The story of how you and your wife settled your difficulties is worth any amount of criticism.

18Assuming we are spiritually fit, we can do all sorts of things alcoholics are not supposed to do. 19People have said we must not go where liquor is served; we must not have it in our homes; we must shun friends who drink; we must avoid

100:4
Path:
15:14, 49:9,
58:1, 66:24,
72:2, 116:11

100:4
Day by Day:
85:15-16, 99:16

100:6
God's Hands:
11:8, 25:10,
45:5, 50:11,
70:23, 84:8,
102:18

100:6
Better Than
Anything:
8:18, 11:13,
16:11, 25:7,
43:1-2, 55:2,
63:18

100:10
Sick:
xiii:5, 7:9, 18:1-
5, 30:13, 44:4,
64:15-18, 92:1,
92:13-14,
101:6, 107:7-8,
118:19, 141:17,
142:3, 149:14,
164:8

100:18
Spiritually Fit:
77:4, 85:11-15,
101:3

100:4-7 The world does not change. We do. Our attitudes and outlook on life are changed as we prove to ourselves that we actually can rely upon God. We live our way into this new way of thinking. We change our actions and our thinking follows. It is a wonderfully practical and effective way of producing the entire psychic change that we must have if we are to live.

100:15-17 Once again, demonstration of spiritual principles in our own lives speaks louder and clearer than any advice we could possibly give others. People tend to follow example and reject advice.

100:18-101:3 We become spiritually fit by working the 12 Steps. By persistently practicing these spiritual exercises we strengthen our ability to apply spiritual principles in our lives. The replacement of our old ideas and attitudes towards life by spiritual means results in our being restored to sanity. We no longer feel a need for alcohol as a solution as we are no longer making ourselves miserable.

moving pictures which show drinking scenes; we must not go into bars; our friends must hide their bottles if we go to their houses; we mustn't think or be reminded about alcohol at all. ¹Our experience shows that this *is* not necessarily so.

²We meet these conditions every day. ³An alcoholic who cannot meet them, still has an alcoholic mind: there is something the matter with his spiritual status. ⁴His only chance for sobriety would be some place like Greenland Ice Cap, and even there an Eskimo might turn up with a bottle of scotch and ruin everything! ⁵Ask any woman who has sent her husband to distant places on the theory he would escape the alcohol problem.

⁶In our belief any scheme of combating alcoholism which proposes to shield the sick man from temptation is doomed to failure. ⁷If the alcoholic tries to shield himself, he may succeed for a time, but usually winds up with a bigger explosion than ever. ⁸We have tried these methods. ⁹These attempts to do the impossible have always failed.

¹⁰So our rule is not to avoid a place where there is drinking, *if we have a legitimate reason for being there.* ¹¹That includes bars, nightclubs, dances, receptions, weddings, even plain ordinary whoopee parties. ¹²To a person who has had experience with an alcoholic, this may seem like tempting Providence, but it isn't.

¹³You will note that we made an important qualification. ¹⁴Therefore, ask yourself on each occasion, "Have I any good social, business, or personal reason for going to this place? ¹⁵Or

101:6-9 Alcohol is not the problem. Our drinking is but a symptom. The root cause of our problem is selfishness and self-centeredness. We turn to God to restore us to sanity. Our obsession to drink is removed as a result of our surrender of our will and our lives to a Power greater than ourselves. There is no need to hide from aspects of life that include drinking. God grants us a daily reprieve from the need and desire to drink.

101:14-102:6 Here are specific instructions to analyze our motivations for attending functions where there will be drinking. We must be absolutely honest with ourselves in this matter as one drink spells disaster. In "The Doctor's Opinion" Dr. Silkworth was very clear that the phenomenon of craving caused by drinking can only be relieved by total abstinence. Thankfully, we have found a method by which we may remain free from alcohol. This review of our motivations is an important part of our program of action.

am I expecting to steal a little vicarious pleasure from the atmosphere of such places?" 102:1If you answer these questions satisfactorily, you need have no apprehension. 2Go or stay away, whatever seems best. 3But be sure you are on solid spiritual ground before you start and that your motive in going is thoroughly good. 4Do not think of what you will get out of the occasion. 5Think of what you can bring to it. 6But if you are shaky, you had better work with another alcoholic instead!

7Why sit with a long face in places where there is drinking, sighing about the good old days. 8If it is a happy occasion, try to increase the pleasure of those there; if a business occasion, go and attend to your business enthusiastically. 9If you are with a person who wants to eat in a bar, by all means go along. 10Let your friends know they are not to change their habits on your account. 11At a proper time and place explain to all your friends why alcohol disagrees with you. 12If you do this thoroughly, few people will ask you to drink. 13While you were drinking, you were withdrawing from life little by little. 14Now you are getting back into the social life of this world. 15Don't start to withdraw again just because your friends drink liquor.

102:4-5
Selfish Program?:
13:18, 14:23, 20:1, 62:2, 70:14, 85:16-18, 93:15, 94:6, 97:3, 120:1, 159:12-13, 164:16

102:6
Work:
15:8-11, 89:1, 119:7, 129:14, 156:10, 181:4

102:4-5 Humility borne of working the steps and God's gift of relief from the burden of self allow us to be useful to others. Rather than seeking satisfaction in life by taking, we find fulfillment in giving to others. At a social event we may feel uncomfortable and afraid that we will not get the things that we want. We may feel isolated or uncomfortable and afraid that we will not get what we want. We are afraid people will not like us, that they will not give us their attention or their respect. These fears drive us mercilessly. We lie, give our opinions, gossip, seek the center of attention or avoid socializing altogether. When we leave we are unhappy with our selves for succumbing once again to our fears and unsatisfied because we did not get what we thought we wanted. The solution is for us to seek to give rather than to take. We can find purpose for our lives by seeking to give to others. We can give others our attention. We can give others our respect.

We can give others our company and our ears. We can make others comfortable and by doing so find comfort for ourselves.

102:6 Nothing works to keep us sober better than intensive work with another alcoholic. We have clear-cut directions for how to carry this message of a solution to others. By practicing these spiritual exercises we maintain and increase our own spiritual fitness.

102:16 Being helpful gives new purpose to our lives. This replaces the slothful indifference and neglect of our responsibilities to God and our fellows that robbed our lives of all meaning and purpose. Our past failings have been transformed by God into powerful tools for good. We can be useful where others cannot. We have been given the priceless treasure of God's grace but we can only keep and increase it by giving it away.

102:16Your job now is to be at the place where you may be of maximum helpfulness to others, so never hesitate to go anywhere, if you can be helpful. 17You should not hesitate to visit the most sordid spot on earth on such an errand. 18Keep on the firing line of life with these motives, and God will keep you unharmed.

19Many of us keep liquor in our homes. 20We often need it to carry green recruits through a severe hangover. 21Some of us still serve it to our friends provided they are not alcoholic. 22But some of us think we should not serve liquor to anyone. 23We never argue this question. 103:1We feel that each family, in the light of their own circumstances, ought to decide for themselves.

2We are careful never to show intolerance or hatred of drinking as an institution. 3Experience shows that such an attitude is not helpful to anyone. 4Every new alcoholic looks for this spirit among us and is immensely relieved when he finds we are not witch-burners. 5A spirit of intolerance might repel alcoholics whose lives could have been saved, had it not been for such stupidity. 6We would not even do the cause of temperate drinking any good, for not one drinker in a thousand likes to be told anything about alcohol by one who hates it.

7Someday we hope that Alcoholics Anonymous will help the public to a better realization of the gravity of the alcoholic problem, but we shall be of little use if our attitude is one of bitterness or hostility. 8Drinkers will not stand for it.

9*After all, our problems were of our own making.* 10*Bottles were only a symbol.* 11*Besides, we have stopped fighting anybody or anything.* 12*We have to!*

102:18 God, rather than any works of our own is the source of our new found power. As long as we humbly acknowledge this fact we will have access to this Power. Ego is the illusion of existence independent of God. We combat the resurgence of ego through the continual development of humility.

103:1-9 We have found a solution to our alcoholism. We have joined together to help those who desire a solution to find one. We are not religious crusaders or anti-alcohol lobbyists. Our only wish is to be useful. God has given us a great gift that we wish to share with those who would have it.

Chapter Eight
TO WIVES

Our drinking affects everyone around us, our friends, our families, our parents, our children and especially our spouses. Here an early member relates the common symptoms of a spouse of an alcoholic. "What symptoms?" You may ask. "I am not the one who is sick!" The truth is that alcoholism exhibited in one we love often harms us in ways that are very much like a sickness. We begin to lose all perspective on what it is we can and what it is we cannot control in our lives and the lives of our loved ones.

In the same way that the authors show us through their experience what alcoholism is in the hope that we may see ourselves and thus perhaps decide to adopt the solution that worked for the authors, so too do the authors describe through their own experience an alcoholic family.

In the chapter To Wives the spouses of alcoholics describe what it's like to be married to an alcoholic (104:12-105:1). The alcoholic's drinking and the spouse's attempts to cope contribute to a household that can only be described as sick (104-108). The baffling nature of alcoholism puzzles us (107:18-21) until we recognize the symptoms of alcoholism. Helping us to identify the problem the authors spell out several different types of alcoholics (108:19-110:17). We are given practical advice on how to deal effectively with each type (110:18-113:26). What we should say to others (114:23-115:10) and what we should tell the children (115:11-14) are questions we can answer by availing ourselves of the experience of those who have overcome problems very similar to ours. We are advised to avoid covering for the alcoholic (115:15-116:11) as in our experience this only makes matters worse by enabling alcoholic behavior to continue. The solution that the authors applied to their situation is clearly spelled out (116:12-15). The reasons why we need to apply the solution to ourselves are stated (116:14-117:2). We are warned of the ups and downs that are to be expected (117:3-118:8). The benefits of patience are extolled (118:9-16) and the pitfalls of resentment (118:17-119:3) and jealousy (119:4-16) are pointed out. Attitudes are suggested that can help us to adopt this new way of life (119:14-120:3). Slips are addressed (120:4-9) and we are told not to blame ourselves for them or try to arrange the affairs of our alcoholic to lessen the chance of temptation. God has either removed the problem or not (120:10-20). Even if our loved one does not recover we can find the solution to our own problems through adopting this way of life.

The experience of those who have gone before us can be a great comfort during such trying times. The hope that the wonderful way of life they have adopted is also available to us gladdens our hearts and encourages us to follow their well trodden path.

The Blueprint

The Alcoholic Home	Wives of alcoholics understand the devastation wrought by this illness.
Illness	Classifying alcoholics helps us to see the stage of alcoholism that our loved one is in.
Solution	What we can expect during the early stages of our loved one's recovery is described.

Chapter Eight
TO WIVES

104:1With few exceptions, our book thus far has spoken of men. 2But what we have said applies quite as much to women. 3Our activities in behalf of women who drink are on the increase. 4There is every evidence that women regain their health as readily as men if they try our suggestions.

5But for every man who drinks others are involved: the wife who trembles in fear of the next debauch; the mother and father who see their son wasting away.

6Among us are wives, relatives, and friends whose problem has been solved, as well as some who have not yet found a happy solution. 7We want the wives of Alcoholics Anonymous to address the wives of men who drink too much. 8What they say will apply to nearly everyone bound by ties of blood or affection to an alcoholic.

104:6 The true nature of our problem may not be readily apparent to us. We may see our problem as being the drinking of a loved one. We find that our real problem is our reaction to the alcoholic. The things we do to cope with this seemingly impossible situation are symptoms of our problem, much as the drinking of an alcoholic is really just a symptom and not the cause of their problem. We did not cause the alcoholic's problem. We cannot control the alcoholic's problem. We can only deal with our own problem.

104:12-107:4 This description of life with an alcoholic is to help us identify with the authors and determine if we face the same difficulties that they have faced and thus be able to benefit from the same remedy. We look for the similarities rather than the differences as individual experiences vary.

105:2-11
Human
Resources:
44:14-45:9,
60:16-61:20

105:8
Frothy:
xxvi:3, 3:19,
90:17

104:9As wives of Alcoholics Anonymous, we would like you to feel that we understand as perhaps few can. 10We want to analyze mistakes we have made. 11We want to leave you with the feeling that no situation is too difficult and no unhappiness too great to be overcome.

12We have traveled a rocky road, there is no mistake about that. 13We have had long rendezvous with hurt pride, frustration, self-pity, misunderstanding, and fear. 14These are not pleasant companions. 15We have been driven to maudlin sympathy, to bitter resentment. 105:1Some of us veered from extreme to extreme, ever hoping that one day our loved ones would be themselves once more.

2Our loyalty, and the desire that our husbands hold up their heads and be like other men have begotten all sorts of predicaments. 3We have been unselfish and self-sacrificing. 4We have told innumerable lies to protect our pride and our husbands' reputations. 5We have prayed, we have begged, we have been patient. 6We have struck out viciously. 7We have run away. 8We have been hysterical. 9We have been terror stricken. 10We have sought sympathy. 11We have had retaliatory love affairs with other men.

12Our homes have been battle-grounds many an evening. 13In the morning we have kissed and made up. 14Our friends have counseled chucking the men and we have done so with finality, only to be back in a little while, hoping, always hoping. 15Our men have sworn great solemn oaths they were through drinking forever. 16We have believed them when no one else could, or would. 17Then, in days, weeks, or months, a fresh outburst.

18We seldom had friends at our homes, never knowing how or when the men of the house would appear. 19We could make few social engagements. 20We came to live almost alone. 21When we were invited out, our husbands sneaked so many drinks that they spoiled the occasion. 22If, on the other hand, they took nothing, their self-pity made them killjoys.

23There was never financial security. 24Positions were

175

106:18
Advice:
xxx:4, 70:2,
73:21, 90:4,
96:11

106:19
Remorseful:
xxvii:1, xxviii:7,
6:7, 37:9, 66:3,
86:12, 109:18

107:3
Addiction:
xxv:2, xxvii:6,
xxviii:15, 3:24,
5:2-6, 6:7-23,
13:4, 21:3,
22:1, 22:17,
23:18, 24:1,
24:3-6, 32:2,
32:8, 39:12,
40:6, 177:8

107:3
Insanity:
xxiv:6, xxvi:9,
5:7, 5:28, 6:23,
23:3, 27:3,
24:15, 33:10,
37:1-9, 37:11,
38:15, 40:10,
41:23, 42:3,
61:17, 66:12,
92:15, 101:3,
107:3, 120:11,
154:17,
157:17-18

always in jeopardy or gone. [105:25]An armored car could not have brought the pay envelopes home. [106:1]The checking account melted like snow in June.

[2]Sometimes there were other women. [3]How heart breaking was this discovery; how cruel to be told they understood our men as we did not!

[4]The bill collectors; the sheriffs; the angry taxi drivers; the policemen; the bums; the pals; and even the ladies they sometimes brought home—our husbands thought we were so inhospitable. [5]"Joykiller, nag, wet blanket"—that's what they said. [6]Next day they would be themselves again and we would forgive and try to forget.

[7]We have tried to hold the love of our children for their father. [8]We have told small tots that father was sick, which was much nearer the truth than we realized. [9]They struck the children, kicked out door panels, smashed treasured crockery, and ripped the keys out of pianos. [10]In the midst of such pandemonium they may have rushed out threatening to live with the other woman forever. [11]In desperation, we have even got tight ourselves—the drunk to end all drunks. [12]The unexpected result was that our husbands seemed to like it.

[13]Perhaps at this point we got a divorce and took the children home to father and mother. [14]Then we were severely criticized by our husband's parents for desertion. [15]Usually we did not leave. [16]We stayed on and on. [17]We finally sought employment ourselves as destitution faced us and our families.

[18]We began to ask medical advice as the sprees got closer together. [19]The alarming physical and mental symptoms, the deepening pail of remorse, depression and inferiority that settled down on our loved ones—these things terrified and distracted us. [107:1]As animals on a treadmill, we have patiently and wearily climbed, falling back in exhaustion after each futile effort to reach solid ground. [2]Most of us have entered the final stage with its commitment to health resorts, sanitariums, hospitals, and jails. [3]Sometimes there were screaming delirium and insanity. [4]Death was often near.

107:5Under these conditions we naturally made mistakes. 107:7-8
Sick:
xiii:5, 7:9, 18:1-
5, 30:13, 44:4,
64:15-18, 92:1,
92:13-14,
100:10, 101:6,
118:19, 141:17,
142:3, 149:14,
164:8
6Some of them rose out of ignorance of alcoholism.
7Sometimes we sensed dimly that we were dealing with sick
men. 8Had we fully understood the nature of the alcoholic
illness, we might have behaved differently.

9How could men who loved their wives and children be so 107:11
Resolves:
xxvii:1, xxviii:7,
5:14-24, 5:30-
6:4, 7:10,
32:11-33:2,
34:8, 38:5,
39:17
unthinking, so callous, so cruel? 10There could be no love in
such persons, we thought. 11And just as we were being convinced of their heartlessness, they would surprise us with fresh
resolves and new attentions. 12For a while they would be their 107:19
Willpower:
xxix:18, 7:10,
11:9, 20:14,
22:11, 24:3-
6,32:13, 33:9,
34:2, 34:12,
40:12, 42:4,
45:2-3, 76:18,
85:19-20, 92:8,
140:5
old sweet selves, only to dash the new structure of affection to
pieces once more. 13Asked why they commenced to drink
again, they would reply with some silly excuse, or none. 14It
was so baffling, so heartbreaking. 15Could we have been so
mistaken in the men we married? 16When drinking, they were
strangers. 17Sometimes they were so inaccessible that it seemed 108:2
We Hope:
xiii:3, xiv:4,
18:6, 29:5-6,
43:4, 44:2,
71:1, 89:19,
153:10, 162:10,
163:1
as though a great wall had been built around them.

18And even if they did not love their families, how could
they be so blind about themselves? 19What had become of
their judgment, their common sense, their will power? 20Why
could they not see that drink meant ruin to them? 21Why was
it, when these dangers were pointed out that they agreed
and then got drunk again immediately?

108:1These are some of the questions which race through
the mind of every girl who has an alcoholic husband. 2We
hope this book has answered some of them. 3Perhaps your
husband has been living in that strange world of alcoholism
where everything is distorted and exaggerated. 4You can see
that he really does love you with his better self. 5Of course,
there is such a thing as incompatibility, but in nearly every
instance the alcoholic only seems to be unloving and inconsiderate; it is usually because he is warped and sickened that
he says and does these appalling things. 6Today most of our
men are better husbands and fathers than ever before.

7Try not to condemn your alcoholic husband no matter what
he says or does. 8He is just another very sick, unreasonable

108:17
The Price:
14:1-3, 155:7

108:18-109:9
Heavy Drinker:
20:23, 139:8,
149:14-16

108:18-
110:17
Classification of
Alcoholics:
xxviii:3, 20:21-
21:4

109:10-24
Alcoholism:
xiii:1, xxviii:3-
18, 18:3-5,
20:8-20, 21:5-
22:7, 24:1,
30:10, 37:13-
38:14, 44:3,
52:6, 56:5,
149:14

109:10-24
Real Alcoholic:
21:3-4, 23:17,
24:1, 30:1,
30:11, 31:5,
33:14, 34:3-4,
35:22, 44:5,
92:7

person. 108:9Treat him, when you can, as though he had pneumonia. 10When he angers you, remember that he is very ill.

11There is an important exception to the foregoing. 12We realize some men are thoroughly bad-intentioned, that no amount of patience will make any difference. 13An alcoholic of this temperament may be quick to use this chapter as a club over your head. 14Don't let him get away with it. 15If you are positive he is one of this type you may feel you had better leave. 16Is it right to let him ruin your life and the lives of your children? 17Especially when he has before him a way to stop his drinkng and abuse if he really wants to pay the price.

18The problem with which you struggle usually falls within one of four categories:

One: Your husband may be only a heavy drinker. 109:1His drinking may be constant or it may be heavy only on certain occasions. 2Perhaps he spends too much money for liquor. 3It may be slowing him up mentally and physically, but he does not see it. 4Sometimes he is a source of embarrassment to you and his friends. 5He is positive he can handle his liquor, that it does him no harm, that drinking is necessary in his business. 6He would probably be insulted if called an alcoholic. 7This world is full of people like him. 8Some will moderate or stop altogether, and some will not. 9Of those who keep on, a good number will become true alcoholics after a while.

10*Two:* Your husband is showing lack of control, for he is unable to stay on the water wagon, even when he wants to. 11He often gets entirely out of hand when drinking. 12He admits this is true, but is positive that he will do better. 13He has begun to try, with or without your cooperation, various means of moderating or staying dry. 14Maybe he is beginning to lose his friends. 15His business may suffer somewhat. 16He is worried at times, and is becoming aware that he cannot drink like other people. 17He sometimes drinks in the morning, and through the

108:18-110:17 We can learn how best to deal with our loved one by determining how far their alcoholism has progressed. Some read- ily identifiable stages of the progression of alcoholism should give us a rough estimate of their condition.

day also, to hold his nervousness in check. ¹⁰⁹:¹⁸He is remorseful after serious drinking bouts and tells you he wants to stop. ¹⁹But when he gets over the spree, he begins to think once more how he can drink moderately next time. ²⁰We think this person is in danger. ²¹These are the earmarks of a real alcoholic. ²²Perhaps he can still tend to business fairly well. ²³He has *by* no means ruined everything. ²⁴As we say among ourselves, *"He wants to want to stop."*

²⁵ *Three:* This husband has gone much further than husband number two. ²⁶Though once like number two, he became worse. ¹¹⁰:¹His friends have slipped away, his home is a near-wreck, and he cannot hold a position. ²Maybe the doctor has been called in, and the weary round of sanitariums and hospitals has begun. ³He admits he cannot drink like other people, but does not see why. ⁴He clings to the notion that he will yet find a way to do so. ⁵He may have come to the point where he desperately wants to stop but cannot. ⁶His case presents additional questions which we shall try to answer for you. ⁷You can be quite hopeful of a situation like this.

⁸*Four:* You may have a husband of whom you completely despair. ⁹He has been placed in one institution after another. ¹⁰He is violent, or appears definitely insane, when drunk. ¹¹Sometimes he drinks on the way home from the hospital. ¹²Perhaps he has had delirium tremens. ¹³Doctors may shake their heads and advise you to have him committed. ¹⁴Maybe you have already been obliged to put him away. ¹⁵This picture may not be as dark as it looks. ¹⁶Many of our husbands were just as far gone. ¹⁷Yet they got well.

¹⁸Let's now go back to husband number one. ¹⁹Oddly enough, he is often difficult to deal with. ²⁰He enjoys drinking. ²¹It stirs his imagination. ²²His friends feel closer over a highball. ²³Perhaps you enjoy drinking with him yourself when he doesn't go too far. ²⁴You have passed happy evenings

109:18
Remorseful:
xxvii:1, xxviii:7,
6:7, 37:9, 66:3,
86:12, 106:19

109:19
Next Time:
xxvii:11, 30:12,
32:5-33:4,
34:5-6, 154:13,
155:13

109:24
Stop:
xlv:2, xxvii:6,
7:10-11, 19:3,
20:8-20, 20:21-
21:2, 22:17,
23:17, 25:2,
31:10-32:2,
32:16-33:2,
33:8-11, 33:15,
34:9-15, 39:2-4,
110:5, 122:14

110:2
Weary:
xxvii:2, 5:5,
6:22, 23:2,
43:6, 48:7,
151:9

110:4
Unwilling:
xxviii:8, 30:1,
39:14-40:1,
44:9, 58:2

110:18-113:36 We can follow the example of the authors' successful experience in these matters. They have been through this before and have learned from their mistakes. We stand a much better chance of helping our alcoholic loved one if we approach them in the ways described here.

together chatting and drinking before your fire. ¹¹⁰:²⁵Perhaps you both like parties which would be dull without liquor. ²⁶We have enjoyed such evening ourselves; we had a good time. ²⁷We know all about liquor as a social lubricant. ²⁸Some, but not all of us, think it has its advantages when reasonably used.

¹¹¹:¹The first principle of success is that you should never be angry. ²Even though your husband becomes unbearable, and you have to leave him temporarily, you should, if you can, go without rancor. ³Patience and good temper are most necessary.

⁴Our next thought is that you should never tell him what he must do about his drinking. ⁵If he gets the idea that you are a nag or a killjoy, your chance of accomplishing anything useful may be zero. ⁶He will use that as an excuse to drink some more. ⁷He will tell you he is misunderstood. ⁸This may lead to lonely evenings for you. ⁹He may seek someone to console him—not always another man.

¹⁰Be determined that your husband's drinking is not going to spoil your relation with your children or your friends. ¹¹They need your companionship and your help. ¹²It is possible to have a full and useful life, though your husband continues to drink. ¹³We know women who are unafraid, even happy, under these conditions. ¹⁴Do not set your heart on reforming your husband. ¹⁵You may be unable to do so, no matter how hard you try.

¹⁶We know these suggestions are sometimes difficult to follow, but you will save many a heartbreak if you can succeed in observing them. ¹⁷Your husband may come to appreciate your reasonableness and patience. ¹⁸This may lay the groundwork for a friendly talk about his alcoholic problem. ¹⁹Try to have him bring up the subject himself. ²⁰Be sure you are not critical during such a discussion. ²¹Attempt instead, to put yourself in his place. ²²Let him see that you want to be helpful rather than critical.

²³When a discussion does arise, you might suggest he read this book, or at least the chapter on alcoholism. ¹¹²:¹Tell him you have been worried, though perhaps needlessly. ²You think he ought to know the subject better, as everyone should have a

clear understanding of the risk he takes if he drinks too much. ¹¹²:³Show him you have confidence in his power to stop or moderate. ⁴Say you do not want to be a wet blanket; that you only want him to take care of his health. ⁵Thus you may succeed in interesting him in alcoholism.

⁶He probably has several alcoholics among his own acquaintances. ⁷You might suggest that you both take an interest in them. ⁸Drinkers like to help other drinkers. ⁹Your husband may be willing to talk to one of them.

¹⁰If this kind of approach does not catch your husband's interest, it may be best to drop the subject, but after a friendly talk your husband will usually revive the topic himself. ¹¹This may take patient waiting, but it will be worth it. ¹²Meanwhile you might try to help the wife of another serious drinker. ¹³If you act upon these principles, your husband may stop or moderate.

¹⁴Suppose, however, that your husband fits the description of number two. ¹⁵The same principles which apply to husband number one should be practiced. ¹⁶But after his next binge, ask him if he would really like to get over drinking for good. ¹⁷Do not ask that he do it for you or anyone else. ¹⁸Just would he *like* to?

¹⁹The chances are he would. ²⁰Show him your copy of this book and tell him what you have found out about alcoholism. ²¹Show him that as alcoholics, the writers of the book understand. ²²Tell him some of the interesting stories you have read. ²³If you think he will be shy of a spiritual remedy, ask him to look at the chapter on alcoholism. ¹¹³:¹Then perhaps he will be interested enough to continue.

²If he is enthusiastic your cooperation will mean a great deal. ³If he is luke-warm, or thinks he is not an alcoholic, we suggest you leave him alone. ⁴Avoid urging him to follow our program. ⁵The seed has been planted in his mind. ⁶He knows that over a hundred men, much like himself, have recovered. ⁷But don't remind him of this after he has been drinking, for he may be angry. ⁸Sooner or later, you are likely to find him

181

reading the book once more. ¹¹³:⁹Wait until repeated stumbling convinces him he must act, for the more you hurry him, the longer his recovery may be delayed.

¹⁰If you have a number three husband, you may be in luck. ¹¹Being certain he wants to stop, you can go to him with this volume as joyfully as though you had struck oil. ¹²He may not share your enthusiasm, but he is practically sure to read the book, and he may go for the program at once. ¹³If he does not, you will probably not have long to wait. ¹⁴Again, you should not crowd him. ¹⁵Let him decide for himself. ¹⁶Cheerfully see him through more sprees. ¹⁷Talk about his condition or this book only when he raises the issue. ¹⁸In some cases it may be better to let someone outside the family present the book. ¹⁹They can urge action without arousing hostility. ²⁰If your husband is otherwise a normal individual, your chances are good at this stage.

²¹You would suppose that men in the fourth classification would be quite hopeless; but that is not so. ²²Many of Alcoholics Anonymous were like that. ²³Everybody had given them up. ²⁴Defeat seemed certain. ²⁵Yet often such men had spectacular and powerful recoveries.

¹¹⁴:¹There are exceptions. ²Some men have been so impaired by alcohol that they cannot stop. ³Sometimes there are cases where alcoholism is complicated by other disorders. ⁴A good doctor or psychiatrist can tell you whether these complications are serious. ⁵In any event, try to have your husband read this book. ⁶His reaction may be one of enthusiasm. ⁷If he is already committed to an institution but can convince you and your doctor that he means business, give him a chance to try our method, unless the doctor thinks his mental condition too abnormal or dangerous. ⁸We make this recommendation with some confidence. ⁹About a year ago a certain state institution released four chronic alcoholics. ¹⁰It was fully expected they would all be back in a few weeks. ¹¹Only one of them has returned. ¹²The others had no relapse at all. ¹³The power of God goes deep!

Historical Note:
114:9 State Hospital: Greystone Psychiatric Hospital, Morris Plains, New Jersey.

114:14You may have the reverse situation on your hands. 15Perhaps you have a husband who is at large, but who should be committed. 16Some men cannot, or will not get over alcoholism. 17When they become too dangerous, we think the kind thing is to lock them up, of course a good doctor should always be consulted. 18The wives and children of such men suffer horribly, but not less than the men themselves.

114:21
Way of life:
xiii:6, 8:19,
13:21, 15:11,
16:6, 42:21,
68:14-23,
79:15, 81:21
84:14, 97:19,
99:11, 117:13,
124:1, 130:10,
134:15, 164:13-
16, tt15:4

19But sometimes you must start life anew. 20We know women who have done it. 21If such women adopt a spiritual way of life, their road will be smoother.

22If your husband is a drinker, you probably worry over what other people are thinking and you hate to meet your friends. 23You draw more and more into yourself and you think everyone is talking about conditions at your home. 24You avoid the subject of drinking, even with your own parents. 115:1You do not know what to tell the children. 2When your husband is bad, you become a trembling recluse, wishing the telephone had never been invented.

3We find that most of this embarrassment is unnecessary. 4While you need not discuss your husband at length, you can quietly let your friends know the nature of his illness. 5But you must be on guard not to embarrass or harm your husband.

6When you have carefully explained to such people that he is a sick person, you will have created a new atmosphere. 7Barriers which have sprung up between you and your friends will disappear with the growth of sympathetic understanding. 8You will no longer be self-conscious, nor feel that you must apologize as though your husband were a weak character. 9He may be anything but that. 10Your new courage, good nature, and lack of self-consciousness will do wonders for you socially.

114:23-115:10 Prudent honesty with others breaks down the walls of secrecy behind which we are imprisoned. We find that humility saves us from humiliation. Many people have had similar experiences with an alcoholic loved one. Our honesty may help them in ways we cannot foresee and perhaps they may have some advice that proves useful to us.

115:11The same principle applies in dealing with the children. 12Unless they actually need protection from their father, it is best not to take sides in any argument he has with them while drinking. 13Use your energies to promote a better understanding all around. 14Then that terrible tension which grips the home of every problem drinker will be lessened.

15Frequently you have felt obliged to tell your husband's employer and his friends that he was sick, when as a matter of fact he was tight. 16Avoid answering these inquiries as much as you can. 17Whenever possible, let your husband explain. 18Your desire to protect him should not cause you to lie to people, when they have a right to know where he is and what he is doing. 19Discuss this with him when he is sober and in good spirits. 116:1Ask him what you should do if he places you in such a position again. 2But be careful not to be resentful about the last time he did so.

3There is another paralyzing fear. 4You may be afraid your husband will lose his position; you are thinking of the disgrace and hard times which will befall you and the children. 5This experience may come to you. 6Or you may already have had it several times. 7Should it happen again, regard it in a different light. 8Maybe it will prove a blessing! 9It may convince your husband he wants to stop drinking forever. 10And now you know that he can stop if he will! 11Time after time, this apparent calamity has been a boon to us, for it opened up a path which led to the discovery of God.

12We have elsewhere remarked how much better life is when lived on a spiritual plane. 13If God can solve the age-old riddle of alcoholism, he can solve your problems too. 14We

---

115:15-116:11 Covering up for the alcoholic only allows the behavior to continue and harms rather than helps our loved one. Allowing the alcoholic to take responsibility for their behavior and suffer the consequences may be the most helpful thing we can do. The delusion that they can continue drinking and get away with it must be smashed. Usually the alcoholic must have no other option before they will take the necessary action

116:12-117:2 The truth is that even though our loved one may quit drinking this will not solve our own problem. Our problem has much the same cause as that of the alcoholic—selfishness and self-centeredness. We turn to spiritual principles for relief from our own symptoms.

wives found that, like everybody else, we were afflicted with
pride, self-pity, vanity, and all the things which go to make
up the self-centered person; and we were not above selfishness or dishonesty. ^{116:15}As our husbands began to apply spiritual principles in their lives, we began to *see* the desirability
of doing so too.

¹⁶At first, some of us did not believe we needed this help.
¹⁷We thought, on the whole, we were pretty good women,
capable of being nicer if our husbands stopped drinking. ¹⁸But
it was a silly idea that we were too good to need God. ¹⁹Now
we try to put spiritual principles to work in every department
of our lives. ²⁰When we do that, we find it solves our problems
too; the ensuing lack of fear, worry and hurt feelings is a wonderful thing. ^{117:1}We urge you to try our program, for nothing
will be so helpful to your husband as the radically changed
attitude toward him which God will show you how to have.
²Go along with your husband if you possibly can.

³If you and your husband find a solution for the pressing
problem of drink, you are, of course, going to be very happy.
⁴But all problems will not be solved at once. ⁵Seed has started
to sprout in a new soil, but growth has only begun. ⁶In spite
of your new-found happiness, there will be ups and downs.
⁷Many of the old problems will still be with you. ⁸This is as it
should be.

⁹The faith and sincerity of both you and your husband will
be put to the test. ¹⁰These work-outs should be regarded as
part of your education, for thus you will be learning to live.
¹¹You will make mistakes, but if you are in earnest, they will
not drag you down. ¹²Instead, you will capitalize them. ¹³A
better way of life will emerge when they are overcome.

¹⁴Some of the snags you will encounter are irritation, hurt-
feelings, and resentments. ¹⁵Your husband will sometimes be
unreasonable, and you will want to criticize. ¹⁶Starting from a

---

117:3-8 If our loved one stops drinking this will, of course, be a big relief. There is much more that must be done on everyones part if we are to live happily.

Stopping drinking is just the beginning of the alcoholics recovery. Likewise, we have much to address in our own character if we are also to recover.

116:14
Self-centered-
ness:
14:2, 56:7,
61:21, 62:2-14,
124:1

117:1
Program:
xiii:2, xxiii:1,
xxix:8, 9:32,
19:13, 20:4-6,
29:1, 42:14,
45:8-9, 58:1-2,
59:7, 72:6,
73:1, 74:15,
85:12-16, 88:6,
94:2, 96:10,
99:16, 113:4,
126:22, 130:10,
147:1, 157:27

117:4
Solve Problem:
xxvi:2, 13:21,
15:4, 17:3,
25:6, 42:20,
43:6, 45:9,
52:8, 52:12,
104:6, 116:13,
118:14, 143:14

117:5
Soil:
12:2

117:12
Capitalize:
18:10-11,
83:23, 84:1,
89:4-5, 89:17,
91:16-19,
123:2, 124:2-
10, 132:20

117:13
Way of life:
xiii:6, 8:19,
13:21, 15:11,
16:6, 42:21,
68:14-23,
79:15, 81:21
84:14, 97:19,
99:11, 114:21,
124:1, 130:10,
134:15, 164:13-
16, tt15:4

speck on the domestic horizon, great thunderclouds of dispute may gather. [117:17]These family dissensions are very dangerous, especially to your husband. [18]Often you must carry the burden of avoiding them or keeping them under control. [19]Never forget that resentment is a deadly hazard to an alcoholic. [20]We do not mean that you have to agree with your husband wherever there is an honest difference of opinion. [21]Just be careful not to disagree in a resentful or critical spirit.

[118:1]You and your husband will find that you can dispose of serious problems easier than you can the trivial ones. [2]Next time you and he have a heated discussion, no matter what the subject, it should be the privilege of either to smile and say, "This is getting serious. I'm sorry I got disturbed. [3]Let's talk about it later." [4]If your husband is trying to live on a spiritual basis, he will also be doing everything in his power to avoid disagreement or contention.

[5]Your husband knows he owes you more than sobriety. [6]He wants to make good. [7]Yet you must not expect too much. [8]His ways of thinking and doing are the habits of years. [9]Patience, tolerance, understanding, and love are the watchwords. [10]Show him these things in yourself and they will be reflected back to you from him. [11]Live and let live is the rule. [12]If you both show a willingness to remedy your own defects, there will be little need to criticize each other.

[13]We women carry with us a picture of the ideal man, the sort of chap we would like our husbands to be. [14]It is the most natural thing in the world, once his liquor problem is solved, to feel that he will now measure up to that cherished vision. [15]The chances are he will not, for like yourself, he is just beginning his development. [16]Be patient.

[17]Another feeling we are very likely to entertain is one of resentment that love and loyalty could not cure our husbands of alcoholism. [18]We do not like the thought that the contents of a

118:1 It does not take much spiritual effort to step out of the way of the tornado that is alcoholism. It takes a great deal of spiritual effort to abandon many of our old failed methods of coping with life and accept the guidance of spiritual principles.

book, or the work of another alcoholic, has accomplished
in a few weeks the end for which we struggled for years.
118:19At such moments we forget that alcoholism is an illness
over which we could not possibly have had any power. 20Your
husband will be the first to say it was your devotion and care
which brought him to the point where he could have a spiritual experience. 119:1Without you he would have gone to
pieces long ago. 2When resentful thoughts come, try to pause
and count your blessings. 3After all, your family is reunited,
alcohol is no longer a problem, and you and your husband
are working together toward an undreamed-of future.

    4Still another difficulty is that you may become jealous of
the attention he bestows on other people, especially alcoholics. 5You have been starving for his companionship, yet
he spends long hours helping other men and their families.
6You feel he should now be yours. 7The fact is that he should
work with other people to maintain his own sobriety.
8Sometimes he will be so interested that he becomes really
neglectful. 9Your house is filled with strangers. 10You may not
like some of them. 11He gets stirred up about their troubles,
but not at all about yours. 12It will do little good if you point
that out and urge more attention for yourself. 13We find it a
real mistake to dampen his enthusiasm for alcoholic work.
14You should join in his efforts as much as you possibly can.
15We suggest you direct some of your thought to the wives of
his new alcoholic friends. 16They need the counsel and love
of a woman who has gone through what you have.

    17It is probably true that you and your husband have been
living too much alone, for drinking many times isolates the
wife of an alcoholic. 18Therefore, you probably need fresh

118:19
Powerless:
11:16, 24:3,
34:11, 45:2-4,
46:12, 50:15,
59:2, 59:8,
60:12, 62:13,
63:6,

118:19
Illness:
xiii:5, 7:9, 18:1-
5, 30:13, 44:4,
64:15-18, 92:1,
92:13-14,
100:10, 101:6,
107:7-8,
141:17, 142:3,
149:14, 164:8

119:7
Intensive:
15:8-11, 89:1,
102:6, 129:14,
156:10, 181:4

119:17-120:3 The alcoholic's neglect of their
spiritual responsibilities and indifference to
the welfare of other people strips meaning
and purpose from their lives. The solution to
this is for them to become involved in a cause
that can overcome self-centeredness. Helping
other alcoholics to recover is just such an
endeavor and is vitally important to their own
continued sobriety. We can restore purpose
and meaning to our own lives in just the
same manner. Our experience enables us to
be useful to others with alcoholic loved ones.
By selflessly helping others we rebuild our
own self-esteem.

interests and a great cause to live for as much as your husband. ¹¹⁹:¹⁹If you cooperate, rather than complain, you will find that his excess enthusiasm will tone down. ²⁰Both of you will awaken to a new sense of responsibility for others. ¹²⁰:¹You, as well as your husband, ought to think of what you can put into life, instead of how much you can take out. ²Inevitably your lives will be fuller for doing so. ³You will lose the old life to find one much better.

⁴Perhaps your husband will make a fair start on the new basis, but just as things are going beautifully, he dismays you by coming home drunk. ⁵If you are satisfied he really wants to get over drinking, you need not be alarmed. ⁶Though it is infinitely better he have no relapse at all, as has been true with many of our men, it is by no means a bad thing in some cases. ⁷Your husband will see at once that he must redouble his spiritual activities if he expects to survive. ⁸You need not remind him of his spiritual deficiency—he will know of it. ⁹Cheer him up and ask him how you can be still more helpful.

¹⁰The slightest sign of fear or intolerance may lessen your husband's chance of recovery. ¹¹In a weak moment he may take your dislike of his high-stepping friends as one of those insanely trivial excuses to drink.

¹²We never, never try to arrange a man's life, so as to shield him from temptation. ¹³The slightest disposition on your part to guide his appointments or his affairs so he will not be tempted will be noticed. ¹⁴Make him feel absolutely free to come and go as he likes. ¹⁵This is important. ¹⁶If he gets drunk, don't blame yourself. ¹⁷God has either removed your husband's liquor problem, or He has not. ¹⁸If not, it had better be found out right away. ¹⁹Then you and your husband can get right down to fundamentals. ²⁰If a repetition is to be prevented, place the problem, along with everything else, in God's hands.

120:4-20 The program suggested in this book is not a self-help program. Rather, it is a God-help program. We learn to rely upon God to solve our problems by applying the spiritual principles contained in the twelve steps. Taking these steps will help us to find a Power greater than ourselves if we are willing to seek in earnest.

121:1We realize we have been giving you much direction and advice. 2We may have seemed to lecture. 3If that is so we are sorry, for we ourselves don't always care for people who lecture us. 4But what we have related is based upon experience, some of it painful. 5We had to learn these things the hard way. 6That is why we are anxious that you understand, that you avoid these unnecessary difficulties.

7So to you out there—who may soon be with us—we say "Good luck and God bless you!"

121:1
Directions:
xiii:2, 20:4-6,
29:1, 45:8-9,
85:22, 86:3

How can the damage done to a family be repaired? How can the hurt feelings, anger, fear, guilt and remorse be assuaged? Practicing these principles in all our affairs means practicing them at home more importantly than anywhere else.

It is easy to talk of spiritual growth, however, it is quite another thing to adopt these principles as the basis for our lives. Thankfully we have the guidance of those who have gone before us to ease our entry into a sober home life. The difficulties we face and the mistakes we are likely to make are laid out in "The Family Afterward."

The pitfalls families may encounter are described. Selfishness and self-centeredness may affect all the members of the family as might the harboring of resentments and being critical or impatient (122:6-13). Ill-considered revelations of past love affairs may damage a marriage (124:11-125:3). Gossip and harsh criticism are to be avoided (125:6-11). Extremes of enthusiasm such as single-minded pursuit of financial success or speaking of nothing else but the new spiritual way of life we have found will hamper the repair of our home life (125:12-126:12). The alcoholic's values and priorities may continue to be out of balance for some time (129:4-7). The re-establishing of family and relationship roles places a burden on many households where the non-alcoholic spouse has been forced to assume sole responsibility for the functioning of the family.

The message we receive from "The Family Afterward" is one of hope that if we use these principles as the basis for our family life we will make strides that bring us closer to those who are most dear to us. Learning from the mistakes of others, we may avoid many of the pitfalls that are common to families in early recovery. We have hope that if we practice these principles we stand the greatest chance of a happy home life.

The Blueprint

The Family is Ill Also	The members of an alcoholic family exhibit some common symptoms that when recognized can be addressed.
Economic Problems	We gain balance in our lives as we recover. Economic issues must take their proper place and not overshadow other important aspects of our lives.
Restoration	Like our health, our families require time to heal.

Chapter Nine
THE FAMILY AFTERWARD

¹²²:¹Our women folk have suggested certain attitudes a wife may take with the husband who is recovering. ²Perhaps they created the impression that he is to be wrapped in cotton wool and placed on a pedestal. ³Successful readjustment means the opposite. ⁴All members of the family should meet upon the common ground of tolerance, understanding, and love. ⁵This involves a process of deflation. ⁶The alcoholic, his wife, his children, his "in-laws," each one is likely to have fixed ideas about the family's attitude towards himself or herself. ⁷Each is interested in having his or her wishes respected. ⁸We find the more one member of a family demands that the others concede to him, the more resentful they become. ⁹This makes for discord and unhappiness.

¹⁰And why? ¹¹Is it not because each wants to play the lead? ¹²Is not each trying to arrange the family show to his liking? ¹³Is he not unconsciously trying to see what he can take from the family life, rather than give?

¹⁴Cessation of drinking is but the first step away from a highly strained, abnormal condition. ¹⁵A doctor said to us, "Years of living with an alcoholic is almost sure to make any wife or child neurotic. ¹⁶The entire family is, to some extent, ill." ¹⁷Let families realize, as they start their journey, that all will not be fair weather. ¹⁸Each in his turn may be footsore and may straggle. ¹²³:¹There will be alluring shortcuts and by-paths down which they may wander and lose their way.

²Suppose we tell you some of the obstacles a family will meet; suppose we suggest how they may be avoided—even

122:8-13
Self-seeking:
60:18-62:14,
61:16, 62:4,
66:4, 67:13,
84:4, 86:16,
88:3

122:14
Stop:
xlv:2, xxvii:6,
7:10-11, 19:3,
20:8-20, 20:21-
21:2, 22:17,
23:17, 25:2,
31:10-32:2,
32:16-33:2,
33:8-11, 33:15,
34:9-15, 39:2-4,
109:24, 110:5

122:14
Elimination:
xxix:7, 19:3,
35:17, 51:1,
63:17, 64:2,
82:19, 103:10

123:2
Converted:
18:10-11,
83:23, 84:1,
89:4-5, 89:17,
91:16-19,
124:2-10,
132:20

122:5-13 The entire family can benefit from the application of spiritual principles. We are all selfish and self-centered in varying degrees. This book suggests a program of action that gives us relief from the frustration we feel as a result of trying to direct life to suit us.

122:14 Stopping drinking is just the beginning of our recovery. There is a great deal of work to be done as we learn to apply spiritual principles in all our affairs. As we recover, we may go through some of the same situations as have the authors. We can ease our way by following their example.

converted to good use for others. ¹²³:³The family of an alcoholic longs for the return of happiness and security. ⁴They remember when father was romantic, thoughtful, and successful. ⁵Today's life is measured against that of other years and, when it falls short, the family may be unhappy.

⁶Family confidence in dad is rising high. ⁷The good old days will soon be back, they think. ⁸Sometimes they demand that dad bring them back instantly! ⁹God, they believe, almost owes this recompense on a long overdue account. ¹⁰But the head of the house has spent years in pulling down the structures of business, romance, friendship, health—these things are now ruined or damaged. ¹¹It will take time to clear away the wreck. ¹²Though old buildings will eventually be replaced by finer ones, the new structures will take years to complete.

¹³Father knows he is to blame; it may take him many seasons of hard work to be restored financially, but he shouldn't be reproached. ¹⁴Perhaps he will never have much money again. ¹⁵But the wise family will admire him for what he is trying to be, rather than for what he is trying to get.

¹⁶Now and then the family will be plagued by spectres from the past, for the drinking career of almost every alcoholic has been marked by escapades, funny, humiliating, shameful, or tragic. ¹⁷The first impulse will be to bury these skeletons in a dark closet and padlock the door. ¹⁸The family may be possessed by the idea that future happiness can be based only upon forgetfulness of the past. ¹²⁴:¹We think that such a view is quite self-centered and in direct conflict with the new way of living.

²Henry Ford once made a wise remark to the effect that experience is the thing of supreme value in life. ³That is true only if one is willing to turn the past to good account. ⁴We grow by our willingness to face and rectify errors and convert them into assets. ⁵The alcoholic's past thus becomes the

---

124:2-10 We allow God to transform our past into our greatest asset by developing humility—a clear recognition of who and what we really are. We are humiliated only by those things that our pride and fear attempt to keep hidden. When we admit our shortcomings to God, ourselves and another human being, we are freed from their power over us. Armed with the truth about ourselves we can be of great use to others.

principal asset of the family, and frequently it is almost the only one!

124:6This painful past may be of infinite value to other families still struggling with their problem. 7We think each family which has been relieved owes something to those which have not, and when the occasion requires, each member of it should be only too willing to bring former mistakes, no matter how grievous, out of their hiding places. 8Showing others who suffer how we were given help, is the very tiring which makes life seem so worth while to us now. 9Cling to the thought that, in God's hands, the dark past is the greatest possession you have—the key to life and happiness for others. 10With it you can avert death and misery for them.

11It is possible to dig up past misdeeds so they become a blight, a veritable plague. 12For example, we know of situations in which the alcoholic or his wife have had love affairs. 13In the first flush of spiritual experience they forgave each other and drew closer together. 14The miracle of reconciliation was at hand. 15Then, under one provocation or another, the aggrieved one would unearth the old affair and angrily cast its ashes about. 16A few of us have had these growing pains and they hurt a great deal. 125:1Husbands and wives have sometimes been obliged to separate for a time until new perspective, new victory over hurt pride, could be rewon. 2In most cases, the alcoholic survived this ordeal without relapse, but not always. 3So we think that unless some good and useful purpose is to be served, past occurrences should not be discussed.

4We families of Alcoholics Anonymous keep few skeletons in the closet. 5Everyone knows about the others alcoholic troubles. 6This is a condition which, in ordinary life, would produce untold grief; there might be scandalous gossip, laughter at the expense of other people, and a tendency to take advantage of intimate information. 7Among us, these are rare

124:9 Key: 66:17

124:14 Miracle: 11:21, 25:1, 27:8, 50:11, 55:7, 57:4, 85:3, 128:12, 133:15

125:2 Relapse: 31:2, 26:7, 30:12, 35:1, 120:6, 147:2

125:3 Our rule is never to attempt to save ourselves by harming others. Though we may feel considerable pain for some of our wrongs, we must bear this burden rather than pass it to another by selfishly revealing our transgression.

occurrences. 125:8We do talk about each other a great deal but almost invariably temper such talk by a spirit of love and tolerance.

9Another principle we observe carefully is that we do not relate intimate experiences of another person unless we are sure he would approve. 10We find it better, when possible, to stick to our own stories. 11A man may criticize or laugh at himself and it will affect others favorably, but criticism or ridicule of him coming from another 12often produces the contrary effect. 13Members of a family should watch such matters carefully, for one careless, inconsiderate remark has been known to raise the very devil. 14We alcoholics are sensitive people. 15It takes some of us a long time to outgrow that serious handicap.

16Many alcoholics are enthusiasts. 17They run to extremes. 18At the beginning of recovery a man will take, as a rule, one of two directions. 19He may either plunge into a frantic attempt to get on his feet in business, or he may be so enthralled by his new life that he talks or thinks of little else. 126:1In either case certain family problems will arise. 2With these we have experience galore.

3We think it dangerous if he rushes headlong at his economic problem. 4The family will be affected also, pleasantly at first, as they feel their money troubles are to be solved, then not so pleasantly as they find themselves neglected. 5Dad may be tired at night and preoccupied by day. 6He may take small interest in the children and may show irritation when reproved for his delinquencies. 7If not irritable, he may seem dull and boring, not gay and affectionate, as the family would like him to be. 8Mother may complain of inattention. 9They are all disappointed, and often let him feel it. 10Beginning with such complaints, a barrier arises. 11He is straining every nerve to make up for lost time. 12He is striving to recover fortune and reputation and feels he is doing very well.

125:10 Alcoholics are not just sensitive, we are plain touchy. Our lack of humility often allows us to be hurt by the slightest reference to any of our failings. Admission of our shortcomings helps us to develop the humility we lack.

126:13Sometimes mother and children don't think so. 14Having been neglected and misused in the past, they think father owes them more than they are getting. 15They want him to make a fuss over them. 16They expect him to give them the nice times they used to have before he drank so much, and to show his contrition for what they suffered. 17But dad doesn't give freely of himself. 18Resentment grows. 19He becomes still less communicative. 20Sometimes he explodes over a trifle. 21The family is mystified. 22They criticize, pointing out how he is falling down on his spiritual program.

23This sort of thing can be avoided. 24Both father and the family are mistaken, though each side may have some justification. 25It is of little use to argue and only makes the impasse worse. 127:1The family must realize that dad, though marvelously improved, is still convalescing. 2They should be thankful he is sober and able to be of this world once more. 3Let them praise his progress. 4Let them remember that his drinking wrought all kinds of damage that may take long to repair. 5If they sense these things, they will not take so seriously his periods of crankiness, depression, or apathy, which will disappear when there is tolerance, love, and spiritual understanding.

6The head of the house ought to remember that he is mainly to blame for what befell his home. 7He can scarcely square the account in his lifetime. 8But he must see the danger of over-concentration on financial success. 9Although financial recovery is on the way for many of us, we found we could not place money first. 10For us, material well-being always followed spiritual progress; it never preceded.

126:22
Program:
xlii:2, xxiii:1,
xxix:8, 9:32,
19:13, 20:4-6,
29:1, 42:14,
45:8-9, 58:1-2,
59:7, 72:6,
73:1, 74:15,
85:12-16, 88:6,
94:2, 96:10,
99:16, 113:4,
117:1, 130:10,
147:1, 157:27

127:10
Straighten Out
Spiritually First:
64:18, 98:1,
98:7-8, 135:15

126:12 We make the decision to turn our will and our lives over to God and then what do we do? We immediately try to wrestle satisfaction out of life by exerting our willpower. Stopping drinking leaves a void in our lives that will quickly be filled by some other obsession if we do not first fill it with God. We may try to fill this void with work, sex or even A.A. meetings. We must strive for balance in our lives and be patient as God fills the void left by drinking once and for all.

127:10 We are humbled for a short time by our powerlessness and turn to God. Our pride and ego will reassert their tyrannical control over us, blocking us off from God, unless we place spiritual growth as our first priority. Being restored to sanity, finances take their proper place in our lives. We find that material well-being comes regardless of our financial situation when we place our trust in God.

127:11Since the home has suffered more than anything else, it is well that a man exert himself there. 12He is not likely to get far in any direction if he fails to show unselfishness and love under his own roof. 13We know there are difficult wives and families, but the man who is getting over alcoholism must remember he did much to make them so.

14As each member of a resentful family begins to see his shortcomings and admits them to the others, he lays a basis for helpful discussion. 15These family talks will be constructive if they can be carried on without heated argument, self-pity, self-justification, or resentful criticism. 16Little by little, mother and children will see they ask too much, and father will see he gives too little. 128:1Giving, rather than getting, will become the guiding principle.

2Assume on the other hand that father has, at the outset, a stirring spiritual experience. 3Over-night, as it were, he is a different man. 4He becomes a religious enthusiast. 5He is unable to focus on anything else. 6As soon as his sobriety begins to be taken as a matter of course, the family may look at their strange new dad with apprehension, then with irritation. 7There is talk about spiritual matters morning, noon and night. 8He may demand that the family find God in a hurry, or exhibit amazing indifference to them and say he is above worldly considerations. 9He may tell mother, who has been religious all her life, that she doesn't know what it's all about, and that she had better get his brand of spirituality while there is yet time.

10When father takes this tack, the family may react unfavorably. 11They may be jealous of a God who has stolen dad's affections. 12While grateful that he drinks no more, they

128:1 The switch in our focus from taking to giving comes from practicing spiritual principles. We have seen for ourselves that always trying to take leads to frustration, discontentment and unhappiness. We learn that by seeking ways to be useful to others, we allow the power of God to work through us. Giving brings us joy and reinforces our gratitude to God as well as building healthy self-esteem.

128:2-17 Having found God through the Twelve Steps, we may mistakenly believe we have discovered the only way to establish a relationship with God. Fearful that we are wrong, we may become dogmatic about our spiritual practices and judgmental of other people. As we become more certain of our own awakening, we become more tolerant of other people's spiritual practices and beliefs.

may not like the idea that God has accomplished the mira- ^{129:3} is rendered below

may not like the idea that God has accomplished the miracle where they failed. 128:13They often forget father was
beyond human aid. 14They may not see why their love and
devotion did not straighten him out. 15Dad is not so spiritual
after all, they say. 16If he means to right his past wrongs, why
all this concern for everyone in the world but his family?
17What about his talk that God will take care of them? 18They
suspect father is a bit balmy!

19He is not so unbalanced as they might think. 20Many of
us have experienced dad's elation. 21We have indulged in
spiritual intoxication. 22Like a gaunt prospector, belt drawn
in over the last ounce of food, our pick struck gold. 23Joy at
our release from a lifetime of frustration knew no bounds.
129:1Father feels he has struck something better than gold.
2For a time he may try to hug the new treasure to himself.
3He may not see at once that he has barely scratched a limitless lode which will pay dividends only if he mines it for the
rest of his life and insists on giving away the entire product.

4If the family cooperates, dad will soon see that he is suffering from a distortion of values. 5He will perceive that his
spiritual growth is lopsided, that for an average man like himself, a spiritual life which does not include his family obligations may not be so perfect after all. 6If the family will
appreciate that dad's current behavior is but a phase of his
development, all will be well. 7In the midst of an understanding and sympathetic family, these vagaries of dad's spiritual infancy will quickly disappear.

8The opposite may happen should the family condemn and
criticize. 9Dad may feel that for years his drinking has placed

129:3
Unselfish:
xxiv:14, xxv:10,
14:23, 20:1,
62:2-3, 67:4,
70:14, 85:16-
18, 93:15, 94:6,
97:3, 159:12-16

128:20 The terrific beating administered by
alcohol hopefully humbles us enough so that
we turn to God. The excitement we feel is like
being in love for the first time. We sometimes
act just as foolishly as a young lover. Soon,
however, the concerns of the material world
demand our attention. This may pull us off the
pink cloud of our newfound spirituality. As we
deal with life, we may begin to take credit for
our successes.

128:21-129:3 It is a divine paradox that by
giving we receive. We have been given the
keys to the greatest treasure of all. To keep
our faith alive, we must continuously work at
carrying the wonderful message of this program—that there is a solution to the seemingly hopeless state of mind and body that is
alcoholism. We must give it away to keep it.

him on the wrong side of every argument, but that now he has become a superior person, with God on his side. 129:10If the family persists in criticism, this fallacy may take a still greater hold on father. 11Instead of treating the family as he should, he may retreat further into himself and feel he has spiritual justification for so doing.

12Though the family does not fully agree with dad's spiritual activities, they should let him have his head. 13Even if he displays a certain amount of neglect and irresponsibility towards the family, it is well to let him go as far as he likes in helping other alcoholics. 14During those first days of convalescence, this will do more to insure his sobriety than anything else. 15Though some of his manifestations are alarming and disagreeable, we think dad will be on a firmer foundation than the man who is placing business or professional success ahead of spiritual development. 130:1He will be less likely to drink again, and anything is preferable to that.

2Those of us who have spent much time in the world of spiritual make-believe have eventually seen the childishness of it. 3This dream world has been replaced by a great sense of purpose, accompanied by a growing consciousness of the power of God in our lives. 4We have come to believe He would like us to keep our heads in the clouds with Him, but that our feet ought to be firmly planted on earth, nevertheless. 5That is where our fellow travelers are, and that is where our work must be done. 6These are the realities for us. 7We have found nothing incompatible between a powerful spiritual experience, and a life of sane and happy usefulness.

8One more suggestion: Whether the family has spiritual

129:13-130:1 Not only must we give it away to keep it, we must give it away to get it. By helping others, we gain meaning and purpose for our lives. We learn how to live this new life by working with those we meet on this path. By helping other's we set the stones in the foundation of our recovery (97:3).

130:3 Until we find a purpose that transcends

our self, we will be unhappy. Working with others is the most successful method of endowing our lives with purpose and meaning. As we persist, we witness for ourselves the power of God acting in our lives. Faith builds upon itself as we come to ever more fully rely upon God.

convictions or not, they may do well to examine the principles by which the alcoholic member is trying to live. 130:9They
can hardly fail to approve these simple principles, though
the head of the house still fails somewhat in practicing them.
10Nothing will help the man who is off on a spiritual tangent
so much as the wife who adopts a sane spiritual program,
making a better practical use of it.

11There will be other profound changes in the household.
12Liquor incapacitated father for so many years that mother
became head of the house. 13She met these responsibilities
gallantly. 14By force of circumstances, she was often obliged
to treat father as a sick or wayward child. 15Even when he
wanted to assert himself, he could not, for his drinking placed
him constantly in the wrong. 131:1Mother made all the plans
and gave the directions. 2When sober, father usually obeyed.
3Thus mother, through no fault of her own, became accustomed to wearing the family trousers. 4Father, coming suddenly to life again, often begins to assert himself. 5This means
trouble, unless the family watches for these tendencies in each
other and come to a friendly agreement about them.

6Drinking isolates most homes from the outside world.
7Father may have laid aside for years all normal activities—
clubs, civic duties, sports. 8When he renews interest in such
things, a feeling of jealousy may arise. 9The family may feel
they hold a mortgage on dad, so big that no equity should
be left for outsiders. 10Instead of developing new channels
of activity for themselves, mother and children may demand
that he stay home and make up the deficiency.

11At the very beginning, the couple ought to frankly face the
fact that each will have to yield here and there, if the family is
going to play an effective part in the new life. 12Father will
necessarily spend much time with other alcoholics, but this
activity should be balanced. 13New acquaintences who know

130:9
Simple:
xxvii:3, 9:32,
14:1, 25:6,
26:20, 28:7,
48:12, 47:11,
50:14-16, 52:8,
57:5, 58:2,
62:21, 88:6

130:10
Program:
xxix:8, xii:2,
xxiii:1, 9:32,
19:13, 20:4-6,
29:1, 42:14,
45:8-9, 58:1-2,
59:7, 72:6,
73:1, 74:15,
85:12-16, 88:6,
94:2, 96:10,
99:16, 113:4,
117:1, 126:22,
147:1, 157:27

130:10
Wife Adopts:
xiii:6, 153:14,
159:17

130:12-131:5 An alcoholic spouse seldom is able to be a full partner in a marriage, instead they become much like a child in their dependency upon the non-alcoholic spouse. As we recover we can begin to take our proper place in the marriage and in the family.

nothing of alcoholism might be made and thoughtful consideration given their needs. [131:14]The problems of the community might engage attention. [15]Though the family has no religious connections, they may wish to make contact with, or take membership in a religious body.

[16]Alcoholics who have derided religious people will be helped by such contacts. [17]Being possessed of a spiritual experience, the alcoholic will find he has much in common with these people, though he may differ with them on many matters. [132:1]If he does not argue about religion, he will make new friends, and is sure to find new avenues of usefulness and pleasure. [2]He and his family can be a bright spot in such congregations. [3]He may bring new hope and new courage to many a priest, minister, or rabbi, who gives his all to minister to our troubled world. [4]We intend the foregoing as a helpful suggestion only. [5]So far as we are concerned, there is nothing obligatory about it. [6]As non-denominational people, we cannot make up others minds for them. [7]Each individual should consult his own conscience.

[8]We have been speaking to you of serious, sometimes tragic things. [9]We have been dealing with alcohol in its worst aspect. [10]But we aren't a glum lot. [11]If newcomers could see no joy or fun in our existence, they wouldn't want it. [12]We absolutely insist on enjoying life. [13]We try not to indulge in cynicism over the state of the nations, nor do we carry the world's troubles on our shoulders. [14]When we see a man sinking into the mire that is alcoholism, we give him first aid and place what we have at his disposal. [15]For his sake, we do recount and almost relive the horrors of our past. [16]But those of us who have tried to shoulder the entire burden and trouble of others, find we are soon overcome by them.

[17]So we think cheerfulness and laughter make for usefulness. [18]Outsiders are sometimes shocked when we burst into

---

132:20 Having recovered from the seemingly hopeless state of mind and body that is alcoholism, we have found hope and so much more in God. Our past has been transformed into a tool to help others and by doing so has given our lives new meaning and direction.

merriment over a seemingly tragic experience out of the past. [132:19]But why shouldn't we laugh? [20]We have recovered, and have been given the power to help others. [21]Everybody knows that those in bad health, and those who seldom play, do not laugh much. [22]So let each family play together or separately, as much as their circumstances warrant. [133:1]We are sure God wants us to be happy, joyous, and free. [2]We cannot subscribe to the belief that this life is a vale of tears, though it once was just that for many of us. [3]But it is clear that we made our own misery. [4]God didn't do it. [5]Avoid then, the deliberate manufacture of misery, but if trouble comes, cheerfully capitalize it as an opportunity to demonstrate His omnipotence.

[6]Now about health: A body badly burned by alcohol does not often recover overnight, nor do twisted thinking and depression vanish in a twinkling. [7]We are convinced that a spiritual mode of living is a most powerful health restorative. [8]We, who have recovered from serious drinking, are miracles of mental health. [9]But we have seen remarkable transformations in our bodies. [10]Hardly one of our crowd now shows any mark of dissipation.

[11]But this does not mean that we disregard human health measures. [12]God has abundantly supplied this world with fine doctors, psychologists, and practitioners of various kinds. [13]Do not hesitate to take your health problems to such persons. [14]Most of them give freely of themselves, that their fellows may enjoy sound minds and bodies. [15]Try to remember that though God has wrought miracles among us, we should never belittle a good doctor or psychiatrist. [16]Their services are often indispensable in treating a newcomer and following his case afterward.

[17]One of the many doctors who had the opportunity of reading this book in manuscript form told us that the use of sweets was often helpful, of course depending upon a doctor's advice. [18]He

132:20
Recovered:
Title Page,
xiii:1, xxiii:10,
17:2-3, 20:3,
29:1, 44:14,
85:14, 90:14,
96:8, 113:6,
133:8, 146:12

132:20
Power to Help
Others:
18:10-11,
83:23, 84:1,
89:4-5, 89:17,
91:16-19,
123:2, 124:2-10

133:15
Miracle:
11:2, 25:1,
27:8, 50:11,
55:7, 57:4,
85:3, 124:14,
128:12

133:11-16
Human Health
Measures:
xxiv:14, xxv:12,
13:4, 30:16,
91:5, 142:18,
143:1-7, 59:15,
160:5

133:5 Few things make as strong a statement about the power of God as one who perseveres in faith through hard times. Much as making amends for our wrongs is a chance to demonstrate God working in our lives.

Hardship and crisis can be our finest hours. It is far easier to be Godly when things are going our way than when our faith is being tested by calamity.

thought all alcoholics should constantly have chocolate available for its quick energy value at times of fatigue. ¹³⁴:¹He added that occasionally in the night a vague craving arose which would be satisfied by candy. ²Many of us have noticed a tendency to eat sweets and have found this practice beneficial.

³A word about sex relations. ⁴Alcohol is so sexually stimulating to some men that they have over-indulged. ⁵Couples are occasionally dismayed to find that when drinking is stopped, the man tends to be impotent. ⁶Unless the reason is understood, there may be an emotional upset. ⁷Some of us had this experience, only to enjoy, in a few months, a finer intimacy than ever. ⁸There should be no hesitancy in consulting a doctor or psychologist if this condition persists. ⁹We do not know of any case where this difficulty lasted long.

¹⁰The alcoholic may find it hard to re-establish friendly relations with his children. ¹¹Their young minds were impressionable while he was drinking. ¹²Without saying so, they may cordially hate him for what he has done to them and to their mother. ¹³The children are sometimes dominated by a pathetic hardness and cynicism. ¹⁴They cannot seem to forgive and forget. ¹⁵This may hang on for months, long after their mother has accepted dad's new way of living and thinking.

¹⁶In time they will see that he is a new man and in their own way they will let him know it. ¹⁷When this happens, they can be invited to join in morning meditation, then they can take part in the daily discussion without rancor or bias. ¹⁸From that point on, progress will be rapid. ¹⁹Marvelous results often follow such a reunion.

¹³⁵:¹Whether the family goes on a spiritual basis or not, the alcoholic member has to if he would recover. ²The others must be convinced of his new status beyond a shadow of a doubt. ³Seeing is believing to most families who have lived with a drinker.

⁴Here is a case in point: One of our friends is a heavy smoker and coffee drinker. ⁵There was no doubt he over-

indulged. [6]Seeing this, and meaning to be helpful, his wife commenced to admonish him about it. [7]He admitted he was overdoing these things, but frankly said that he was not ready to stop. [135:8]His wife is one of those persons who really feel there is something rather sinful about these commodities, so she nagged, and her intolerance finally threw him into a fit of anger. [9]He got drunk.

[10]Of course our friend was wrong—dead wrong. [11]He had to painfully admit that and mend his spiritual fences. [12]Though he is now a most effective member of Alcoholics Anonymous, he still smokes and drinks coffee, but neither his wife nor anyone else stands in judgment. [13]She sees she was wrong to make a burning issue out of such a matter when his more serious ailments were being rapidly cured.

[14]We have three little mottoes which are apropos. [15]Here they are: "FIRST THINGS FIRST" "LIVE AND LET LIVE" and "EASY DOES IT."

135:15
First Things First:
64:18, 98:1, 98:7-8, 127:10

135:15
Live and Let Live:
19:18, 28:9, 67:2, 67:10, 70:21, 83:6, 84:23, 103:2, 118:9, 125:5

135:15
Easy Does It:
86:20-24

135:14 Our motto "First Things First" guides us when we are confused about priorities. We stop drinking first and then we address our other problems. We place spiritual progress first, then other aspects of our lives fall into their proper place. "Live and Let Live" reminds us that patience and tolerance of others is our code. "Easy Does It" suggests to us that recovery takes time and that we should patiently persist in practicing spiritual principles.

What should one do with an alcoholic employee? Before being presented with the explanation of alcoholism as an illness that affects both the body and the mind, we may have thought the alcoholic was foolish and irresponsible. Now we can see that while actually very sick the alcoholic who adopts this solution can recover.

Practical measures that can be taken to deal successfully with an alcoholic employee are given in the chapter "To Employers". A suggested approach is illustrated (141:19-142:17). The criteria for evaluating whether an employee should be retained is if the employer believes the employee is sincere in wanting to quit drinking (142:8). Medical treatment for detoxification is recommended for the alcoholic (142:19). Directions are given for supervisors and executives caught between acting in the best interests of the firm and covering for their subordinates and hoping that the situation will improve (147:6-148:6).

Alcoholism is so common that most companies have experience dealing with alcoholic employees. Retaining valuable employees is in the best interest of all concerned.

The Blueprint

The Alcoholic Employee · An executive shares his understanding of the problem.

Successfully Approaching the Employee · How to most effectively direct your employee toward help is discussed here.

Chapter Ten
TO EMPLOYERS

136:1One of our friends, whose gripping story you will read, has spent much of his life in the world of big business. 2He has hired and fired hundreds of men. 3He knows the alcoholic as the employer sees him. 4His present views ought to prove exceptionally useful to business men everywhere.

5But let him tell you:

6I was at one time assistant manager of a corporation department employing sixty-six hundred men. 7One day my secretary came in saying that Mr. B— insisted on speaking with me. 8I told her to say that I was not interested. 9I had warned him several times that he had but one more chance. 10Not long afterward he had called me from Hartford on two successive days, so drunk he could hardly speak. 11I told him he was through—finally and forever.

12My secretary returned to say that it was not Mr. B— on the phone; it was Mr. B—'s brother, and he wished to give me a message. 13I still expected a plea for clemency, but these words came through the receiver: 14"I just wanted to tell you Paul jumped from a hotel window in Hartford last Saturday. 15He left us a note saying you were the best boss he ever had, and that you were not to blame in any way."

16Another time, as I opened a letter which lay on my desk, a newspaper clipping fell out. 137:1It was the obituary of one of the best salesman I ever had. 2After two weeks of drinking, he had placed his toe on the trigger of a loaded shotgun—the barrel was in his mouth. 3I had discharged him for drinking six weeks before.

4Still another experience: A woman's voice came faintly over long distance from Virginia. 5She wanted to know if her husband's company insurance was still in force. 16Four days before he had hanged himself in his woodshed. 7I had been obliged to discharge him for drinking, though he was brilliant, alert, and one of the best organizers I have ever known.

137:8Here were three exceptional men lost to this world because I did not understand alcoholism as I do now.

9What irony—I became an alcoholic myself! 10And but for the intervention of an understanding person, I might have followed in their footsteps. 11My downfall cost the business community unknown thousands of dollars, for it takes real money to train a man for an executive position. 12This kind of waste goes on unabated. 13We think the business fabric is shot through with a situation which might be helped by better understanding all around.

14Nearly every modern employer feels a moral responsibility for the well-being of his help, and he tries to meet these responsibilities. 15That he has not always done so for the alcoholic is easily understood. 16To him the alcoholic has often seemed a fool of the first magnitude. 17Because of the employee's special ability, or of his own strong personal attachment to him, the employer has sometimes kept such a man at work long beyond a reasonable period. 18Some employers have tried every known remedy. 19In only a few instances have there been a lack of patience and tolerance. 138:1And we, who have imposed on the best of employers, can scarcely blame them if they have been short with us.

2Here, for instance, is a typical example: An officer of one of the largest banking institutions in America knows I no longer drink. 3One day he told me about an executive of the same bank, who, from his description, was undoubtedly alcoholic. 4This seemed to me like an opportunity to be helpful, so I spent two hours talking about alcoholism, the malady, and described the symptoms and results as well as I could. 5His comment was: "Very interesting. 6But I'm sure this man is done

---

138:2-139:6 It is ironic that we, who have thought ourselves so unique, follow a pattern that is so easily recognizable that our experiences can be considered typical. Typical for an alcoholic that is. Our behavior patterns are usually so abnormal that anyone familiar with alcoholism and its symptoms can not help but recognize the source of our problem. Likewise, we can see the symptoms of the problem displayed in the lives of other sufferers. Our own experiences allow us to be helpful when we are presented with an opportunity.

drinking. [138:7]He has just returned from a three-months leave of absence, has taken a cure, looks fine, and to clinch the matter, the board of directors told him this was his last chance."

[8]The only answer I could make was that if the man followed the usual pattern, he would go on a bigger bust than ever. [9]I felt this was inevitable and wondered if the bank were doing the man an injustice. [10]Why not bring him in contact with some of our alcoholic crowd? [11]He might have a chance. [12]I pointed out I had had nothing to drink whatever for three years, and this in the face of difficulties that would have made nine out of ten men drink their heads off. [13]Why not at least afford him an opportunity to hear my story? [14]"Oh no," said my friend, "this chap is either through with liquor, or he is minus a job. [15]If he has your will power and guts, he will make the grade."

[16]I wanted to throw up my hands in discouragement, for I saw that I had failed to help my banker friend understand. [17]He simply could not believe that his brother-executive suffered from a serious illness. [139:1]There was nothing to do but wait.

[2]Presently the man did slip and was fired. [3]Following his discharge, we contacted him. [4]Without much ado, he accepted the principles and procedure that had helped us. [5]He is undoubtedly on the road to recovery. [6]To me, this incident illustrates lack of understanding as to what really ails the alcoholic, and lack of knowledge as to what part employers might profitably take in salvaging their sick employees.

[7]If you desire to help it might be well to disregard your own drinking, or lack of it. [8]Whether you are a hard drinker, a

139:4 Accept: xxix:8, xxx:1, 12:18-19, 14:4, 42:19, 47:12, 60:14, 145:3

139:8 Hard: (Drinker) 20:23, 108:18-109:9, 149:14-16

139:8-14 Moderate: (Drinkers) 20:21, 34:9-15

206:6 Misunderstand: 18:5, 20:19, 42:5, 63:15, 74:5, 112:21, 140:14

139:4 The principles are guides to our behavior and ideas, outlooks and attitudes that we must adopt if we are to recover. The procedures are the simple program of action outlined in this book. One example is the Third Step. We adopt a new attitude about God during our Third Step, the attitude that from now on God will direct our lives. We follow the procedure of turning our will and our life over to God in a prayer. From then on we use our Third Step decision as a guiding principle in our lives. We adopt these new ideas and practice these principles so that God might give us mastery over our problems (155:15).

139:6 What really ails the alcoholic is not so much weakness of character or low morals but a mental and physical illness. We offer a treatment for this illness. This chapter explains how an employer may best present this program of recovery to an alcoholic employee.

moderate drinker, or a teetotaler, you may have some pretty strong opinions, perhaps prejudices. 139:9Those who drink moderately may be more annoyed with an alcoholic than a total abstainer would be. 10Drinking occasionally, and understanding your own reactions, it is possible for you to become quite sure of many things, which, so far as the alcoholic is concerned, are not always so. 11As a moderate drinker, you can take your liquor or leave it alone. 12Whenever you want to, you control your drinking. 13Of an evening, you can go on a mild bender, get up in the morning, shake your head, and go to business. 14To you, liquor is no real problem. 15You cannot see why it should be to anyone else, save the spineless and stupid.

16When dealing with an alcoholic, there may be a natural annoyance that a man could be so weak, stupid and irresponsible. 17Even when you understand the malady better, you may find this feeling rising.

18A look at the alcoholic in your organization is many times illuminating. 19Is he not usually brilliant, fast-thinking, imaginative and likeable? 20When sober, does he not work hard and have a knack of getting things done? 140:1If he had these qualities and did not drink would he be worth retaining? 2Should he have the same consideration as other ailing employees? 3Is he worth salvaging? 4If your decision is yes, whether the reason be humanitarian, or business, or both, then the following suggestions may be helpful.

5Can you discard the feeling that you are dealing only with habit, with stubborness, or a weak will? 6If this presents difficulty re-reading chapters two and three, where the alcoholic sickness is discussed at length might be worth while. 7You, as a business man, want to know the necessities before considering the result. 8If you concede that your employee is ill, can he be forgiven for what he has done in the past? 9Can his past absurdities be forgotten? 10Can it be appreciated that he has been a victim of crooked thinking, directly caused by the action of alcohol on his brain?

11I well remember the shock I received when a prominent

doctor in Chicago told me of cases where pressure of the spinal fluid actually ruptured the brain. 140:12No wonder an alcoholic is strangely irrational. 13Who wouldn't be, with such a fevered brain? 14Normal drinkers are not so affected, nor can they understand the abberations of the alcoholic.

15Your man has probably been trying to conceal a number of scrapes, perhaps pretty messy ones. 16They may be disgusting. 17You may be at a loss to understand how such a seemingly above-board chap could be so involved. 18But these scrapes can generally be charged, no matter how bad, to the abnormal action of alcohol on his mind. 19When drinking, or getting over a bout, an alcoholic, sometimes the model of honesty when normal, will do incredible things. 141:1Afterward, his revulsion will be terrible. 2Nearly always, these antics indicate nothing more than temporary conditions.

3This is not to say that all alcoholics are honest and upright when not drinking. 4Of course that isn't so, and such people often may impose on you. 5Seeing your attempt to understand and help, some men will try to take advantage of your kindness. 6If you are sure your man does not want to stop, he may as well be discharged: the sooner the better. 7You are not doing him a favor by keeping him on. 8Firing such an individual may prove a blessing to him. 9It may be just the jolt he needs. 10I know, in my own particular case, that nothing my company could have done would have stopped me, for so long as I was able to hold my position, I could not possibly realize how serious my situation was. 11Had they fired me first, and had they then taken steps to see that I was presented with the solution contained in this book, I might have returned to them six months later, a well man.

12But there are many men who want to stop, and with them you can go far. 13Your understanding treatment of their cases will pay dividends.

14Perhaps you have such a man in mind. 15He wants to quit drinking, and you want to help him, even if it be only a matter of good business. 16You now know more about alcoholism.

140:14
Misunderstand:
18:5, 20:19,
42:5, 63:15,
74:5, 112:21

141:7
No Favor:
95:12, 96:19-
97:1, 97:16,
98:6, 115:17

141:12
Want to Stop:
xiv:2, 5:18,
25:13, 28:7,
57:11, 58:9,
70:8, 73:5,
96:1-8, 114:7,
147:3, 159:5,
161:11, 120:5

141:12
Stop:
xiv:2, xxvii:6,
7:10-11, 19:3,
20:8-20, 20:21-
21:2, 22:17,
23:17, 25:2,
31:10-32:2,
32:16-33:2,
33:8-11, 33:15,
34:9-15, 39:2-4,
109:24, 110:5,
122:14

141:17You can see that he is mentally and physically sick. 18You are willing to overlook his past performances. 19Suppose an approach is made something like this:

State that you know about his drinking, that it must stop. 20You might say you appreciate his abilities, would like to keep him, but cannot, if he continues to drink. 142:1A firm attitude at this point has helped many of us.

2Next he can be assured that you do not intend to lecture, moralize, or condemn; that if this was done formerly, it was because of misunderstanding. 3If possible express a lack of hard feeling toward him. 4At this point, it might be well to explain alcoholism, the sickness. 5Say that you believe he is a gravely-ill person, with this qualification—being perhaps fatally ill, does he want to get well immediately? 6You ask because many alcoholics, being warped and drugged, do not want to quit. 7But does he? 8Will he take every necessary step, submit to anything to get well, to stop drinking forever?

9If he says yes, does he really mean it, or down inside does he think he is fooling you, and that after rest and treatment he will be able to get away with a few drinks now and then? 10We believe a man should be thoroughly probed on these points. 11Be satisfied he is not deceiving himself or you.

12Whether you mention this book is a matter for your discretion. 13If he temporizes and still thinks he can ever drink again, even beer, he might as well be discharged after the next bender which, if an alcoholic, he is almost certain to have. 14He should understand that emphatically. 15Either you are dealing with a man who can and will get well, or you are not. 16If not,

---

142:2-18 These techniques for approaching alcoholics are repeated several times throughout this book. They work. They are the result of considerable experience bringing alcoholics to the solution. All one can do is present the solution to an alcoholic employee. It is up to the alcoholic to put it to use.

142:13-17 To recover, an alcoholic must abandon all reservations. The idea that a period of abstinence will qualify the alcoholic to drink normally must be smashed. Switching types of drinks or moderating will have temporary benefits at best. Soon, the alcoholic will be in as much difficulty as ever. Hanging on to any of these threadbare ideas will almost certainly prevent the alcoholic from recovering.

why waste time with him? 142:17This may seem severe, but it is usually the best course.

18After satisfying yourself that your man wants to recover and that he will go to any extreme to do so, you may suggest a definite course of action. 19For most alcoholics who are drinking, or who are just getting over a spree, a certain amount of physical treatment is desirable, even imperative. 143:1The matter of physical treatment should, of course, be referred to your own doctor. 2Whatever the method, its object is to thoroughly clear mind and body of the effects of alcohol. 3In competent hands, this seldom takes long, nor is it very expensive. 4Your man will fare better if placed in such physical condition that he can think straight and no longer craves liquor. 5If you propose such a procedure to him, it may be necessary to advance the cost of treatment, but we believe it should be made plain that any expense will later be deducted from his pay. 6It is better for him to feel fully responsible.

7If your man accepts your offer, it should be pointed out that physical treatment is but a small part of the picture. 8Though you are providing him with the best possible medical attention, he should understand that he must undergo a change of heart. 9To get over drinking will require a transformation of thought and attitude. 10We all had to place recovery above everything, for without recovery we would have lost both home and business.

11Can you have every confidence in his ability to recover? 12While on the subject of confidence, can you adopt the attitude that so far as you are concerned, this will be a strictly personal matter, that his alcoholic derelictions, the treatment about to be undertaken, will never be discussed without his consent? 13It might be well to have a long chat with him on his return.

14To return to the subject matter of this book: It contains full suggestions by which the employee may solve his problem.

142:18
Suggest:
xxviii:18, 12:9,
19:13, 59:7,
86:3, 92:4,
94:13, 104:4,
143:14, 144:2,
144:10, 153:10,
164:5

142:18
Any Extreme:
14:4, 42:16,
58:9, 60:2,
76:15, 76:19,
79:5, 80:2,
90:13, 94:15,
112:18, 158:8

142:19
Physical
Treatment:
xxiv:14, xxv:12,
13:4, 30:16,
91:5, 143:1-7,
159:15, 160:5

143:9
Attitude:
25:8, 26:20,
27:12, 50:13,
55:16, 63:1,
72:2, 84:5,
86:1, 99:13,
150:2

143:8
Heart:
11:19, 55:11,
55:20

143:9
Transformation:
xxvii:2, xxvii:3,
xxvii:10, 12:1-2,
14:4-8, 25:8-10,
27:9-12, 44:3-4,
84:25, 158:10,
569:1

143:14
Precisely:
xiii:2, 20:4-6,
29:1, 45:4-9,
85:22, 86:3,
tt34:12

143:7 Stopping drinking is merely a change in behavior. Attending A.A. meetings is only the adoption of a new behavior. It is our experience that alcoholics must willingly seek a Power greater than themselves if they are to recover. It seems only God can bring about the necessary entire psychic change.

144:2
Suggest:
Xxviii:18, 12:9,
19:13, 59:7,
86:3, 92:4,
94:13, 104:4,
142:18, 143:14,
144:10, 153:10,
164:5

144:3
Last Word:
28:6, 95:19,
164:5

144:6
Remedy:
xxiv:1, xxix:1,
17:1-3, 31:1,
39:19, 112:23

144:8
Book:
xxix:8, xxx:1,
17:12-14, 20:4-
5, 90:19, 92:9,
94:19, 96:10,
111:23, 112:21,
113:18, 142:12,
153:10, 164:5

¹⁴⁴:¹To you, some of the ideas which it contains are novel. ²Perhaps you are not quite in sympathy with the approach we suggest. ³By no means do we offer it as the last word on this subject, but so far as we are concerned, it has worked with us. ⁴After all, are you not looking for results rather than methods? ⁵Whether your employee likes it or not, he will learn the grim truth about alcoholism. ⁶That won't hurt him a bit, though he does not go for this remedy.

⁷We suggest you draw the book to the attention of the doctor who is to attend your patient during treatment. ⁸If the book is read the moment the patient is able, while acutely depressed, realization of his condition may come to him.

⁹We hope the doctor will tell the patient the truth about his condition, whatever that happens to be. ¹⁰When the man is presented with this volume it is best that no one tell him he must abide by its suggestions. ¹¹The man must decide for himself.

¹²You are betting, of course, that your changed attitude and the contents of this book will turn the trick. ¹³In some cases it will, and in others it may not. ¹⁴But we think that if you persevere, the percentage of successes will gratify you. ¹⁵When our work spreads and our numbers increase, we hope your employees may be put in personal contact with some of us. ¹⁶Meanwhile, we are sure a great deal can be accomplished by the use of the book alone.

144:1-11 We may disagree with the program of recovery that the authors suggest, but we can not argue with A.A.'s 60+ years of success helping millions of alcoholics in over 140 countries around the world. This program works for those who want it. If the alcoholic would prefer to try another method to recover, by all means encourage it. A.A. will always be here to help if the alcoholic ever does desire it. This is a suggested program. It will only work if the alcoholic voluntarily decides to give it a try. Though many of us have voluntarily adopted this program only after involuntary attendance at A.A. meetings dictated by our spouse's, a judge's or an employer's order. Despite any amount of coercion in the end the decision to apply this solution rests solely with the alcoholic.

144:8 We are most receptive to this message when our ego has been deflated after yet another failure of will power to control our drinking. Soon the delusion that we can control our drinking will overpower our memory of repeated failure and we will repeat the insane experiment of that first drink. Recognition of the hopelessness of one's condition will produce a willingness to seek help from a Power greater than oneself.

145:3
Accepted:
xxix:8, xxx:1,
12:18-19, 14:4,
42:19, 47:12,
139:4, 60:14

145:3
Honesty:
(Rigorous)
3:4, 58:5, 73:5,
83:16, 146:18

145:9
Resentment:
13:11, 15:6,
18:5, 36:4,
62:1, 64:15-
67:19, 65:5,
66:7-13, 70:18,
84:19, 86:5,
117:19

¹⁴⁴:¹⁷On your employee's return, talk with him. ¹⁸Ask him if he thinks he has the answer. ¹⁹If he feels free to discuss his problems with you, if he knows you understand, and will not be upset by anything he wishes to say, he will probably be off to a fast start.

¹⁴⁵:¹In this connection, can you remain undisturbed if the man proceeds to tell you shocking things? ²He may, for example, reveal that he has padded his expense account, or that he has planned to take your best customers away from you. ³In fact, he may say almost anything if he has accepted our solution, which, as you know, demands rigorous honesty. ⁴Can you charge this off as you would a bad account and start fresh with him? ⁵If he owes you money you may wish to make terms.

⁶If he speaks of his home situation, you can undoubtedly make helpful suggestions. ⁷Can he talk frankly with you so long as he does not bear business tales or criticize his associates? ⁸With this kind of employee such an attitude will command undying loyalty.

⁹The greatest enemies of we alcoholics are resentment, jealousy, envy, frustration, and fear. ¹⁰Wherever men are gathered together in business, there will be rivalries, and, arising out of these, a certain amount of office politics. ¹¹Sometimes we alcoholics have an idea that people are trying to pull us down. ¹²Often this is not so at all. ¹³But sometimes our drinking will be used politically.

¹⁴One instance comes to mind in which a malicious individual was always making friendly little jokes about an alcoholic's drinking exploits. ¹⁵In this way he was slyly carrying tales. ¹⁶In another case, an alcoholic was sent to a hospital for treatment. ¹⁷Only a few knew of it at first, but

144:16 Following the clear-cut directions in this book has resulted in our experiencing a deep and effective spiritual awakening. We open ourselves to God's gift of recovery by practicing the principles outlined in this book. We have found it very helpful to work through these steps with someone who has already recovered. Directions for contacting A.A. can be found in the back of this book.

145:9 We have specific methods for dealing with these troubles. Our Third Step will do much to alleviate feelings of frustration. The Fourth Step teaches us how to deal successfully with resentment and fear. We find relief from jealousy and envy in steps Seven and Nine.

within a short time, it was bill-boarded throughout the entire company. ¹⁴⁵:¹⁸Naturally this sort of thing decreased the man's chance of recovery. ¹⁹The employer can many times protect the victim from this kind of talk. ¹⁴⁶:¹The employer cannot play favorites, but he can always defend a man from needless provocation and unfair criticism.

²As a class, alcoholics are energetic people. ³They work hard and they play hard. ⁴Your man should be on his mettle to make good. ⁵Being somewhat weakened, and faced with physical and mental readjustment to a life which knows no alcohol, he may overdo. ⁶You may have to curb his desire to work sixteen hours a day. ⁷You may need to encourage him to play once in a while. ⁸He may wish to do a lot for other alcoholics and something of the sort may come up during business hours. ⁹A reasonable amount of latitude will be helpful. ¹⁰This work is necessary to maintain his sobriety.

¹¹After your man has gone along without drinking a few months, you may be able to make use of his services with other employees who are giving you the alcoholic runaround—provided, of course, they are willing to have a third party in the picture. ¹²An alcoholic who has recovered, but holds a relatively unimportant job, can talk to a man with a better position. ¹³Being on radically different basis of life, he will never take advantage of the situation.

¹⁴Your man may be trusted. ¹⁵Long experience with alcoholic excuses naturally arouses suspicion. ¹⁶When his wife next calls saying he is sick, you might jump to the conclusion he is drunk. ¹⁷If he is, and is still trying to recover, he will tell you about it, even if it means the loss of his job. ¹⁸For he knows he must be honest if he would live at all. ¹⁹He will appreciate knowing you are not bothering your head about him at all, that you are not suspicious, nor are you trying to run his life so he will be shielded from temptation to drink. ¹⁴⁷:¹If he is conscientiously following the Program of Recovery he can go anywhere your business may call him.

²In case he does stumble, even once, you will have to decide

whether to let him go. 147:3If you are sure he doesn't mean business, there is no doubt you should discharge him. 4If, on the contrary, you are sure he is doing his utmost, you may wish to give him another chance. 5But you should feel under no obligation to keep him on, for your obligation has been well discharged already.

6There is another thing you might wish to do. 7If your organization is a large one, your junior executives might be provided with this book. 8You might let them know you have no quarrel with the alcoholics of your organization. 9These juniors are often in a difficult position. 10Men under them are frequently their friends. 11So, for one reason or another, they cover these men, hoping matters will take a turn for the better. 12They often jeopardize their own positions by trying to help serious drinkers who should have been fired long ago, or else given an opportunity to get well.

13After reading this book, a junior executive can go to such a man and say approximately this, "Look here, Ed. 14Do you want to stop drinking or not? 15You put me on the spot every time you get drunk. 16It isn't fair to me or the firm. 17I have been learning something about alcoholism. 18If you are an alcoholic, you are a mighty sick man. 19You act like one. 20The firm wants to help you get over it, and if you are interested, there is a way out. 21If you do, your past will be forgotten and the fact that you went away for treatment will not be mentioned. 148:1But if you cannot, or will not stop drinking, I think you ought to resign."

2Your junior executive may not agree with the contents of our book. 3He need not, and often should not, show it to his alcoholic prospect. 4But at least he will understand the problem and will no longer be misted by ordinary promises. 5He will be able to take a position with such a man which is eminently fair and square. 6He will have no further reason for covering up an alcoholic employee.

7It boils right down to this: No man should be fired just because he is alcoholic. 8If he wants to stop, he should be

147:2
Stumble:
26:7, 30:12,
31:2, 35:1,
120:6, 125:2

147:3
Honest:
(Means
Business)
xiv:2, 5:18,
25:13, 28:7,
57:11, 58:9,
70:8, 73:5,
96:1-8, 114:7,
159:5, 161:11,
120:5

215

149:14
Alcoholism:
xiii:1,18:3-5,
21:3-4, 73:6-17

149:14
Description: (Of
alcoholism)
xiii:1, xxviii:3-
18, 18:3-5,
20:8-20, 21:5-
22:7, 24:1,
30:10, 37:13-
38:14, 44:3,
52:6, 56:5,
109:10-22

149:14
Sick:
xiii:5, 7:9, 18:1-
5, 30:13, 44:4,
64:15-18, 92:1,
92:13-14,
100:10, 101:6,
107:7-8,
118:19, 141:17,
142:3, 164:8

149:14-16
Whoopee:
20:23, 108:18-
109:9, 139:8

afforded a real chance. [148:9]If he cannot, or does not want to stop, he should be discharged. [10]The exceptions are few.

[11]We think this method of approach will accomplish several things. [12]It will permit the rehabilitation of good men. [13]At the same time you will feel no reluctance to rid yourself of those who cannot, or will not, stop. [14]Alcoholism may be causing your organization considerable damage in its waste of time, men and reputation. [15]We hope our suggestions will help you plug up this sometimes serious leak. [16]We think we are sensible when we urge that you stop this waste and give your worth-while man a chance.

[17]The other day an approach was made to the vice-president of a large industrial concern. [18]He remarked: "I'm mighty glad you fellows got over your drinking. [19]But the policy of this company is not to interfere with the habits of our employees. [20]If a man drinks so much that his job suffers, we fire him. [21]I don't see how you can be of any help to us, for as you see, we don't have any alcoholic problem." [149:1]This same company spends millions for research every year. [2]Their cost of production is figured to a fine decimal point. [3]They have recreational facilities. [4]There is company insurance. [5]There is a real interest, both humanitarian and business, in the well-being of employees. [6]But alcoholism—well, they just don't believe they have it.

[7]Perhaps this is a typical attitude. [8]We, who have collectively seen a great deal of business life, at least from the alcoholic angle, had to smile at this gentleman's sincere opinion. [9]He might be shocked if he knew how much alcoholism is costing his organization a year. [10]That company may harbor many actual or potential alcoholics. [11]We believe that managers of large enterprises often have little idea how prevalent this problem is. [12]Even if you feel your organization has no alcoholic problem, it might pay to take another look down the line. [13]You may make some interesting discoveries.

[14]Of course, this chapter refers to alcoholics, sick people, deranged men. [15]What our friend, the vice-president, had in

mind, was the habitual or whoopee drinker. [149:16]As to them, his policy is undoubtedly sound, but he did not distinguish between such people and the alcoholic.

[17]It is not to be expected that an alcoholic employee will receive a disproportionate amount of time and attention. [18]He should not be made a favorite. [19]The right kind of man, the kind who recovers, will not want this sort of thing. [20]He will not impose. [21]Far from it. [22]He will work like the devil, and thank you to his dying day.

[23]Today, I own a little company. [24]There are two alcoholic employees, who produce as much as five normal salesmen. [150:1]But why not? [2]They have a new attitude, and they have been saved from a living death. [3]I have enjoyed every moment spent in getting them straightened out. *

150:2
Attitude:
25:8, 26:20,
27:12, 50:13,
55:16, 63:1,
72:2, 84:5,
86:1, 99:13,
143:9

* See appendix—The Alcoholic Foundation. We may be able to carry on a limited correspondence.

Historical Note:
149:23 The author of this chapter—Hank P. owned the Honest Dealers Company, an automobile polish distributorship.
149:24 The two employees were Bill W., the primary contributor to this book, and Jimmy B., who wrote the story "The Vicious Cycle" included in the second and third editions of this book. Jimmy B. was the force behind including the provision "as we understand him" when referencing God (See page 248 third edition).

What are we to do? If we are to leave our old lives of drinking what then? Where are we to find fellowship with others of like mind? What substitute do these people have to offer for our life of drinking?

The vision offered us is one of usefulness and purpose for our lives. We have seen how our common troubles allow us to be useful to others like us. We can be useful in a way that no one else can. Here we are shown how the authors built a fellowship. A.A. is a society of recovered alcoholics able to work together in brotherly and harmonious action. A.A. is a fellowship of people who travel a common path as they apply this solution to their problems and help others to find this path that really leads somewhere.

This chapter, like many of the earlier chapters, opens with a portrayal of the alcoholic drinker so accurate that we are able to see our illness parallel that of the people who have gone before us. They have shown us the path they took to recovery. Should we wish to adopt their way of life, we are assured that we will enjoy the same results as the authors. The results are nothing short of miraculous, when we travel from the despair of alcoholism to the joy of a useful and satisfying life.

We have been shown a way of life that affords us access to an Unlimited Source of Power. The foundation stone of this way of life is helping others to discover this real solution to their problems. By working with others we will find fellowship in Alcoholics Anonymous.

The Blueprint

More than a Substitute for Drinking	Awakening spiritually as the result of these steps, we find meaning and purpose in a way of life vastly superior to any we had ever dreamed possible.
Beginnings of the Fellowship	The first meeting of Bill W. and Dr. Bob, co-founders of Alcoholics Anonymous, is described followed by the stories of how the third and fourth members were approached and accepted the program outlined in this book.
Growth of the Fellowship	Alcoholics who had recovered spread this message. Today the Alcoholics Anonymous program is practiced around the world, in many different languages, by millions of people.

Chapter Eleven
A VISION FOR YOU

^{151:1}For most normal folks, drinking means conviviality, companionship, and colorful imagination. ²It means release from care, boredom, and worry. ³It is joyous intimacy with friends, and a feeling that life is good. ⁴But not so with us in those last days of heavy drinking. ⁵The old pleasures were gone. ⁶They were but memories. ⁷Never could we recapture the great moments of the past. ⁸There was an insistent yearning to enjoy life as we once did and a heartbreaking obsession that some new miracle of control would enable us to do it. ⁹There was always one more attempt—and one more failure.

¹⁰The less people tolerated us, the more we withdrew from society, from life itself. ¹¹As we became subjects of King Alcohol, shivering denizens of his mad realm, the chilling vapor that is loneliness settled down. ¹²It thickened, ever becoming blacker. ¹³Some of us sought out sordid places, hoping to find understanding companionship and approval. ¹⁴Momentarily we did—then would come oblivion and the awful awakening to face the hideous Four Horsemen— Terror, Bewilderment, Frustration, Despair. ¹⁵Unhappy drinkers who read this page will understand!

¹⁶Now and then a serious drinker, being dry at the moment says, "I don't miss it at all. ¹⁷Feel better. ¹⁸Work better. ¹⁹Having a better time." ²⁰As ex-alcoholics, we smile at such a sally. ^{152:1}We know our friend is like a boy whistling in the

---

151:7
Recapture:
xxviii:17, 9:7,
30:11

151:8
Obsession:
23:13, 30:4,
155:9

151:8
True:
xxvi:9, 5:7,
30:4, 40:12,
92:12, 155:13

151:9
Repeated:
(Over and
Over)
xxvii:2, 5:5,
6:22, 23:2,
26:8, 34:2,
43:6, 48:7

151:11
Shivered:
12:12

151:14
Terror:
6:7-9, 6-23,
13:4

151:20
Ex-alcoholic:
xxiv:12

151:1 We are not anti-alcohol, anti-drinking or anti-anything. People who are able to control their drinking have no need to abstain. We do not concern ourselves whatsoever with anyone else's decision to drink or not.

151:4-9 One old timer said that "Once we are pickled, we can never be cucumbers again." The truth of this statement has been borne out in the vast experience of A.A. members.

Once we lose our ability to control our drinking, it is gone forever.

151:14 We experience terror that we are out of control, bewilderment that despite our firm resolve we have gotten drunk again, frustration that our willpower can not bring about the life that we desire, and despair that we will ever rise out of the mire into which we are sinking.

dark to keep up his spirits. [152:2]He fools himself. [3]Inwardly he would give anything to take half a dozen drinks and get away with them. [4]He will presently try the old game again, for he isn't happy about his sobriety. [5]He cannot picture life without alcohol. [6]Some day he will be unable to imagine life either with alcohol or without it. [7]Then he will know loneliness such as few do. [8]He will be at the jumping-off place. [9]He will wish for the end.

[10]We have shown how we got out from under. [11]You say: "Yes, I'm willing. [12]But am I to be consigned to a life where I shall be stupid, boring and glum, like some righteous people I see? [13]I know I must get along without liquor, but how can I? [14]Have you a sufficient substitute?"

[15]Yes, there is a substitute, and it is vastly more than that. [16]It is a Fellowship in Alcoholics Anonymous. [17]There you will find release from care, boredom, and worry. [18]Your imagination will be fired. [19]Life will mean something at last. [20]The most satisfactory years of your existence lie ahead. [21]Thus we find The Fellowship, and so will you.

[22]"How is that to come about?" you ask. [23]"Where am I to find these people?"

[24]You are going to meet these new friends in your own community. [25]Near you alcoholics are dying helplessly like people in a sinking ship. [26]If you live in a large place, there are hundreds. [27]High and low, rich and poor, these are future Fellows of Alcoholics Anonymous. [28]Among them you will make lifelong friends. [29]You will be bound to them with new and wonderful ties, for you will escape disaster together and you will commence shoulder to shoulder your common

---

152:12 What could be more stupid than to kill oneself through excess and addiction? What could be more boring that to be blocked off from God, from our fellows, and from life itself by our attitudes, outlook and behaviors? What could be more glum than the destruction of all things worthwhile in life brought about by alcoholism? We very quickly find our new way of life vastly superior to our old life.

152:15-153:2 Learning to give of ourselves fills the hole in our spirit caused by our former slothful indifference to our responsibilities and to the welfare of others. The incalculable benefits of self-sacrifice replace the baleful results of selfishness. To awaken spiritually and find fellowship with others united in a great purpose gives us a satisfaction and sense of fulfillment we never dreamed possible.

journey. ¹⁵³:¹Then you will know what it means to give of your-self, that others may survive and rediscover life. ²You will learn the full meaning of "Love thy neighbor as thyself."

³It may seem incredible that these men are to become happy, respected, and useful once more. ⁴How can they rise out of such misery, bad repute and hopelessness? ⁵The prac-tical answer is that since these things have happened among us, they can happen with you. ⁶Should you wish them above all else, and be willing to make use of our experience, we are sure they will come. ⁷The age of miracles is still with us. ⁸Our own recovery proves that!

⁹Our hope is that when this chip of a book is launched on the world tide of alcoholism, defeated drinkers will seize upon it, to follow its suggestions. ¹⁰Many, we are sure, will rise to their feet and march on. ¹¹They will approach still other sick ones and Fellowships of Alcoholics Anonymous may spring up in each city and hamlet, havens for those who must find a way out.

¹²In the chapter "Working With Others" you gathered an idea of how we approach and aid others to health. ¹³Suppose now that through you several families have adopted this way of life. ¹⁴You will want to know more of how to proceed from that point. ¹⁵Perhaps the best way of treating you to a glimpse of your future will be to describe the growth of the Fellowship among us. ¹⁶Here is a brief account:

¹⁷Nearly four years ago, one of our number made a journey to a certain western city. ¹⁸From the business standpoint, his trip came off badly. ¹⁹Had he been successful in his enterprise,

153:3
Useful:
8:19, 13:18,
19:18, 20:1,
42:21, 49:13,
52:6, 76:7,
77:4, 84:2,
86:12, 89:17,
102:16, 130:7,
132:1, 132:17,
158:17

153:9
Book:
xxix:8, xxx:1,
17:12-14, 20:4-
5, 90:19, 92:9,
94:19, 96:10,
111:23, 112:21,
113:18, 142:12,
144:8, 164:5

153:9
Defeated:
28:2

153:9
Suggest:
xxviii:18, 12:9,
19:13, 59:7,
86:3, 92:4,
94:13, 104:4,
142:18, 143:14,
144:2, 144:10,
164:5

153:13
Way of life:
(Family)
xiii:6, 130:10,
159:17

153:15
Fellowship:
xiii:10, xxiii:9,
15:11, 15:19,
17:7, 44:8,
45:13, 89:7-10,
90:15, 94:18,
95:10, 96:7,
152:16, 152:21,
159:7, 160:1,
161:8, 162:10,
164:4, 164:17

Historical Note:
153:17 Bill W. traveled in 1935 to Akron, Ohio.

153:6 We must place the attainment of spir-itual progress above our desire for the satis-faction of our self-will. We hold most tightly to our will. To make progress we "let go and let God." We learn to do this by following the authors' example. We do what they did and we get the same results. We receive access to a Miracle powerful enough to transform our lives.

153:9-15 We are unwilling to reach for help until we realize we are defeated. The authors help us to see the truth by explaining the physical craving and mental obsession that makes the alcoholic seem beyond hope. We learn to approach others in the same way. We may study how to build a fellowship in the same manner. We follow the example of those who have gone before.

he would have been set on his feet financially, which, at the time, seemed vitally important. ¹⁵⁴:¹But his venture wound up in a law suit and bogged down completely. ²The proceding was shot through with much hard feeling and controversy.

³Bitterly discouraged, he found himself in a strange place, discredited and almost broke. ⁴Still physically weak, and sober but a few months, he saw that his predicament was dangerous. ⁵He wanted so much to talk with someone, but whom?

⁶One dismal afternoon he paced a hotel lobby wondering how his bill was to be paid. ⁷At one end of the room stood a glass covered directory of local churches. ⁸Down the lobby a door opened into an attractive bar. ⁹He could see the gay crowd inside. ¹⁰In there he would find companionship and release. ¹¹Unless he took some drinks, he might not have the courage to scrape an acquaintance, and would have a lonely week-end.

¹²Of course, he couldn't drink, but why not sit hopefully at a table, a bottle of ginger ale before him? ¹³Then after all, had he not been sober six months now? ¹⁴Perhaps he could handle, say, three drinks—no more! ¹⁵Fear gripped him. ¹⁶He was on thin ice. ¹⁷Again it was the old, insidious insanity—that first drink. ¹⁸With a shiver, he turned away and walked down the lobby to the church directory. ¹⁹Music and gay chatter still floated to him from the bar.

²⁰But what about his responsibilities—his family and the men who would die because they would not know how to get well, ah-yes, those other alcoholics? ²¹There must be many such in this town. ²²He would phone a clergyman. ²³His sanity returned, and he thanked God. ¹⁵⁵:¹Selecting a church at random from the directory, he stepped into a booth and lifted the receiver.

²His call to the clergyman led him presently to a certain resident of the town, who, though formerly able and respected, was then nearing the nadir of alcoholic despair. ³It was the usual situation: home in jeopardy, wife ill, children distracted,

Definitions:
154:2 Nadir: the lowest point.

Historical Note:
154:6 Bill stayed at the Mayflower Hotel in Akron, Ohio.
154:22 The clergyman was Walter F. Tunks, Rector of St. Paul's Episcopal Church in Akron, Ohio.
155:2 Dr. Bob, co-founder of A.A. is the person referred to.

bills in arrears, and standing damaged. [155:4]He had a desperate desire to stop, but saw no way out; for he had earnestly tried many avenues of escape. [5]Painfully aware of being somehow abnormal, the man did not fully realize what it means to be alcoholic.

[6]When our friend related his experience, the man agreed that no amount of willpower he might muster could stop his drinking for long. [7]A spiritual experience, he conceded, was absolutely necessary, but the price seemed high upon the basis suggested. [8]He told how he lived in constant worry about those who might find out about his alcoholism. [9]He had, of course, the familiar alcoholic obsession that few knew of his drinking. [10]Why, he argued, should he lose the remainder of his business, only to bring still more suffering to his family, by foolishly admitting his plight to people from whom he made his livelihood? [11]He would do anything, he said, but that.

[12]Being intrigued, however, he invited our friend to his home. [13]Some time later, and just as he thought he was getting control of his liquor situation, he went on a roaring bender. [14]For him, this was the spree that ended all sprees. [15]He saw that he would have to face his problems squarely, that God might give him mastery.

[156:1]One morning he took the bull by the horns and set out to tell those he feared what his trouble had been. [2]He found himself surprisingly well received, and learned that many knew of his drinking. [3]Stepping into his car, he made the rounds of people he had hurt. [4]He trembled as he went about, for this might mean ruin, particularly to a person in his line of business.

[5]At midnight he came home exhausted, but very happy. [6]He has not had a drink since. [7]As we shall see, he now means a

Historical Note:
156:6 Dr. Bob sobered up on June 10, 1935. He was 55 years old. This day is counted as the birthdate of A.A.

155:3-5 The effects of alcoholism are plain to see. Circumstances may differ but the destruction of all things worthwhile in life, bewilderment and despair of those involved are clear signs of alcoholism.

155:11 A reservation, in this instance pride disguised as prudence, hindered Dr. Bob's recovery. Until our reservations are abandoned and we become willing to do what is necessary, we will not recover.

Margin references:
155:9 Obsession: 23:13, 30:4, 151:8
155:11 Anything, But That: 13:6, 14:4, 32:11, 33:8, 50:16, 63:16
155:13 Getting Control: xxvi:9, 5:7, 30:4, 40:12, 92:12, 151:8
155:13 Time: xxviii:11, 30:12, 32:5-33:4, 34:5-6, 109:19, 154:13
155:13 Delusion: 30:9, 32:13, 40:11, 61:17, 62:4, 154:13
155:15 Mastery: 66:22, 88:6
156:6 It Works: xxix:14, xxx:2, 13:9 26:18, 56:21, 88:4, 158:16

great deal to his community, and the major liabilities of thirty years of hard drinking have been repaired in four.

156:8But life was not easy for the two friends. 9Plenty of difficulties presented themselves. 10Both saw that they must keep spiritually active. 11One day they called up the head nurse of a local hospital. 12They explained their need and inquired if she had a first class alcoholic prospect.

13She replied, "Yes, we've got a corker. 14He's just beaten up a couple of nurses. 15Goes off his head completely when drinking. 16But he's a grand chap when sober, though he's been in here six times in the last four months. 17Understand he was once a well-known lawyer in town, but just now we've got him strapped down tight."

18Here was a prospect all right, but, by the description, none too promising. 19The use of spiritual principles in such cases was not so well understood as it is now. 157:1But one of the friends said, "Put him in a private room. 2We'll be down."

3Two days later, a future Fellow of Alcoholics Anonymous stared glassily at the strangers beside his bed. 4"Who are you fellows, and why this private room? 5I was always in a ward before."

6Said one of the visitors, "We're giving you a treatment for alcoholism."

7Hopelessness was written large on the man's face as he replied: "Oh, but that's no use. 8Nothing would fix me. 9I'm a goner. 10The last three times, I got drunk on the way home from here. 11I'm afraid to go out the door. 12I can't understand it."

Historical Note:
156:11 The Head Nurse was Mrs. Hall at Akron City Hospital.
156:18 The prospect was Bill D. author of "Alcoholics Anonymous Number Three" appearing in the second and third editions of this book.

157:7-158:28 This man had taken his first step (157:8-9). The techniques Bill and Bob used (157:13 & 157:18-19) to help the man see his drinking patterns and diagnose his alcoholic condition were successful (157:13-20). After the prospect knew what the problem was, he was presented with the solution (157:28). Being willing to believe in a Power greater than himself the man was at Step Three (158:3-6). Taking the Third Step the man began to awaken spiritually (158:8-10). The result was that he recovered from alcoholism (158:11).

157:13For an hour, the two friends told him about their drinking experiences. 14Over and over, he would say: "That's me. 15That's me. 16I drink like that."

17The man in the bed was told of the acute poisoning from which he suffered, how it deteriorates the body of an alcoholic and warps his mind. 18There was much talk about the mental state preceding the first drink.

19"Yes, that's me," said the sick man, "the very image. 20You fellows know your stuff all right, but I don't see what good it'll do. 21You fellows are somebody. 22I was once, but I'm a nobody now. 23From what you tell me, I know more than ever I can't stop." 24At this both the visitors burst into a laugh. 25Said the future Fellow Anonymous: "Damn little to laugh about that I can see."

26The two friends spoke of their spiritual experience and told him about the course of action they carried out

27He interrupted: "I used to be strong for the church, but that won't fix it. 158:1I've prayed to God on hangover mornings and sworn that I'd never touch another drop but by nine o'clock I'd be boiled as an owl."

2Next day found the prospect more receptive. 3He had been thinking it over. 4"Maybe you're right," he said. 5"God ought to be able to do anything." 6Then he added, "He sure didn't do much for me when I was trying to fight this booze racket alone."

7On the third day the lawyer gave his life to the care and direction of his Creator, and said he was perfectly willing to do anything necessary. 8His wife came, scarcely daring to be hopeful, but she thought she saw something different about her husband already. 9He had begun to have a spiritual experience.

10That afternoon he put on his clothes and walked from the hospital a free man. 11He entered a political campaign, making

157:18
Insanity of the first drink:
8:14, 22:9, 23:2, 23:9, 24:6, 35:2, 37:6, 40:10, 41:20, 43:14-16,154:17

157:18
No Defense:
xxvii:13-xxviii:1, 24:1-6, 22:17, 24:7-8, 33:10, 35:2, 37:7, 40:12, 41:21, 42:4, 43:14-16, 92:3-8

157:24-25
Laughter:
16:7-8, 132:10-20, 160:8, 161:12

157:26
Course of Action:
59:7, 72:6, 73:1, 74:15, 85:12-16, 88:6, 94:2, 96:10, 99:16, 113:4, 117:1, 126:22, 130:10, 147:1

157:26
Tell:
20:6

158:7
Do Anything:
14:4, 42:16, 58:9, 60:2, 76:15, 76:19, 79:5, 80:2, 90:13, 94:15, 112:18, 142:8, 142:18

158:7
Step Three:
13:5, 59:10, 60:14, 63:9-12

158:9
Spiritual Experience:
xxvii:2, xxvii:3, xxvii:10, 12:1-2, 14:4-8, 25:8-10, 27:9-12, 44:3-4, 84:25, 143:9

speeches, frequenting men's gathering places of all sorts, often staying up all night. [158:12]He lost the race by only a narrow margin. [13]But he had found God and in finding God had found himself.

[14]That was in June, 1935. [15]He never drank again. [16]He too, has become a respected and useful member of his community. [17]He has helped other men recover, and is a power in the church from which he was long absent.

[18]So, you see, there were three alcoholics in that town, who now felt they had to give to others what they had found, or be sunk. [19]After several failures to find others, a fourth turned up. [20]He came through an acquaintance who had heard the good news. [21]He proved to be a devil may-care young fellow whose parents could not make out whether he wanted to stop drinking or not. [22]They were deeply religious people, much shocked by their son's refusal to have anything to do with the church. [159:1]He suffered horribly from his sprees, but it seemed as if nothing could be done for him. [2]He consented, however, to go to the hospital, where he occupied the very room recently vacated by the lawyer.

[3]He had three visitors. [4]After a bit, he said: "The way you fellows put this spiritual stuff makes sense. [5]I'm ready to do business. [6]I guess the old folks were right after all." [7]So one more was added to the Fellowship.

[8]All this time our friend of the hotel lobby incident remained in that town. [9]He was there three months. [10]He now returned home, leaving behind his first acquaintance, the lawyer, and the devil-may-care chap. [11]These men had found

Historical Notes:
158:15 Bill D. sobered up on June 26, 1935.
158: 21 A.A. number 4 was Ernie G. who authored "The Seven Month Slip" appearing in the first edition of this book.

158:13 We fear that we may lose our identity by turning our will and our lives over to the care of God. The truth is that by so doing we are freed from the control of alcohol. We are also freed from the control of all the failed ideas, attitudes, fears and underlying motivations that prevent us from being who we really are and who we really want to be. The removal of these influences that warp our characters allows us to finally find our true selves.

158:22-159:7 No one can see the inner motivations of another person. We must not be too quick to judge who will accept our message and who will not. We do our best and God will do the rest.

something brand new in life. ¹⁵⁹ˑ¹²Though they knew they must help other alcoholics if they would remain sober, that motive became secondary. ¹³It was transcended by the happiness they found in giving themselves for others. ¹⁴They shared their homes, their slender resources, and gladly devoted their spare hours to fellow-sufferers. ¹⁵They were willing, by day or night, to place a new man in the hospital and visit him afterward. ¹⁶They grew in numbers. ¹⁷They experienced a few distressing failures, but in those cases, they made an effort to bring the man's family into a spiritual way of living, thus relieving much worry and suffering.

¹⁸A year and six months later these three had succeeded with seven more. ¹⁹Seeing much of each other, scarce an evening passed that someone's home did not shelter a little gathering of men and women, happy in their release, and constantly thinking how they might present their discovery to some newcomer. ²⁰In addition to these casual get-togethers, it became customary to set apart one night a week for a meeting to be attended by anyone or everyone interested in a spiritual way of life. ¹⁶⁰ˑ¹Aside from fellowship and sociability, the prime object was to provide a time and place where new people might bring their problems.

²Outsiders became interested. ³One man and his wife placed their large home at the disposal of this strangely assorted crowd. ⁴This couple has since become so fascinated that they have dedicated their home to the work. ⁵Many a

159:12-13
Selfish
Program?:
13:18, 14:23,
20:1, 62:2,
70:14, 85:16-
18, 93:15, 94:6,
97:3, 102:4-5,
120:1, 164:16

159:12-16
Unselfish:
xxiv:14, xxv:10,
14:23, 20:1,
62:2-3, 67:4,
70:14, 85:16-
18, 93:15, 94:6,
97:3, 129:3

159:15
Hospitalization:
xxiv:14, xxv:12,
13:4, 30:16,
91:5, 142:18,
143:1-7, 160:5

159:17
Way of life:
(Family)
xiii:6, 130:10,
153:14

159:19
Constant:
20:1, 85:16-18,
85:28, 87:20,
164:7

159:19-161:8
Meetings:
15:19

160:1
Fellowship:
xiii:10, xxiii:9,
15:11, 15:19,
17:7, 44:8,
45:13, 89:7-10,
90:15, 94:18,
95:10, 96:7,
152:16, 152:21,
153:16, 159:7

Historical Note:
160:3 T. Henry and Clarace Williams were members of the Oxford Group.

159:12-13 A.A. is not a program based on selfishness. Selfishness is the root of our problems. It is by the abandonment of selfishness and the adoption of self-sacrifice that we are able to use the power of God. This is not a theory, we have to live it, and by doing so we acquire the undeniable proof of our own experience.

159:15 Some mistaken people may disparage the efforts of those who take a prospect to a hospital and call it twelve step work.

Coupled with subsequent visits, this can be twelve step work at its finest and most effective. This type of self-sacrifice and service is what has enabled our fellowship to grow.

159:19-160:1 The beginning of A.A. meetings is described here. Recovery from alcoholism is gained through practicing the spiritual principles which we learn by taking the Twelve Steps. A.A. meetings are an opportunity for us to carry this message to newcomers.

distracted wife has visited this house to find loving and understanding companionship among women who knew their problem, to hear from the lips of men like their husbands what had happened to them, to be advised how her own wayward mate might be hospitalized and approached when next he stumbled.

160:6Many a man, yet dazed from his hospital experience, has stepped over the threshold of that home into freedom. 7Many an alcoholic who entered there came away with an answer. 8He succumbed to that gay crowd inside, who laughed at their misfortune and understood him. 9Impressed by those who visited him at the hospital, he capitulated entirely, when, later, in an upper room of this house, he heard the story of some man whose experience closely tallied with his own. 10The expression on the faces of the women, that indefinable something in the eyes of the men, the stimulating and electric atmosphere of the place, conspired to let him know that here was haven at last.

11The very practical approach to his problems, the absence of intolerance of any kind, the informality, the genuine democracy, the uncanny understanding which these people had were irresistible. 12He and his wife would leave elated by the thought of what they could now do for some stricken acquaintance and his family. 161:1They knew they had a host of new friends; it seemed they had known these strangers always. 2They had seen miracles, and one was to come to them. 3They had visioned The Great Reality—their loving and All Powerful Creator.

4Now, this house will hardly accommodate its weekly visitors, for they number sixty or eighty as a rule. 5Alcoholics are being attracted from far and near. 6From surrounding towns, families drive long distances to be present. 7A community thirty miles away has fifteen Fellows of Alcoholics

Historical Note:
161:7 Cleveland, Ohio is the community referred to here.

160:11-161:14 These are the attributes of A.A. that attract people. There is no need for promotion. Here we are. You may join us if you wish.

Anonymous. ¹⁶¹:⁸Being a large place, we think that some day its Fellowship will number many hundreds.

⁹But life among Alcoholics Anonymous is more than attending gatherings and visiting hospitals. ¹⁰Cleaning up old scrapes, helping to settle family differences, explaining the disinherited son to his irate parents, lending money and securing jobs for each other, when justified—these are every-day occurrences. ¹¹No one is too discredited, nor has sunk too low to be welcomed cordially—if he means business. ¹²Social distinctions, petty rivalries and jealousies—these are laughed out of countenance. ¹³Being wrecked in the same vessel, being restored and united under one God, with hearts and minds attuned to the welfare of others, the things which matter so much to some people no longer signify much to them. ¹⁴How could they?

¹⁵Under only slightly different conditions, the same thing is taking place in several eastern cities. ¹⁶In one of these there is a well-known hospital for the treatment of alcoholic and drug addiction. ¹⁶²:¹Four years ago one of our number was a patient there. ²Many of us have felt, for the first time, the Presence and Power of God within its walls. ³We are greatly indebted to the doctor in attendance there, for he, although it might preju-dice his own work, has told us his belief in our work.

⁴Every few days this doctor suggests our approach to one of his patients. ⁵Understanding our work, he can do this with an eye to selecting those who are willing and able to recover on a spiritual basis. ⁶Many of us, former patients, go there to help. ⁷&⁸Then, in this eastern city, there are informal meetings such as we have described to you, where you may see thirty or forty, there are the same fast friendships, there is the same

Historical Notes:
161:16 Charles B. Towns Hospital was located in New York, New York.
162:1 Bill W. had been sober for over four years when this book was first published in April, 1939.
162:3 Dr. William D. Silkworth authored the Doctor's Opinion appearing in this book.
162:7 New York is the Eastern City mentioned here.

161:12-14 When faced with alcoholic destruc-tion, we were able to set aside our prejudice against spiritual principles. Having been restored to sanity, we see the artificial barri-ers we place between ourselves and others as impediments to usefulness. We set aside our differences and work harmoniously together to carry our good news to those who suffer from alcoholism.

161:11 Honest: (Means Business) xiv:2, 5:18, 25:13, 28:7, 57:11, 58:9, 70:8, 73:5, 96:1-8, 114:7, 120:5, 147:3, 159:5

161:12 Laughter: 16:7-8, 132:10-20, 157:25-26, 160:8

161:12-14 Vessel: 17:8-14

161:13 Restored: 57:3, 57:8, 59:9, 84:25, 101:3, 120:17

162:1 Years: xxx:2, xxiii:6, xxix:14, 13:9, 32:12, 158:15-16

162:2 Presence: 12:27, 51:3, 56:13-18, 63:6, 85:21-23

helpfulness to one another as you find among our western friends. ¹⁶²:⁹There is a good bit of travel between East and West and we foresee a great increase in this helpful interchange.

¹⁰Some day we hope that every alcoholic who journeys will find a Fellowship of Alcoholics Anonymous at his destination. ¹¹To some extent this is already true. ¹²Some of us are salesmen and go about. ¹³Little clusters of twos and threes and fives of us have sprung up in other communities, through contact with our two larger centers. ¹⁴Those of us who travel drop in as often as we can. ¹⁵This practice enables us to lend a hand, at the same time avoiding certain alluring distractions of the road, about which any traveling man can inform you.

¹⁶Thus we grow. ¹⁷And so can you, though you be but one man with this book in your hand. ¹⁶³:¹We believe and hope it contains all you will need to begin.

²We know what you are thinking. ³You are saying to yourself: "I'm jittery and alone. ⁴I couldn't do that." ⁵But you can. ⁶You forget that you have just now tapped a source of power so much greater than yourself. ⁷To duplicate, with such backing, what we have accomplished is only a matter of willingness, patience and labor.

⁸We know a former alcoholic who was living in a large community. ⁹He had lived there but a few weeks when he found that the place probably contained more alcoholics per square mile than any city in the country. ¹⁰This was only a few days ago at this writing. ¹¹The authorities were much concerned. ¹²He got in touch with a prominent psychiatrist who has undertaken certain responsibilities for the mental health of the community. ¹³The doctor proved to be able and exceedingly anxious to adopt any workable method of handling

Historical Notes:
163:8 Hank P., the author of the chapter "To Employers" and the story "The Unbeliever" lived in Mountclair, New Jersey.
163:12 The psychiatrist was Dr. Howard of Mountclair, NJ.

163:6-7 We have tapped into a limitless source of Power. Free of blockage caused by selfish motives we can become effective conduits for this Power. We need willingness to set aside our own selfish self-interest, patience to accept the time-table of God, and hard work to keep our faith alive.

the situation. 163:14So he inquired, what did our friend have on the ball?

15Our friend proceeded to tell him. 16And with such good effect that the doctor agreed to a test among his patients and certain other alcoholics from a clinic which he attends. 17Arrangements were also made with the chief psychiatrist of a large public hospital to select still others from the stream of misery which flows through that institution.

18So our fellow worker will soon have friends galore. 19Some of them may sink and perhaps never get up, but if our experience is a criterion, more than half of those approached will become Fellows of Alcoholics Anonymous. 20When a few men in this city have found themselves, and have discovered the joy of helping others to face life again, there will be no stopping until everyone in that town has had his opportunity to recover—if he can and will.

164:1Still you may say: "But I will not have the benefit of contact with you who write this book." 2We cannot be sure. 3God will determine that, so you must remember that your real reliance is always upon Him. 4He will show you how to create the Fellowship you crave.*

5Our book is meant to be suggestive only. 6We realize we know only a little. 7God will constantly disclose more to you and to us. 8Ask him in your morning meditation what you can do each day for the man who is still sick. 9The answers will come, if your own house is in order. 10But obviously you cannot transmit something you haven't got. 11See to it that your relationship with Him is right, and great events will come to pass for you and countless others. 12This is the Great Fact for us.

Historical Note:
163:17 Dr. Russell E. Blaisdell was the chief psychiatrist at Rockland State Hospital in New York State.

163:18 Friends Galore: 89:8

164:3 Reliance: 20:1, 45:21, 52:8, 68:10, 68:14, 85:15, 80:13, 87:5, 98:9, 99:21, 100:1

164:5 Suggestive Only: 28:6, 95:19, 144:3

164:5 Suggest: xxviii:18, 12:9, 19:13, 59:7, 86:3, 92:4, 94:13, 104:4, 142:18, 143:14, 144:2, 144:10, 153:10

164:7 Constantly: 20:1, 85:16-18, 85:28, 87:20, 159:19

164:8 Prayer: xxx4, 13:15-20, 59:18, 63:9-12, 67:5, 68:22, 69:18, 69:22, 70:12, 75:17, 76:5, 76:6-9, 76:18, 79:5, 82:5, 83:6, 84:20, 85:26-86:3, 86:13, 86:16, 86:21, 87:6-11, 87:14-18, 87:19-20

164:12 The Great Fact: 11:22, 17:12, 25:8-10, 51:3, 55:11, 119:18, 130:3, 161:3

164:3 We learn to rely on God by taking the Twelve Steps. Direct personal experience with God working to solve our problems produces unshakable faith. Sharing our solution with others keeps our faith alive and vital.

164:5-7 The authors describe what life was like for them, the way of life they have now adopted, and what the results have been for them. This kit of spiritual tools is laid at our feet. It is up to us whether we will pick them up or not.

164:13
Abandon:
25:11, 58:14,
59:5, 63:13,
63:16, 66:8,
68:13, 98:18-19

164:16
Give Freely:
13:18, 14:23,
20:1, 62:2,
70:14, 85:16-
18, 93:15, 94:6,
97:3, 102:4-5,
120:1, 159:12-
13

[13]Abandon yourself to God as you understand God. [14]Admit your faults to him and your fellows. [164:15]Clear away the wreckage of your past. [16]Give freely of what you find, and join us. [17]We shall be with you, in the Fellowship of The Spirit, and you will surely meet some of us as you trudge the Road of Happy Destiny.

[18]May God bless you and keep you—until then.

*See appendix—The Alcoholic Foundation. It may be we shall be able to carry on a limited correspondence.

164:13-16 The main object of this book is to show us how to bring these things about. We learn how to do these things by practicing the Twelve Steps. We keep what we find by giving it away.

PROFILE OF
DR. BOB
1879-1951

Dr. Bob, a co-founder of A.A., was rebellious as a youth. He started drinking as a youth when he found a jug of booze and continued to enjoy drinking until in his college years when it began to cause him trouble. He attended Dartmouth College and received his medical degree from Brush University.

Dr. Bob opened his medical practice in Akron, Ohio in 1912 and practiced medicine as a surgeon until 1948. During prohibition he was able to write himself prescriptions for whiskey. Dr. Bob's alcoholism progressed along a familiar path leading inevitably to the destruction of all things worthwhile in life. Dr. Bob checked into sanitariums to dry out at least a dozen times.

Dr. Bob and his wife Anne began attending meetings of the Oxford Group, a Christian fellowship. Anne's Oxford Group friend, Henrietta Seiberling introduced Bill W. to Dr. Bob. Bill was on a business trip to Akron and contacted Henrietta through the Reverend Walter Tunks whose name Bill found on a readerboard at the Mayflower Hotel where he was staying.

Dr. Bob and Bill, both originally from Vermont, quickly identified with each other as alcoholics and talked for hours at their first meeting. Dr. Bob saw that Bill had been able to stay sober for six months by attempting to help other alcoholics gain sobriety. After one final spree Dr. Bob sobered never to drink again. He was 55 years old and his June 10, 1935 sobriety date is counted as the birthdate of A.A.

Dr. Bob and Bill began to try helping alcoholics soon after Dr. Bob sobered. Their first attempt failed but soon they had several alcoholics who were sober by following their path. Dr. Bob continued to work with alcoholics, at Akron City Hospital and then for a dozen years at St. Thomas Hospital where he worked with his nurse Teddy and Sister Mary Ignatia.

Dr. Bob and his wife Anne relied heavily on the Bible for inspiration and direction. Many of A.A.'s fundamental ideas came from Anne's spiritual studies. "Faith without works is dead" was one of Anne's favorite passages. Other terms that came from Anne were: "the unmanageability of our lives," "our lack of power," "the spiritual experience" and "one day at a time."

Dr. Bob's wise counsel and prudence kept A.A. on a steady path during it's early years. On the Sunday before Dr. Bob died he advised Bill to "keep it simple."

PERSONAL STORIES

I was born in a small New England village of about seven thousand souls. The general moral standard was, as I recall it, far above the average.

No beer or liquor was sold in the neighborhood, except at the State liquor agency where perhaps one might procure a pint if he could convince the agent that he really needed it. Without this proof the expectant purchaser would be forced to depart empty handed with none of what I later came to believe was the great panacea for all human ills. Men who had liquor shipped in from Boston or New York by express were looked upon with great distrust and disfavor by most of the good townspeople. The town was well supplied with churches and schools in which I pursued my early educational activities.

My father was a professional man of recognized ability and both my father and mother were most active in church affairs. Both father and mother were considerably above the average in intelligence.

Unfortunately for me I was the only child, which perhaps engendered the selfishness which played such an important part in bringing on my alcoholism.

From childhood through high school I was more or less forced to go to church, Sunday School and evening service, Monday night Christian Endeavor and sometimes to Wednesday evening prayer meeting. This had the effect of making me resolve that when I was free from parental domination, I would never again darken the doors of a church. This resolution I kept steadfastly for the next *forty* years, except when circumstances made it seem unwise to absent myself.

After high school came four years in one of the best colleges in the country where drinking seemed to be a major extra-curricular activity. Almost everyone seemed to do it. I did it more and more, and had lots of fun without much grief, either physical or financial. I seemed to be able to snap back the next morning better than most of my fellow drinkers, who were cursed (or perhaps blessed) with a great deal of morning-after nausea. Never once in my life have I had a headache, which fact leads me to believe that I was an alcoholic almost from the start. My whole life seemed to be centered around doing what I wanted to do, without regard for the rights, wishes, or privileges of anyone else; a state of mind which became more and more predominant as the years passed. I was graduated with "summa cum laude" in the eyes of the drinking fraternity, but not in the eyes of the Dean.

The next three years I spent in Boston, Chicago, and Montreal in the employ of a large manufacturing concern, selling railway supplies, gas engines of all sorts, and many other items of heavy hardware. During these years, I drank as much as my purse permitted, still without paying too great a penalty, although I was beginning to have morning "jitters" at times. I lost only a half day's work during these three years.

My next move was to take up the study of medicine, entering one of the largest universities in the country. There I took up the business of drinking with much greater earnestness than I had previously shown. On account of my enormous capacity for beer, I was elected to membership in one of the drinking societies, and soon became one of the leading spirits. Many mornings I have gone to classes, and even though fully prepared, would turn and walk back to the fraternity house because of my jitters, not daring to enter the classroom for fear of making a scene should I be called on for recitation.

This went from bad to worse until sophomore spring when, after a prolonged period of drinking, I made up my mind that I could not complete my course, so I packed my grip and went South and spent a month on a large farm owned by a friend of mine. When I got the fog out of my brain, I decided that quitting school was very foolish and that I had better return and continue my work. When I reached school, I discovered the faculty had other ideas on the subject. After much argument they allowed me to return and take my exams, all of which I passed creditably. But they were much disgusted and told me they would attempt to struggle along without my presence. After many painful discussions, they finally gave me my credits and I migrated to another of the leading universities of the country and entered as a Junior that Fall.

There my drinking became so much worse that the boys in the fraternity house where I lived felt forced to send for my father, who made a long journey in the vain endeavor to get me straightened around. This had little effect however for I kept on drinking and used a great deal more hard liquor than in former years.

Coming up to final exams I went on a particularly strenuous spree.

When I went in to write the examinations, my hand trembled so I could not hold a pencil. I passed in at least three absolutely blank books. I was, of course, soon on the carpet and the upshot was that I had to go back for two more quarters and remain absolutely dry, if I wished to graduate. This I did, and proved myself satisfactory to the faculty, both in deportment and scholastically.

I conducted myself so creditably that I was able to secure a much coveted internship in a western city, where I spent two years. During these two years I was kept so busy that I hardly left the hospital at all. Consequently, I could not get into any trouble.

When those two years were up, I opened an office downtown. Then I had some money, all the time in the world, and considerable stomach trouble. I soon discovered that a couple of drinks would alleviate my gastric distress, at least for a few hours at a time, so it was not at all difficult for me to return to my former excessive indulgence.

By this time I was beginning to pay very dearly physically and, in hope of relief, voluntarily incarcerated myself at least a dozen times in one of the local sanitariums. I was between Scylla and Charybdis now, because if I did not drink my stomach tortured me, and if I did, my nerves did the same thing. After three years of this, I wound up in the local hospital where they attempted to help me, but I would get my friends to smuggle me a quart, or I would steal the alcohol about the building, so that I got rapidly worse.

Finally my father had to send a doctor out from my home town who managed to get me back there some way and I was in bed about two months before I could venture out of the house. I stayed about town a couple of months more and returned to resume my practice. I think I must have been thoroughly scared by what had happened, or by the doctor, or probably both, so that I did not touch a drink again until the country went dry.

With the passing of the Eighteenth Amendment I felt quite safe. I knew everyone would buy a few bottles, or cases, of liquor as their exchequers permitted, and it would soon be gone. Therefore it would make no great difference, even if I should do some drinking. At that time I was not aware of the almost unlimited supply the government made it possible for us doctors to obtain, neither had I any knowledge of the bootlegger who soon appeared on the horizon. I drank with moderation at first, but it took me only a relatively short time to drift back into the old habits which had wound up so disastrously before.

During the next few years, I developed two distinct phobias. One was the fear of not sleeping, and the other was the fear of running out of liquor. Not being a man of means, I knew that if I did not stay sober enough to earn money, I would run out of liquor. Most of the time, therefore, I did not take the morning drink which I craved so badly, but instead would fill up on large doses of sedatives to quiet the jitters, which distressed me terribly. Occasionally, I would yield to the morning craving, but if I did, it would be only a few hours before I would be quite unfit for work. This would lessen my chances of smuggling some home that evening, which in turn would mean a night of futile tossing around in bed followed by a morning of unbearable jitters. During the subsequent fifteen years I had sense enough never to go to the hospital if I had been drinking, and very seldom did I receive patients. I would sometimes hide out in one of the clubs of which I was a member, and had the habit at times of registering at a hotel under a fictitious name. But my friends usually found me and I would go home if they promised that I should not be scolded.

If my wife were planning to go out in the afternoon, I would get a large supply of liquor and smuggle it home and hide it in the coal bin, the clothes chute, over door jambs, over beams in the cellar and in cracks in the cellar tile. I also made use of old trunks and chests, the old can container, and even the ash container. The water tank on the toilet I never used, because that looked too easy. I found out later that my wife inspected it frequently. I used to put eight or twelve ounce bottles of alcohol in a fur lined glove and toss it onto the back airing porch when winter days got dark enough. My bootlegger had hidden alcohol at the back steps where I could get it at my convenience. Sometimes I would bring it in my pockets, but they were inspected, and that became too risky. I used also to put it up in four ounce bottles and stick several in my stocking tops. This worked nicely until my wife and I went to see Wallace Beery in "Tugboat Annie," after which the pant-leg and stocking racket were out!

I will not take space to relate all my hospital or sanitarium experiences.

During all this time we became more or less ostracized by our friends. We could not be invited out because I would surely get tight and my wife dared not invite people in for the same reason. My phobia for sleeplessness demanded that I get drunk every night, but in order to get more liquor for the next night, I had to stay sober during the day, at least up to four o'clock. This routine went on with few interruptions for seventeen years. It was really a horrible nightmare, this earning money, getting liquor, smuggling it home, getting drunk, morning jitters, taking large doses of sedatives to make it possible for me to earn more money, and so on ad nauseam. I used to promise my wife, my friends, and my children that I would drink no more—promises which seldom kept me sober even through the day, though I was very sincere when I made them.

For the benefit of those experimentally inclined, I should mention the so-called beer experiment. When beer first came back, I thought that I was safe. I could drink all I wanted of that. It was harmless; nobody ever got drunk on beer. So I filled the cellar full, with the permission of my good wife. It was not long before I was drinking at least a case and a half a day. I put on thirty pounds weight in about two months, looked like a pig, and was uncomfortable from shortness of breath. It then occurred to me that after one was all smelled up with beer nobody could tell what had been drunk, so I began to fortify my beer with straight alcohol. Of course, the result was very bad, and that ended the beer experiment.

About the time of the beer experiment I was thrown in with a crowd of people who attracted me because of their seeming poise, health, and happiness. They spoke with great freedom from embarrassment, which I could never do, and they seemed very much at ease on all occasions and appeared very healthy. More than these attributes, they seemed to be happy. I was self conscious and ill at ease most of the time, my health was at the breaking point, and I was thoroughly miserable. I sensed they had something I did not have, from which I might readily profit. I learned that it was something of a spiritual nature, which did not appeal to me very much, but I thought it could do no harm. I gave the matter much time and study for the next two and a half years, but still got tight every night nevertheless. I read everything

I could find, and talked to everyone who I thought knew anything about it.

My good wife became deeply interested and it was her interest that sustained mine, though I at no time sensed that it might be an answer to my liquor problem. How my wife kept her faith and courage during all those years, I'll never know, but she did. If she had not, I know I would have been dead a long time ago. For some reason, we alcoholics seem to have the gift of picking out the world's finest women. Why they should be subjected to the tortures we inflicted upon them, I cannot explain.

About this time a lady called up my wife one Saturday afternoon, saying she wanted me to come over that evening to meet a friend of hers who might help me. It was the day before Mother's Day and I had come home plastered, carrying a big potted plant which I set down on the table and forthwith went upstairs and passed out. The next day she called again. Wishing to be polite, though I felt very badly, I said, "Let's make the call," and extracted from my wife a promise that we would not stay over fifteen minutes.

We entered her house at exactly five o'clock and it was eleven fifteen when we left. I had a couple of shorter talks with this man afterward, and stopped drinking abruptly. This dry spell lasted for about three weeks; Then I went to Atlantic City to attend several days' meeting of a National Society of which I was a member. I drank all the Scotch they had on the train and bought several quarts on my way to the hotel. This was on Sunday. I got tight that night, stayed sober Monday till after the dinner and then proceeded to get tight again. I drank all I dared in the bar, and then went to my room to finish the job. Tuesday I started in the morning, getting well organized by noon. I did not want to disgrace myself, so I then checked out. I bought some more liquor on the way to the depot. I had to wait some time for the train. I remember nothing from then on until I woke up at a friend's house, in a town near home. These good people notified my wife, who sent my newly-made friend over to get me. He came and got me home and to bed, gave me a few drinks that night, and one bottle of beer the next morning.

That was June 10, 1935, and that was my last drink. As I write nearly four years have passed.

The question which might naturally come into your mind would be: "what did the man do or say that was different from what others had done or said?" It must be remembered that I had read a great deal and talked to everyone who knew, or thought they knew, anything about the subject of alcoholism. This man was a man who had experienced many years of frightful drinking, who had had most all the drunkard's experience known to man, but who had been cured by the very means I had been trying to employ, that is to say, the spiritual approach. He gave me information about the subject of alcoholism which was undoubtedly helpful. *Of far more importance was the fact that he was the first living human with whom I had ever talked, who knew what he was talking about in regard to alcoholism from actual experience. In other words, he talked my language.* He knew all the answers, and certainly not because he had picked them up in his reading.

It is a most wonderful blessing to be relieved of the terrible curse with which I was afflicted. My health is good and I have regained my self-respect and the respect of my colleagues. My home life is ideal and my business is as good as can be expected in these uncertain times.

I spend a great deal of time passing on what I learned to others who want and need it badly. I do it for four reasons:

1. Sense of duty.
2. It is a pleasure.
3. Because in so doing I am paying my debt to the man who took time to pass it on to me.
4. Because every time I do it I take out a little more insurance for myself against a possible slip.

Unlike most of our crowd, I did not get over my craving for liquor much during the first two and one half years of abstinence. It was almost always with me. But at no time have I been anywhere near yielding. I used to get terribly upset when I saw my friends drink and knew I could not, but I schooled myself to believe that though I once had the same privilege, I had abused it so frightfully that it was withdrawn. So it doesn't behoove me to squawk about it, for after all, nobody ever used to throw me down and pour any liquor down my throat.

If you think you are an atheist, an agnostic, a skeptic, or have any other form of intellectual pride which keeps you from accepting what is in this book, I feel sorry for you. If you still think you are strong enough to beat the game alone, that is your affair. But if you really and truly want to quit drinking liquor for good and all, and sincerely feel that you must have some help, we know that we have an answer for you. It never fails if you go about it with one half the zeal you have been in the habit of showing when getting another drink.

Your Heavenly Father will never let you down!

DULL . . . listless . . . semicomatose . . . I lay on my bed in a famous hospital for alcoholics. Death or worse had been my sentence.

What was the difference? What difference did anything make? Why think of those things which were gone—why worry about the results of my drunken escapades? What the hell were the odds if my wife had discovered the mistress situation? Two swell boys . . . sure . . . but what difference would a corpse or an asylum imprisoned father make to them? . . . thoughts stop whirling in my head . . . that's the worst of this sobering-up process . . . the old think tank is geared in high-high . . . what do I mean high-high . . . where did that come from . . . oh yes, that first Cadillac I had, it had four speeds . . . had a high-high gear . .

insane asylum . . . how that bus could scamper . . . yes . . . even then liquor probably poisoned me. What had the little doctor said this morning . . . thoughts hesitate a moment . . . stop your mad turning . . . what was I thinking about . . . oh yes, the doctor.

This morning I reminded Doc this was my tenth visit. I had spent a couple of thousand dollars on these trips and those I had financed for the plastered play girls who also couldn't sober up. Jackie was a honey until she got plastered and then she was a hellion. Wonder what gutter she's in now. Where was I? Oh . . . I asked the doctor to tell me the truth. He owed it to me for the amount of money I had spent. He faltered. Said I'd been drunk that's all. God! Didn't I know that?

But Doc, you're evading. Tell me honestly what is the matter with me. I'll be all right did you say? But Doc, you've said that before. You said once that if I stopped for a year I would be over the habit and would never drink again. I didn't drink for over a year, but I did start to drink again.

Tell me what is the matter with me. I'm an alcoholic? Ha ha and ho ho! As if I didn't know that! But aside from your fancy name for a plain drunk, tell me why I drink. You say a true alcoholic is something different from a plain drunk? What do you mean . . . let me have it cold . . . brief and with no trimmings.

An alcoholic is a person who has an allergy to alcohol? Is poisoned by it? One drink does something to the chemical make-up of the body? That drink effects the nerves and in a certain number of hours another drink is medically demanded? And so the vicious cycle is started? An ever smaller amount of time between drinks to stop those screaming, twitching, invisible wires called nerves?

I know that history Doc . . . how the spiral tightens . . . a drink . . . unconscious . . . awake . . . drink . . . unconscious . . . poured into the hospital . . . suffer the agonies of hell . . . the shakes . . . thoughts running wild . . . brain unleashed . . . engine without a governor. But hell Doc, I don't want to drink! I've got one of the stubbornest will powers known in business. I stick at things. I get them done. I've stuck on the wagon for months. And not been bothered by it . . . and then suddenly, incomprehensibly, an empty glass in my hand and another spiral started. How did the Doc explain that one?

He couldn't. That was one of the mysteries of true alcoholism. A famous medical foundation had spent a fortune trying to segregate the reasons for the alcoholic as compared to the plain hard, heavy drinker. Had tried to find the cause. And all they had been able to determine as a fact was that the majority of the alcohol in every drink taken by the alcoholic went to the fluid in which the brain floated. Why a man ever started when he knew those things was one of the things that could not be fathomed. Only the damn fool public believed it a matter of weak will power. Fear . . . ostracism . . . loss of family . . . loss of position . . . the gutter . . . nothing stopped the alcoholic.

Doc! What do you mean—nothing! What! An incurable disease? Doc, you're kidding me! You're trying to scare me into stopping! What's that you say? You wish you were? What are those tears in your eyes Doc? What's that? Forty years you've spent at this alcoholic business and you have yet to see a true alcoholic cured? Your life defeated and wasted? Oh, come, come Doc . . . what would some of us do without you? If even to only sober up. But Doc . . . let's have it. What is going to be my history from here on out? Some vital organ will stop or the mad house with a wet brain? How soon? Within two years? But, Doc, I've got to do something about it! I'll see doctors . . . I'll go to sanitariums. Surely the medical profession knows something about it. So little, you say? But why? Messy. Yes, I'll admit there is nothing messier than an alcoholic drunk.

What's that Doc? You know a couple of fellows that were steady customers here that haven't been drunk for about ten months? You say

they claim they are cured? And they make an avocation of passing it
on to others? What have they got? You don't know . . . and you don't
believe they are cured . . . well why tell me about it? A fine fellow you
say, plenty of money, and you're sure it isn't a racket . . . just wants to
be helpful . . . call him up for me will you, Doc?

How Doc had hated to tell me. Thoughts stop knocking at my door.
Why can't I get drunk like other people, get up next morning, toss my
head a couple of time and go to work? Why do I have to shake so I can't
hold the razor? Why does every little muscle inside me have to feel like
a crawling worm? Why do even my vocal cords quiver so words are gib-
berish until I've had a big drink? Poison! Of course! But how could
anyone understand such a necessity for a drink that it has to be loaded
with pepper to keep it from bouncing? Can any mortal understand
such secret shame in having to have a drink as to make a person keep
the bottles hidden all over the house. The morning drink . . . shame
and necessity . . . weakness . . . remorse. But what do the family know
about it? What do doctors know about it? Little Doc was right, they
know nothing. They just say "Be strong"—"Don't take that drink"—
"Suffer it through."

What the hell do they know about suffering? Not sickness. Not a belly
ache—oh yes, your guts get so sore that you cannot place your hands
on them . . . oh sure, every time you go you twist and writhe in pain.
What the hell does any non-alcoholic know about suffering? Thoughts
. . . stop this mad merry-go-round. And worst of all this mental suffering—the hating yourself—the feeling of absurd, irrational weakness-
the unworthiness. Out that window! Use the gun in the drawer! What
about poison? Go out in a garage and start the car. Yeah, that's the
way out . . . but then people'll say "He was plastered." I can't leave that
story behind. That's worse than cowardly.

Isn't there someone who understands? Thoughts . . . please, oh
please, stop . . . I'm going nuts . . . or am I nuts now? Never . . . never
again will I take another drink, not even a glass of beer . . . even that
starts it. Never . . . never . . . never again . . . and yet I've said that a
dozen times and inexplicably I've found an empty glass in my hand
and the whole story repeated.

My Lord, the tragedy that sprang out of her eyes when I came home with a breath on me . . . and fear. The smiles wiped off the kids' faces. Terror stalking through the house. Yes . . . that changed it from a home into a house. Not drunk yet, but they knew what was coming. Mr. Hyde was moving in.

And so I'm going to die. Or a wet brain. What was it that fellow said who was here this afternoon? Damn fool thought . . . get out of my mind. Now I know I'm going nuts. And science knows nothing about it. And psychiatrists. I've spent plenty on them. Thoughts, go away! No . . . I don't want to think about what that fellow said this afternoon.

He's trying . . . idealistic as hell . . . nice fellow, too. Oh, why do I have to suffer with this revolving brain? Why can't I sleep? What was it he said? Oh yes, came in and told about his terrific drunks, his trips up here, this same thing I'm going through. Yes, he's an alcoholic all right. And then he told me he knew he was cured. Told me he was peaceful . . . (I'll never know peace again) . . . that he didn't carry constant fear around with him. Happy because he felt free. But it's screwy. He said so himself. But he did get my confidence when he started to tell what he had gone through. It was so exactly like my case. He knows what this torture *is*. He raised my hopes so high; it looked as though he had something. I don't know, I guess I was so sold that I expected him to spring some kind of a pill and I asked him desperately what it was.

And he said "God."

And I laughed.

A ball bat across my face would have been no greater shock. I was so high with hope and expectation. How can a man be so heartless? He said that it sounded screwy but it worked, at least it had with him . . . said he was not a religionist . . . in fact didn't go to church much . . . my ears came up at that . . . his unconventionality attracted me . . . said that some approaches to religion were screwy . . . talked about how the simplest truth in the world had been often all balled up by complicating it . . . that attracted me . . . get out of my mind . . . what a fine religious bird I'd be . . . imagine the glee of the gang at me getting religion . . . phooey . . . thoughts, please slow down . . . why don't they give me something to go to sleep . . . lie down in green pastures. . . the guy's nuts . . . forget him.

And so it's the mad house for me . . . glad mother is dead, she won't
have to suffer that . . . if I'm going nuts maybe it'd be better to be crazy
the way he is . . . at least the kids wouldn't have the insane father whis-
per to carry through life . . . life's cruel . . . the punyminded, curtain-
hiding gossips . . . "didn't you know his father was committed for
insanity?" What a sly label that would be to hang on those boys . . .
damn the gossiping, reputation-shredding, busybodies who put their
noses into other people's business.

He'd laid in this same dump . . . suffered . . . gone through hell . . .
made up his mind to get well . . . studied alcoholism . . . Jung. . . Blank
Medical Foundation . . . asylums . . . Hopkins . . . many said incurable
disease . . . impossible . . . nearly all known cures had been through
religion . . . revolted him . . . made a study of religion . . . more he studied the more it was bunk to him . . . not understandable . . . self-hypnotism . . . and then the thought hit him that people had it all twisted
up. They were trying to pour everyone into molds, put a tag on them,
tell them what they had to do and how they had to do it, for the salvation of their own souls. When as a matter of fact people were through
worrying about their souls, they wanted action right here and now. A
lot of tripe was usually built up around the simplest and most beautiful ideas in the world.

And how did he put the idea . . . bunk . . . bunk . . . why in hell am
I still thinking about him . . . in hell . . . that's good . . . I am in hell.
He said: "*I* came to the conclusion that there is SOMETHING. I know
not what It is, but It is bigger than I. If I will acknowledge It, if I will
humble myself, if I will give in and bow in submission to that SOME-
THING and then try to lead a life as fully in accord with my idea of
good as possible, I will be in tune." And later the word good contracted
in his mind to God.

But mister, I can't see any guy with long white whiskers up there just
Waiting for me to make a plea . . . and what did he answer . . . said I
was trying to complicate it . . . why did I insist on making It human . . .
all I had to do was believe in some power greater than myself and
knuckle down to It . . . and I said maybe, but tell me mister why are
you wasting your time up here? Don't hand me any bunk about it being
more blessed to give than to receive . . . asked him what this thing cost

and he laughed. He said it wasn't a waste of time . . . in doping it out he had thought of something somebody had said. A person never knew a lesson until he tried to pass it on to someone else. And that he had found out every time he tried to pass this on It became more vivid to him. So if we wanted to get hard boiled about it, he owed me, I didn't owe him. That's a new slant . . . the guy's crazy as a loon . . . get away from him brain . . . picture me going around telling other people how to run their lives . . . if I could only go to sleep . . . that sedative doesn't seem to take hold. He could visualize a great fellowship of us . . .quietly passing this from alcoholic to alcoholic . . . nothing organized . . . not ministers . . . not missionaries . . . what a story . . . thought we'd have to do it to get well . . . some kind of a miracle had happened in his life . . . common sense guy at that . . . his plan does fire the imagination.

Told him it sounded like self hypnotism to me and he said what of it . . . didn't care if it was yogi-sire, self-hypnotism, or anything else . . . four of them were well. But it's so damn hypocritical . . . I get beat every other way and then I turn around and lay it in God's lap . . . damned if I ever would turn to God . . . what a low-down, cowardly, despicable trick that would be . . . don't believe in God anyway . . . just a lot of hooey to keep the masses in subjugation . . .world's worst inquisitions have been practiced in His name . . . and he said . . . do I have to turn into an inquisitionist . . . if I don't knuckle down, I die . . .why the low-down missionary . . . what a bastardly screw to put on a person . . . a witch burner, that's what he is . . . the hell with him and all his damn theories . . . witch burner.

Sleep, please come to my door . . . that last was the eight hundred and eighty-fifth sheep over the fence . . . guess I'll put in some black ones . . . sheep . . . shepherds . . . wise men . . . what was that story . . . hell there I go back on that same line . . . told him I couldn't understand and I couldn't believe anything I couldn't understand. He said he supposed then that I didn't use electricity. No one actually understood where it came from or what it was. Nuts to him. He's got too many answers. What did he think the nub of the whole thing was? Subjugate self to some power above . . . ask for help . . . mean it . . . try to pass it on. Asked him what he was going to name this? Said it would be fatal to give it any kind of a tag . . . to have any sort of formality.

I'm going nuts . . . tried to get him into an argument about miracles . . . about Immaculate Conception . . . about stars leading three wise men . . . Jonah and the whale. He wanted to know what difference those things made . . . he didn't even bother his head about them . . . if he did, he would get tight again. So I asked him what he thought about the Bible. Said he read it, and used those things he understood. He didn't take the Bible literally as an instruction book, for there was no nonsense you could not make out of it that way.

Thought I had him when I asked about the past sins I had committed. Guess I've done everything in the book . . . I supposed I would have to adopt the attitude that all was forgiven . . . here I am pure and clean as the driven snow . . . or else I was to go through life flogging myself mentally . . . bah. But he had the answer for that one too. Said he couldn't call back the hellish things he had done, but he figured life might be a ledger page. If he did a little good here and there, maybe the score would be evened up some day. On the other hand, if he continued as he had been going there would be nothing but debit items on the sheet. Kind of common sense.

This is ridiculous . . . have I lost all power of logic . . . would I fall for all that religious line . . . let's see if I can't get to thinking straight . . . that's it . . . I'm trying to do too much thinking . . . just calm myself . . . quietly . . . quiet now . . . relax every muscle . . . start at the toes and move up . . . insane . . . wet brain . . . those boys . . . what a mess my life is . . . mistress . . . how I hate her . . . ah . . . I know what's the matter . . . that fellow gave me an emotional upset . . . I'll list every reason I couldn't accept his way of thinking. After laughing at this religious stuff all these years I'd be a hypocrite. That's one. Second, if there was a God, why all this suffering? Wait a minute, he said that was one of the troubles, we tried to give God some form. Make It just a Power that will help. Third, it sounds like the Salvation Army. Told him that and he said he was not going around singing on any street corners but nevertheless the Salvation Army did a great work. Simply, if he heard of a guy suffering the torments, he told him his story and belief.

There I go thinking again . . . just started to get calmed down . . . sleep . . . boys . . . insane . . . death . . . mistress . . . life all messed up . . .

business. Now listen, take hold . . . what am I going to do? NEVER . . . that's final and in caps. Never . . . that's net no discount. Never . . . never . . . and my mind is made up. NEVER am I going to be such a cowardly low down dog as to acknowledge God. The two faced, gossiping Babbitts can go around with their sanctimonious mouthings, their miserable worshipping, their Bible quotations, their holier-than-thou, their nicey-nice, Sunday-worshipping, Monday-robbing actions, but never will they find me acknowledging God. Let me laugh . . . I'd like to shriek with insane glee . . . my mind's made up . . . insane, there it *is* again.

Brrr, this floor is cold on my knees . . . why are the tears running like a river down my cheeks . . . God, have mercy on my soul!

I was born in Europe, in Alsace to be exact, shortly after it had become German and practically grew up with "good Rhine wine" of song and story. My parents had some vague ideas of making a priest out of me and for some years I attended the Franciscan school at Basle, Switzerland, just across the border, about six miles from my home. But, although I was a good Catholic, the monastic life had little appeal for me.

Very early I became apprenticed to harness-making and acquired considerable knowledge of upholstering. My daily consumption of wine was about a quart, but that was common where I lived. Everybody drank wine. And it is true that there was no great amount of drunkenness. But I can remember, in my teens, that there were a few characters who caused the village heads to nod pityingly and sometimes in anger as they paused to say, "That sot, Henri" and "Ce pauvre Jules," who drank too much. They were undoubtedly the alcoholics of our village.

Military service was compulsory and I did my stretch with the class of my age, goose-stepping in German barracks and taking part in the Boxer Rebellion in China, my first time at any great distance from home. In foreign parts many a soldier who has been abstemious at home learns to use new and potent drinks. So I indulged with my comrades in everything the Far East had to offer. I cannot say, however, that I acquired any craving for hard liquor as a result. When I got back to Germany I settled down to finish my apprenticeship, drinking the wine of the country as usual.

Many friends of my family had emigrated to America, so at 24 I decided that the United States offered me the opportunity I was never likely to find in my native land. I came directly to a growing industrial city in the middle west, where I have lived practically ever since. I was warmly welcomed by friends of my youth who had preceded me. For weeks after my arrival I was feted and entertained in the already large colony of Alsatians in the city, among the Germans in their saloons and clubs. I early decided that the wine of America was very inferior stuff and took up beer instead.

I soon found work at my trade in harness-making. It was still an age of horses. But I discovered that harness and saddle-making in America was different than anything I had known. Every man in the shop was a specialist and instead of having a variety of jobs to do every day, I was compelled to sit all day long at a bench doing the same thing endlessly. I found it very monotonous and, wanting a change, I found it when I got work as an upholsterer in a large furniture store.

Fond of singing, I joined a German singing society which had good club headquarters. There I sat in the evenings, enjoying with my friends our memories of the "old country," singing the old songs we all knew, playing simple card games for drinks and consuming great quantities of beer.

At that time I could go into any saloon, have one or two beers, walk out and forget about it. I had no desire whatever to sit down at a table and stay a whole morning or afternoon drinking. Certainly at that time I was one of those who "can take it or leave it alone." There had never been any drunkards in my family. I came of good stock, of men and women who drank wine all their lives as a beverage, and while they occasionally got drunk at special celebrations, they were up and about their business the next day.

Prohibition came. Having regard for the law of the land, I resigned myself to the will of the national legislators and quit drinking altogether, not because I had found it harmful, but because I couldn't get what I was accustomed to drink. You can all remember that in the first few months after the change, a great many men, who had formerly been used to a few beers every day or an occasional drink of whiskey, simply quit all alcoholic drinks. For the great majority of us, however, that condition didn't last. We saw very early that prohibition wasn't going to work. It wasn't very long before home-brewing was an institution and men began to search feverishly for old recipe books on winemaking.

But I hardly tasted anything for two years and started in business for myself, rounding a mattress factory which is today an important industrial enterprise in our city. I was doing very well with that and general upholstering work, and there was every indication that I would be financially independent by the time I reached middle age. By this time I was married and was paying for a home. Like most immigrants I wanted to be somebody and have something and I was very happy and contented as I felt success crown my efforts. I missed the old social times, of course, but had no definite craving even for beer.

Successful home-brewers among my friends began to invite me to their homes. I decided that if these fellows could make it I would try it myself and so I did. It wasn't very long until I had developed a pretty good brew with uniformity and plenty of authority. I knew the stuff I was making was a lot stronger than I had been used to, but never suspected that steady drinking of it might develop a taste for something even stronger.

It wasn't long before the bootlegger was an established institution in this, as in other towns. I was doing well in business and in going around town I was frequently invited to have a drink in a speakeasy. I condoned my domestic brewing and the bootleggers and their business. More and more I formed the habit of doing some of my business in the speakeasy and after a time did not need that as an excuse. The "speaks" usually sold whiskey. Beer was too bulky and it couldn't be kept in a jug under the counter ready to be dumped when John Law would come around. I was now forming an entirely new drinking technique. Before long I had a definite taste for hard liquor, knew nausea and headaches I had never known before, but as in the old days, I suffered them out.

Gradually, however, I'd suffer so much that I simply had to have the morning-after drink.

I became what is called a periodical drinker. I was eased out of the business I had rounded and was reduced to doing general upholstery in a small shop at the back of my house. My wife upbraided me often and plenty when she saw that my "periodicals" were gradually losing me what business I could get. I began to bring bottles in. I had them hidden away in the house and all over my shop in careful concealment. I had all the usual experiences of the alcoholic for I was certainly one by this time. Sometimes, after sobering up after a bout of several weeks, I would righteously resolve to quit. With a great deal of determination, I would throw out full pints—pour them out and smash the bottles— firmly resolved never to take another drink of the stuff. I was going to straighten up.

In four or five days I would be hunting all over the place, at home and in my workshop for the bottles I had destroyed, cursing myself for being a damned fool. My "periodicals" became more frequent until I reached the point where I wanted to devote all my time to drinking, working as little as possible and then only when the necessity of my family demanded it. As soon as I had satisfied that, what I earned as an upholsterer went for liquor. I would promise to have jobs done and never do them. My customers lost confidence in me to the point where I retained what business I had only because I was a well-trained and reputedly fine craftsman. "Best in the business, when he's sober," my customers would say and I still had a following who would give me work though they deplored my habits because they knew the job would be well done when they eventually got it.

I had always been a good Catholic, possibly not so devoted as I should have been, but fairly regular in my attendance at services. I had never doubted the existence of the Supreme Being but now I began to absent myself from my church where I had formerly been a member of the choir. Unfortunately, I had no desire to consult my priest about my drinking. In fact I was scared to talk to him about it, for I feared the kind of talk he would give me. Unlike many other Catholics who frequently take pledges for definite periods—a year, two years or for good, I never had any desire to "take a pledge" before the priest. And yet, realizing at last that liquor really had me, I wanted to quit. My wife wrote away for advertised cures for the liquor habit and gave them to me in coffee. I even got them myself and tried them. None of the various cures of this kind were any good.

My experiences differ very little from the experiences of other alcoholics but if ever a man was firmly in the grip of a power that could lead only to ruin and disgrace, I was that man.

I had the usual array of friends who tried to stop me in my drinking career. I can hear them yet. Kindly for the most part, yet blind and almost wholly without understanding, they had the approach that every alcoholic knows:

"Can't you be a man?"

"You can cut it out."

"You've got a good wife; you could have the best business in town. What's the matter with you anyway?"

Every alcoholic has heard those familiar phrases from well-meaning friends. And they were my friends, too. In their way they did what they could, helped me at different times to get on my feet after a particularly bad time, aided me in unraveling my tangled business affairs, suggested this and suggested that. They all wanted to help me. But none of them knew how. Not one of them had the answer I wanted.

My wife got talking to a local merchant one day. He was known as a deeply religious man. He was undoubtedly a fundamentalist with strong leanings toward evangelistic preaching. He knew me and something of my reputation. My wife asked him to help her if he could. So he came to see me, bringing a friend along. He found me drunk and in bed. This man had never been an alcoholic and his approach to me was the familiar one of the emotional seeker after souls. Well, there I was, lying in an alcoholic stupor with occasional flashes of emotional self-pity, in pretty much the same condition as the drunk who plunges to the sawdust at the appeal of a religious orator.

Good, honest and sincere man, he prayed at my bedside and I promised to go to church with him to hear an evangelist. He didn't wait for me to come to his office, he came after me. I heard the evangelist but was not impressed. The service was entirely foreign to what I had been accustomed to in my religious observance since childhood. I have no doubt of the preacher's sincerity and seek not at all to belittle his work, but I was unaffected. So I got no answer.

There are alcoholics who have been without any consciousness of God all their lives; there are some who are actual haters of the idea of a Supreme Being; there are others, like myself, who have never given up a belief in the Almighty, but who have always felt that God is far off. And that's the way I felt. I had a closer sense of God during the mass at church, a feeling of His presence, but in everyday life He seemed to be at a distance from me and more as a righteous judge, than an all-wise, pitying Father to the human race.

Then occurred the event that saved me. An alcoholic came to see me who is a doctor. He didn't talk like a preacher at all. In fact his language was perfectly suited to my understanding. He had no desire to know anything except whether I was definite about my desire to quit drinking. I told him with all the sincerity at my command that I did. Even then he went into no great detail about how he and a crowd of alcoholics, with whom he associated, had mastered their difficulty.

Instead he told me that some of them wanted to talk to me and would be over to see me.

This doctor had imparted his knowledge to just a few other men at that time—not more than four or five—they now number more than seventy persons. And, because as I have discovered since, it is part of the "treatment" that these men be sent to see and talk with alcoholics who want to quit, he kept them busy. He had already imbued them with his own spirit until they were ready and willing at all times to go where sent, and as a doctor he well knew that this mission and duty would strengthen them as it later helped me. The visits from these men impressed me at once. Where preaching and prayers had touched me very little, I was immediately impressed with desire for further knowledge of these men.

"There must be something to it," I said to myself. "Why would these busy men take the time to come to see me? They understand my problem. Like me, they've tried this remedy and that remedy but never found one that worked. But whatever it is they are using now, it seems to keep them sober."

Certainly I could see they were sober. The third man who came to see me had been one of the greatest business-getters his company had ever employed. From the top of the heap in a few years he had skidded to becoming a shuffling customer, still entering the better barrooms but welcomed by neither mine host nor his patrons. His own business was practically gone, he told me, when he discovered the answer.

"You've been trying man's ways and they always fail," he told me. "You can't win unless you try God's Way."

I had never heard of the remedy expressed in just this language. In a few sentences he made God seem personal to me, explained Him as a being who was interested in me, the alcoholic, and that all I needed to do was to be willing to follow His way for me; that as long as I followed it I would be able to overcome my desire for liquor.

Well, there I was, willing to try it, but I didn't know how, except in a vague way. I knew somehow that it meant more than just going to church and living a moral life. If that was all, then I was a little doubtful that it was the answer I was looking for.

He went on talking and told me that he had found the plan has a basis of love and the practice of Christ's injunction, "Love thy neighbor as thyself." Taking that as a foundation, he reasoned that if a man followed that rule he could not be selfish. I could see that. And he further said that God could not accept me as a sincere follower of His Divine Law unless I was ready to be thoroughly honest about it.

That was perfectly logical. My church taught that. I had always known that in theory. We talked, too, about personal morals. Every man has his problem of this kind but we didn't discuss it very much. My visitor well knew, that as I tried to follow God I would get to studying these things out for myself.

We talked things over a long time. I saw readily that I couldn't afford to quibble. I already believed in God, had always done so. Was ready to give my will to Him. That's what it came to.

That day I gave my will to God and asked to be directed. But I have never thought of that as something to do and then forget about. I very early came to see that there had to be a continual renewal of that simple deal with God; that I had perpetually to keep the bargain. So I began to pray; to place my problems in God's hands.

For a long time I kept on trying, in a pretty dumb way at first, I know, but very earnestly. I didn't want to be a fake. And I began putting in practice what I was learning every day. It wasn't very long until my doctor friend sent me to tell another alcoholic what my experience had been. This duty together with my weekly meetings with my fellow alcoholics and my daily renewal of the contract I originally made with God have kept me sober when nothing else ever did.

I have been sober for three years now. The first few months were hard. Many things happened; business trials, little worries, and feelings of general despondency came near driving me to the bottle, but I made progress. As I go along I seem to get strength daily to be able to resist more easily. And when I get upset, cross-grained and out of tune with my fellow man I know that I am out of tune with God. Searching where I have been at fault, it is not hard to discover and get right again, for I have proven to myself and to many others who know me that God can keep a man sober if he will let Him.

Being a Catholic, it is natural that I should attend my own church which I do regularly. I partake of its sacraments which have a new and deeper meaning to me now. I realize what it is to be in the presence of God right in my own home and I realize it deeply when I am at church. For when a man is truly trying to do God's will instead of his own, he is very conscious of being in the presence of God always, wherever he may be.

To my lot falls the rather doubtful distinction of being the only "lady" alcoholic in our particular section. Perhaps it is because of a desire for a "supporting cast" of my own sex that I am praying for inspiration to tell my story in a manner that may give other women who have this problem the courage to see it in its true light and seek the help that has given me a new lease on life.

When the idea was first presented to me that *I was an alcoholic*, my mind simply refused to accept it. Horrors! How disgraceful! What humiliation! How preposterous! Why, I loathed the taste of liquor. Drinking was simply a means of escape when my sorrows became too great for me to endure. Even after it had been explained to me that alcoholism is a disease, I could not realize that I had it. I was still ashamed, still wanted to hide behind the screen of reasons made up of "unjust treatment," "unhappiness," "tired and dejected," and the dozens of other things that I thought lay at the root of my search for oblivion by means of whiskey or gin.

In any case, I felt quite sure that I was *not* an alcoholic. However, since I have faced the fact, and it surely is a fact, I have been able to use the help that is so freely given when we learn how to be really truthful with ourselves.

The path by which I have come to this blessed help was long and devious. It led through the mazes and perplexities of an unhappy marriage and divorce, and a dark time of separation from my grown children, and a readjustment of life at an age when most women feel pretty sure of a home and security.

But I *have* reached the source of help. I *have* learned to recognize and acknowledge the underlying cause of my disease; selfishness, self-pity and resentment. A few short months ago those three words applied to me would have aroused as much indignation in my heart as the word alcoholic. The ability to accept them as my own has been derived from trying, with the unending help of God, to live with certain goals in mind.

Coming to the grim fact of alcoholism, I wish I could present the awful reality of its insidiousness in such a way that no one could ever again fail to recognize the comfortable, easy steps that lead down to the edge of the precipice, and show how those steps suddenly disappeared when the great gulf yawned before me. I couldn't possibly turn and get back to solid earth again that way.

The first step is called "The first drink in the morning to pull you out of a hangover."

I remember so well when I got onto that step. I had been drinking just like most of the young married crowd I knew. For a couple of years it went on, at parties and at "speakeasies," as they were then called, and with cocktails after matinees. Just going the rounds and having a good time.

Then came the morning when I had my first case of jitters. Someone suggested a little of the "hair of the dog that bit me." A half hour after that drink I was sitting on top of the world, thinking how simple it was to cure shaky nerves. How wonderful liquor was, in only a few minutes my head had stopped aching, my spirits were back to normal and all was well in this very fine world.

Unfortunately, there was a catch to it—I was an alcoholic. As time went on the one drink in the morning had to be taken a little earlier—it had to be followed by a second one in an hour or so, before I really felt equal to getting on with the business of living.

Gradually I found at parties the service was a little slow; the rest of the crowd being pretty happy and carefree after the second round. My reaction was inclined to be just the opposite. Something had to be done about that so I'd just help myself to a fast one, sometimes openly, but as time went on and my need became more acute, I often did it on the quiet.

In the meantime, the morning-after treatment was developing into something quite stupendous. The eye-openers were becoming earlier, bigger, more frequent, and suddenly, it was lunch time!

Perhaps there was a plan for the afternoon—a bridge or tea, or just callers. My breath had to be accounted for, so along came such alibis as a touch of grippe or some other ailment for which I'd just taken a hot whiskey and lemon. Or "someone" had been in for lunch and we had just had a couple of cocktails. Then came the period of brazening it out—going to social gatherings well fortified against the jitters; next the phone call in the morning "Terribly sorry that I can't make it this afternoon, I have an awful headache;" then simply forgetting that there were engagements at all; spending two or three days drinking, sleeping it off, and waking to start all over again.

Of course, I had the well known excuses; my husband was failing to come home for dinner or hadn't been home for several days; he was spending money which was needed to pay bills; he had always been a drinker; I had never known anything about it until I was almost thirty years old and he gave me my first drink. Oh, I had them all down, letter perfect—all the excuses, reasons and justifications. What I did not know was that I was being destroyed by selfishness, self-pity and resentment.

There were the swearing-off periods and the "goings on the wagon" —they would last anywhere from two weeks to three or four months. Once, after a very severe illness of six weeks' duration (caused by drinking), I didn't touch anything of an alcoholic nature for almost a year. I thought I had it licked that time, but all of a sudden things were worse than ever. I found fear had no effect.

Next came the hospitalization, not a regular sanitarium, but a local hospital where my doctor would ship me when I'd get where I had to call him in. That poor man—I wish he could read this for he would know then it was no fault of his I wasn't cured.

When I was divorced, I thought the cause had been removed. I felt that being away from what I had considered injustice and ill-treatment would solve the problem of my unhappiness. In a little over a year I was in the alcoholic ward of a public hospital!

It was there that L— came to me. I had known her very slightly ten years before. My ex-husband brought her to me hoping that she could help. She did. From the hospital I went home with her.

There, her husband told me the secret of his rebirth. It is not really a secret at all, but something free and open to all of us. He asked me if I believed in God or some power greater than myself. Well, I did believe in God, but at that time I hadn't any idea what He is. As a child I had been taught my "Now I lay me" and "Our Father which art in Heaven." I had been sent to Sunday School and taken to church. I had been baptized and confirmed. I had been taught to realize there is a God and to "love" him. *But though I had been taught all these things, I had never learned them.*

When B— (L's husband) began to talk about God, I felt pretty low in my mind. I thought God was something that I, and lots of other people like me, had to worry along without. Yet I had always had the "prayer habit." In fact I used to say in my mind "Now, if God answers this prayer, I'll know there *is* a God." It was a great system, only somehow it didn't seem to work!

Finally B— put it to me this way: "You admit you've made a mess of things trying to run them your way, are you willing to give up? Are you willing to say: 'Here it is God, all mixed up. I don't know how to unmix it, I'll leave it to you.'" Well, I couldn't quite do that. I wasn't feeling very well, and I was afraid that later when the fog wore off, I'd want to back out. So we let it rest a few days. L and B sent me to stay with some friends of theirs out of town. I'd never seen them before. The man of that house, P— had given up drinking three months before. After I had been there a few days, I saw that P— and his wife had something that made them mighty hopeful and happy. But I got a little uneasy going into a perfect stranger's home and staying day after day. I said this to P— and his reply was: "Why, you don't know how much it is helping me to have you here." Was that a surprise! Always before that when I was recovering from a tailspin I'd been just a pain in the neck to everyone. So, I began to sense in a small way just what these spiritual principles were all about.

Finally I very self-consciously and briefly asked God to show me how to do what He wanted me to do. My prayer was just about as weak and helpless a thing as one could imagine, but it taught me how to open my mouth and pray earnestly and sincerely. However, I had not quite made the grade. I was full of fears, shames, and other "bug-a-boos" and two weeks later an incident occurred that put me on the toboggan again. I seemed to feel that the hurt of that incident was too great to endure without some "release." So I forsook Spirit in favor of "spirits" and that evening I was well on the way to a long session with my old enemy "liquor." I begged the person in whose home I was living not to let anyone know, but she, having good sense, got in touch right away with those who had helped me before and very shortly they had rallied round.

I was eased out of the mess and in a day or two I had a long talk with one of the crowd. I dragged out all my sins of commission and omission, I told everything I could think of that might be the cause of creating a fear situation, a remorse situation, or a shame situation. It was pretty terrible, I thought then, to lay myself bare that way, but I know now that such is the first step away from the edge of the precipice.

Things went very well for quite a while, then came a dull rainy day. I was alone. The weather and my self-pity began to cook up a nice dish of the blues for me. There was liquor in the house and I found myself suggesting to myself "Just one drink will make me feel so much more cheerful." Well, I got the Bible and "Victorious Living" and sitting down in full view of the bottle of whiskey, I commenced to read. I also prayed. But I didn't say "I must not take that drink because I owe it to so and so not to." I didn't say "I won't take that drink because I'm strong enough to resist temptation." I didn't say "I must not" or "I will not" at all. I simply prayed and read and in half an hour I got up and was absolutely free of the urge for a drink.

It might be very grand to be able to say "Finis" right here, but I see now I hadn't gone all the way I was intended to go. I was still coddling and nursing my two pets, self-pity and resentment. Naturally, I came a cropper once more. This time I went to the telephone (after I had taken about two drinks) and called L to tell her what I had done. She asked me to promise that I would not take another drink before someone came to me. Well, I had learned enough about truthfulness to refuse to give that promise. Had I been living after the old pattern, I would have been ashamed to call for help. In fact I should not have wanted help. I should have tried to hide the fact that I was drinking and continued until I again wound up behind the "eight ball." I was taken back to B's home where I stayed for three weeks. The drinking ended the morning after I got there, but the suffering continued for some time. I felt desperate and I questioned my ability to really avail myself of the help that the others had received and applied so successfully. Gradually, however, God began to clear my channels so that real understanding began to come. Then was the time when full realization and acknowledgment came to me. It was realization and acknowledgment of the fact that I was full of self-pity and resentment, realization of the fact that I had not fully given my problems to God. *I was still trying to do my own fixing.*

That was more than a year ago. Since then, although circumstances are no different, for there are still trials and hardships and hurts and disappointments and disillusionments, self-pity and resentment are being eliminated. In this past year I haven't been tempted once. I have no more idea of taking a drink to aid me through a difficult period than I would if I had never drank. But I know absolutely that the minute I close my channels with sorrow for myself, or being hurt by, or resentful toward anyone, I am in horrible danger.

I know that my victory is none of my human doing. I know that I must keep myself worthy of Divine help. And the glorious thing is this: I am free, I am happy, and perhaps I am going to have the blessed opportunity of "passing it on." I say in all reverence—Amen.

TWO ROSY-CHEEKED children stand at the top of a long hill as the glow of the winter sunset lights up the snow covered country-side. "It's time to go home," says my sister. She is the eldest. After one more exhilarating trip on the sled, we plod homeward through the deep snow. The light from an oil lamp shines from an upstairs window of our home. We stamp the snow from our boots and rush in to the warmth of the coal stove which is supposed to heat upstairs as well. "Hello dearies," calls Mother from above, "get your wet things off."

"Where's Father?" I ask, having gotten a whiff of sausage cooking through the kitchen door and thinking of supper.

"He went down to the swamp," replies Mother. "He should be home soon."

Father is an Episcopal minister and his work takes him over long drives on bad roads. His parishioners are limited in number, but his friends are many, for to him race, creed, or social position make no difference. It is not long before he drives up in the old buggy. Both he and old Maud are glad to get home. The drive was long and cold but he was thankful for the hot bricks which some thoughtful person had given him for his feet. Soon supper is on the table. Father says grace, which delays my attack on the buckwheat cakes and sausage. What an appetite!

A big setter lies asleep near the stove. He begins to make queer sounds and his feet twitch. What is he after in his dreams? More cakes and sausage. At last I am filled. Father goes to his study to write some letters. Mother plays the piano and we sing. Father finishes his letters and we all join in several exciting games of Parcheesi. Then Father is persuaded to read aloud some more of "The Rose and the Ring."

Bed-time comes. I climb to my room in the attic. It is cold so there is no delay. I crawl under a pile of blankets and blow out the candle. The wind is rising and howls around the house. But I am safe and warm. I fall into a dreamless sleep.

I am in church. Father is delivering his sermon. A wasp is crawling up the back of the lady in front of me. I wonder if it will reach her neck. Shucks! It has flown away. Ho, hum, maybe the watermelons are ripe in Mr. Jones' patch. That's an idea! Benny will know, but Mr. Jones will not know what happened to some of them, if they are. At last! The message has been delivered.

"Let your light so shine before men that they may see your good works." I hunt for my nickel to drop in the plate so that mine will be seen.

Father comes forward in the chancel of the church. "The peace of God which passes all understanding, keep your hearts and minds." Hooray! Just a hymn and then church will be over until next week!

I am in another fellow's room at college. "Freshman," said he to me, "do you ever take a drink?" I hesitated. Father had never directly spoken to me about drinking and he never drank any, so far as I knew. Mother hated liquor and feared a drunken man. Her brother had been a drinker and had died in a state hospital for the insane. But his life was unmentionable, so far as I was concerned. I had never had a drink but I had seen enough merriment in the boys who were drinking to be interested. I would never be like the village drunkard at home. How a lot of people despised him! Just a weakling!

"Well," said the older boy, "Do you?"

"Once in a while," I lied. I could not let him think I was a sissy.

He poured out two drinks. "Here's looking at you," said he. I gulped it down and choked. I didn't like it, but I would not say so. No, never! A mellow glow stole over me. Say! This wasn't so bad after all. In fact, it was darn good. Sure I'd have another. The glow increased. Other boys came in. My tongue loosened. Everyone laughed loudly. I was witty. I had no inferiorities.

Why, I wasn't even ashamed of my skinny legs! This was the real thing!

A haze filled the room. The electric light began to move. Then two bulbs appeared. The faces of the other boys grew dim. How sick I felt. I staggered to the bathroom. Shouldn't have drunk so much or so fast. But I knew how to handle it now. I'd drink like a gentleman after this.

And so I met John Barleycorn. The grand fellow who at my call made me "a hale fellow, well met," who gave me such a fine voice, as we sang "Hail, hail, the gang's all here," and "Sweet Adeline," who gave me freedom from fear and feelings of inferiority. Good old John! He was my pal, all right.

Final exams of my senior year and I may somehow graduate. I would never have tried, but Mother counts on it so. A case of measles saved me from being kicked out during my Sophomore year. Bells, bells, bells! Class, library, laboratory! Am I tired!

But the end is in sight. My last and an easy one. I gaze at the board with its questions. Can't remember the answer to the first. I'll try the second. No soap there. Say this is getting serious! I don't seem to remember anything. I concentrate on one of the questions. I don't seem to be able to keep my mind on what I am doing. I get uneasy. If I don't get started soon, won't have time to finish. No use. I can't think.

Oh! An idea, I leave the room, which the honor system allows. I go to my room. I pour out half a tumbler of grain alcohol and fill it with ginger ale. Oh, boy! Now back to the exam. My pen moves rapidly. I know enough of the answers to get by. Good old John Barleycorn! He can certainly be depended on. What a wonderful power he has over the mind! He has given me my diploma!

Underweight! How I hate that word. Three attempts to enlist in the service, and three failures because of being skinny. True, I have recently recovered from pneumonia and have an alibi, but my friends are in the war, or going, and I am not. To hell with it all! I visit a friend who is awaiting orders. The atmosphere of "eat, drink, and be merry" prevails and I absorb it. I drink a lot every night. I can hold a lot now, more than the others.

I am examined for the draft and pass the physical exam. What a dirty deal! Drafted! The shame of it. I am to go to camp on November 13th. The Armistice is signed on the 11th and the draft is called off. Never in the service! The war leaves me with a pair of blankets, a toilet kit, a sweater knit by my sister, and a still greater inferiority.

It is ten o'clock of a Saturday night. I am working hard on the books of a subsidiary company of a large corporation. I have had experience in selling, collecting, and accounting, and am on my way up the ladder.

Then the crack-up. Cotton struck the skids and collections went cold. A twenty three million dollar surplus wiped out. Offices closed up and workers discharged. I, and the books of my division have been transferred to the head office. I have no assistance and am working nights, Saturdays and Sundays. My salary has been cut. My wife and new baby are fortunately staying with relatives. What a life! I feel exhausted. The doctor has told me that if I don't give up inside work, I'll have tuberculosis. But what am I to do? I have a family to support and have no time to be looking for another job.

Oh, well. I reach for the bottle which I just got from George, the elevator boy.

I am a traveling salesman. The day is over and business has been not so good. I'll go to bed. I wish I were home with the family and not in this dingy hotel.

Well-well-look who's here! Good old Charlie! It's great to see him. How's the boy? A drink? You bet your life! We buy a gallon of "corn" because it is so cheap. Yet I am fairly steady when I go to bed.

Morning comes. I feel horribly. A little drink will put me on my feet. But it takes others to keep me there.

I see some prospects. I am too miserable to care if they give me an order or not. My breath would knock out a mule, I learn from a friend. Back at the hotel and more to drink. I come to early in the morning. My mind is fairly clear, but inwardly I am undergoing torture. My nerves are screaming in agony. I go to the drug store and it is not open. I wait. Minutes are interminable. Will the store never open? At last! I hurry in. The druggist fixes me up a bromide. I go back to the hotel and lie down. I wait. I am going crazy. The bromides have no effect. I get a doctor. He gives me a hypodermic. Blessed peace!

And I blame this experience on the quality of the liquor.

I am a real estate salesman. "What is the price of that house," I ask the head of the firm I work for. He names me a price. Then he says, "That is what the builders are asking, but we will add on $500.00 and split it, if you can close the deal." The prospect signs the contract for the full amount. My boss buys the property and sells to the prospect. I get my commission and $250.00 extra and everything is Jake. But is it? Something is sour. So let's have a drink!

I become a teacher in a boy's school. I am happy in my work. I like the boys and we have lots of fun, in class and out.

An unhappy mother comes to me about her boy, for she knows I am fond of him. They expected him to get high marks and he has not the ability to do it. So he altered his report card through fear of his father.

And his dishonesty has been discovered. Why are there so many foolish parents, and why is there so much unhappiness in these homes?

The doctors' bills are heavy and the bank account is low. My wife's parents come to our assistance. I am filled with hurt pride and self-pity. I seem to get no sympathy for my illness and have no appreciation of the love behind the gift.

I call the boot-legger and fill up my charred keg. But I do not wait for the charred keg to work. I get drunk. My wife is extremely unhappy. Her father comes to sit with me. He never says an unkind word. He is a real friend but I do not appreciate him.

We are staying with my wife's father. Her mother is in critical condition at a hospital. The wind is moaning in the pine trees. I cannot sleep. I must get myself together. I sneak down stairs and get a bottle of whiskey from the cellaret. I pour drinks down my throat. My father-in-law appears. "Have a drink?" I ask. He makes no reply, and hardly seems to see me. His wife dies that night.

Mother has been dying of cancer for a long time. She is near the end and now in a hospital. I have been drinking a lot, but never get drunk. Mother must never know. I see her about to go.

I return to the hotel where I am staying and get gin from the bell-boy. I drink and go to bed; I take a few the next morning and go see my mother once more. I cannot stand it. I go back to the hotel and get more gin. I drink steadily. I come to at three in the morning. The indescribable torture has me again. I turn on the light. I must get out of the room or I shall jump out of the window. I walk miles. No use. I go to the hospital, where I have made friends with the night superintendent. She puts me to bed and gives me a hypodermic. Oh, wonderful peace!

Mother and Father die the same year. What is life all about anyway? The world is crazy. Read the newspapers. Everything is a racket. Education is a racket. Medicine is a racket. Religion is a racket. How could there be a loving God who would allow so much suffering and sorrow? Bah! Don't talk to me about religion. For what were my children ever born? I wish I were dead!

I am at the hospital to see my wife. We have another child. But she is not glad to see me. I have been drinking while the baby was arriving. Her father stays with her.

My parents estates are settled at last. I have some money. I'll try farming. It will be a good life. I'll farm on a large scale and make a good thing of it. But the deluge descends. Lack of judgment, bad management, a hurricane, and the depression create debts in ever-increasing number. But the stills are operating throughout the country-side.

It is a cold, bleak day in November. I have fought hard to stop drinking. Each battle has ended in defeat. I tell my wife I cannot stop drinking. She begs me to go to a hospital for alcoholics which has been recommended. I say I will go. She makes the arrangements, but I will not go. I'll do it all myself. This time I'm off of it for good. I'll just take a few beers now and then.

It is the last day of the following October, a dark, rainy morning. I come to in a pile of hay in a barn. I look for liquor and can't find any. I wander to a stable and drink five bottles of beer. I must get some liquor. Suddenly I feel hopeless, unable to go on. I go home. My wife is in the living room. She had looked for me last evening after I left the car and wandered off into the night. She had looked for me this morning. She has reached the end of her rope. There is no use trying any more, for there is nothing to try. "Don't say anything," I say to her. "*I* am going to do something."

I am in the hospital for alcoholics. I am an alcoholic. The insane asylum lies ahead. Could I have myself locked up at home? One more foolish idea. I might go out West on a ranch where I couldn't get anything to drink. I might do that. Another foolish idea. I wish I were dead, as I have often wished before. I am too yellow to kill myself. But maybe—. The thought stays in my mind.

Four alcoholics play bridge in a smoke-filled room. Anything to get my mind from myself. The game is over and the other three leave. I start to clean up the debris. One man comes back, closing the door behind him.

He looks at me. "You think you are hopeless, don't you?" he asks. "I know it," I reply.

"Well, you're not," says the man. "There are men on the streets of New York today who were worse than you, and they don't drink anymore."

"What are you doing here then?" I ask.

"I went out of here nine days ago saying that I was going to be honest, and I wasn't," he answers.

A fanatic, I thought to myself, but I was polite. "What is it?" I inquire.

Then he asks me if I believe in a power greater than myself, whether I call that power God, Allah, Confucius, Prime Cause, Divine Mind, or any other name. I told him that I believe in electricity and other forces of nature, but as for a God, if there is one, He has never done anything for me. Then he asks me if I am willing to right all the wrongs I have ever done to anyone, no matter how wrong I thought they were. Am I willing to be honest with myself about myself and tell someone about myself, and am I willing to think of other people and of their needs instead of myself; to get rid of the drink problem?

"I'll do anything," I reply.

"Then all of your troubles are over," says the man and leaves the room. The man is in bad mental shape certainly. I pick up a book and try to read, but cannot concentrate. I get in bed and turn out the light. But I cannot sleep. Suddenly a thought comes. Can all the worthwhile people I have known be wrong about God? Then I find myself thinking about myself, and a few things that I had wanted to forget. I begin to see I am not the person I had thought myself, that I had judged myself by comparing myself to others, and always to my own advantage. It is a shock.

Then comes a thought that is like A Voice. "Who are you to say there is no God?" It rings in my head, I can't get rid of it.

I get out of bed and go to the man's room. He is reading. "I must ask you a question," I say to the man. "How does prayer fit into this thing?"

"Well," he answers, "you've probably tried praying like I have. When you've been in a jam you've said, 'God, please do this or that' and if it turned out your way that was the last of it and if it didn't you've said 'There isn't any God' or 'He doesn't do anything for me'. Is that right?"

"Yes" I reply.

"That isn't the way," he continued. "The thing I do is to say, 'God here I am and here are all my troubles. I've made a mess of things and can't do anything about it. You take me, and all my troubles, and do anything you want with me.' Does that answer your question?"

"Yes, it does," I answer. I return to bed. It doesn't make sense. Suddenly I feel a wave of utter hopelessness sweep over me. I am in the bottom of hell. And there a tremendous hope is born. It might be true.

I tumble out of bed onto my knees. I know not what I say. But slowly a great peace comes to me. I feel lifted up. I believe in God. I crawl back into bed and sleep like a child.

Some men and women come to visit my friend of the night before. He invites me to meet them. They are a joyous crowd. I have never seen people that joyous before. We talk. I tell them of the Peace, and that I believe in God. I think of my wife. I must write her. One girl suggests that I phone her. What a wonderful idea.

My wife hears my voice and knows I have found the answer to life. She comes to New York. I get out of the hospital and we visit some of these new-found friends. What a glorious time we have!

I am home again. I have lost the fellowship. Those that understand me are far away. The same old problems and worries surround me. Members of my family annoy me. Nothing seems to be working out right. I am blue and unhappy. Maybe a drink—I put on my hat and dash off in the car.

Get into the lives of other people, is one thing the fellows in New York had said. I go to see a man I had been asked to visit and tell him my story. I feel much better! I have forgotten about a drink.

I am on a train, headed for a city. I have left my wife at home, sick, and I have been unkind to her in leaving. I am very unhappy. Maybe a few drinks when I get to the city will help. A great fear seizes me. I talk to the stranger in the seat with me. The fear and the insane idea is taken away.

Things are not going so well at home. I am learning that I cannot have my own way as I used to. I blame my wife and children. Anger possesses me, anger such as I have never felt before. I will not stand for it. I pack my bag and leave. I stay with understanding friends.

I see where I have been wrong in some respects. I do not feel angry any more. I return home and say I am sorry for my wrong. I am quiet again. But I have not seen yet that I should do some constructive acts of love without expecting any return. I shall learn this after some more explosions.

I am blue again. I want to sell the place and move away. I want to get where I can find some alcoholics to help, and where I can have some fellowship. A man calls me on the phone. Will I take a young fellow who has been drinking for two weeks to live with me? Soon I have others who are alcoholics and some who have other problems.

I begin to play God. I feel that I can fix them all. I do not fix anyone, but I am getting part of a tremendous education and I have made some new friends.

Nothing is right. Finances are in bad shape. I must find a way to make some money. The family seems to think of nothing but spending. People annoy me. I try to read. I try to pray. Gloom surrounds me. Why has God left me? I mope around the house. I will not go out and I will not enter into anything. What is the matter? I cannot understand. I will not be that way.

I'll get drunk! It is a cold-blooded idea. It is premeditated. I fix up a little apartment over the garage with books and drinking water. I am going to town to get some liquor and food. I shall not drink until I get back to the apartment. Then I shall lock myself in and read. And as I read, I shall take little drinks at long intervals. I shall get myself "mellow" and stay that way.

I get in the car and drive off. Halfway down the driveway a thought strikes me. I'll be honest anyway. I'll tell my wife what I am going to do. I back up to the door and go into the house. I call my wife into a room where we can talk privately. I tell her quietly what I intend to do. She says nothing. She does not get excited. She maintains a perfect calm.

When I am through speaking, the whole idea has become absurd. Not a trace of fear is in me. I laugh at the insanity of it. We talk of other things. Strength has come from weakness.

I cannot see the cause of this temptation now. But I am to learn later that it began with the desire for my own material success becoming greater than the interest in the welfare of my fellow man. I learn more of that foundation stone of character, which is honesty. I learn that when we act upon the highest conception of honesty which is given us, our sense of honesty becomes more acute.

I learn that honesty is truth, and the truth shall make us free!

Sensuality, drunkenness, and worldliness satisfy a man for a time, but their power is a decreasing one. God produces harmony in those who receive His Spirit and follow Its dictates.

Today as I become more harmonized within, I become more in tune with all of God's wonderful creation. The singing of the birds, the sighing of the wind, the patter of raindrops, the roll of thunder, the laughter of happy children, add to the symphony with which I am in tune. The heaving ocean, the driving rain, autumn leaves, the stars of heaven, the perfume of flowers, music, a smile, and a host of other things tell me of the glory of God.

There are periods of darkness, but the stars are shining, no matter how black the night. There are disturbances, but I have learned that if I seek patience and open-mindedness, understanding will come. And with it, direction by the Spirit of God. The dawn comes and with it more understanding, the peace that passes understanding, and the joy of living that is not disturbed by the wildness of circumstances or people around me. Fears, resentments, pride, worldly desires, worry, and self-pity no longer possess me. Ever-increasing are the number of true friends, ever-growing is the capacity for love, ever-widening is the horizon of understanding. And above all else comes a greater thankfulness to, and a greater love for Our Father in heaven.

The S.S. "Falcon" of the Red D. Line, bound from New York to Maracaibo, Venezuela, glided up the bay, and docked at the wharf in the port of La Guayra on a hot tropical afternoon early in 1927. I was a passenger on that boat bound for the oil fields of Maracaibo as an employee of the X Oil Company, under a two year contract at a good salary and maintenance. There I hoped to buckle down to two years of hard work, and save some money, but above all to avoid any long, continued drinking that would interfere with my work, because that had cost me too many jobs in the past.

Not that I was going to give up drinking entirely; no, such a step would be too drastic. But down here in the oil fields with a bunch of hard working, hard drinking good fellows, I, too, would learn how to handle my liquor and not let it get the best of me again. Such an environment would surely do the trick, would surely teach me to drink moderately with the best of them and keep me away from those long, disastrous sprees. I was still young, I could make the grade, and this was my chance to do it. At last I had the real answer, and my troubles were over!

Red and I, who had become bosom shipboard companions on the way down from New York, stood at the rail watching the activity on the dock incident to getting the vessel secured alongside. Red was also on his way to Maracaibo to work for the same company, and we agreed that so long as we were going to be here overnight, we might as well go ashore together and look the town over.

Red was a swell fellow who might take a drink now and then, who might even get drunk once in a while, but he could handle his liquor and did not go to any great excesses. Thousands of other fellows like him, who have been my drinking companions from time to time, were in no way responsible for the way I drank, or what I did, or the way liquor affected me.

So off we went, Red and I, to do the town—and do it we did.

After a few drinks we decided there wasn't much else to do in town except to make a round of the "cantinas," have a good time, get back to the ship early and get a good night's rest. So what harm would a little drinking do now, I reasoned. Especially with one full day and two nights ahead to get over it.

We visited every "cantina" along the straggling main street of La Guayra, and feeling high, wide and handsome, Red and I decided to return to the ship. When we rolled down to the dock we found that our ship had been berthed off from the wharf about thirty feet and that it was necessary to take a tender out to her. No such ordinary method would satisfy Red and myself, so we decided to climb the stern hawser hand over hand to get on board. The flip of a coin decided that I would go first; so off I started, hand over hand, up the hawser.

Now even a good experienced sailor, perfectly sober, would never attempt such a foolhardy feat and, as was to be expected, about half way up the hawser I slipped and fell into the bay with a loud splash. I remember nothing more until next morning. The captain of the boat said to me "Young man, it is true that God looks after drunken fools and little children. You probably don't know it, but this bay is infested with man-eating sharks and usually a man overboard is a goner. How close you were to death, you don't realize, but I do."

Yes, I was lucky to be saved! But it wasn't until ten years later, after I had time and time again tempted Fate by going on protracted benders that I was really saved not until after I had been fired from job after job, tried the patience of my family to the breaking point, alienated what might have been many, many good, lasting friendships, taken my dear wife through more sorrow and heartaches than any one woman should bear in a lifetime; after doctors, hospitals, psychiatrists, rest cures, changes of scenery and all the other paraphernalia that go with the alcoholic's futile attempts to quit drinking. Finally I dimly began to get the realization that during twenty years of continual drinking every expedient I had tried, (and I had tried them all) had failed me. I hated to admit the fact even to myself, that I just couldn't lick booze. I was licked. I was desperate. I was scared.

I was born in 1900, my father was a hardworking man who did the very best he could to support his family of four on a small income. Mother was very good to us, kind, patient, and loving. As soon as we were old enough my mother sent us to Sunday School and it so happened that as I grew older I took quite an active interest, becoming successively a teacher and later Superintendent of a small Sunday School in uptown New York.

When the United States entered the World War in April 1917, I was under age but, like most other youngsters of that period, wanted very much to get into the fray. My parents, of course, would not hear of this but told me to be sensible and wait until I was eighteen. Being young and restless, however, and fired by the military spirit of the times, I ran away from home to join the Army in another city.

There I joined up. I didn't get into any of the actual hostilities at the front, but later, after the Armistice, served with the United States forces occupying the Rhineland, working my way up to a good non-commissioned rank.

While serving abroad I started to drink. This, of course, was entirely my own choice. Drinking by a soldier during those times was viewed with a degree of indulgence by both superiors and civilians. It seems to me, as I recall it now, that even then I wasn't satisfied to drink like the normal fellow.

Most of the United States Army of Occupation were sent back home in 1921 but my appetite for travel had been whetted, and having heard terrible stories of Prohibition in the United States, I wanted to remain in Europe where "a man could raise a thirst."

Subsequently I went to Russia, then to England, and back to Germany; working in various capacities, my drinking increasing and my drunken escapades getting worse. So back home in 1924 with the sincere desire to stop drinking and the hope that the Prohibition I had heard so much about would enable me to do it—in other words—that it would keep me away from it.

I secured a good position, but it wasn't long before I was initiated into the mysteries of the speakeasy to such an extent that I soon found myself once more jobless. After looking around for some time, I found that my foreign experience would help me in securing work in South America. So, full of hope once more, resolved that at last I was on the wagon to stay, I sailed for the tropics. A little over a year was all the company I then worked for would stand of my continual drinking and ever-lengthening benders. So they had me poured on a boat and shipped back to New York.

This time I was really through. I promised my family and friends, who helped me get along while looking for another job, that I would never take another drink as long as I lived—and I meant it. But alas!

After several successive jobs in and around New York had been lost, and it isn't necessary to tell you the cause, I was sure that the only thing that would enable me to get off the stuff was a change of scenery. With the help of patient, long-suffering friends, I finally persuaded an oil company that I could do a good job for them in the oil fields of Maracaibo.

But it was the same thing all over again!

Back to the United States. I really sobered up for a while—long enough to establish a connection with my present employers. During this time I met the girl who is now my wife. At last here was the real thing—I was in love. I would do anything for her. Yes, I would give up drinking. I would never, never do anything to even remotely affect the happiness that now came into my life. My worries were over, my problem was solved. I had sown my wild oats and now I was going to settle down to be a good husband and live a normal happy life.

And so we were married.

Supported by my new found happiness, my abstinence this time lasted about six months. Then a New Year's party we gave started me off on a long bender. The thing about this episode that is impressed on my mind is how earnestly and sincerely I then promised my wife that I would absolutely and positively this time give up drinking—and again I meant it.

No matter what we tried, and my wife helped me in each new experiment to the best of her ability and understanding, failure was always the result, and each time greater hopelessness.

The next step was doctors, a succession of them, with occasional hospitalization. I remember one doctor who thought a course of seventy-two injections, three a week, after two weeks in a private hospital, would supply the deficiency in my system that would enable me to stop drinking. The night after the seventy-second injection I was paralyzed drunk and a couple of days later talked myself out of being committed to the City Hospital.

My long-suffering employers had a long talk with me and told me that they were only willing to give me one last final chance because during my short periods of sobriety I had shown them that I could do good work. I knew they meant it and that it was the last chance they would ever give me.

I also knew that my wife couldn't stand it much longer.

Somehow or other I felt that I had been cheated—that I had not really been cured at the sanitarium even though I felt good physically. So I talked it over with my wife who said there must be something somewhere that would help me. She persuaded me to go back to the sanitarium and consult Dr.—, which thank God I did.

He told me everything had been done for me that was medically possible but that unless I decided to quit I was licked. "But doctor," I said, "I have decided time and time again to quit drinking and I was sincere each time, but each time I slipped again and each time it got worse." The doctor smiled and said, "Yes, yes, I've heard that story hundreds of times. You really never made a decision, you just made declarations. You've got to decide and if you really want to quit drinking I know of some fellows who can help you. Would you like to meet them?"

Would a condemned man like a reprieve? Of course I wanted to meet them. I was so scared and so desperate that I was willing to try anything. Thus it was that I met that band of life-savers, Alcoholics Anonymous.

The first thing Bill told me was his own story, which paralleled mine in most respects, and then said that for three years he had had no trouble. It was plain to see that he was a supremely happy man—that he possessed a happiness and peacefulness I had for years envied in men.

What he told me made sense because I knew that everything that I, my wife, my family and my friends had tried had failed. I had always believed in God even though I was not a devout church-goer. Many times in my life I had prayed for the things I wanted God to do for me, but it had never occurred to me that He, in His Infinite Wisdom knew much better than I what I should have, and be, and do, and that if I simply turned the decision over to Him, I would be led along the right path.

At the conclusion of our first interview, Bill suggested that I think it over and come back to see him within a few days if I was interested. Fully realizing the utter futility with which my own efforts had met in the past, and somehow or other sensing that delay might be dangerous, I was back to see him the next day.

At first it seemed a wild, crazy idea to me, but because of the fact that everything else I had tried had failed, because everything seemed so hopeless, and because it worked with these fellows who all had been through the same hell that I had been through, I was willing, at least, to have a try.

To my utter astonishment, when I did give their method a fair trial, it not only worked, but was so amazingly easy and simple that I said to them, "Where have you been all my life?"

That was in February, 1937, and life took on an entirely different meaning. It was plain to see that my wife was radiantly happy. All of the differences that we seemed to have been having, all of the tenseness, the worry, confusion, the hectic days and nights that my drinking had poured into our life together, vanished. There was peace. There was real love. There was kindness and consideration. There was everything that goes into the fabric of a happy normal existence together.

My employers, of course, the same as the writers of these stories, must remain anonymous. But I would be very thoughtless if I did not take this opportunity to acknowledge what they did for me. They kept me on, giving me chance after chance, hoping I suppose, that some day I would find the answer, although they themselves did not know what it might be. They do now, however.

A tremendous change took place in my work, in my relationship with my employers, in my association with my co-workers and in my dealings with our customers. Crazy as the idea seemed when broached to me by these men who had found it worked, God did come right into my work when permitted, as He had come into the other activities connected with my life.

With this sort of lubricant the wheels turned so much more smoothly that it seemed as if the whole machine operated on a much better basis than heretofore. Promotion that I had longed for previously, but hadn't deserved, was given to me. Soon another followed; more confidence, more trust, more responsibility and finally a key executive position in that same organization which so charitably kept me on in a minor position through the period of my drunkenness.

You can't laugh that off. Come into my home and see what a happy one it is. Look into my office, it is a happy human beehive of activity.

Look into any phase of my life and you will see joy and happiness, a sense of usefulness in the scheme of things, where formerly there was fear, sorrow and utter futility.

A DIFFERENT SLANT

I PROBABLY have one of the shortest stories in this whole volume and it is short because there is one point I wish to get over to an occasional man who may be in my position.

Partner in one of this country's nationally known concerns, happily married with fine children, sufficient income to indulge my whims and future security from the financial standpoint should paint a picture in which there would be no possibility of a man becoming an alcoholic from the psychological standpoint. I had nothing to escape from and I am known as a conservative, sound business man.

I had missed going to my office several times while I tapered off and brought myself to sobriety. This time, though, I found I could not taper off, I could not stop and I had to be hospitalized. That was the greatest shock to my pride I ever had. Such a blow that I made the firm resolve to never again taste as much as one glass of beer. Careful thought and analysis went into that decision.

The doctor at this hospital told me vaguely of the work of men who called themselves Alcoholics Anonymous and asked if I wanted one of them to call upon me. I was sure I needed no outside help, but in order to be polite to the doctor and hoping he would forget it, I assented.

I was embarrassed when a chap called at my house one evening and told me about himself. He quickly sensed my slight resentment and made it plain to me that none of the crowd were missionaries, nor did they feel it their duty to try to help anyone who did not want help. I think I closed the talk by saying I was glad I was not an alcoholic and sorry he had been bothered by me.

Within sixty days, after leaving the hospital the second time, I was pounding at his door, willing to do anything to conquer the vicious thing that had conquered me.

The point I hope I have made is—even a man with everything from the material standpoint, a man with tremendous pride and the will power to function in all ordinary circumstances can become an alcoholic and find himself as hopeless and helpless as the man who has a multitude of worries and troubles.

The annual post-game banquet was winding up. The last rolling "R" of the speaker's hearty Caledonian accent died away sonorously. The company of students and alumni, all Scots, began to adjourn to the spacious bar for stronger stuff than the comparatively innocuous wines on the tables. A goal-scorer in a soccer game between my school and its centuries-old rival, I rated some popularity and the admiration of the moment expressed in famous ales and whiskey and soda. I was the son of a clergyman and just past sixteen years of age.

Waking in my hotel room the next day, I groaned. I didn't want to see or talk to anyone. Then someone raised my head and put a glass to my lips. "What you need is *a* hair of the dog that bit you,' get this into you."

The smell of the stuff sickened me. I grimaced, gulped the draught down and fell back on the bed. Somehow it stayed down and in about fifteen minutes I began to feel better and managed to eat a fair breakfast. That was my first experience of the "morning after" drink.

Back to college and my apprenticeship to a well-known lawyer, the students in their various clubs and societies, tippled enormously. I gave up the law but stayed in school to graduate. Through these college years in a city of well over a million inhabitants I learned all the better barrooms. Burns and Byron and other colorful profligates were the literary idols in the gang of "bloods" with whom I was a popular figure. I thought I was a gay dog and this was the life.

With nothing but a liberal arts education, very definitely estranged from my family and already married, soon after graduation I became a bookmaker's clerk on the British racing circuits, far better off financially than the average professional man. I moved in a gay crowd in the various "pubs" and sporting clubs. My wife traveled with me, but with a baby coming I decided to settle in a large city where I got a job with a commission agent which is a polite term for a hand-book operator. My job was to collect bets and betting-slips in the business section, a lucrative spot. My boss, in his way, was "big business." Drinking was all in the day's work.

One evening, the book, after checking up, was very definitely in the red for plenty through a piece of studied carelessness on my part, and my boss, very shrewd and able, fired me with a parting statement to the effect that once was enough. With a good stake I sailed for New York. I knew I was through among the English "bookies."

Tom Sharkey's brawling bar on 14th Street and the famous wine-room at the back were headquarters for me. I soon ran through my stake. Some college friends got me jobs when I finally had to go to work, but I didn't stick to them. I wanted to travel. Making my way to Pittsburgh, I met other former friends and got a job in a large factory where piecemakers were making good money. My fellow-workers were mostly good Saturday night drinkers and I was right with them. Young and able to travel with the best of them, I managed to hold my job and keep my end up in the bar-rooms.

One of my keenest memories is of meeting Jack London who came in unannounced one night to our favorite saloon, made a rousing speech, and later set up the drinks all evening.

I quit the factory and got a job on a small newspaper, going from that to a Pittsburgh daily, long ago defunct. Following a big drunk on that sheet where I was doing leg-work and rewrite, a feeling of nostalgia made me buy a ticket for Liverpool and I returned to Britain.

During my visit there, renewing acquaintance with former friends I soon spent most of my money. I wanted to roam again and through relatives got a supercargo job on an Australian packet which allowed me to visit my people in Australia where I was born. But I didn't stay long. I was soon back in Liverpool. Coming out of a pub near the Cunard pier I saw the Lusitania standing out in the middle of the Mersey. She had just come in and was scheduled to sail in two days. In my mind's eye I saw Broadway again and Tom Sharkey's bar; the roar of the subway was in my ears. Saying goodbye to my wife and baby, I was treading Manhattan's streets in a little more than a week. Again I spent my bankroll, by no means as thick as the one I had when I first saw the skyline of Gotham. I was soon broke, this time without train-fare to go anywhere. I got my first introduction to "riding the rods and making a blind."

In my early twenties the hardships of hobo life did not discourage me but I had no wish to become just a tramp. Forced to detrain from an empty gondola on the other side of Chicago by a terrific rainstorm which drenched me to the skin, I hit the first factory building I saw for a job. That job began a series of brief working spells, each one ending in a "drunk" and the urge to travel. My migrations extended for over a year as far west as Omaha. Drifting back to Ohio, I landed on a small newspaper and later was impressed into the direction of boy-welfare work at the local "Y". I stayed sober for four years except for a one-night carousel in Chicago. I stayed so sober that I used to keep a quart of medicinal whiskey in my bureau which I used to taper off the occasional newspaper alcoholics who were sent to see me.

Lots of times, vain-gloriously, I used to take the bottle out, look at it and say, "I've got you licked."

The war was getting along. Curious about it, feeling I was missing something, absolutely without any illusions about the aftermath, with no pronounced feeling of patriotism, I joined up with a Canadian regiment, serving a little over two years. Slight casualties, complicated however by a long and serious illness, were my only mishaps. Remarkably enough, I was a very abstemious soldier. My four years of abstinence had something to do with it, but soldiering is a tough enough game for a sober man, and I had no yen for full-pack slogging through mud with a cognac or vin rouge hangover.

Discharged in 1919, I really made up for my dry spell.

Quebec, Toronto, Buffalo, and finally Pittsburgh, were the scenes of man-sized drunks until I had gone through my readjusted discharge pay, a fair sum.

I again became a reporter on a Pittsburgh daily. I applied for a publicity job and got it. My wife came over from Scotland and we started housekeeping in a large Ohio city.

The new job lasted five years. Every encouragement was given me with frequent salary increases, but the sober times between "periods" became shorter. I myself could see deterioration in my work, from being physically and mentally affected by liquor, although I had not yet reached the point where all I wanted was more to drink. Successive Monday morning hangovers, which despite mid-week resolutions to do better, came with unfailing regularity, eventually causing me to quit my job. Washington, D.C. and news-gathering agency work followed with many parties. I couldn't stand the pace. My drinking was never the spaced doses of the careful tippler; it was always gluttonous.

Returning to the town I had left three months before, I became editor of a monthly magazine, soon had additional publicity and advertising accounts and the money rolled in. The strain of overwork soon led me to the bottle again. My wife made several attempts to get me to stop and I had the usual visits from persons who would always ask me "Why?" As if I knew! Offered the job of advertising manager for an eastern automotive company, I moved to Philadelphia to begin life anew. In three months John Barleycorn had me kicked out.

I did six years of newspaper advertising, and trade journal work with many, many drunks of drab and dreary hue woven into the pattern of my life. I visited my family just once in that time. An old avocation, the collection of first editions, rare books and Americana, fascinated me between times. I had some financial success through no ability of my own, and, when jobless and almost wiped out in 1930, I began to trade and sell my collection and much of the proceeds went to keep my apartment stocked with liquor and almost every night saw me helpless to bed.

I tried to help myself. I even began to go the rounds of the churches. I listened to famous ministers—found nothing. I began to know the inside of jails and workhouses. My family would have nothing to do with me, in fact couldn't, because I couldn't spare any of my money which I needed for drink to support them. My last venture, a book shop, was hastened to closed doors by my steady intoxication. Then I had an idea.

Loading a car with good old books to sell to collectors, librarians, universities and historical societies, I started out to travel the country. I stayed sober during the trip except for an occasional bottle of beer because funds barely met expenses. When I hit Houston, Texas, I found employment in a large bookstore. Need I say here that in a very short time I was walking along a prairie highway with arm extended and thumb pointed? In the two succeeding years I held ten different jobs ranging from newspaper copy-desk and rewrite, to traffic director for an oil field equipment company. Always in between there were intervals of being broke, riding freights and hitch-hiking interminable distances from one big town to another in three states. Now on a new job I was always thinking about payday and how much liquor I could buy and the pleasure I could have.

I knew I was a drunkard. Enduring all the hangover hells that every alcoholic experiences, I made the usual resolutions. My thoughts sometimes turned to the idea that there must be a remedy. I have stood listening to street-corner preachers tell how they did beat the game. They seemed to be happy in their fashion, they and the little group of supporters, but always pride of intellect stopped me from seeking what they evidently had. Sniffing at emotional religion I walked away. I was an honest agnostic but definitely not a hater of the church or its adherents. What philosophy I had was thoroughly paganistic—all my life was devoted to a search for pleasure. I wanted to do nothing except what it pleased me to do and when I wanted to do it.

Federal Theater in Texas gave me an administrative job which I held for a year, only because I worked hard and productively when I worked, and because my very tolerant chief ascribed my frequent lapses to a bohemian temperament. When it was closed through Washington edict I began with Federal Writers in San Antonio. In those days my system was always to drink up my last pay check and believe that necessity would bring the next job. A friend who knew I would soon be broke mounted guard over me when I left my job of writing the histories of Texas cities and put me aboard a bus for the town I had left almost five years before.

In five years a good many persons had forgotten that I had been somewhat notorious. I had arrived drunk but promised my wife I would keep sober, and I knew I could get work if I did. Of course, I didn't keep sober. My wife and family stood by me for ten weeks and then, quite justifiably, ejected me. I managed to maintain myself with odd jobs, did ten weeks in a social rescue institution and at length wound up in a secondhand bookstore in an adjacent town as manager. While there I was called to the hospital in my home town to see a former partner who had insisted that I visit him. I found my friend was there for alcoholism and now he was insisting that he had found the only cure. I listened to him, rather tolerantly. I noticed a Bible on his table and it amazed me. I had never known him to be anything but a good healthy pagan with a propensity for getting into liquor jams and scrapes. As he talked I gathered vaguely, (because he was a faltering beginner then just as I am now) that to be relieved of alcoholism I would have to be different.

Some days later, after he had been discharged, a stranger came into my shop in the nearby town. He introduced himself and began to tell me about a bunch of some 60 former drinkers and drunkards who met once a week, and he invited me to go with him to the next meeting. I thanked him, pleaded business engagements and promised I'd go with him at some future date.

"Anyhow, I'm on the wagon now," I said. "I'm doing a job I like and it's quiet where I live, practically no temptations. I don't feel bothered about liquor."

He looked at me quizzically. He knew too well that didn't mean a thing just as I knew in my heart that it would be only a question of time—a few days, a week, or even a month, it was inevitable—till I would be off on another bender. The time came just a week later. And as I look back on the events of two months, I can clearly see that I had been circling around, half-afraid of encountering the remedy for my situation, half-wanting it, deferring fulfillment of my promise to get in touch with the doctor I had heard about. An accident while drunk laid me low for about three weeks. As soon as I could get up and walk I started to drink again and kept up until my friend of the hospital, who, in his first try at the new way of life had stubbed his toe in Chicago but had come back to the town to take counsel and make a new start, picked me up and got me into a hospital.

I had been drinking heavily from one state of semi–coma to another and it was several days before I got "defogged" but subconsciously I was in earnest about wanting to quit liquor forever. It was no momentary emotionalism born of self-pity in a maudlin condition. I was seeking something and I was ready to learn. I did not need to be told that my efforts were and would be unavailing if I did not get help. The doctor who came to see me almost at once did not assail me with any new doctrines; he made sure that I had a need and that I wanted to have that need filled and little by little I learned how my need could be met. The story of Alcoholics Anonymous fascinated me. Singly and in groups of two or three, they came to visit me. Some of them I had known for years, good two-fisted drinkers who had disappeared from their former haunts. I had missed them myself from the barrooms of the town.

There were business men, professional men, and factory workers. All sorts were represented and their relation of experiences and how they had found the only remedy, added to their human existence as sober men, laid the foundation of a very necessary faith. Indeed, I was beginning to see that I would require implicit faith, like a small child, if I was going to get anywhere or so it appeared as I lay in that hospital. The big thing was that these men were all sober and evidently had something I didn't have. Whatever it was, I wanted it.

I left the hospital on a meeting night. I was greeted warmly, honestly, and with a true ring of sincerity by everyone present. That night I was taken home by a former alcoholic and his wife. They did not show me to my room and wish me a good night's rest. Instead, over coffee cups, this man and his wife told me what had been done for them. They were earnest and obviously trying to help me on the road I had chosen. They will never know how much their talk with me has helped. The hospitality of their home and their fine fellowship were mine freely.

I had never, since the believing days of childhood, been able to conceive an authority directing the universe. But I had never been a flippant, wise-cracking sneerer at the few persons I had met who had impressed me as Christian men and women, or at any institutions whose sincerity of purpose I could see. No conviction was necessary to establish my status as a miserable failure at managing my own life. I began to read the Bible daily and to go over a simple devotional exercise as a way to begin each day.

Gradually I began to understand.

I cannot say that my taste for liquor has entirely *dis*appeared. It has been that way with some, but it has not been with me and may never be. Neither can I honestly say that I have forgotten the "fleshpots of Egypt." I haven't. But I can remember the urge of the Prodigal Son to return to his Father that he might taste of the husks that the swine did eat.

Formerly in the acute mental and physical pain during the remorseful periods succeeding each drunk, I found my recollection of the misery I had gone through a bolsterer of resolution and afterward, perhaps, a deterrent for a time. But in those days I had no one to whom I might take my troubles. Today I have. Today I have Someone who will always hear me; I have a warm fellowship among men who understand my problems; I have tasks to do and am glad to do them, to see others who are alcoholics and to help them in any way I can to become sober men.

When I was graduated from high-school the World War was on in full blast. I was too young for the army but old enough to man a machine for the production of the means of wholesale destruction. I became a machine-hand at high wages. Machinery appealed to me anyway, because I had always wanted to be a mechanical engineer. Keen to learn as many different operations as possible, I insisted on being transferred from one operation to another until I had a good practical knowledge of all machines in a standard machine shop. With that equipment I was ready to travel for broader experience and in seven years had worked in the leading industrial centers in the eastern states, supplementing my shop work with night classes in marine engineering.

I had the good times of the period but confined my drinking to weekends, with an occasional party after work in the evenings. But I was unsettled and dissatisfied, and in a sense disgusted with going from job to job and achieving nothing more than a weekly pay envelope. I wasn't particularly interested in making a lot of money, but I wanted to be comfortable and independent as soon as possible.

So I married at that time, and for a while it seemed that I had found the solution to my urge for moving around. Most people settle down when they marry and I thought I'd have the same experience, that my wife and I would chose a place where we could establish a home and bring up a family. I had the dream of wearing carpet slippers in a life of comparative ease by the time I was forty. It didn't work out that way. After the newness of being married had worn off a little the old wander business got me again.

In 1924, I brought my wife to a growing city in the middle west where work was always plentiful. I had been in and out of work several times before and I could always get a job in the engineering department of its largest industrial plant. I early acquired the spirit of the organization which had a real reputation for constructive education of its workers. It encouraged ambition and aided latent talent to develop. I was keen about my work and strove always to place myself in line for promotion. I had a thorough knowledge of the mechanical needs of the plant and when I was offered a job in the purchasing department's mechanical section I took it.

We were now resident in sort of a workers' paradise, a beautifully landscaped district where employees were encouraged to buy homes from the company. We had a boy about two years after I started with the company and with his advent I began to take marriage seriously. My boy was going to have the best I could give him. He would never have to work through the years as I had done. We had a very nice circle of acquaintance where we lived, nice neighbors and my colleagues in the engineering department and later in purchasing were good people, many of them bent on getting ahead and enjoying the good things of life while they climbed. We had nice parties with very little drinking, just enough to give a little Saturday night glow to things—never enough to get beyond control.

Fateful and fatal came the month of October in the year 1929. Work slowed down. Reassuring statements from financial leaders maintained our confidence that industry would soon be on an even keel again. But the boat kept rocking. In our organization, as in many others, the purchasing department found its work lessened by executive order. Personnel was cut down. Those who were left went around working furiously at whatever there was to do, looking furtively at each other wondering who would be next to go. I wondered if the long hours of overtime with no pay would be recognized in the cutting down program. I lay awake lots of nights just like any other man who sees what he has built up threatened with destruction.

I was laid off. I took it hard for I had been doing a good job and I thought as a man often will, that it might have been somebody else who should get the axe. Yet there was a sense of relief. It had happened. And partly through resentment and partly from a sense of freedom I went out and got pretty well intoxicated. I stayed drunk for three days, something very unusual for me, who had very seldom lost a day's work from drinking.

My experience soon helped me to a fairly important job in the engineering department of another company. My work took me out of town quite a bit, never at any great distance from home, but frequently overnight.

Sometimes I wouldn't have to report at the office for a week, but I was always in touch by phone. In a way I was practically my own boss and being away from office discipline I was an easy victim to temptation. And temptation certainly existed. I had a wide acquaintance among the vendors to our company who liked me and were very friendly. At first I turned down the countless offers I had to take a drink, but it wasn't long before I was taking plenty.

I'd get back into town after a trip, pretty well organized from my day's imbibing. It was only a step from this daily drinking to successive bouts with absence from my route. I would phone and my chief couldn't tell from my voice whether I had been drinking or not, but gradually learned of my escapades and warned me of the consequences to myself and my job. Finally when my lapses impaired my efficiency and some pressure was brought to bear on the chief, he let me go. That was in 1932.

I found myself back exactly where I had started when I came to town. I was still a good mechanic and could always get a job as an hourly rated machine operator. This seemed to be the only thing which offered and once more I discarded the white collar for the overalls and canvas gloves. I had spent more than half a dozen good years and had got exactly nowhere, so I did my first really serious drinking. I was good for at least ten days or two weeks off every two months I worked, getting drunk and then half-heartedly sobering up. This went on for almost three years. My wife did the best she could to help me at first, but eventually lost patience and gave up trying to do anything with me at all. I was thrown into one hospital after another, got sobered up, discharged, and ready for another bout. What money I had saved dwindled and I turned everything I had into cash to keep on drinking.

In one hospital, a Catholic Institution, one of the sisters had talked religion to me and had brought a priest in to see me. Both were sorry for me and assured me that I would find relief in Mother Church. I wanted none of it. "If I couldn't stop drinking of my own free will, I was certainly not going to drag God into it," I thought.

During another hospital stay a minister whom I liked and respected came to see me. To me, he was just another non-alcoholic who was unable, even by the added benefit and authority of the cloth, to do anything for an alcoholic.

I sat down one day to figure things out. I was no good to myself, my wife, or my growing boy. My drinking had even affected him; he was a nervous, irritable child, getting along badly at school, making poor grades because the father he knew was a sot and an unpredictable one. My insurance was sufficient to take care of my wife and child for a fresh start by themselves and I decided that I'd simply move out of the world for good. I took a killing dose of bichloride of mercury.

They rushed me to the hospital. The emergency physicians applied the immediate remedies but shook their heads. There wasn't a chance, they said. And for days it was touch and go. One day the chief resident physician came in on his daily rounds. He had often seen me there before for alcoholism.

Standing at my bedside he showed more than professional interest, tried to buoy me up with the desire to live. He asked me if I would really like to quit drinking and have another try at living. One clings to life no matter how miserable. I told him I would and that I would try again. He said he was going to send another doctor to see me, to help me.

This doctor came and sat beside my bed. He tried to cheer me up about my future, pointed out I was still a young man with the world to lick and insisted that I could do it if I really wanted to stop drinking. Without telling me what it was, he said he had an answer to my problem and condition that really worked. Then he told me very simply the story of his own life, a life of generous tippling after professional hours for more than three decades until he had lost almost everything a man can lose, and how he had found and applied the remedy with complete success. He felt sure I could do the same. Day after day he called on me in the hospital and spent hours talking to me.

He simply asked me to make a practical application of beliefs I already held theoretically but had forgotten all my life. I believed in a God who ruled the universe. The doctor submitted to me the idea of God as a father who would not willingly let any of his children perish and suggested that most, if not *all* of our troubles, come from being completely out of touch with the idea of God, with God Himself. All my life, he said, I had been doing things of my own human will as opposed to God's will and that the only certain way for me to stop drinking was to submit my will to God and let Him handle my difficulties.

I had never looked on my situation in that way, had always felt myself very remote indeed from a Supreme Being. "Doc," as I shall call him hereinafter, was pretty positive that God's law was the Law of Love and that all my resentful feelings which I had fed and cultivated with liquor were the result of either conscious or unconscious, it didn't matter which, disobedience to that law. Was I willing to submit my will? I said I would try to do so. While I was still at the hospital his visits were supplemented by visits from a young fellow who had been a heavy drinker for years but had run into "Doc" and had tried his remedy.

At that time, the ex-alcoholics in this town, who have now grown to considerable proportions, numbered only Doc and two other fellows. To help themselves and compare notes they met once a week in a private house and talked things over. As soon as I came from the hospital I went with them. The meeting was without formality. Taking love as the basic command I discovered that my faithful attempt to practice a law of love led me to clear myself of certain dishonesties.

I went back to my job. New men came and we were glad to visit them. I found that new friends helped me to keep straight and the sight of every new alcoholic in the hospital was a real object lesson to me. I could see in them myself as I had been, something I had never been able to picture before.

Now I come to the hard part of my story. It would be great to say I progressed to a point of splendid fulfillment, but it wouldn't be true. My later experience points a moral derived from a hard and bitter lesson. I went along peacefully for two years after God had helped me quit drinking. And then something happened. I was enjoying the friendship of my ex-alcoholic fellows and getting along quite well in my work and in my small social circle. I had largely won back the respect of *my* former friends and the confidence of *my* employer. I was feeling fine—too fine. Gradually I began to take the plan I was trying to follow apart. After all, I asked myself, did I really have to follow any plan at all to stay sober? Here I was, dry for two years and getting along all right. It wouldn't hurt if I just carried on and missed a meeting or two. If not present in the flesh I'd be there in spirit, I said in excuse, for I felt a little bit guilty about staying away.

And I began to neglect my daily communication with God. Nothing happened—not immediately at any rate. Then came the thought that I could stand on my own feet now. When that thought came to mind—that God might have been all very well for the early days or months of my sobriety but I didn't need Him now—I was a gone coon. I got clear away from the life I had been attempting to lead. I was in real danger. It was just a step from that kind of thinking to the idea that my two years training in total abstinence was just what I needed to be able to handle a glass of beer. I began to taste. I became fatalistic about things and soon was drinking deliberately knowing I'd get drunk, stay drunk, and what would inevitably happen.

My friends came to my aid. They tried to help me, but I didn't want help. I was ashamed and preferred not to see them come around. And they knew that as long as I didn't want to quit, as long as I preferred my own will instead of God's will, the remedy simply could not be applied. It is a striking thought that God never forces anyone to do His will, that His help is ever available but has to be sought in all earnestness and humility.

This condition lasted for months, during which time I had voluntarily entered a private institution to get straightened out. On the last occasion when I came out of the fog, I asked God to help me again. Shamefaced as I was, I went back to the fellowship. They made me welcome, offered me collectively and individually all the help I might need. They treated me as though nothing had happened. And I feel that it is the most telling tribute to the efficacy of this remedy that during my period of relapse I still knew this remedy would work with me if I would let it, but I was too stubborn to admit it.

That was a year ago. Depend upon it I stay mighty close to what has proven to be good for me. I don't dare risk getting very far away. And I have found that in simple faith I get results by placing my life in God's hands every day, by asking Him to keep me a sober man for 24 hours, and trying to do His will. He has never let me down yet.

STRANGELY ENOUGH, or by some queer quirk, I became acquainted with the hilarious life just at the time in my life when I was beginning to really settle down to a common-sense, sane, domestic life. My wife became pregnant and the doctor recommended the use of Porter Ale . . . so . . . I bought a six gallon crock and a few bottles, listened to advice from amateur brewmeisters, and was off on my beer manufacturing career on a small scale (for the time being). Somehow or other, I must have misunderstood the doctor's instructions, for I not only made the beer for my wife, I also drank it for her.

As time went on, I found that it was customary to open a few bottles whenever visitors dropped in. That being the case, it didn't take me long to figure out that my meager manufacturing facilities were entirely inadequate to the manufacture of beer for social and domestic consumption. From that point on, I secured crocks of ten gallon capacity and really took quite an active interest in the manufacture of home brew.

We were having card parties with limburger and beer quite regularly. Eventually, of course, what with all the hilarity that could be provoked with a few gallons of beer, there seemed to be no need of bridge or poker playing for entertainment. Well . . . we all know how those things go. The parties waxed more liquid up with me, and when it did, I was a mental, physical, and nervous wreck.

I arrived at the stage where I couldn't quite make it to the office some mornings. Then I would send an excuse of illness. But the firm became violently ill with my drunkenness and their course of treatment was to remove their ulcer in the form of me from their payroll, amid much fanfare and very personal and slighting remarks and insinuations.

During this time, I had been threatened, beaten, kissed, praised and damned alternately by relatives, family, friends and strangers, but of course it all went for naught. How many times I swore off in the morning and got drunk before sunset I don't know. I was on the toboggan and really making time.

After being fired, I lined up with a new finance company that was just starting in business, and took the position of business promotion man, contacting automobile dealers. WOW . . . was that something??? While working in an office, there was some semblance of restraint, but,

oh boy, when I got on the outside with this new company without supervision, did I go to town???

I really worked for several weeks, and having had a fairly wide
acquaintance with the dealer trade, it was not difficult for me to line
enough of them up to give me a very substantial volume of business
with a minimum of effort.

Now I was getting drunk all the time. It wasn't necessary to report
to the office in person every day, and when I did go in, it was just to
make an appearance and bounce right out again. Was that a merry-go-
round for the eight months that it lasted? ? ?

Finally this company also became ill and I was once more looking
for a job. Then I learned something else. I learned that a person just
can't find a job hanging in a dive or barroom all day and all night, as
jobs don't seem to turn up in those places. I became convinced of that
because I spent most of my time there and nary a job turned up. By
this time, my chances of getting lined up in my chosen business were
shot. Everyone had my umber and wouldn't hire me at any price.

I have omitted details of transgressions that I made when drunk for
several reasons. One is that I don't remember too many of them, as I
was one of those drunks who could be on his feet and attend a meeting or a party, engage in a conversation with people and do things that
any nearly normal person would do, and the next day, not remember
a thing about where I was, what I did, who I saw, or how I got home.
(That condition was a distinct handicap to me in trying to vindicate
myself with the not so patient wife).

I also committed other indiscretions of which I see no particular
point in relating. Anyone who is a rummy or is close to rummies knows
what all those things amount to without having to be told about them.

Things eventually came to the point where I had no friends. I did-
n't care to go visiting unless the parties we might visit had plenty of
liquor on hand and I could get stinking drunk. Fact is, that I was always
well on my way before I would undertake to go visiting at all. (Naturally,
this condition was also a source of great delight to my wife.)

After holding good positions, making better than average income
for over ten years, I was in debt, had no clothes to speak of, no money,
no friends, and no one any longer tolerating me but my wife. My son

had absolutely no use for me. Even some of the saloonkeepers where I had spent so much time and money, requested that I stay away from their places. Finally, an old business acquaintance of mine, whom I hadn't seen for several years offered me a job. I was on that job a month and drunk most of the time.

Just at this time my wife heard of a doctor in another city who had been very successful with drunks. She offered me the alternative of going to see him or her leaving me for good and all. Well . . . I had a job, and I really wanted desperately to stop drinking, but couldn't, so I readily agreed to visit the doctor she recommended.

That was the turning point of my life. My wife accompanied me on my visit and the doctor really told me some things that in my state of jitters nearly knocked me out of the chair. He talked about himself, but I was sure it was me. He mentioned lies, deceptions, etc. in the course of his story in the presence of the one person in the world I wouldn't want to know such things. How did he know all this? I had never seen him before, and at the time hoped to hell I would never see him again. However, he explained to me that he had been just such a rummy as I, only for a much longer period of time.

He advised me to enter the particular hospital to which staff he was connected and I readily agreed. In all honesty though, I was skeptical, but I wanted so definitely to quit drinking that I would have welcomed any sort of physical torture or pain to accomplish the result.

I made arrangements to enter the hospital three days later and promptly went out and got stiff for three days. It was with grim foreboding and advanced jitters that I checked in at the hospital. Of course, I had no hint or intimation as to what the treatment was to consist of. Was I to be surprised!

After being in the hospital for several days, a plan of living was outlined to me. A very simple plan that I find much joy and happiness in following. It is impossible to put on paper all the benefits I have derived . . . physical, mental, domestic, spiritual, and monetary. This is no idle talk. It is the truth.

From a physical standpoint, I gained 16 pounds in the first two months I was off liquor. I eat three good meals a day now, and really enjoy them. I sleep like a baby, and never give a thought to such a thing as insomnia. I feel as I did when I was fifteen years younger.

Mentally—I know where I was last night, the night before, and the nights before that. Also, I have no fear of anything. I have self confidence and assurance that cannot be confused with the cockiness or noise-making I once possessed. I can think clearly and am helped much in my thinking and judgment by my spiritual development which grows daily.

From a domestic standpoint, we really have a home now. I am anxious to get home after dark. My wife is ever glad to see me come in. My youngster has adopted me. Our home is always full of friends and visitors (No home brew as an inducement).

Spiritually . . . I have found a Friend who never lets me down and is ever eager to help. I can actually take my problems to Him and He does give me comfort, peace, and radiant happiness.

From a monetary standpoint . . . in the past nine months, I have reduced my reckless debts to almost nothing, and have had money to get along comfortably. I still have my job, and just prior to the writing of this narrative, I received an advancement.

For all of these blessings, I thank Him.

AT FOURTEEN years of age, when I should have been at home under the supervision of my parents, I was in the United States army serving a one year enlistment. I found myself with a bunch of men none too good for a fourteen year old kid who passed easily for eighteen. I transferred my hero-worshipping to these men of the world. I suppose the worst damage done in that year in the army barracks was the development of an almost unconscious admiration for their apparently jolly sort of living.

Once out of uniform I went to Mexico where I worked for an oil company. Here I learned to take on a good cargo of beer and hold it. Later I rode the range in the Texas cow country and often went to town with the boys to "whoop it up on payday." By the time I returned to my home in the middle west I had learned several patterns of living, to say nothing of a cock-sure attitude that I needed no advice from anyone.

The next ten years are sketchy. During this time I married and established my own home and everything was lovely for a time. Soon I was having a good time getting around the law in speakeasies. Oh yes, I outsmarted our national laws but I was not quite successful in evading the old moral law.

I was working for a large industrial concern and had been promoted to a supervisional job. In spite of big parties, I was for three or four years able to be on the job the next morning. Then gradually the hangovers became more persistent and I found myself not only needing a few shots of liquor before I could go to work at all, but finally found it advisable to stay at home and sober up by the taper-off method. My bosses tried to give me some good advice. When that didn't help they tried more drastic measures, laying me off without pay. They covered up my too frequent absences many times in order to keep them from the attention of the higher officials in the company.

My attitude was that I could handle my liquor whenever I wanted to go about it seriously, and I considered my absences no worse than those of other employees and officials who were getting away with murder in their drinking.

One does not have to use his imagination much to realize that this sort of drinking is hard on the matrimonial relationship. After proving myself neither faithful nor capable of being temperate, my wife left me and obtained a judicial separation. This gave me a really good excuse to get drunk.

In the years 1933 and 1934 I was fired several times, but always got my job back on my promises to do better. On the last occasion I was reduced to the labor gang in the plant. I made a terrific effort to stay sober and prove myself capable of better things. I succeeded pretty well and one day I was called into the production chief's office and told I had met with the approval of the executive department and to be ready to start on a better job.

This good news seemed to justify a mild celebration with a few beers. Exactly four days later I reported for work only to find that they too knew about the "mild" celebration and that they had decided to check me out altogether. After a time I went back and was assigned to one of the hardest jobs in the factory. I was in bad shape physically and after six months of this, I quit, going on a drunk with my last pay check.

Then I began to find that the friends with whom I had been drinking for some time seemed to disappear. This made me resentful and I found myself many times feeling that everybody was against me. Bootleg joints became my hangouts. I sold my books, car, and even clothing in order to buy a few drinks.

I am certain that my family kept me from gravitating to flophouses and gutters. I am eternally thankful to them that they never threw me out or refused me help when I was drinking. Of course I didn't appreciate their kindness then, and I began to stay away from home on protracted drinking spells.

Somehow my family heard of two men in town who had found a way to quit drinking. They suggested that I contact these men but I retorted, "If I can't handle my liquor with my own will power then I had better jump over the viaduct."

Another of my usual drinking spells came on. I drank for about ten days with no food except coffee before I was sick enough to start the battle back to sobriety with the accompanying shakes, night sweats, jittery nerves, and horrible dreams. This time I felt that I really needed some help. I told my mother she could call the doctor who was the center of the little group of former drinkers. She did.

I allowed myself to be taken to a hospital where it took several days for my head to clear and my nerves to settle. Then, one day I had a couple of visitors, one a man from New York and the other a local attorney. During our conversation I learned that they had been as bad as myself in this drinking, and that they had found relief and had been able to make a come-back. Later they went into more detail and put it to me very straight that I'd have to give over my desires and attitudes to a power higher than myself which would give me new desires and attitudes.

Here was religion put to me in a different way and presented by three past-masters in liquor guzzling. On the strength of their stories I decided to give it a try. And it worked, as long as I allowed it to do so.

After a year of learning new ways of living, new attitudes and desires, I became self-confident and then careless. I suppose you would say I got to feeling too sure of myself and Zowie! First it was a beer on Saturday nights and then it was a fine drunk. I knew exactly what I had done to bring myself to this old grief. I had tried to handle my life on the strength of my own ideas and plans instead of looking to God for the inspiration and the strength.

But I didn't do anything about it. I thought "to hell with everybody. I'm going to do as I please." So I floundered around for seven months refusing help from any quarter. But one day I volunteered to take another drunk on a trip to sober him up. When we got back to town we were both drunk and went to a hotel to sober up. Then I began to reason the thing out. I had been a sober, happy man for a year, living decently and trying to follow the will of God. Now I was unshaven, unkempt, ill-looking, bleary-eyed. I decided then and there and went back to my friends who offered me help and who never lectured me on my seven month failure.

That was more than a year ago. I don't say now that I can do anything. I only know that as long as I seek God's help to the best of my ability, just so long will liquor never bother me.

Coming from a farm boyhood with the common education of the little red schoolhouse, I had worked during the war and afterwards for seven years at high wages in a booming industrial town, had saved considerable money and finally married an able, well educated woman who had an unusual gift of common sense and far more than the average business vision, a true helpmate in every way.

In our early twenties, we were both ambitious and had boundless faith in our ability to succeed. We talked over the future all the time, exchanged ideas and really planned our way in life. Just working in a factory, even at highly-paid piece work, and saving out of my wages, did not seem to us to be the best way to do. We talked things over and decided to strike out for ourselves. Our first venture, a neighborhood grocery store, prospered. Another neighborhood store, in an ideal location at a nearby summer resort, looked good to us. We bought it and started in to make it go. Then came a business slump affecting the whole country. With fewer customers I had lots of time on my hands and was getting to like high-powered home brew and the potent liquors of prohibition days entirely too well. That didn't help the business. We finally shut up shop.

Jobs were scarce, but by persistence I again found a factory job. In a few months the factory closed down.

We had again accumulated a small stake and since the job situation showed no improvement, we thought we would try business again.

This time we opened a restaurant in a semi-rural section and for a time all went well. My wife opened up in the morning, did all the baking and cooking and waited on trade. I relieved her later in the day and stayed open late to catch every possible bit of business. Our place became a regular hang-out for groups of latecomers who showed up with a bottle every now and then.

I told myself that I was one man who could handle my liquor because I was always on my feet at closing time. I talked knowingly about spacing my drinks, about taking only a measured shot, and about the folly of gulping down big drinks. Yes sir, I was never going to be one of those "rummies" who let liquor get the best of them. Young and strong, I could throw off the effects of the previous night's drinking and stand the nausea the following morning, even abstaining from taking a drink until the afternoon. But before long the idea of suffering for a few hours didn't seem so good.

The morning drink became the first act of the daily routine. I had now become a "regular." I had my regular remedy—a stiff shot to start the day and no waiting till a specified time. I used to wait for the need, soon I was craving the stuff so much that I didn't wait for that. My wife could see that it was gripping me. She warned me, gently at first, with quiet seriousness. Was I going to pave the way to losing this business just when it needed to be nursed along? We began to run behind. My wife, anxious for the goal we had set out to reach, and seeing the result if I didn't brace up, talked straight from the shoulder. We had words. I left in a passion.

Our separation lasted a week, I did a lot of thinking, and went back to my wife. Quieter, somewhat remorseful, we talked things over. Our situation was worse than I had anticipated. We got a buyer for the place and sold out. We still had some money left.

I had always been a natural mechanic, handy with tools. We moved back into town with a slim bankroll and, still determined never to be a factory hand again, I looked around and finding a workshop location with a house adjacent I started a sheet-metal shop. I had chosen a very difficult time to start up. My business practically vanished on account of the depression.

There were no jobs of any kind. We fell far behind on our rent and other obligations. Our cupboard was often bare. With every penny needed for food and shelter, and wearing old clothes with nothing new except what our two youngsters needed, I didn't touch a drop for two years. I went after business. I slugged doorbells all over the town asking for jobs. My wife rang bells with me, taking one side of the street while I worked the other. We left nothing undone to keep going, but we were still far behind, so far that at the low point we could see eviction and our belongings in the street.

I braced myself to talk to our landlord who was connected with a large real estate firm managing many properties. We were behind six months in our rent and they saw that the only way to get their back rent was to give me a couple of small jobs. My wife learned to use the tools to shape and fashion material when I was doing the installation work. The real estate firm liked my work and began to give me more jobs. In those grim days, with babies to feed, I couldn't spend what little money came in for drink. I stayed sober. My wife and I even started back to church, began paying our dues.

They were thin years, those depression years. For three years in succession, Christmas in our little family was just the 25th of December. Our customers saw us as two earnest young people trying to get along and as times improved a little we began to get better jobs. Now we could hire some competent workmen and bought a car and a few small trucks. We prospered and moved into a better-equipped house.

My pockets, which hadn't jingled for years, now held folding money. The first greenbacks grew into a roll with a rubber band around it. I became well-known to real estate firms, business men, and politicians. I was well-liked, popular with everyone. Following a prosperous season came a quiet period. With time on our hands I had a drinking spell. It lasted for a month, but with the aid of my wife, I checked myself in time. "Remember how we lost the store! Remember our restaurant!" my wife said. Yes, I could remember. Those times were too recent and their memory too bitter. I solemnly swore off and once more climbed aboard the wagon, this time for nine long months.

Business kept up. It became evident that by careful handling we might eventually have something pretty good, a sufficient income to provide a good living for us all and ensure a good education for our children.

My business is seasonal. Fall and early winter are rush times. The first few months of the year are quiet. But though business slackened, I got around making contracts, lining up future work and meeting people who would be able to put work in my way. Not yet sensing any great danger, in spite of past experiences, I seldom refused the invitations of business friends to have a drink. In a short time I was drinking every day and eventually much more than I had ever done before, for I always had a roll in my pocket.

At first I was even more jolly than usual when I came home in the evening to my wife and family. But the joking good fellow who was the husband and father they had known, gave place to a man who slammed the door when he came in. My wife, genuinely alarmed now as week after week went past without any sign that I was going to quit, tried to reason with me, but the old arguments didn't work this time.

Summer came on with its demand for roof repairs and spouting installations. My wife often started the men to work in the morning, did shop jobs, kept the books, and in addition, ran the house and looked after the family.

For eight months my daily routine was steady drinking. Even after slumping in bed late at night in a semi-stupor, I would get up at all hours and drive to some all-night spot where I could get what I wanted. I was going to have a good time in spite of hell and high water. I became increasingly surly when at home. I was the boss. I was master in my own house, wasn't I? I became morose, with few lucid moments between drinks. I would listen to no arguments and certainly attempts to reason with me were futile. Unknown to me, my wife influenced some of my friends and business associates to drop in casually. They were mostly non-drinkers and generally ended up by mildly upbraiding me.

"A fine lot of Job's comforters," I would say. I felt that everybody was against me, thought bitterly of my wife as being of little help and told myself I wasn't getting the breaks, that everybody was making a mountain out of a molehill and so, to hell with everything! I still had money and with money I could always buy bottled happiness. And still my wife kept trying. She got our pastor to talk to me. It was no good.

Drinking and staying drunk without cessation, even my splendid constitution began to give way. My wife called doctors who gave me temporary relief. Then my wife left me after a bitter quarrel, taking the children with her. *My* pride was hurt and I began to regard myself as an injured husband and an unappreciated father who, deep in his heart, just doted on his children. I went to *see* her and demanded to see them. I up and told her that I didn't care whether she came back or not, that I wanted the children. My wife, wise woman, thought she still had a chance to have me, save our home for the children. She threw aside her sense of injury, spoke right up to me and said she was coming back, that forbidding her the house wouldn't work, that she had helped me get what I had and was going to cross its threshold and resume its management. She did just that.

When she opened the door she was appalled at the sight of it, cur-
tains down, dishes and utensils unwashed, dirty glasses and empty bottles everywhere.

Every alcoholic reaches the end of the tether some day. For me there
came a day when, physically and mentally, I was unable to make my way
to a saloon for a drink. I went to bed. I told my wife for the first time
that I wanted to quit drinking, but couldn't. I asked her to do something for me; I had never done this before. I realized that I needed
help. Somehow in talking with a lady doctor, my wife had heard of
another doctor who in some mysterious way had stopped drinking after
thirty years and had been successful in helping a few other alcoholics
to become sober men. As a last resort, my wife appealed to this doctor,
who insisted on a certain situation before he could help; his experience had taught him that unless that situation existed nothing could
be done for the alcoholic.

"Does your husband want to stop drinking, or is he merely temporarily uncomfortable? Has he come to the end of the road?" he asked
my wife.

She told him that for the first time I had expressed a desire to quit,
that I had asked her in desperation to try to do something—anything,
to help me stop. He said he would see me the following morning.

With every part of my being craving a drink, I could hardly sit still
when I got up to await the visit from the man she had talked to on the
phone, but something kept me in the house. I wanted to hear what
this fellow had to offer and since he was a medical man I had some
preconceived notions ready for him when he came. I was pretty jittery
when my wife opened the door to admit a tall, somewhat brusque professional man who, from his speech, was obviously an Easterner. I don't
know what I had expected, but his salutation, designed to shake me
up, I can now see, had almost the same effect as the hosing with cold
water in a Turkish bath.

"I hear you're another rummy," he said as he smiled and sat down
beside me. I let him talk. Gradually he drew me out until what I did
tell him gave him a picture of my experience. And then he put it to
me plainly. "If you are perfectly sure that you want to quit drinking for
good, if you are serious about it, if you don't merely wish to get well so

that you can take up drinking again at some future date, you can be relieved," he said.

I told him that I had never wanted anything as much in my life as to be able to quit using liquor, and I meant every word of it.

"The first thing to do with your husband," he said, turning to my wife, "is to get him to a hospital and have him 'defogged.' I'll make the necessary arrangements."

He didn't go into any further explanation, not even to my wife. That evening I was in a hospital bed. The next day the doctor called. He told me that several former alcoholics were now dry as a result of following a certain prescribed course of action and that some of them would be in to see me. My wife came to see me faithfully. She, too, had been learning, perhaps more quickly than I was doing, through talking with the doctor who by this time was getting down to brass tacks with me. My friend was the human agency employed by an all-wise Father to bring me into a pathway of life.

It is an easy matter to repeat and orally affirm a faith. Here were these men who visited me and they, like myself, had tried everything else and although it was plain to be seen none of them were perfect, they were living proof that the sincere attempt to follow the cardinal teachings of Jesus Christ was keeping them sober. If it could do that for others, I was resolved to try it, believing it could do something for me also.

I went home after four days, my mind clear, feeling much better physically and, what was far more important, with something better than just will power to aid me. I got to know others of these alcoholics whose human center was my doctor. They came to our home. I met their wives and families. They invited my wife and myself to their homes. I learned that it would be well to begin the day with morning devotion which is the custom in our house now.

It was almost a year when I began to get a little careless. One day I hoisted a few drinks, arriving home far from sober. My wife and I talked it over, both knowing it had happened because I had stopped following the plan. I acknowledged my fault to God and asked His help to keep to the course I had to follow.

Our home is a happy one. My children no longer hide when they

see me coming. My business has improved. And—this is important—
I try to do what I can for my fellow alcoholics. In our town there are
some 70 of us, ready and willing to spend our time to show the way to
sobriety and sanity to men who are like what we used to be.

A WARD OF THE PROBATE COURT

AT ABOUT the time of my graduation from high school, a state university was established in our city. On the call for an office assistant, I was recommended by my superintendent, and got the position. I was rather his choice and pride, but a few years later, I met him in a nearby city and "panhandled" him for two "bucks" for drinks.

I grew with this institution and advanced in position. I took a year off for attendance at an engineering college. At college I refrained from any hilarious celebrating or drinking.

War was declared. I was away from home on business at the State Capitol where my mother couldn't raise objections and I enlisted. Overseas I was on five fronts from Alsace up to the North Sea. Upon relief from the lines—back in the rest area—"vin rouge" and "cognac" helped in the let down from trying circumstances. I was introduced to the exhilaration of intoxication. The old spirit, "What the hell? Heinie may have you tagged," didn't help toward any moderation in drinking then. We had many casualties but one of the real catastrophes was the loss of a pal, a lieutenant who died from the D.T.'s over there, after it was all over. This didn't slow me up and back in the States I had a big fling before returning home.

My plans were to cover up with my mother and the girl I was to marry, that I had become addicted to alcohol. But I exposed the fact on the day our engagement was announced. On the way I met a training camp buddy, got drunk and missed the party. Booze had got over its first real blow on me. I saw her briefly that night but didn't have the guts to face her people. The romance was over.

To forget, I engaged in a super-active life in social, fraternal, and civic promotion in my community. This all outside my position in the President's Office of the State University. I became a leader—the big flash in the pan. I organized and was first commander of the American Legion Post—raised funds and built a fine memorial Club House. Was Secretary of Elks, Eagles, Chamber of Commerce, City Club, and active as an operator and officer in political circles. I was always a good fellow and controlled my drinking, indulging only in sprees in private clubs or away from home.

I was deposed from the executive position at the college by a political change in the governorship of the State. I knew the sales manager of the Securities Division of a large utility corporation in Wall Street, and started out to sell securities. The issues and the market were good and I had a fine opportunity. I was away from home and I began to drink heavily. To get away from my drinking associates, I managed to be transferred to another city, but this didn't help. Booze had me, my sales and commissions diminished, I remained almost in a continuous stupor on my drawing account until I was released.

I braced up, got sober, and made a good connection with a steamship agency, a concern promoting European travel and study at most all important universities in Europe. Those were the bath-tub gin days and for drinking in and about my office, I held out in this position for only a year.

I was now engaged to be married and fortunately I got another position as salesman for a large corporation. I worked hard, was successful, and drinking became periodical. I was married and my wife soon learned that I was no social drinker. I tried hard to control it, but could not. There were many separations and she would return home. I would make pledges and a sincere effort and then my top would blow off again. I began here to take sanitarium treatments to satisfy my wife and my folks.

I had a great capacity for drink and work. With the help of Turkish baths, Bromo-seltzer and aspirin, I held to the job. I became top-notcher in the entire sales force of the country. I was assigned to more special territory and finally into the market of keenest competition. I was top rate in salary, won bonus awards and was bringing in the volume. But there was always the drawback my excessive drinking made at times. I was called in once, twice, and warned. Finally I wasn't to be tolerated any longer, although I was doing a good job. I had lasted five and a half years.

I lost my wife along with my job and fine income. This was a terrible jolt. I tried for a hook-up, but I had a black eye marring a good record. I became discouraged and depressed. I sought relief with booze. There began the four black years of my life.

I had returned home to the community where I had been so prominent. These were dry days still and I hung out at the clubs with bars. I got so I would last on a job but a few days, just until I could get an advance for drinks. I began to get entangled with the law—arrested for driving while intoxicated and drunken and disorderly conduct.

My folks heard of the cure at the State Hospital. I was picked up drunk and sent there by the Probate Court. I was administered paraldehyde and came to in a receiving ward among lunatics. I was transferred to another ward of less violent cases and I found a little group of alcoholics and "junkers" (dope addicts). I learned from them the seriousness of being a ward of the Probate Court. I felt then if I ever got released the old devil alcohol would never get me in a jam like this again. In times of great distress such *as* this, I would pray to God for help.

I was fortunate and was released after eleven days and nights barred up in the laughing academy—"bug-house." That was enough. I wanted no more of it. I took a job as manager of a club and put myself to the old acid test. I was going to really assert my will power. I even tended bar part of the time, but never imbibed a bit. This lasted about three months.

I went to an annual convention of my overseas division and came to locked up in a cheap hotel room, new shoes, suit coat, hat and purse missing. I must have slipped badly.

Then followed much drinking and trouble. After a few arrests for intoxication, the law decided another sojourn to the State Hospital would tame me. They jumped the stay this time from eleven days to eleven weeks. It was getting tough for me. I came out in good physical condition and held a fear of getting probated again, thinking the siege might be eleven months. I got another job and stayed dry for about two months and off to the races again. I became terribly weak- couldn't eat and tried to get nourishment from booze and mostly only bootleg at that. One time, I just made it into a hospital and another time a police patrol took me to the hospital instead of the jail. I suffered badly from insomnia. As many as three shots in the arm had no effect.

I would get in shape and back at it again. I was going to battle it to the finish. The time came when I was to be paid my soldier's bonus. I had the limit or maximum coming. Friends advised my folks to send me to a Veterans Hospital before I got this money in my hands. I was probated again, held in a county jail for two weeks and sent again to the asylum.

This was my summer sort for three months. I was on the waiting list for the Veterans Hospital but I got into such wonderful physical condition from eating and working out of doors that I was released.

I reached home full of resentment against my folks for their having my money tied up under a guardianship. I went out and got saturated and landed in jail—I had been free from the asylum about eight hours. Behind the bars again so soon—this was bad. However, I was freed again next day and this was my last confinement with the law. I began to use my head, I continued to drink but kept under cover or hid in the "jungles" with the bums.

In a few months an old friend came along. He located me a few times in saloons. We had been drinking pals in the early days, particularly at the club houses. He had heard of my predicament. He himself had quit drinking and looked fine. He encouraged me to visit him in a nearby city.

I wanted to quit drinking, but hadn't much faith in ever getting away from it. I agreed to go into a hospital as the patient of a doctor who had been an alcoholic for many years and was now a new man.

It is almost uncanny—in just eight days I left there a different person. This doctor in plain words was a wonderful guy—he spent many hours with me telling me his experience with alcohol. Others of his band, which was then small, visited me—told me their stories. They were all strangers to me, but treated me as a friend. I was impressed with their interest and fellowship. I learned the secret. They had a religious experience. I was willing, and renewed my acquaintance with God and acknowledged Him as a reality.

I found it easy. I came to life and have been free now for two years. I hope never to take another drink. I am building up a reputation again and nearly every day am complimented on my appearance.

I have a new outlook on life. I look forward to each day with happiness because of the real enjoyment it is to me to be sane, sober, and respectable. I was existing really from one drink until the next, with no perception about circumstances, conditions, or even nature's elements. My acquaintance with God—lost and forgotten when I was a young man—is renewed. God is all-loving and all-forgiving. The memories of my past are being dimmed by the life I now aspire to.

FOURTEEN years old and strong, I was ready—an American Whittington who knew a better way to get places than by walking. The "clear the way"' whistle of a fast freight thundering over the crossing on the tracks a mile away was a siren call. Sneaking away from my farm home one night, I made my way to the distant yards. Ducking along a lane between two made-up trains that seemed endless, I made my way to the edge of the yards. Here and there I passed a silent, waiting figure. Then a little group talking among themselves. Edging in, I listened eagerly. I had met my first hoboes. They talked of places I had never heard of. This town was good. A fellow could get by on the Bowery all winter if he knew the ropes; that other town was "hostile;" thirty days for "vag" awaited you in another if you didn't hit the cinders before the road "bulls" fine-combed the train.

Then they noticed me. Somehow a new kid is always an object of interest to the adventurers of the rails. "Where ye makin' for, Kid?"

I had heard one of them mention "Dee-troit" and it seemed as good an answer as any. I had no plans, just wanted to get away—anywhere— just away!

"That Michigan Manifest will be along any minute now; I think she's moving." The tall hobo who had spoken grabbed me by the arm. "Come on, kid. We'll help you."

Suddenly I felt big. I had gotten away! The two hoboes talked, the tall one about getting work in Detroit, the other arguing for staying on the road. Then the one who had boosted me up began to quiz me. I told him I had run away from the farm. In a sort of halting way he told me not to get the train habit or it would get me until I would always want to be moving. The rocking motion of the car as the train increased speed became a cradle song in my ears. I fell asleep.

It was way past dawn when I awoke. My two companions were already sitting up and talking. The day wore on. We passed through small towns. Soon the train was threading its way between factories and huge warehouses, crossing tracks with brisk clatter, coming into a large railway yard. Brakes went on. They helped me off. We were in Detroit.

My hobo friends parted at a street corner. The tall one took me along right into town and got a room for both of us with "Mother Kelly," a kindly Irish landlady if there ever was one. "Sit tight, kid," he said. "I'll see you through as much as I can. Got to find a job."

He got a job. For almost two years he looked after me. He was always vigilant, steering me past the snares and pitfalls that are always in the path of a growing boy. This hobo, Tom Casey, who never talked much about himself or his experience except as a warning illustration of "What not to do," made me start a bank account and keep it growing. It is to him I owe the fact that I didn't become a "road kid," that I never became a hobo. Came a day when he left me. The road was calling him, he explained, although that never seemed to me to be the reason. I never saw Tom Casey again, but from this man I received my first lesson in the guiding and compelling principle of the Good Life. "Love thy neighbor as thyself."

I was city-wise by this time, uncontaminated to be sure, thanks to my friend. No longer a "boy rube in the big town." I found a job quickly enough but I missed Tom. I began to hang around pool rooms and it was inevitable that I soon learned to handle a schooner of beer and an occasional "shot." Jobs were plentiful. If I didn't feel right in the morning after a night with the "corner gang" I didn't go to work. I lost jobs. My bank account dwindled, disappeared entirely. My new barroom friends were little help. I was broke.

It was summer and the park benches, hard and uncomfortable as they were, appealed to me more than the squalid "flops" of the city's slums. So I slept out a few nights. Young and full of energy, I hunted for work. The war was on and work was easy to get. I became a machine-shop hand, progressing rapidly from drill-press to milling machine to lathe. I could quit a job one day and have a new one the next with more money. Soon I again had a good boarding-house, clothes and money. But I never started another bank account. "Plenty of time for that," I thought. My weekends were spent in my conception of "a good time," finally becoming regular carousals and debauches over Saturday and Sunday. I had the usual experiences of being slipped a "Mickey Finn" and getting slugged and rolled for my money. These had no deterrent effect. I could always get jobs and live comfortably again in a few weeks. Soon, however, I tired of the weary routine of working and drinking. I began to dislike the city. Somehow my boyhood days on the farm didn't seem to be so bad at a distance.

No, I didn't go home, but found work not too far away. I still drank. I soon got restless and took a freight for a Michigan city, arriving there broke late at night. I set out to look for friends. They helped me find work. Slowly I began to climb the industrial job ladder once more and eventually achieved a responsible position as a machine setter in a large plant. I was sitting on top of the world again. The sense of accomplishment I had now told me that I had earned the right to have enjoyable weekends once more. The weekends began to extend to Tuesday and Wednesday until I frequently worked only from Thursday to Saturday with the bottle always in my mind. In a vague sort of way I had set a time to quit drinking but that was at least fifteen years away and "What the hell!" I said to myself. "I'm going to have a good time while I'm young."

Then I was fired. Piqued, I drank up my last pay check and when I got sober again found another job then another—and another in quick succession. I was soon back on the park benches. And once more I got a break when everything seemed dark. An old friend volunteered to get me a job driving a bus. He said he would buy me a uniform and give me the hospitality of his home if I would promise to quit drinking. Of course I promised. I had been working about three days when the bus line superintendent called me into his office.

"Young fellow," he said, "In your application you state that you don't use alcoholic liquors. Now, we always check a man's references and three of the firms you have worked for say you're a highly capable man, but you have the drink habit."

I looked at him. It was all true, I admitted, but I had been out of work such a long time that I had welcomed this job as an opportunity to redeem myself. I told him what I had promised my friend, that I was sincerely doing my best and not drinking a drop. I asked him to give me a chance.

"Somehow I think you are in earnest," he said. "I believe you mean it. I'll give you a chance and help you to make good."

He shook my hand in friendship and encouragement. I strode from his office with high hope. "John Barleycorn will never make a bum out of me again," I told myself with determination.

For three months I drove my route steadily with never a hitch. My employers were satisfied. I felt pretty good. I was really on the wagon this time, wasn't I?

Yes indeed, I was on the wagon for good.

I soon repaid my debt to my friend for his stake in me and even saved a little money. The feeling of security increased. It was summer and, hot and tired at the end of the day, I began to stop in at a speakeasy on my way home. Detroit beer was good then, almost like old-time pre-prohibition stuff. "This is the way to do it," I would say to myself. "Stick to beer. After all, it's really a food and it sure hits the spot after a trick of wheeling that job around in this man's town. It's the hard liquor that gets a man down. Beer for mine."

Even then with all the hard lessons of bitter experience behind me I did not realize that thinking along that line was a definite red light on my road in life—a real danger signal.

The evening glass of beer led, as usual, to the night when I didn't get away from the bar until midnight. I began to need a bracer in the morning. Beer, I knew from experience was simply no good as a bracer—all right as a thirst quencher perhaps, but lacking action and authority the next morning. I needed a jolt.

The morning jolt became a habit. Then it got to be several jolts until I was generally pretty well organized when I started to work. Spacing my drinks over the day I managed not to appear drunk, just comfortable, as I drove along the crowded thoroughfares of the city. Then came the accident.

On one of the avenues a man darted from between parked cars right in my path. I swung the bus sharply over to keep from hitting him but couldn't quite make it. He died in the hospital. Passenger and sidewalk witnesses absolved me completely. Even if I had been completely sober I couldn't have cleared him. The company investigation immediately after the accident showed me blameless but my superiors knew I had been drinking. They fired me—not for the accident—but for drinking on the job.

Well, once more I felt I had enough of city life and found a job on an upstate farm. While there I met a young school-teacher, fell in love with her and she with me. We were married. Farm work was not very remunerative for a young couple so we went successively to Pontiac,

Michigan and later to an industrial city in Ohio. For economy's sake we had been living with my wife's people, but somehow we never seemed able to get ahead. I was still drinking but not so much as formerly, or so it seemed to me.

The new location seemed ideal—no acquaintances, no entanglements, no boon companions to entice me. I made up my mind to leave liquor alone and get ahead. But I forgot one boon companion, one who was always at my elbow, one who followed me from city to farm and back to city. I had forgotten about John Barleycorn.

Even so, the good resolutions held for a time—new job, comfortable home, and understanding helpmate, they all helped. We had a son and soon came another. We began to make friends and moved in a small social circle of my fellow-workers and their wives and families. Those were still bootleg days. Drinks were always available but nobody seemed to get very drunk. We just had a good time, welcome surcease after a week of toil. Here were none of the rowdy debauches that I had known, I had discovered "social drinking" how to "drink like a gentleman and hold my liquor." There is no point in reiterating the recurrence of experience already described. The "social drinking" didn't hold up. I became the bootlegger's first morning customer. How I ever managed to hold the job I had I don't know. I began to receive the usual warnings from my superiors. They had no effect. I had now come to an ever-deepening realization that I was a drunkard, that there was no help for me.

I told my wife that. She sought counsel of her friends and my friends. They came and talked with me. Reverend gentlemen, who knew nothing of my problem, pointed me to the age-old religious formula. I would have none of it. It left me cold. Now, with hope gone, I haunted the mean thoroughfares of speakeasy districts, with my mind on nothing but the next drink. I managed to work enough to maintain a slim hold on my job. Then I began to reason with myself.

"What good are you?" I would say. "Your wife and children would be better off if they never saw you again. Why don't you get away and never come back? Let them forget about you. Get away—get away anywhere-that's the thing to do."

That night, coatless and hatless, I hopped a freight for Pittsburgh.

The following day I walked the streets of the Smoky City. I offered to work at a roadside stand for a meal. I got the meal, walked on, sat down by the roadside to think.

"What a heel I've turned out to be!" I soliloquized. "My wife and two kids back there—no money—what can they do? I should have another try at it. Maybe I'll never get well, but at least I can earn a dollar or two now and then—for them."

I took another freight back home. Despite my absence, my job was still open. I went to work, but it was no go. I would throw a few dollars at my wife on payday and drink up what was left. I hated my surroundings, hated my job, my fellow-workers—the whole town. I tried Detroit again, landing there with a broken arm. How I got it I'll never know for I was far gone in drink when I left. My wife's relatives returned me to my home in a few days. I became morose, mooning around the house by myself. Seeing me come home, my wife would leave a little money on the table, grab the children and flee. I was increasingly ugly. Now, all hope was gone entirely. I made several attempts on my life. My wife had to hide any knives and hammers. She feared for her own safety. I feared for my mind feared that I was breaking—that I would end up insane. Finally the fear got so terrible that I asked my wife to have me "put away" legally. There came a morning when, alone in my room, I began to wreck it, breaking the furniture, destroying everything in sight. Desperate, my wife had to employ the means I had suggested to her in the depths of alcoholic despair. Loath to have me committed to the state asylum, still trying to save something from the wreckage of my life and hers, she had me placed in a hospital, hoping against hope to save me.

I was placed under restraint. The treatment was strenuous—no alcohol—just bromides and sleeping potions. The nights were successions of physical and mental agony. It was weeks before I could sit still for any length of time. I didn't want to talk to anyone and cared less to listen. That gradually wore off and one day I fell into casual conversation with another patient—another alcoholic. We began to compare notes. I told him frankly that I was in despair, that no thinking I had ever been able to do had shown me a way of escape, that all my attempts to try will power (well meaning persons had often said, "Why don't you use your willpower?"—as if willpower were a faculty one could turn on and off like a faucet!) had been of no avail.

"Being in here and getting fixed up temporarily," I told him bitterly, "is no good. I know that only too well. I can see nothing but the same old story over again. I'm simply unable to quit. When I get out of here I'm going to blow town."

My fellow-patient and new found acquaintance looked at me a long time in silence and finally spoke. From the most unexpected quarter in the world, from a man who was in the same position I was in, from a fellow-alcoholic, came the first ray of hope I had seen.

"Listen fellow," he said, looking at me with ten times the earnestness of the many good citizens and other well-intentioned persons who had tried their best to help me. "Listen to me. I know a way out. I know the only answer. And I know it works."

I stared at him in amazement. There were several mild mental cases in the place and, little as I knew about their exhibitions of tendencies, I knew that even in a normal conversation, strange ideas might be expected. Was this fellow perhaps a little balmy—a wee bit off? Here was a man, an admitted alcoholic like myself, trying to tell me he knew the remedy for my situation. I wanted to hear what he had to suggest but made the reservation that he was probably a little "nutty." At the same time I was ready to listen, like any drowning man, to grasp at even a straw.

My friend smiled, he knew what I was thinking. "Yes," he continued. "Forget that I'm here. Forget that I'm just another 'rummy.' But I had the answer once—the only answer."

He seemed to be recalling his very recent past. Looking at me earnestly, his voice impressive in its sincerity, he went on. "For more than a year before coming here I was a sober man, thoroughly dry. I wasn't just on the wagon. I was dry! And I would still be dry if I had stuck to the plan which kept me sober all that time."

Let me say here that he later went back to the very plan he told me about and has since been sober for more than a year for the second time.

He told me his own story briefly and went on to tell me of a certain cure for alcoholism—the only certain cure. I had anticipated hearing of some new treatment, some newly discovered panacea that I had not heard of, something which no doubt combined drugs and mental healing. But it was neither one nor the other; it was certainly not a mixture of any kind.

He spoke of some 30 men in my town who were ready to take me by the hand and call me by my first name. They would be friends without canting or ranting. He told me they met once a week to talk over their experiences, how they tried to help each other, how they spent their time in helping men like me.

"I know it sounds strange, incredible, maybe," he said. "I slipped, got drunk after being sober for a year, but I'm going back to try again. I know it works."

Helpless, without faith in myself or anyone else, entirely doubtful that the fellow really had something, I began to ask questions. I had to be interested or go crazy.

"How do you go about this—where do I have to go?" I asked.

"You don't have to go anywhere," he said. "Someone will come to you if you want them to." He didn't go into any detail, just told me that much and little more. I did some thinking that afternoon. Calling one of the nurses I asked her to get in touch with my wife and have her come to see me that evening.

She came during visiting hours. She expected, I know, to hear me plead for instant release from the place. I didn't talk about that. In my lame way I told her the story. It made little impression.

"It doesn't sound right," she said. "If this plan—and for the life of me I don't quite get it from what you've told me—if this plan is successful, why is this fellow back here himself?"

I was stumped. I was too ignorant about the thing myself to be capable of explaining it clearly to her. "I don't know," I said. 'I'll admit it sounds queer, the way this fellow is and all that, but somehow I feel there's something to it. Anyhow, I want to know more about it."

She went away skeptically. But the next day I had a visitor, a doctor who had been himself an alcoholic. He told me little more about the plan. He was kindly, didn't offer any cut and dried formula to overcome my life-long difficulty. He presented no religious nostrums, suggested no saving rituals. Later he sent some of the other ex-alcoholics to see me.

A few days later my fellow-alcoholic was released, and shortly afterward I was allowed to go home also. Through the man who had first told me of the plan I was introduced to several other former alcoholics. They told me their experiences. Many were men of former affluence and position. Some had hit even lower levels than I had.

The first Wednesday evening after my release found me a somewhat shame-faced but intensely curious attendant at a gathering in a private home in this city. Some forty others were present. For the first time I saw a fellowship I had never known in actual operation. I could actually feel it. I learned that this could be mine, that I could win my way to sobriety and sanity if I would follow a few precepts, simple in statement, but profound and far-reaching in their effect if followed. It penetrated to my inner consciousness that the mere offering of lip-service wasn't enough. Still ignorant, still a little doubting, but in deadly earnest, I made up my mind to make an honest effort to try.

That was two years ago. The way has not been easy. The new way of living was strange at first, but all my thoughts were on it. The going was sometimes slow; halting were my steps among the difficulties of the path. But always, when troubles came, when doubts assailed and temptation was strong and the old desire returned, I knew where to go for aid. Helping others also strengthened me and helped me to grow.

Today I have achieved, through all these things, a measure of happiness and contentment I had never known before. Material success has mattered little. But I know that my wants will be taken care of.

I expect to have difficulties every day of my life, I expect to encounter stops and hindrances, but now there is a difference. I have a new and tried foundation for every new day.

THE SALESMAN

I LEARNED to drink in a workmanlike manner when the law of the land said I couldn't and what started out as a young man's fun became a habit which in its later existence laid me by the heels many a time and almost finished my career.

Teen years were uneventful with me. I was raised on a farm but saw little future in farming. I was going to be a business man, took a business college course, acquired a truck and stand in the city market of a nearby town, and started off. I brought produce from my folks' place and sold it to city customers and there were plenty of them with bulging pocketbooks.

Back of me was the normal life of a farmer's son. My parents were unusually understanding people. My father was a life-long comrade till the day of his death. The business theory I had learned in college was now being practiced and I was equipped beyond many of my competitors to be materially successful. Soon I had expanded until I was represented in all the city markets and also in another city. In 1921 I had the forerunner of the later depression and my customers disappeared. Successively I had to close my stands and was finally wiped out altogether. Being a young man of affairs, I had begun to do a little business and social drinking and now with time on my hands, I seemed to do more of it.

Following a year of factory work, during which time I got married, I got a job with a grocer as clerk. My grocer-employer was an expert winemaker and I had free access to his cellar. The work was monotonous in the extreme, behind a counter all day when I had been used to driving around attending to business, meeting people and building for what I thought was a great future. I mark, too, as a milestone, the death of my father, whom I missed greatly.

I kept hitting the wine, with just occasional use of liquor.

Leaving the grocery I went back into the produce business and out among people, went back to liquor again and got my first warning to quit before it got me.

I was anxious to get with a concern which would give me an opportunity to build up again, and landed a job with a nationally known biscuit company. I was assigned to a good business region, covering several important towns, and almost at once began to earn real money. In a very short time I was the star salesman of the company, winning a reputation as a business-getter. Naturally I drank with my better customers for on my route I had many stops where that was good business. But I had things rather well under control and in the early days on this job I seldom wound up my day's work with any visible effects of drinking.

I had a private brewery at home which was now producing 15 gallons a week most of which I drank myself. It is typical of the attitude I had toward alcohol at that time that, when a fire threatened total destruction of my home and garage, I rushed to the cellar and rescued my most precious possessions—a keg of wine and all the beer I could carry, and got pretty indignant when my better half suggested that I had better get some of the needed effects out of the house before it burned down.

My home-brewing gradually became a bore and I began to carry home bottles of powerful bootleg whiskey, starting with half a pint every night and winding up with a quart as my daily after-supper allowance. For a time I kept on the job spacing my drinks en route and very little of them in the morning hours. I just couldn't wait until I got home to drink. In a very short time I became an all-day drinker.

Chain-store managers and quantity buyers were both my guests and hosts and every now and then we had prodigious parties. Finally, in a re-organization shakeup resulting in new district managers with a pretty poor territory deal for me, I gave the company two weeks notice and quit. I had bought a home but in the year and a half following I had little income and finally lost that. I became satisfied with just enough to live on and buy the liquor I wanted. Then I landed in the hospital when my car was hit by a truck. My car was ruined entirely. That loss and my injuries plus the recriminations of my wife sort of sobered me up. When I got out of the hospital I stayed sober for six weeks and had made up my mind to quit.

I went back in the business where I had been a successful salesman, but with another company. When I started with this concern I talked things over with my wife and made her some very solemn promises. I wasn't going to touch another drop of liquor.

By this time prohibition was a thing of the past and saloons and clubs where I was well known as a good customer and a good spender became my patrons. I rolled up business until I was again a star, but after the first four months on the new job I began to slip. It is not unusual in the drinking experience of any man that after a time of sobriety he comes to the conclusion that he "can handle it." In no time at all liquor again became the most important thing in my life and every day became like another, steady drinking in every saloon and club on my route. I would get to headquarters every night in a top-heavy condition, just able to maintain equilibrium. I began to get warnings and was repeatedly fired and taken on again. My wife's parents died about this time in unfortunate circumstances. All my troubles seemed to be piling up on me and liquor was the only refuge I knew.

Some nights I wouldn't go home at all and when I did go home I was displeased when my wife had supper ready and equally angry when she didn't. I didn't want to eat at all and frequently when I underestimated my consumption of the amount of liquor I brought home, I made extra trips back to town to renew the supply. My morning ration when I started out was five double whiskies before I could do any business at all. I would go into a saloon, trembling like a leaf, tired in appearance and deathly sick, I would down two double whiskies, feel the glow and become almost immediately transformed. In half an hour I would be able to navigate pretty well and start out on my route. My daily reports became almost illegible and finally, following arrest for driving while intoxicated and on my job at that, I got scared and stayed sober for several days. Not long afterward I was fired for good.

My wife suggested I go to my old home in the country, which I did. Continued drinking convinced my wife I was a hopeless case and she entered suit for divorce. I got another job, but didn't stop drinking. I kept on working although my physical condition was such as to have required extensive hospitalization. For years I hadn't had a peaceful nights' sleep and never knew a clear head in the morning. I had lost my wife, and had become resigned to going to bed some night and never waking again.

Every drunkard has one or two friends who haven't entirely given up hope for him, but I came to the point where I had none. That is, none but my Mother, and she, devoted soul, had tried everything with me. Through her, people came to me and talked, but nothing they said—some were ministers and others good church members—helped me a particle. I would agree with them when they were with me and as fast as they went away, I'd go after my bottle. Nothing suggested to me seemed to offer a way out.

I was getting to a place where I wanted to quit drinking but didn't know how. My Mother heard of a doctor who had been having marked success with alcoholics. She asked me if I'd like to talk to him and I agreed to go with her.

I had known, of course, of the various cures and after we had discussed the matter of my drinking fairly thoroughly, the doctor suggested that I go into the local hospital for a short time. I was very skeptical, even after the doctor hinted there was more to his plan than medical treatment. He told me of several men whom I knew who had been relieved and invited me to meet a few of them who got together every week. I promised I would be on deck at their next meeting but told him I had little faith in any hospital treatments. Meeting night, I was as good as my word and met the small group. The doctor was there but somehow I felt quite outside of the circle. The meeting was informal, nevertheless I was little impressed. It is true they did no psalm singing, nor was there any set ritual, but I just didn't care for anything religious. If I had thought of God at all in the years of drinking, it was with a faint idea that when I came to die I would sort of fix things up with Him.

I say that the meeting did not impress me. However, I could see men whom I had known as good, hardworking drunkards apparently in their right minds, but I just couldn't see where I came into the picture. I went home, stayed sober for a few days, but was soon back to my regular quota of liquor every day.

Some six months later, after a terrific binge, in a maudlin and helpless state, I made my way to the doctor's home. He gave me medical treatment and had me taken to the home of one of my relatives. I told him I had come to the point where I was ready for the remedy, the only remedy. He sent two of the members to see me. They were both kindly to me, told me what they had gone through and how they had overcome their fight with liquor. They made it very plain that I had to seek God, that I had to state my case to Him and ask for help. Prayer was something I had long forgotten. I think my first sincere utterance must have sounded pretty weak. I didn't experience any sudden change, and the desire for liquor wasn't taken away overnight, but I began to enjoy meeting these people and began to exchange the liquor habit for something that has helped me in every way. Every morning I read a part of the Bible and ask God to carry me through the day safely.

There is another part I want to talk about—a very important part. I think I would have had much more difficulty in getting straightened out if I hadn't been almost immediately put to work. I don't mean getting back on my job as salesman. I mean something that is necessary to my continued happiness. While I was still shakily trying to rebuild my job of selling, the doctor sent me to see another alcoholic who was in the hospital. All the doctor asked me to do was tell my story. I told it, not any too well perhaps, but as simply and as earnestly as I knew how.

I've been sober for two years, kept that way by submitting my natural will to the Higher Power and that is all there is to it. That submission wasn't just a single act, however. It became a daily duty; it had to be that. Daily I am renewed in strength and I have never come to the point where I have wanted to say, "Thanks God, I think I can paddle my own canoe now," for which I am thankful.

I have been reunited with my wife, making good in business, and paying off debts as I am able. I wish I could find words to tell my story more graphically. My former friends and employers are amazed and see in me a living proof that the remedy I have used really works. I have been fortunate to be surrounded with friends ever ready to help, but I firmly believe any man can get the same result if he will sincerely work at it God's way.

FIRED AGAIN

IT SEEMS to me that I never did do things normally. When I learned to dance I had to go dancing every night in the week if possible; when I worked or studied I wanted no interruptions or distractions. Wherever I worked I wanted to be the highest paid man in the place or I was irritated; and of course when I drank I could never seem to stop until I was saturated. I was usually hard to get along with as a boy; if the others wouldn't play my way I'd go home.

The town we lived in when I was a child was rather new and raw, peopled largely by immigrants who seemed to be constantly getting married with free drinks and eats for anybody who cared to come. We kids usually managed to get to these celebrations, and although supposed to have soda pop we could get ourselves one or two beers. With this sort of background and more money than was good for me, it was fairly easy to start getting drunk before I was sixteen.

After I left home I earned rather decent salaries but was never satisfied with my position, salary, or the treatment accorded me by my employer. I very seldom stayed on one job for more than six months until I was married at the age of 28, at which time I had already begun to lose jobs because of my drinking. Whenever things went wrong I knew that a few drinks would make everything rosy, my fears, doubts and worries would vanish and I would always promise myself that the next time I would stop short of getting plastered. Somehow things seldom worked out that way though.

I was irritated by the efforts of so many doctors, ministers, lawyers, employers, relatives and friends who remonstrated with me, none of whom knew from personal experience what I was up against. I'd fall down, get up, work a while, get my debts paid (at least the most pressing ones) drink moderately for a few days or weeks, but eventually get myself so messed up in tanglefoot that I'd lose another job. In one year *(1916) I* quit two jobs because I thought I'd be discharged anyhow and was fired outright from five more, which is more jobs than many men have in a lifetime. Had I remained sober, any one of them would have led to advancement because they were with growing companies and in my chosen field of engineering.

After being discharged for the fifth time that year, I drank more than ever, cadging drinks and meals where I could, and running up a large rooming-house account. My brother took me home and my folks talked me into going to a sanitarium for thirty days. This place was operated by a physician who was a personal friend of the family and I was his only patient at the time. The doctor did his best, saw that I got into good physical condition, tried to straighten out the mental quirks he thought partly responsible for my drinking, and I left with the firm resolve never to drink again.

Before I left the sanitarium I answered an advertisement for an engineer in a small Ohio town and after an interview, obtained the position. In three days after leaving the sanitarium I had a job I liked at a satisfactory salary in a small town with basic living costs (board, room and laundry) amounting only to about 15% of my salary. I was all set, sober, working in a congenial atmosphere for a firm that had more profitable business than they knew what to do with. I made some beautiful plans. I could save enough in a few years to complete my formal education and there were no saloons in the town to trip me up. So what? So at the end of the week I was drunk again for no particular reason at all that I could understand. In about three months I was out of a job again, but in the meantime two things of major importance had happened. I had fallen in love and war had been declared.

I had learned my lesson. I knew definitely that I couldn't take even one drink. I wanted to get married so I planned very earnestly to get another job, stay sober, and save some money. I went to Pittsburgh on Sunday, called on a manufacturer of rolling-mill equipment and on Monday, got a position and went to work. I was first paid at the end of the second week, was drunk before the end of the day and couldn't be bothered with going to work the next Monday.

Why did I take that first drink? I honestly don't know. Anyhow I nearly went crazy that summer and really developed some sort of mental disturbance. The night clerk of the small hotel where I was staying saw me go out about three in the morning in pajamas and slippers and had a policeman take me back into my room. I suppose he was used to screwy drunks or he would have taken me to jail instead. I stayed there a few days and sweated the alcohol out of my system, went to the office to collect the balance of my salary, paid my room rent, and found I had just enough money to get home. So home I went, sick, broke, discouraged and despairing of ever attaining a normal, happy life.

After two or three weeks of idleness at home, I obtained a subordinate position with a former employer, doing the lowest grade of drafting work on an hourly basis. I kept reasonably sober for several months, went to see my fiancee one or two weekends, was advanced rapidly in salary and responsibility, had a date set for the wedding and then inadvertently learned that one of the men working under my direction was receiving about forty dollars more per month than I was, which burnt me up to such an extent I quit after an argument, took my money, packed my personal effects, left them at the corner drug store, and went downtown and got plastered. Knowing that I would be greeted with tears, sorrowful sympathy and more grief when I got home, I stayed away until I was again destitute.

I was really worried sick about my drinking so father again advanced the money for treatment. This time I took a three-day cure and left with the firm resolve never to drink again, got a better position then I'd had before and actually did keep sober for several months, saved some money, paid my debts and again made plans to get married. But the desire for a drink was with me constantly after the first week or two, and the memory of how sick I had been from liquor and the agonies of the treatment I had undergone faded into the background. I had only begun to restore the confidence of my associates, family, friends and myself before I was off again, without any excuse this time. The wedding was again postponed and it looked very much as though it would never take place. My employer did not turn me loose but I was in another nice jam nevertheless. After considerable fumbling around mentally as to what to do I went back to the three-day cure for the second time.

After this treatment I got along a little better, was married in the spring of 1919 and did very little drinking for several years. I got along very well with my work, had a happy home life, but when away from home with little likelihood of being caught at it, I'd go on a mild binge. The thought of what would happen if my wife caught me drinking served to keep me reasonably straight for several years. My work became increasingly more important. I had many outside interests and drinking became less of a factor in my life, but I did continue to tipple some during my out-of-town trips and it was because of this tendency that things finally became all snarled up at home.

I was sent to New York on business and later stopped at a night club where I had been drunk before. I certainly must have been very tight and it is quite likely that I was "Mickey Finned" for I woke up about noon the next day in my hotel without a cent. I had to borrow money to get home on but didn't bother to start back till several days later. When I got there I found a sick child, a distracted wife and had lost another job paying $7,000 a year. This, however, was not the worst of it. I must have given my business card to one of the girls at the night club for she started to send me announcements of another clip-joint where she was employed and writing me long hand "come on" notes, one of which fell into my wife's hands. I'll leave what happened after that to the reader's imagination.

I went back into the business of getting and losing jobs and eventually got to the point where I didn't seem to have any sense of responsibility to myself or to my family. I'd miss important family anniversaries, forget to come home for Christmas and in general wouldn't go home until I was exhausted physically and flat broke. About four years ago I didn't come home on Christmas Eve but arrived there about six o'clock on Christmas morning, minus the tree I had promised to get, but with an enormous package of liquor on board. I took the three-day cure again with the usual results but about three weeks later I went to a party and decided a few beers wouldn't hurt me; however I didn't get back to work for three days and a short while later had lost my job and was again at the bottom of things. My wife obtained employment on a relief basis and I finally got straightened out with my employer who placed me in another position in a nearby city which I also lost by the end of the year.

So it went until about a year ago when a neighbor happened to hear me trying to get into the house and asked my wife whether I had been having some drinking difficulties. This, of course, disturbed my wife but our neighbor was not just inquisitive. She had heard of the work of an ex-alcoholic doctor who was busily engaged in passing on the benefits he had received from another who had found the answer to his difficulties with liquor. As a result of this my wife saw the doctor.

Then I talked with him, spent a few days in a local hospital and haven't had a drink since.

While in the hospital about twenty men called on me and told me of their experiences and the help they had received. Of the twenty I happened to know five, three of whom I had never seen completely sober. I became convinced then and there that if these men had learned something that could keep them sober, I also could profit from the same knowledge. Before leaving the hospital, two of these men, convinced of my sincerity of purpose, imparted to me the necessary knowledge and mental tools which have resulted in my complete sobriety for thirteen months, and an assurance that I need never, so long as I live, drink anything of an alcoholic nature if I kept on the right track.

My health is better, I enjoy a fellowship which gives me a happier life than I have ever known, and my family joins me in a daily expression of gratitude.

THE FEARFUL ONE

WHEN I was 21, I was taken suddenly and violently ill and was ill for seven years. As a result of this illness I was left with a poorish nervous system and a curious phobia. As this has a large place in my story, I will try to explain it clearly. After I had been ill some months, I grew strong enough to get out of doors a little each day, but found I couldn't get farther than the nearest corner without becoming totally panic stricken. As soon as I turned back home the panic would vanish. I gradually overcame this particular phase of the trouble by setting myself longer distances to walk each day. Similarly I learned later to take short street car rides, then longer ones, and so forth, until I appeared to be doing most of the things other people do daily. But the things I did not have to do each day, or at least frequently, remained unconquered and a source of great but secret embarrassment to me.

So I went on for years, planning always to sidestep the things I was afraid of, but concealing my fear from everyone. Those years of illness were not all total invalidism. I made a good living part of the time, but was continually falling down and having to get up and start over again. The whole process gave me a licked feeling, especially when, towards the end of my twenties, I had to give up the presidency of a small company which was just turning the corner to real success.

Shortly after this, I was successfully operated on and became a physically well man. But the surgeon did not remove the phobia, that remained with me.

During the period of my illness I was not especially interested in liquor. I was not a teetotaler, but I was just a "social drinker." However, when I was about thirty, my mother died. I went to pieces as I had become very dependent on my parents through my illness. When I began to get on *my* feet again I discovered that whiskey was a fine relief from the terrific nervous headaches I had developed. Long after the headaches were gone, however, I kept discovering other difficulties for which whiskey was a grand cure. During the ensuing ten years I once, by sheer will power, remained dry for five weeks.

I had many business opportunities during those ten years which, although I tried to keep them in my grasp, slipped through my fingers. A lovely wife came and went. She tried her best and our baby's birth put me on my mettle for all of six months, but after that, worse and more of it. When my wife finally took the baby and left, did I square my shoulders and go to work to prove to her and to the world that I was a man? I did not. I stayed drunk for a solid month.

The next two years were simply a drawn-out process of less and less work and more and more liquor. They ended eventually at the home of a very dear friend whose family were out of town. I had been politely but firmly kicked out of the house where I had been boarding, and although I seemed to be able to find money to buy drinks, I couldn't find enough to pay advance room rent anywhere.

One night, sure my number was up, I chucked my "pride" and told this friend a good deal of my situation. He was a man of considerable means and he might have done what many men would have done in such a case. He might have handed me fifty dollars and said that I ought to pull myself together and make a new start. I have thanked God more than once that that was just what he did not do.

Instead, he took me out, bought me three more drinks, put me to bed and yanked me bodily out of town the next noon to a city 200 miles away and into the arms of one of the most extraordinary bunch of men in the United States. Here, while in the hospital, men with clear eyes and happy faces came to see me and told me the story of their lives. Some of them were hard to believe, but it didn't take a lot of brain work to see they had something I could use. And it was so simple. The sum and substance of it seemed to be that if I would turn to God, it was very probable that He could do a better job with my life than I had.

When I got out of the hospital, I was invited to stay in the home of one of the fellows. Here I found myself suddenly and uncontrollably seized with the old panic. I was in a strange house, in a strange city, and fear gripped me. I shut myself in my room. I couldn't sit down, I couldn't stand up, I couldn't lie down, couldn't leave because I had nowhere to go and no money to take me. Any attempt at reasoning accomplished nothing.

Suddenly in this maelstrom I grasped at a straw. Maybe God would help me—just maybe, mind you. I was willing to give Him a chance, but with considerable doubt. I got down on my knees—something I hadn't done in thirty years. I asked Him if He would let me hand over all these fears and this panic to Him. I lay down on the bed and went to sleep like a baby. An hour later I awoke to a new world. I could scarcely credit my senses, but that terrible phobia which had wrecked my life for eighteen years, was gone. Utterly gone. And in its place was a power and fearlessness which is a bit hard to get accustomed to.

All that happened nearly six months ago. In those six months a new life has opened before me. It isn't that I have been cured of an ordinarily incurable disease. I have found a joy in living that has nothing to do with money or material success. I know that incomparable happiness that comes from helping some other fellow get straightened out. Don't get me wrong. We are not a bunch of angels. None of us has any notion of becoming such. But we know that we can never go completely back to old ways because we are traveling upward through service to others and in trying to be honest, decent, and loving toward the world, instead of sliding and slipping around in a life of drinking, cheating, lying and doing what we like.

IN MAY 1936, after a prolonged period of alcoholism, my friends, my associates, my superiors, and those people who really loved me in spite of embarrassments too numerous to mention, finally left me because they had come to the conclusion that I didn't have any idea of doing or trying to do the right thing.

I was a spineless individual who didn't care a rap for anyone or anything—I was hopeless and knew it—and then in my extremity, The Divine Comforter, "Truth" came to me in a barroom where I had spent the major portion of six weeks.

The Divine Comforter, in my experience, came in the guise of a former drinking companion whom I had assisted home on several occasions. Because of physical infirmities brought about by alcoholic excess, he had been unable to walk a distance of three blocks to his home unassisted, when I last saw him. Now he approached me, and to my amazement he was sober and appeared greatly improved in physical condition.

He induced me to take a ride with him, and as we rode along told me of the marvelous thing that had come into his life. He had more than a practical idea of my difficulties, he also had a logical and practical idea as to how they might be overcome.

He started the conversation by explaining acute alcoholism and stated very bluntly that I was an alcoholic. This was news to me in spite of the fact that I had promised everybody East of the Mississippi, if they would take time to listen, that I was through with drink. At the time I made these promises, I honestly wanted to quit drinking, but for some unknown reason hadn't seemed able to. He told me why I failed.

He then suggested that I accompany him to a local doctor who had been helpful to him. It took forty-eight hours of persuasion and quite a few drinks to fortify myself, but I finally agreed to go. The doctor turned out to be one who had been an alcoholic himself, and in gratitude for the release he had found and because he understood the true meaning of the phrase "Brotherly Love" was spending a great portion of his time helping unfortunate individuals like myself.

With the help and advice of these two individuals and two or three associates, I was able, for the first time in two and a half years, to stay sober for six weeks, and then disastrously tried the beer experiment. For some time I couldn't get hold of myself, but gradually came out of hiding and exposed myself again to this influence which had been so helpful.

July 2, 1936, I again contacted the two individuals, and since that day I have never had a drink. However, because of the difficulties I encountered as the result of the beer experiment, I was unable for some time to find reality in this new way of life. I was doubtful, fearful, full of self-pity, afraid to humiliate myself.

This unreality lasted until December 11th, when I was faced with the absolute necessity of raising a sum of money. For the first time came the realization that I was faced with a difficulty from which I seemed unable to extricate myself. Of course, I took time out to bemoan the fact that "after all I'd done, this had to happen to me" but on the advice of my wife, I reluctantly went to a banker.

I told him my story completely. I went to him believing that my need was money. I went there as a last resort to attempt to pry it loose to meet my needs. My need was not money, but again I had been led to the proper source. After having related my story to the banker, who knew my reputation not only as an alcoholic but as an individual who didn't pay his bills, he said, "I know something of what you are trying to do, and I believe you are on the right track. Are you right with the Father who knows your needs before you ask? If so, you are not dependent upon this bank or any individual in it, or any rules by which we operate, because your help comes from an ever present and all powerful Father. I am going to do everything I can to secure this loan for you. However, I don't want anything that happens here to throw you off the track, I want you to leave here feeling that you have done everything you could to secure these funds, and go about your business. Your business is business with God's work. I don't know whether that calls for you to go and collect a bill, sell some new contract, or to sit quietly and pray, but your Father knows and if you will but permit Him, He will direct you."

I had again found reality. My needs were met from another entirely unexpected source.

The manifestations of this ever present Power in my experience since 1936 are too numerous to mention. Let suffice to say that I am profoundly grateful for the opportunities I have had of seeing and knowing "TRUTH."

SMILE WITH ME, AT ME

AT THE age of eighteen I finished high school and during my last year there my studies were dropping away to be replaced by dancing, going out nights, and thinking of a good time as most of the boys of my age did. I secured a job with a well known telegraph company which lasted about a year, due to the fact I thought I was too clever for a $7.00 a week job which did not supply me with enough money for my pleasures, such as taking girls out, etc. I was not at all satisfied with my small wages.

Now, I was a very good violinist at the time and was offered jobs with some well known orchestras, but my parents objected to my being a professional musician although my last year in high school was mostly spent playing for dances and giving exhibition dances at most of the fraternity affairs. Now naturally I was far from satisfied with my seven dollars a week wages, so when I came across a boy neighbor of mine on the subway one night (by the way I read in the newspaper that this same boy died four days ago) he told me he was a host in a celebrated Restaurant and Cabaret, and that his salary ran $14.00 per week and he made $50.00 a week in tips. Well, think of being paid for dancing with the carefree ladies of the afternoon and receiving all that sum, and me working for only $7.00 per. The following day I went straight uptown to Broadway and never did go back to my old job.

This was the beginning of a long stretch of high-flying as I thought, only to find out when I was forty-one years old to be very low-flying. I worked in this restaurant until I was twenty-one, then we went into the world war. I joined the navy. My enlistment pleased the owner of my cabaret so much that he offered me a good job at the end of my federal service.

The day I walked in to his establishment with my release from active duty, he said, "You are my assistant manager from now on." Well, this pleased me as you can imagine and my hat from then on would not fit.

Now, all this time my taste for liquor was constantly growing although it was no habit and I had no craving. In other words, if I had a date and wanted a drink with the girl friend I would, otherwise I would not think of it at all.

In six months time I found I was too good for this job and a competitive restaurateur, or a chain of the best well-known night clubs

offered me a better position which I accepted. This night life was starting to tell and show its marks and together with the slump in that sort
of business at the time, I decided to apply for a job with a well known
ballet master who drilled many choruses for Broadway shows.

I was this man's assistant and I really had to work very hard for the
little money I received, sometimes twelve hours or more a day, but I
got the experience and honor which was just what I was looking for.
This was one time when my work interfered with my drinking. This job
came to an end one evening when I was drinking quite heavily. A certain prominent actress inquired of Professor X, my boss, if I would be
interested to sign an eighty week contract for a vaudeville tour. It seems
she could use me as a partner in her act. Now, a very nice woman, Miss
J. who was office clerk and pianist for the boss, overheard the conversation and told both Mr. X and Miss Z that I would not be interested.

On hearing this I went out and drank enough to cause plenty of trouble, slapping Miss J. and doing an all round drunk act in the studio.

This was the end of my high-flying among the white lights. I was only
twenty-four years old and I came home to settle down; in fact I had to.
I was broke both financially and in spirit.

Being a radio operator in the navy, I became interested in amateur
radio. I got a federal license and made a transmitting radio set and
would often sit up half the night trying to reach out all over the country. Broadcasting radio was just in its infancy then, so I began to make
small receiving sets for my friends and neighbors.

Finally I worked up quite a business and opened a store, then two
stores, with eleven people working for me.

Now here is where Old Barleycorn showed his hidden strength. I
found that in order to have a paying business I had to make friends,
not the kind I was used to, but ordinary, sane, hard working people.
In order to do this I should not drink, but I found that I could not stop.

I will never forget the first time I realized this. Every Saturday, my
wife and I would go to some tavern. I would take a bottle of wine, gin,
or the like, and we would spend an evening dancing, drinking, etc.
(This was fourteen years ago.)

I was practically a pioneer in the radio business and that must
account for people putting up with me as they did. However, within

three years time I had lost both stores, I won't say entirely due to my drinking, but at least if I had been physically and mentally fit, I could have survived and kept a small business going.

Now from this time up to about a year ago, I drifted from one job to another. I peddled brushes, did odd jobs such as painting, and finally got established with a well known piano company as assistant service manager.

Then came the big crash of 1929 this particular company abolished their radio department. For two years I worked for one of my old competitors who owned a radio store. He put up with my drinking until I was in such a physical breakdown that I had to quit.

All this time my troubles at home were getting worse. My whole family blamed my failure on the alcoholic question and so the usual arguments would start the instant I came in the house. This naturally made me go out and drink some more. If I had no money, I would borrow, beg, or even steal enough for a bottle.

My wife fortunately went to business which was our only salvation. Our little boy was six years old at the time and due to the fact we needed someone to care for him during the day we moved in with my family. Now the trouble did start, because I not only had my wife to face every evening, but three of the elders of the family. My wife did everything for me she possibly could. First she got in touch with a well known psychiatrist and I went faithfully to him for a few months. This particular doctor was such a nervous individual, I thought he had the St. Vitus' dance and I really thought he needed some kind of treatment more than I did. He advised hospitalization from three months to a year.

Well, this was all out of order as far as I was concerned. In the first place I had an idea that my wife wanted to put me away in a state institution where maybe I would be stuck for the rest of my life. In the second place, I wanted to go, if anywhere, to a private institution and that was far beyond our financial means. In the third place, I knew that that would be no cure, because I reasoned that it would be like taking candy out of a young child's reach. The instant I would come out a free man I would go right back to old Alky again. In this one thing I found out later I was perfectly right.

What I thought and wanted at the time was "not to want to want to take a drink." This phrase is a very important link in my story. I knew this could only be done by myself, but how could I accomplish it? Well, this was the main question.

The point was always that when I did drink, I wanted all the time not to, and that alone wasn't enough. At the time I felt like a drink, I did not want to take it at all, but I had to, it seemed. So if you can grasp what I mean, I wished I would not want that drink. Am I nuts, or do you get me?

To get back to the doctor. If anything, these visits made me worse, and worst of all, everyone told me I wanted to drink and that was all there was to that. After going to as many as six or eight other doctors, some of my own friends advised my wife to make her plans for the future as I was a hopeless case, had no backbone, no will power, and would end up in the gutter.

Well, here I was, a man with much ability, a violinist, a radio engineer, a ballet master, and at this point took up hair dressing, so that added one more to the list. Can you beat it? I knew there must be some way out of all this mess. Everyone told me to stop my drinking, but none could tell me how, until I met a friend and believe me he turned out to be a true friend, something I never had until this past year.

One morning, after one of my escapades, my wife informed me I was to go with her to a public hospital or she would pack up and leave with our boy. My father, being a physician for forty years, put me in a private New York hospital. I was there ten days and was put in physical shape, and above everything else put on the right path to recovery and happiness.

My friend first asked me if I really wanted to stop drinking, and if I did, would I do anything no matter what it was in order to? I knew there was only one thing left to do if I wished to live and not enter an insane asylum where I knew I would eventually wind up.

Making up my mind that I would, he said, "Fine." And went on to explain the simple steps to take. After spending an hour or two with me that day he returned two days later and went into the subject more thoroughly. He explained he had been in the same hospital with the same malady and after taking these steps after his discharge, had not taken a drink in three years and also there were about sixty others that had this same experience. All these fellows got together on Sunday evenings and brought their wives and everybody spent a very pleasant time together.

Well, after I met all these people, I was more than surprised to find a very interesting, sociable, and friendly crowd. They seemed to take more interest in me than all of my old fraternity brothers or Broadway pals had ever done.

There were no dues or expenses whatsoever. I went along for about fourteen weeks, partly keeping these ideas, and so one afternoon I thought it would do no harm to take a couple of drinks and no more. Saying to myself, "I have this thing in hand now, I can be a moderate drinker." Here I made a fatal mistake. After all my past experience, again I thought I could handle the situation only to find out one week later it was the same old thing. I repeated the same thing over again and another week again.

Finally I was back at the hospital, although I went under protest. My wife had expected to take two weeks vacation in the country with me, but instead had to use this money for the hospital expenses. During my one week stay, I held this as a grudge against her. The result was I got drunk three days after I was discharged from the hospital. And she left me for two weeks. During this period of time I drank heavily, being upset not only over her absence, but perfectly at sea as to how I could ever get back on my feet and make a new start again.

There was no mistake about it. There was something that I failed to do in those simple steps. So I carefully went over each day as best I could since my first drink after the fourteen weeks of sobriety, and found I had slipped away from quite a few of some of the most important things which I should do in order to keep sober.

Certainly I was down now—ashamed to face my new friends—my own family giving me up as lost and everyone saying, "The system didn't work, did it?"

This last remark was more than too much for me. Why should this fellowship of hard working fellows be jeopardized by me? It worked for them. As a matter of fact, not one who has kept faithfully to it has ever slipped.

One morning, after a sleepless night worrying over what I could do to straighten myself out, I went to my room alone—took my Bible in hand and asked Him, the One Power, that I might open to a good place to read and I read. "For I delight in the law of God after the inward man. But I see a different law in my members, warring against the law of my mind and bringing me into captivity under the law of sin which is in my members. Wretched man that I am! Who shall deliver me out of the body of this death?"

That was enough for me—I started to understand. Here were the words of Paul, a great teacher. When then if I had slipped? Now, I could understand.

From that day I gave and still give and always will, time everyday to read the word of God and let Him do all the caring. Who am I to try to run myself or anyone else?

A CLOSE SHAVE

THE YEAR 1890 witnessed my advent as the youngest of five sons to a fine Christian mother and a hard working blacksmith father. At the age of eight my father used to send me after his pail of beer and it was by lapping the foam off the beer that I first discovered that the taste was much to my liking. By the time I was fourteen, at which time I quit school, I had found that wine and hard cider were also pleasing to my palate. The next six years I spent learning the art of barbering and by the end of this period I had become both a proficient barber and an earnest drinker.

During the next 10 or 12 years I was able to acquire several lucrative shops, some with poolrooms and restaurants attached. It seemed quite impossible however for me to stand prosperity so I would drink myself out of one situation, get myself together a bit, develop another, and then repeat the performance.

The time came when I could no longer refinance myself so I began to float about the country, getting a job here and there as I could, but invariably I got fired in a short time because of my unreliability.

My marriage, which occurred in 1910 about the time I started my successful ownership of shops, resulted in our having a family of ten children who were usually desperately in need because I used my slender income for booze instead of providing for them.

I finally secured a job in a shop in a town of about 4,500 people, where I now live. My reputation for drinking soon became more or less generally known. About this time a deacon and the pastor of one of the local churches used to come in the shop for their work and were constantly inviting me to church and Bible classes, which invitations irritated me very much. I earnestly wished they would mind their own business.

I finally did accept one or two invitations to social functions at the home of one of these men, and was received so cordially that the barrier between us was partially lowered.

I did not stop drinking however, though my feeling toward these men was kindly. They at last persuaded me to go to a nearby town to have a talk with a doctor who had had a great deal of experience with this type of trouble. I listened to the man for two hours, and although my mind was quite foggy, I retained a good deal of what he said. I feel that the combined effort of these three Christian gentlemen made it possible for me to have a vital spiritual experience. This occurred in March, 1937.

For about six years previous to this time I was never at any time completely free from the influence of liquor.

Since that time I have regained the love of my family and the respect of the community, and can truthfully say that the past two years have been the happiest of my life.

I have busied myself a great deal during these two years in helping others who were afflicted as I was, and the combined efforts of the deacon, the pastor, and myself, have resulted in nine other men finding a way out of difficulties which were identical with mine. I feel this activity has played an important part in my mastery of this most devastating habit.

WHY GO into the drinking pattern that is so much the same with all of us? Three times I had left the hospital with hope that I was saying goodbye forever. And here I was again.

The first day there I told the kindly doctor that I was a thoroughly hopeless case and would probably continue to return as long as I could beg, borrow, or steal the money to get in. On the second day he told me that he knew of something that would keep me off liquor for life. I laughed at him. Yes, indeed, I would do anything or take anything that would produce such results, but there wasn't anything. On the third day a man came to talk with me. He was an alcoholic who had stopped! He talked about alcoholism and a spiritual way of life. I was deeply impressed by his seriousness, but nothing that he said made sense to me. He spoke about God, and a power greater than one's self. I remember being very careful not to say anything that might shake his faith in whatever it was he believed! I was deeply grateful to him for taking the trouble to talk with me, but what he had was not for me. I had thought much about religion and had come to rather definite conclusions. There was no God. The universe was an inexplicable phenomenon. In spite of my sorry state and outlook, there were many beautiful things in life, but no beauty. There were truths discoverable about life, but no truth. There were people who were good, kind, considerate, but no such thing as goodness. I had read rather extensively, but when people began to talk in such ultimates I was lost. I could find in life no eternal purpose nor anything that might be labeled "divine guidance." War, illness, cruelty, stupidity, poverty and greed were not and could not be the product of any purposeful creation. The whole thing simply didn't make sense.

About this I felt no deep emotion. I had struggled with the problem during late adolescence, but had long since ceased to give it anxious thought. Many people believe in a god of some sort and worship him in various ways. That was excellent. I thought it nice that so many people, poor misguided souls, could find so simple a solution to their problems. If this world proved too hopelessly disillusioning they could always seek comfort in a more pleasant existence promised in a world to come, where wrongs would be righted and justice tempered with tender mercy would prevail. But none of that was for me. I had enough courage and intellectual honesty to face life as I saw it without recourse to a self-erected deity.

The next day another man visited me. He, too, had been an alcoholic and stopped drinking. He pointed out that I had found myself unable to handle my liquor problem by myself. He had been in the same position, yet he hadn't had a drink in over three years! He told me of other men who had found sobriety through the recognition of some power beyond themselves. If I cared to I was to consider myself invited to a gathering the following Tuesday where I would meet other alcoholics who had stopped.

With the knowledge I now have, it is hard for me to recall how screwy the whole thing sounded—the blind leading the blind, a union of drunks, all banded together in some kind of a spiritual belief! What could be more idiotic! But . . . these men were sober! Nuts!

I returned to my despairing wife with this incoherent story of a bunch of drunks who had found a cure for their alcoholism through some kind of spiritual exercise and who held regular meetings where, as far as I could figure out, they went through some kind of spiritual exercise! She was very nearly convinced that my mental balance had now been completely and probably permanently destroyed. The only rational support I could find for giving it a try was that it was vouched for by the kindly doctor whom she had met on several occasions at the hospital. That and the fact that nothing else worked.

May I stop at this point and address a few sentences direct to agnostic or atheistically inclined alcoholics: You can't take less stock in the references made to God in this book than I would have if this book had been available to me at that time. To you those references have no meaning. They have simply used a name that people give to a fond delusion. All your life, except possibly in early childhood, when you conceived of an enormous figure with a flowing white beard somewhere beyond the clouds, it has meant nothing. You have now too much intelligence and honesty to allow of such delusions. Even if you could, you are too proud to affirm a belief now that you are in desperate trouble, that you denied when things were rosy. Or, you might possibly persuade yourself to believe in some creative force, or algebraic "X," but what earthly good would an "X" be in solving such a problem as you face? And, even admitting, from your knowledge of psychology, it is possible you might acquire such delusions, how could you possibly believe in them if you recognized them as delusions? Some such thinking must have been going on in your mind as you have weighed these incredible experiences against your own inability to cope with a problem that is gradually destroying your personality. Rest assured that such questions were in my mind. I could see no satisfactory solution to any of them. But I kept hard to the only thing that seemed to hold out any hope, and gradually my difficulties were lessened. I have not given up my intellect for the sake of my soul, nor have I destroyed my integrity to preserve my health and sanity. *All I had feared to lose I have gained and all I feared to gain I have lost.*

But to conclude my story: The following Tuesday, hardly daring to hope and fearful of the worst, my wife and I attended our first gathering with former alcoholic slaves who had been made free through the rediscovery of a power for good, found through a spiritual attitude toward life. I know that I have never before been so inspired. It was not anything that happened. Because nothing happened. Nor yet by anything that was said, but more by an atmosphere created by friendliness, sincerity, honesty, confidence, and good cheer. I couldn't believe that these men could have been drunks, and yet gradually I learned their stories, alcoholics every one!

That was, with me, the beginning of a new life. It would be difficult, if not impossible, for me to put into words the change that has taken place in me. I have since learned that with many members the change has been almost instantaneous. This was not the case with me. I was tremendously inspired at first, but my basic thinking was not altered that evening nor did I expect any profound change. I felt that while the spiritual aspect of what these men had was not for me, I did believe strongly in the emphasis they put on the need to help others. I felt that if I could have the inspiration of these gatherings and if I could have an opportunity to try to help others that the two together would re-enforce my own will-power and thus be of tremendous assistance. But gradually, in a manner I can not explain, I began to re-examine the beliefs I had thought beyond criticism. Almost imperceptibly my whole attitude toward life underwent a silent revolution. I lost many worries and gained confidence. I found myself saying and thinking things that a short time ago I would have condemned as platitudes! A belief in the basic spirituality of life has grown and with it belief in a supreme and guiding power for good.

In the process of this change I can recognize two immensely significant steps for me. The first step I took when I admitted to myself for the first time that all my previous thinking might be wrong. The second step came when I first consciously wished to believe. As a result of this experience I am convinced that to seek is to find, to ask is to be given. The day never passes that I do not silently cry out in thankfulness, not merely for my release from alcohol, but even more for a change that has given life new meaning, dignity, and beauty.

"HELLO Pal."

"Hello, Buddy!"

"Have a drink?"

"Got one!"

"Come over on the next stool I'm lonesome. Hell of a world."

"You said it, brother—hell of a world."

"You taking rye? Mine's gin. God, I'm up against it now!"

"How's 'at?"

"Oh, same old hell-hell-hell. She's going to leave me now!"

"Your wife?"

"Yeah. How am I going to live? Can't go home like this; too damn drunk to stay out. Can't land in jail will if I stay out—ruin my business—business going anyway—break her heart. Where is she you ask? She's at the store, working I guess, probably eating her heart out waiting for me. What time is it? Seven o'clock? Store's been closed an hour. She's gone home by now. Well, what the hell. Have one more—then I'll go."

That is a hazy recollection of my last debauch. Nearly a year ago now. By the time my new "bar fly friend" and I had soaked up several more, I was shedding tears and he, in the tender throes of drunken sympathy, was working out a guaranteed plan whereby my wife would greet me with great joy and out-spread arms as soon as we got home.

Yes "we" were going to my home. He was the finest fixer in the world. He knew all about how to handle wives. He admitted that!

So, two drunks, now lifetime buddies, stumbled out arm in arm headed up the hill towards home.

A draft of cool air cleared some of the fog away from my befuddled brain. "Wait a minute, what's this so-and-so-plan of yours? I got to know about it," I said. "I got to know what you're going to say and what I say."

The plan was a honey! All he had to do was to lead me up to the apartment, ring the bell, ask my wife if I was her husband, and then tell her he had found me down at the river about to jump from the bridge and had saved my life.

"That's all there is to it," he kept mumbling over and over, "works every time—never fails."

On up the hill we staggered, then my "life saver" got a better idea that would clinch the deal. He'd have to go home first and put on clean linen. Couldn't let the nice lady see a dirty shirt.

That sounded all right. Maybe he'd have a bottle at his home. So we stumbled up to his place, a dreary third floor back room, on a third rate street.

I have a hazy recollection of that place, but have never been able to find it since. There was a photograph of a quite pretty girl on his dresser. He told me it was a picture of his wife and that she had kicked him out because he was drunk. "You know how women are," he said.

Some fixer!

He did put on a clean shirt all right and then reached into a drawer and pulled out a .38 caliber revolver. That gave me quite a sobering shock. I reached for the gun realizing in a hazy way that here was trouble.

He began to pull the trigger and every moment I expected to hear an explosion, but the gun was empty. He proved it!

Then he got a new idea. To reconcile my wife and make her happy, he would tell her the gun was mine, that I stood on the bridge, with the gun at my head and that he snatched it away just in time to save my life.

God Almighty must have, at that moment, granted me a flash of sanity. I quickly excused myself while he was completing his toilet and, on the pretext of phoning my wife, rushed noisily down the stairs and ran down the street with all my might.

Some blocks away I came to a drug store, bought a pint of gin, and drank half of it in several large gulps, staggered on up to my apartment, and tumbled into bed, fully dressed and dead drunk.

This wasn't any new terror for my wife. This sort of thing had been going on for several years, only I was getting worse and worse with each drunken spree and more difficult to handle.

Only the previous day I had been in an accident. A Good Samaritan saw my condition and got me away quickly, before the police came, and drove me back to my home.

I was dreadfully drunk that day and my wife consulted a lawyer as preliminary to entering divorce action. I swore to her that I wouldn't drink again and within 24 hours, here I was in bed dead drunk.

Several months previously I had spent a week in a New York hospital for alcoholics and came out feeling that everything would be all right. Then I began to think that I had the thing licked. I could practice a little controlled drinking. I knew I couldn't take much but just one drink before dinner. That went all right, too. Sure I had it licked now! The next step was to take one quick one at noon and cover it up with a milk shake. To make it doubly sure, I'd have ice cream put into the milk shake, and then, so help me, I don't know what the next step down was, but I surely landed at the bottom with an awful, heartbreaking thud.

The next morning was June 7th. I recall the date so well because the sixth is my daughter's birthday. And that, by the grace of God, was my last spree.

That morning I was afraid to open my eyes, surely my wife would have kept her promise and left me. I loved my wife. It is a paradox I know, but I did and do.

When I did stir, there she was sitting at my bedside,

"Come on," she said, "get up, bathe, shave and dress. We're going to New York this morning."

"New York!" I said, "To the hospital?"

"Yes."

"I haven't any money to pay a hospital."

"I know you haven't," she said, "but I arranged it all last night over long distance and I'm going to give you that one chance, once again. If you let me down this time, that's all there is."

Well, I went into that hospital again feeling like a whipped cur. My wife pleaded with the doctor to please do something to save her husband, to save her home, to save our business, and our self-respect.

The doctor assured us that he really had something for me this time that would work and with that faint hope, we separated; she to hurry back home, 150 miles away, and carry on the work of two people and I to sit trembling and fearful there in what seemed to me, a shameful place.

Four days later a man called on me and seemed interested to know how I was coming along. He told me that he, too, had been there several times but had now found relief.

That night another man came. He, too, had suffered the same trouble and told how he and the other fellow and several more had been released from alcohol.

Then the next day a fine fellow came, and in a halting but effective way, told how he had placed himself in God's hand and keeping. Almost before I knew it, I was asking God to clean me up.

I suppose there are many who feel a strong resentment against such a spiritual approach. Some of Alcoholics Anonymous whom I have met since that day tell me they had difficulty in accepting a simple, day to day, plan of faith. In my case I was ripe for such an opportunity, perhaps because of early religious training. I have always, it seems, had a keen sense of the fact and presence of God.

That, too, like loving my wife and at the same time hurting her so dreadfully, is paradoxical, but it's a fact. I knew that God, was there with infinite love and yet, somehow, I kept on drifting further and further away. But now I do feel that my heart and mind are "tuned in" and by His grace there will be no more alcoholic "static."

After making this final agreement (not just another resolution) to let God to be first in my life, the whole outlook and horizon brightened up in a manner which I am unable to describe except to say that it was "glorious."

The following day was Monday and my ex-alcoholic friend insisted that I check out from the hospital and come over to his home in Jersey. I did that and there I found a lovely wife and children all so "happy about the whole thing."

The next night I was taken to a meeting, at the home of an ex-alcoholic in Brooklyn, where to my surprise, there were more than 30 men like myself, telling of a liberty of living unmatched by anything I had ever seen.

Since returning to my home, life has been so different. I have paid off the old debts, have money enough now for decent clothes and some to use in helping others, a thing which I enjoy doing but didn't do when I had to contribute so generously to alcohol.

I am trying to help other alcoholics. At this writing there are four of us working, all of whom have been kicked around dreadfully.

There is no "cocky" feeling about this for me. I know I am an alcoholic and while I used to call on God to help me, my conclusion is that

I was simply asking God to help me drink alcohol without its hurting me which is a far different thing than asking him to help me not to drink at all.

So here I stand, living day to day, in His presence, and it is wonderful. This prodigal came home.

During the first week of March, 1937, through the grace of God, I ended 20 years of a life made practically useless because I could not do two things.

First, I was unable to not take a drink.

Second, I was unable to take a drink without getting drunk.

Perhaps a third as important as the other two should be added; my being unwilling to admit either of the first two.

With the result I kept trying to drink without getting drunk, and kept making a nightmare of my life, causing suffering and hardship to all those relatives and friends who tried so hard to help me and whom, when I was sober, I took the greatest pleasure in pleasing.

The first time I drank anything strong, or in greater quantity than a glass of beer, I got disgustingly drunk and missed the dinner which had been arranged for me in honor of my coming marriage.

I had to be taken home and remained in bed the following day; more sick than I thought a human could be and live. Yet, until two years ago I periodically did the same thing.

Making money was always pretty easy when I was sober and worked.

All right when sober—absolutely helpless with a drink aboard. But I seemed to have had the idea that making money or a living was something to take or let alone.

I got into the real estate business—began to neglect business, sometimes with four houses under construction, wouldn't see any of them for a week or even longer—sometimes paid good money for an option, then forgot to exercise it. I made and lost plenty of money in the market.

Understand, I wasn't actually drunk all of this time but there seemed always to be an excuse to have a drink, and this first one, more and more often lead to my becoming drunk. As time went on, periods between drunks got shorter and I was full of fear; fear that I wouldn't be able to do anything I agreed to do; fear of meeting men; worrying about what they might know of my drinking and its results; all of which made me quite useless whether I was sober or drunk.

Thus I drifted. Breaking promises to my wife, my mother, and a host of other relatives and friends who stood more from me and tried harder than humans should be expected to, to help me.

I always seemed to pick the most inopportune time for a binge. An important business deal to be closed might find me in another city. Once when entrusted to purchase for a large customer, I agreed to meet his representative in New York. I spent the time waiting for a train in a bar; arrived in New York tight; stayed tight the week; and came home by a route twice the distance from New York.

Worked weeks, by long distance, wire, letters, and personal calls, to contact possible business connections under proper conditions and finally succeeded, only to show up tight or get tight and insult the man who's friendship, or respect meant so much.

Each time there was the feeling of regret, inability to understand why, but a firm determination that it would never happen again—but it did—in fact the periods between became increasingly shorter, and the duration of each binge longer.

During the aforementioned period, I had spent thousands of dollars, my home was broken up; half a dozen cars smashed up; I had been picked up by police for driving while intoxicated—plain drunk; had sponged and borrowed money; cashed rubber checks; and made such a general nuisance of myself that I lost all the friends I had. At least they felt unwilling to be a party to financing me while I made a more complete ass of my self. And I, on my side was ashamed to face any of them when I was sober.

My friends secured jobs for me; I made good on them for a time. I advanced quickly to night superintendent in a factory but it wasn't long until I was missing, or worse, turning up drunk; was warned—warned again; finally fired. I was later re-hired as a factory hand and mighty glad to have it—advance again—then back to the bottom—always the same process.

I drank continuously and when I drank, sooner or later, and generally sooner, I got drunk and threw everything away.

During the early part of 1935 my brother secured my release from the city jail. On that day by sincere but non-alcoholic friends I was shown what might be done about my drinking with the help of God.

I asked for this help, gratefully accepted it, and in addition to losing my desire for drink, asked for and received the same help in other matters. I began to earn my living and in my new found security, was unashamed to meet people I had avoided for years with happy results.

Things continued well, I had two or three advancements to better jobs with greater earning power. My every need was being met as long as I accepted and acknowledged the Divine Help which was so generously given.

I find now, as I look back, that this period covered about six or eight months, then I began to think how smart I was; to wonder if my superiors realized what they had in me; if they were not pretty small about the money they paid me; as these thoughts grew, my feeling of gratefulness grew less. I was neglecting to ask for help—when I received it as I always did, I neglected to acknowledge it. Instead I took great credit for myself. I began to take credit for the non-drinking too—it came to me strongly that I had conquered the drinking habit myself—I became convinced of my great will power.

Then someone suggested a glass of beer—I had one. This was even better than I thought—I could take a drink and not get drunk. So another day, another beer until it was regular every day. Now I was indeed in the saddle concerning drink—could take it or leave it alone. Just to prove it to myself, I decided to march right past the place I usually stopped for beer, and I felt pretty good as I went to the parking lot for my car. The longer I drove the greater was my pride that I had finally licked liquor. I was sure I had—so sure in fact that I stopped and had a beer before I went home. In my smugness I continued to drink beer and began occasionally to drink liquor.

So it went until inevitably, "as darkness follows the sun," I got drunk and was right back where I had been fifteen years before, slipping into a binge every now and then—never knowing when they would come—nor where I would wind up.

This lasted about eight months—I didn't miss much time from work—did spend one ten day stretch in the hospital after a beating I got while drunk—was warned a few times by my superiors—but was "getting by."

In the meantime I had heard of some men who, like myself, were what I had always scoffed at being—alcoholics. I had been invited to see them, but after twenty years of drinking, I felt there was nothing wrong with me. *They* might need it; *they* might be queer; but not me. I wasn't going to get drunk again.

Of course I did, again and again, until these men not only contacted me but took me under their wing.

After a few days of "degoofing" in a hospital, these men came to me one by one and told me of their experiences. They didn't lecture —didn't tell me I should quit. But they did tell me *how* to quit. THAT WAS IMPORTANT and simple too.

Their suggestion was that we simply acknowledge we had made a pretty dismal failure of our lives, that we accept as truth and act upon what we had always been taught and known, that there was a kind and merciful God; that we were His children; and, that if we would let Him, He would help us.

I had certainly made a mess of my life. From the age of 20 I had thrown aside everything God had seen fit to endow me with. Why not avail myself of this all wise, ever-present help?

This I did. I ask for, accept, and acknowledge this help, and know that so long as I do, I shall never take a drink and what is more important, though impossible without the first, all other phases of my life have been helped.

There are, it seems to me, four steps to be taken by one who is a victim of alcoholism.

First: Have a real desire to quit.

Second: Admit you can't. (This is hardest.)

Third: Ask for His ever present help.

Fourth: Accept and acknowledge this help.

FIRED! Still, I got a new and better job. One which gave me more time to relax and where drinking was permitted during working hours. People were beginning to criticize my drinking habits and I scoffed at them. Hadn't I earned ten thousand dollars that year? And wasn't this the middle of the depression? Who were they to say that I couldn't handle my liquor? A year of this and I was fired.

Other jobs followed with the same net result. After each experience of this kind I would sit down and figure out the reason why it happened. I always found a good reason, and usually people accepted it and gave me another chance. For weeks, sometimes months, I wouldn't touch a drop and because I could do this, I reasoned that there was a real excuse for that last bender, and since that excuse no longer existed I could start to drink moderately again.

I usually did—for a while. Then I would step up the consumption about one glass per day until I reached the stage where all of the past unhappy experiences associated with drinking were brought back to my mind. Soon I was crying in my beer, full of self-pity, and off again to a flying start toward a floundering finish.

How many times this happened, I don't know. I don't even want to know. I do know that during this period I completely smashed nine new automobiles and was never scratched. Even this didn't convince me that there might be a God who was looking out for me in answer to the prayers of others. I made many friends and abused them terribly. I didn't want to, but when it was a question of a friendship or a drink, I usually took the drink.

In a final effort to escape, I went to New York thinking I could leave my reputation and troubles behind me. It didn't work. I was hired by eight nationally known organizations and fired just as quickly when they had checked my references. The world was against me. They wouldn't give me a chance. So I continued my drinking and took any mediocre job I could get.

Occasionally I dropped into a church half hoping that I might absorb something, anything, that might help a little bit. On one of these visits I saw and met a girl who I felt could be the answer to all of my problems. I told her all about myself and how I felt sure that with her friendship and love everything could and would be different. Although born in New York she was "from Missouri." I would have to show her first. She had seen other girls try to reform men by marrying them and she knew it didn't work.

She suggested praying and having faith and a lot of things that seemed silly at the time, but I really got down to business and started doing some serious bargaining with God. I prayed and prayed. In all earnestness I said, "If You will get this girl for me then I'll stop drinking for You." And "If You will only get me my original job back, I'll drink moderately for You." I soon found out that God didn't work that way because I didn't get the girl or the job.

Six months later I was sitting in a small hotel on the west side of New York full of remorse and desperate because I didn't know what would happen next. A middle-aged man approached me and said in a very sincere voice, "Do you really want to stop drinking?" Immediately I answered "Yes," because I knew that was the correct answer. He wrote down a name and address and said, "When you are sure you do, go and see this man." He walked away.

I began to think, "Did I really want to quit? Why should I? If I couldn't have this girl and I couldn't ever have a good job again, why in the hell should I quit?" I tucked the address into my pocket along with a nickel for subway fare, just in case I ever decided to really quit. I started drinking again, but could get no happiness or release regardless of the number of drinks.

Occasionally I would check up to see if the address and the nickel were still safe, because I was being tortured with one thought this girl had given to me. "You must be decent for your own sake. And because you want to be decent, not because some one else wants you to be."

A week later I found myself in the presence of the man whose address was in my pocket. His story was incredible. I couldn't believe it, but he had the proof. I met men whose stories convinced me that in the ranks of men who had been heavy drinkers I was an amateur and a sissy.

What I heard was hard to believe but I wanted to believe it. What's more I wanted to try it and see if it wouldn't work for me.

It worked, and is still working. For weeks I was bitter against society. Why didn't some one put me wise to this before? Why did I have to go on like that for years making my parents unhappy, abusing friends, and passing up opportunities? It wasn't fair that I should be the instrument to make people unhappy.

I believe now that I was given this experience so that I might understand and be of use in helping others to find a solution to this and other problems.

When I decided to do something about my problem, I was reconciled to the fact that it might be necessary for me to wash dishes, scrub floors, or do some menial task for possibly many years in order to reestablish myself as a sober, sane, and reliable person. Although I still wanted and hoped for the better things in life, I was prepared to accept whatever was due me.

Once I became sincere, good things began to happen to me. My first experience in overcoming fear was three weeks later when I applied for a position with a national organization. After numerous questions I was finally asked why I had left the company I had been with six years. I replied that I had been fired for being a drunk. The manager was flabbergasted and so completely astounded by the truth that he refused to believe me. I referred him to my former employer but he refused to write him—but he did give me the job.

It has been three and a half years since I made that decision. Those years have been the happiest years of my life. The little girl, who was big enough to tell me the nasty truth when I needed it, is now my wife.

Eight months ago I went to another city to set up a new business. I had sufficient money to last me several months. What I wanted to accomplish could have been done under ordinary circumstances in about two weeks. The obstacles I have encountered and overcome are hard to enumerate. At least twenty times I have been sure that I would be doing business within the next twenty-four hours and at least twenty times something has happened which later made it seem that the business never would get started.

While I am writing this I happen to be at the low point of the twenty first time. Money is exhausted. All recent developments have been unfavorable, everything seems on the surface to be wrong. Yet I am not discouraged. I am not blue. I feel no bitterness toward these people who have tried to obstruct the progress of the business, and somehow I feel because I have tried hard, played square, and met situations, that something good will come from this whole experience. It may not come the way I want it, but I sincerely believe that it will come the way that it is best.

IN EARLY youth I believe I had some of the tendencies that lead to alcoholism. I refer to attempted escapes from reality.

At fifteen and sixteen although free at home to drink small amounts of beer and wine, I drank considerable quantities of stronger liquors at school and other places. Not enough to cause serious worry, but enough apparently to give me occasionally what I thought I wanted. Escape? A feeling of superiority? I do not know.

I decided I'd had enough of school, which decision was probably shared by the schools. The next few years were spent in civil engineering work, travel sports and a little idleness, and I seem to have avoided alcoholic difficulties of the more pronounced kind.

Immediately before marriage and in the short time before sailing for France, alcohol began to take a real part in my life. A year and a half in war time France postponed the inevitable and the post war period of hopes and plans brought me nearer and nearer to the point where I eventually found myself to be an alcoholic. Not that I would have admitted it then, having the alcoholic's usual facility for deception, both to self and others.

Divorced, sometimes suspecting that drinking was the basis for most of my troubles but never admitting it, I had enough left in health, interests of various kinds and luck to carry on with considerable success.

About this time I stopped all social drinking. I became a periodical drunkard, the sprees lasting from three days to three weeks and the dry intervals lasting from three weeks to four months.

During one of the best years, I made a happy marriage and the age of thirty-five found me with the following: a beautiful little home presided over by a kind, understanding, and lovely wife; a partnership in a firm I had helped to found years before; more than a comfortable income; many luxuries and many friends; opportunity to follow my interests and hobbies; a love of my work; pride in my success; great health; optimism and hope on the credit side. On the other hand, I had a growing, gnawing fear of my recurring trouble.

I slipped by far too easy stages to the bottom in less than eight years. Not a pleasant place, the bottom. Sometimes I slept in a cheap hotel or rooming house, sometimes a flop house, sometimes the back room of a police station and once in a doorway; many times in the alcoholic ward at a hospital, and once in a subway toilet. Sometimes decently fed, clothed and housed, I worked at my business on commission with a large firm; sometimes I dared not appear there cold, hungry with torn clothes, shaking body and muddled brain advertising what I had become. Helpless, hopeless, bitter.

Sometimes I was apparently on the way back, and sometimes writhing in bed for days at a time, terrorized by the fear of insanity and by the specters of people without faces, people with horrible faces, people grimacing and laughing at me and my misery. Tortured by dreams from which I would awake with a scream of agony and bathed in cold sweat. Tortured by day dreams of what might have been, dreams of the kindness, faith and love that had been heaped upon me.

Due to this last however, and to what little remained of my former self and perhaps to some lingering power of spiritual faith, I became somewhat better, not well, but better.

This helped me to take stock and to try to do some clear thinking. I found my inventory somewhat mixed, but as my thoughts became clearer, I grew much better and at last arrived at that point where for the first time in several years I could see some light and hope ahead of me. Through a haze of doubt and skepticism I began to realize, partly at least, many things in myself which had greased the path I had pursued, and some vague thoughts and ideas came to me that are now crystallizing with the help of the men I have been happy to join.

What thoughts and ideas? The answer is short, although the road to it is long and tedious.

My intelligence, instead of drawing me further away from spiritual faith is bringing me closer to it. I no longer react in quite the same way when my will and desires are apparently frustrated.

The simple words "Thy Will Be Done" and the simple ideas of honesty and of helping others are taking on a new meaning for me. I should not be surprised to find myself coming to the astounding conclusion that God, whoever or whatever He may be, is eminently more capable of running this universe that I am. At last I believe I am on my way.

I HAVE the misfortune, or I should say the good fortune of being an alcoholic's wife. I say misfortune because of the worry and grief that goes with drinking, and good fortune because we found a new way of living.

My husband did not drink, to my knowledge, for several years after we were married. Then we started on an occasional Saturday night party. As I drank nothing except an occasional highball I soon became what was called a "wet blanket." The parties became more frequent and more often I was left at home.

I would sit up and wait for him. As each car passed the house I would return to walking the floor and crying and feeling so sorry for myself, thinking, "Here I am left at home to take care of the baby and him out having a good time."

When he did return sometimes on Sunday and sometimes a week later, it usually called for a scene. If he was still drunk I would put him to bed and cry some more. If he was sober it would mean I would say all the things I had been thinking and cry some more. He usually got drunk again.

I finally went to work as the bills worried me. I thought if I worked and got the bills paid he would quit drinking. He had no money in the bank but would write checks as he knew I would pay them for the boy's sake and in the hopes that each time would be the last.

I thought I should have a lot of credit, as I was paying his bills, taking care of the house and baby, besides my work, making as much money as he was, doing without things I wanted so he could have a good time.

I always went to church and thought I was living a Christian life. After my husband came in contact with Alcoholics Anonymous I thought our troubles were over as I was sure all our trouble was his drinking.

I soon found out that there was a lot wrong with me. I was selfish with my money, time, and thoughts. I was selfish about my time because I was always tired and had no time left for my family's pleasure or to do God's work. All I did was go to Sunday School and Church on Sunday with the boy and thought that was all God wanted me to do. I would be irritable and lose my temper and say all manner of things which usually called for another drunk and me pitying myself all over again.

Since giving my husband's problem to God I have found a peace and happiness. I know that when I try to take care of the problems of my husband I am a stumbling block as my husband has to take his problems to God the same as I do.

My husband and I now talk over our problems and trust in a Divine Power. We have now started to live. When we live with God we want for nothing.

There is a principle, which is a bar against all information, which is proof against all arguments and which can not fail to keep a man in everlasting ignorance—that principle is contempt prior to investigation.
—HERBERT SPENCER

THE above quotation is descriptive of the mental attitudes of many alcoholics when the subject of religion, as a cure, is first brought to their attention. It is only when a man has tried everything else, when in utter desperation and terrific need he turns to something bigger than himself, that he gets a glimpse of the way out. It is then that contempt is replaced by hope, and hope by fulfillment.

In this personal story I have endeavored to relate something of my experience in the search for spiritual help rather than a description of the neurotic drinking that made the search necessary. After all, the pattern of most alcoholic experiences fits a pretty general mold. Experiences differ because of circumstances, environment, and temperament, but the after effects, both physical and mental, are almost identical. It makes but little difference how or why a man becomes an alcoholic once this disease manifests itself. The preventive measures adopted for alcoholic tendencies in the future will have to be found in a more progressive program of mental hygiene and medical research than is now obtainable.

It is important that at present we believe there is only one sure pathway to recovery for any alcoholic.

In my own case I was not entirely ignorant of the causes that led me into excessive drinking. In a desperate effort to eliminate these causes, to find a means to better mental and physical health, I investigated the alcoholic problem from every angle. Medicine, psychology, psychiatry, and psychoanalysis absorbed my interest and supplied me with a great deal of general and specific information. It led me in the end, however, to the fact that for me here was a mental and physical disease that science had placed in the category of "incurables." Briefly, all that this study and research ever did for me was to show something about WHY I drank. It substantiated a fact I had known all along, that my drinking was symptomatic. It did point out a road to better mental health but it demanded something of me in return that I did not have to give. It asked of me a *power* of self-will but it did not take into consideration that this self-will was already drugged with poison—that it was very sick. Intuitively I also knew that a person constrained to temperance by the domination of will is no more *cured* of his vice than if he were locked up in prison. I knew that somehow, some way, the mental stream, the emotions, must be purified before the right pathway could be followed.

It was about this time that I began "flirting" with religion as a possible way out. I approached the subject in a wary, none too reverent, attitude. I believed in an omnipotent God or Deity, but the orthodox approach through the church, with its dogma and ritual, left me unmoved. The more I struggled to gain an intelligent grasp upon spiritual development, the more confused I became. On the other hand a purely materialistic viewpoint that postulated a "mechanical order of things" seemed too negative even to entertain. As an artist I had spent too much time communing with nature—trying to place upon canvas or paper my emotional feelings, not to know that a tremendous spiritual power was back of the universe. There was, however, so much that seemed illogical or sentimental about religion in general—so many doubts assailed me, so many problems to be confronted—yet there was within myself a strong and urgent desire for spiritual satisfaction. The occasional periods in which I felt a spiritual emotion, I immediately examined with all the ardor of the inveterate analyst. Was this emotion just a form of religious ecstasy? Was it fear? Was it just blind belief or had I tapped something?

"Most men," wrote Thoreau, "lead lives of quiet desperation." It was the articulation of this despair that led to my drinking in the beginning. Religion, so far, had only added to my desperation. I drank more than ever.

A seed had been planted, however, and a short time afterward I met the man who has for the past five years devoted a great deal of time and energy to helping alcoholics. Looking back on that meeting, the simplicity of his talk with me is amazing. He told me very little but what I already knew, in part, but what he did have to say was bereft of all fancy spiritual phraseology—it was simple Christianity imparted with Divine Power. The next day I met over twenty men who had achieved a mental rebirth from alcoholism. Here again it was not so much what these men told me in regard to their experiences that was impressive, as it was a sense or feeling that an invisible influence was at work. What was it this man had and these other men exemplified without their knowing? They were human every-day sort of people. They certainly were not pious. They had no "holier than thou" attitude. They were not reformers, and their concepts of religion in some cases were almost inarticulate. But they had *something!* Was it just their sincerity that was magnetic? Yes, they certainly were sincere, but much more than that emanated from them. Was it their great and terrible need, now being fulfilled, that made me feel a vibratory force that was new and strange? Now I was getting closer and suddenly, it seemed to me, I had the answer. These men were but instruments. Of themselves they were nothing.

Here at last was a demonstration of spiritual law at work. Here was spiritual law working through human lives just as definitely and with the same phenomena expressed in the physical laws that govern the material world.

These men were like lamps supplied with current from a huge spiritual dynamo and controlled by the rheostat of their souls. They burned dim, bright, or brilliant, depending upon the degree and progress of their contact. And this contact could only be maintained just so long as they obeyed that spiritual law.

These men were thinking straight—therefore their actions corresponded to their thoughts. They had given themselves, *their minds,* over to a higher power for *direction.* Here, it seemed to me, in the one word "Thought"—was the crux of the whole spiritual quest. That "As a man thinketh in his heart, so is he" and so is his health, his environment, his failure, or his success in life.

How foolish I had been in my quest for spiritual help. How selfish and egotistical I had been to think that I could approach God *intellectually.* In the very struggle to obtain faith I had lost it. I had given to the term faith a religious significance only. I had failed. to see that faith was "our common everyday manner of thinking." That good and evil were but end results of certain uniform and reliable spiritual laws. Obviously, my own thinking had been decidedly wrong. Normal most of the time, it was abnormal at the wrong times. Like everyone's thinking, it was a mixture of good and bad, but mainly it was uncontrolled.

I had been sticking my chin out and getting socked by spiritual law until I was punch drunk. If one could become humble, if he could become "*as a little child*" before this powerful spiritual thought force, the pathway could be discovered.

The day I made my first efforts in this direction an entire new world opened up for me. Drinking as a vicious habit was washed completely out of my consciousness. I have never even been tempted to take a drink since. As a matter of fact there are so many other things within myself that need correction that the drink habit looks silly in comparison. Please do not assume that all this is but an exposition of spiritual pride. A chart of my spiritual progress would look like the "graph" of a business that had been hit by everything but an earthquake. But there has been progress. It has cured me of a vicious habit. Where my life had been full of mental turmoil there is now an ever increasing depth of calmness. Where there was a hit or miss attitude toward living there is now new direction and force.

The approaches of man to God are many and varied. My conception of God as Universal Mind is after all but one man's approach to and concept of the Supreme Being. To me it makes sense, opens up a fascinating field of endeavor and is a challenge, the acceptance of which can make of life the "Adventure Magnificent."

AFTER the breaking up of our home, my father went west and took up his work and became fairly successful.

Then it was decided that I should be sent to a preparatory school so to a midwestern school I was sent. It didn't last long for I got into a jam and left.

I went to Chicago, wrote my father and he sent me fare to come on west, which I did. I started in to High School after I got there, but I had no companionship, for my Father was away most of the day and when he came in he always spent the evenings reading and studying.

This all caused me to become very bitter towards anything religious, because I felt that I was only in his way when he wanted to read his religious books and he took only enough interest in me to leave a dollar on the dresser each morning to buy my meals with. It caused me to become so hostile towards anything religious that I formed a hatred against religion which I was to carry for years.

During the time which I spent by myself, I had found that I could buy wine and loaf around saloons and it wasn't long before I had formed a taste for drink. I was only about fourteen years old then, but I looked eighteen.

When vacation time came I wanted to go to San Francisco. My father willingly let me go and after seeing the sights of that city I decided I wanted to go to sea and see the world, so it was only a short time before I found myself signed as an apprentice at sea and leading a new life.

In the meantime my mother had married again. I knew she was well taken care of so my letters were few and my visits home were years apart, and through the selfish interest I had taken in myself I never gave a thought to how worried she might be over me. I had become a person wrapped up in my own life only and giving no thought of anyone else.

Starting to sea out of San Francisco brought me in and out of port there a great deal so I considered San Francisco my home, and as I had arrived there about 1905 I knew the old San Francisco of before the earthquake where the lid was off and vice flourished at all times.

In my young life I saw all and knew all and considered myself well able to play the game as others did.

I developed into a steady drinker and, when going to sea, was sure

I took enough liquor along to take care of me for the trip. When we arrived at a foreign port we would go ashore and proceed to see the sights which mostly started at the first saloon. If American liquor was not to be had or was too high in cost then we would drink their native drink, and as I look back it hardly seems possible that I have a brain left to remember with for I have done about everything possible to destroy it by over-indulgence in alcohol.

I have been to most of the ports in this world; have stayed in some for some time; have put in a winter in Alaska; lived in the tropics; but no time did I ever find a place where I could not get liquor.

I quit the sea when I was just past 20. I had become interested in construction work, also had studied some art and learned the Freco decorating trade. Eventually I went into the building trade and have followed that ever since.

I had always made good wages or made good at contracting, but was ever a rolling stone, never staying in one place long and drinking just the same as in my seafaring days.

I had always a certain respect for myself and I carried my liquor well for years; knew enough not to make a show of myself and stopped when I had enough.

Then came the war. I was 29 years old and was in Texas when I went into the army and went overseas from there. After leaving Texas I found out that we were stopping in my home town for an hour and I received permission to call my mother when we arrived there, so fortunately I was able to get her down to the train before I left. I had not been home in years and I then told her if I came back alive I would come home to stay.

I had not been in the service long before I was a high ranking noncommissioned officer, for I had learned army discipline years before in the army transport service and while in this country and when behind the lines in France this gave me a chance to get my liquor when my buddies couldn't.

But when we got to the front lines it was the firsttime in years that I was unable to get my daily share of alcohol but, when it was possible, I never missed.

On into Germany for six months where I made up for lost time.

"Schnapps" was barred to American Troops but I got mine. After coming back to the U.S. I received an honorable discharge and came back to my home and mother.

Then I started trying to break away from liquor but it did not last. The last few years found me in all kinds of mix-ups for I had at last developed into an alcoholic.

When I drank I would get to the state where it required a doctor to straighten me out. The times I have had to rely upon doctors are numerous. I even tried sanitariums for relief. I had plenty of suffering thrown in but still I would drift back again to that first drink and off again I went.

I wanted to quit but each time I drank it was worse than before. The misery that my mother went through was unbelievable for I had become her sole support. I was willing to try anything if I could only get a release from this curse. I knew it was breaking up my home and I was losing everyone that was dear to me.

For a few months I was successful in discontinuing drinking. Then all of a sudden I fell again. I lost my position and thought I was through.

When I was told of a doctor who had been successful in overcoming alcohol and was asked to go and see him in a nearby city, I consented but with a feeling that it was just another cure.

From him and a number of other men, however, found it was possible to become a man again. He suggested my entrance into a hospital to clear my mind and build me up. Meals had become a thing of the past for me. I had lost all appetite for food but forced myself to eat a little to survive.

This doctor told me that unless I was sincere in wanting to quit drinking, I would be wasting his time and mine and also money in doing this. My answer was I would try anything that would release me.

I went into the hospital and started to build my body up again through proper nourishment, and my mind through a different method than I had ever known of.

A religious awakening was conveyed to me through some unseen force. I at one time would have laughed at such a possibility because I had tried it and failed because I had not applied it properly. I, at last, was shown the way by these men to whom I am now most grateful.

I am now 50 years old, unmarried, have become sane and sensible again, have made my mother happy and brought back those who were dear to me, have made many new friends, mix where I never mixed before, received back my old position. I have the respect of my fellow men and have learned how to actually live and really enjoy life. It has been nearly a year and a half since I have found this new life and I know as long as I do the few things that God requires me to do, I never will take another drink.

LONE ENDEAVOR

AS A mother looked idly through a small medical journal, an article written by a doctor on alcoholism caught her attention. Anything in reference to this subject was worthy of perusal, for her son, an only child, had been drinking uncontrollably for years. Each year of his drinking had added new heartaches, though every small ray of hope had been investigated, and though he had tried desperately to stop. But little had been accomplished. He was occasionally able to remain sober for short periods at a time, but things constantly became worse.

So this mother read the short medical article with a heavy heart, for she was constantly on the alert to find something which might prove helpful to her son.

The article gave only a vague hint of the solution found by many alcoholics, which is fully covered in this book, but the mother immediately wrote to the doctor explaining her heart-breaking problem, and requesting further information. She felt there must be help somewhere, and surely if other men had recovered from alcoholism, her son also had a chance.

The doctor turned her letter over to Alcoholics Anonymous. It ended as follows:

"God knows if you can help my son, it will bring happiness to many of us who love him and ache with him in his futile efforts to overcome his problem. Please accept my gratitude for whatever you may be able to do and let me hear from you."

A few days later the following letter was sent to this mother. It was our initial effort to help others through the book alone.

"About a hundred men, here in the east, have found a solution for alcoholism that really works. We are now preparing a book hoping to help others who suffer in the same way, and are enclosing a rough copy of the first two chapters. As soon as possible we will forward rough copy of the rest of the proposed book."

We received no answer for some time, and later wrote again:

"We are sending you a pre-publication multilith copy of 'ALCO-
HOLICS ANONYMOUS.' We would appreciate hearing about
your son's condition and his reaction to this volume, as this is the
first time we have had an opportunity of trying to help an alcoholic at long distance. Won't you please write?
            Sincerely,
            Alcoholics Anonymous"

After another period of silence from the far west, during which time
we began to think this book was inadequate without personal contact,
we received a long letter from the son, himself. A letter which we feel
will be of tremendous help to others who live in distant places, who
feel alone and totally unable to work this program out by themselves.
A letter which encompasses a man's solitary effort to take what we had
to offer and carry the program through alone. Alone except for one
book and the help which printed pages could give; alone until he had
tried our program of recovery and found spiritual comfort and help.
    He wrote as follows:

"I want to thank you from the bottom of my heart for your letters
and for 'ALCOHOLICS ANONYMOUS.' I have read this book
from cover to cover and it is really the first time I have read anything dealing with alcoholism that made sense and showing understanding of the problems of the alcoholic.
    "I found the personal stories very accurate as pertaining to my
own experience; any one of them might have been my own story.
    "I started drinking in 1917 when I was 18. I enlisted in the army,
soon became a non-commissioned officer, went overseas as a
sergeant. I associated with older men, drank, gambled, and ran
around with them, sampling everything France had to offer.
    "Upon my return from France I continued drinking. At that
time I could get plenty tight at night, get up in the morning and
go to work feeling O.K. The following fifteen years were one drunk
after another which, of course, as they got worse, meant one job

after another. Police Department truck driving, etc. Then in an attempt to get away from it all I enlisted in the U.S. Marine Corps. In 13 months time I drank very little and was promoted to Gunnery Sergeant, a rank that usually takes 10 or 12 years to obtain, if ever. I started drinking again. In six months I was reduced to Line Sergeant. I transferred to get away from my former associates.

"Then came several years in China. China of all places for a man who wanted to stay away from booze. My four years over, I did not re-enlist.

"Came more jobs selling automobiles, real estate, etc. Then down to odd jobs. I was drinking so much no one could take a chance by giving me a steady job, such as I could easily have handled if I left the liquor alone. I married and the booze split that up. My mother was a nervous wreck. I was getting arrested for drinking three or four times a year. I had myself committed on two different occasions to State Hospitals, but soon after discharge, I was back at it again. Two years ago I went to a private hospital for a liquor cure. A week after getting out I was curious as to what would happen if I took a drink. I took it nothing happened. I took another—why go further. I went back to the private hospital, came out and was O.K. for a few months—then at it again.

"Now previous to this and at the time of these cures, I was working at a State Hospital for the insane. I saw continually the effects of liquor but did it help me to leave it alone? No—it did not. But it did make me realize that if I did not, I would end up in the "bughouse" and someone else would be carrying the keys. After several years of working at mental institutions always in a violent ward, on account of my six feet and 210 lbs., I realized there was too much nervous tension and every couple of months I would 'blow up' and be off drunk for a week or ten days.

"I left mental work and got a job at the County General Hospital where I am now in a medical ward. We get quite a few patients with D.T.s, all broken out with wine sores, etc. I steadied down a bit, but not enough. I was off 'sick' for several days every six or eight weeks.

"I married again. A good Catholic girl whose people were used to having liquor, especially wine around the house always. She of course could not understand about my drinking—as far as that's concerned, neither could I. And all this time my poor mother and wife became more and more worried.

"Mother had heard of your wonderful work and wrote a doctor. You answered with letters, and finally the book. Before the book arrived and after reading the chapters I knew that the only way to combat this curse was to ask the help of that greater Power, God. I realized it even though I was then on a binge!

"I contacted a friend of mine who is liaison officer of the Disabled Veterans of the World War. He made arrangements for my care in a State Sanitarium which specializes in alcoholism. I wanted to get the liquor out of my system and start this new idea right. I explained my absence as 'Flu' and under the care of the head psychiatrist spent most of the time from Sept. 1, 1938 till Jan. 15, 1939 at the hospital having my appendix removed and a ventral hernia fixed up.

"Six weeks ago I returned from the sanitarium and your book was here waiting for me. I read, more than that I pored over it so as not to miss anything. I thought to myself, yes, this is the only way. God is my only chance. I have prayed before but I guess not the right way. I have followed out the suggestions in the book, I am happier this moment than I have been in years. I'm sure I have found the solution, thanks to ALCOHOLICS ANONYMOUS.

"I have had talks with another man, an attorney, who was at the sanitarium when I was. He has my book now and he is very much enthused.

"I go down to the sanitarium every week for a check-up and medicine which they give me, just a tonic, no sedatives. The manager has asked me to contact some of his patients along our line. How I told him I would appreciate his letting me do so!

"Would you put me in touch with some 'A.A.s' out here? I know it would help me and help me to help others.

"I hope you can make sense out of this letter. I could write so much more but this I have written just as it popped into my head.

"Please let me hear from you."

This man's lone struggle was impressive. Wouldn't the story of his solitary recovery be helpful to many others who would have to start out by themselves with only this book to aid them?

So we immediately sent him a wire:

JUST RECEIVED LETTER. MAY WE HAVE YOUR PERMISSION TO USE LETTER ANONYMOUSLY IN BOOK AS FIRST EXAMPLE OF WHAT MIGHT BE ACCOMPLISHED WITHOUT PERSONAL CONTACT. IMPORTANT YOU WIRE THIS PERMISSION AS BOOK IS GOING TO PRINTER.

ALCOHOLICS ANONYMOUS

His wire arrived next day:

PERMISSION GRANTED WITH PLEASURE. LOTS OF LUCK.

THE ALCOHOLIC FOUNDATION

IN OUR text we have shown the alcoholic how he may recover but we realize that many will want to write us.

To receive these inquiries, to administer royalties from this book and such other funds as may come to hand, a Trust has been created known as The Alcoholic Foundation. Three Trustees are members of Alcoholics Anonymous, the other four are well-known business and professional men who have volunteered their services. The Trust states these four (who are not of Alcoholics Anonymous) or their successors, shall always constitute a majority of the Board of Trustees.

We must frankly state however, that under present conditions, we shall be unable to reply to all inquiries, as our members, in their spare time, may attend to most of the correspondence. Nevertheless we shall strenuously attempt to communicate with those men and women who are able to report that they are staying sober and working with other alcoholics. Once we have such an active nucleus, we can then perhaps refer to them those inquiries which originate in their respective localities. Starting with small but active centers created in this fashion, we are hopeful that fellowships will spring up and grow very much as they have among us.

The Alcoholic Foundation is our sole agency of its kind. We have agreed that all business engagements touching on our alcoholic work shall have the approval of its trustees. People who state they represent The Alcoholic Foundation should be asked for credentials and if unsatisfactory, these ought to be checked with the Foundation at once. We welcome inquiry by scientific, medical and religious societies.

This volume is published by the Works Publishing Company, organized and financed mostly by small subscriptions by our members. This company donates the customary royalty from each copy of ALCOHOLICS ANONYMOUS to The Alcoholic Foundation.

To order this book, send your check or money order for $3.50 to:
Book orders ONLY to
Works Publishing Co.
Church Street Annex
Post Office Box 657
New York City

General Correspondence to
The Alcoholic Foundation
Church Street Annex
Post Office
Box 658
New York City

Note: The above information refers to conditions applicable in 1939
The current address of A.A. is:
Alcoholics Anonymous
P.O. Box 459, Grand Central Station
New York, NY 10163
U.S.A.

WHEN this book appeared in April 1939 there were approximately 100 A.A. members. Two thirds of them were at Akron, Ohio, or nearby communities in the northern part of that state. Most of the remainder were in or near New York City and a few others were scattered along the Atlantic Seaboard. The work had then been in existence over four years. It had been satisfactorily demonstrated that at least two out of three alcoholics who wished to get well could apparently do so, notwithstanding the fact that their chance of recovery upon any other medical or spiritual basis had been almost nil—a small percentage at best.

Publication of the book, which set down our experience and methods at length, opened a new and unexplored phase which meant an attempt to carry the work to other localities, widespread publicity, and the exposure of our methods to the test of approval or disapproval by religion, medicine, and the general public, an uncharted field indeed. Would theologians complain of our lack of orthodoxy? Would physicians frown upon the idea of banding together great numbers of alcoholics for mutual aid through a spiritual common denominator? Would reviewers and columnists ridicule the spiritual content of the work, thus prejudicing the men and women we were trying to help? Would alcoholic men and women and their families be convinced by the book and the attendant publicity that here at last was a solution? Such were the uncertainties of April 1939.

Remarkable as it may seem none of these anticipated difficulties has materialized. Clergymen of all faiths, Catholic, Protestant and Jewish, have united in generous approval of our activities. The Christian Science Monitor gave this book a favorable editorial review. Physicians who have observed us at close range are almost unanimous in their opinion that our methods are sound and the results most promising.

Best of all is the fact that alcoholics and their familes seize upon this book, perceive its practical application to their problems, and often take action by writing to The Alcoholic Foundation Office (Box 459, Grand Central Annex, New York 17) inquiring how they may get in touch with the nearest A.A. center, or asking directions for starting groups in their own communities. Innumerable inquiries have been answered by personal letter, relating those anxious to get well to the nearest A.A. membership. In notable instances The Alcoholic

Foundation* has fostered the creation of new centers about enthusiastic alcoholics who have derived their inspiration from the book alone.
In some cases the book has acted as a specific for alcoholism, for we
are in touch with men who have worked out their own recovery by simply following out the suggestions of the book.

Besides maintaining a correspondence with new people, our central
office keeps in touch with men who have recovered in established centers, who travel to other communities, or who find employment in new
places. Such individuals turn up sooner or later where new groups are
in process of formation contributing to their success and relating them
to the older memberships.

When it is considered that we have increased one hundred fold in
the last five years and when it is remembered that we are growing by a
sort of geometrical progression, each alcoholic as a part of his own
treatment working with others, one begins to ask how far A.A. may go.
Though we alcoholics are plagued with over active imaginations, we
shall surely have thousands of new members every year.

Then, too, it should be remembered that for each alcoholic, three
or four other persons are vitally affected spiritually as well as economically. Even now it is evident that these collateral benefits of our work
are large.

Cleveland, Ohio, is an interesting example. In the Fall of 1939
approximately 5 Cleveland alcoholics were attending meetings with
the already large group at Akron, Ohio. The *Cleveland Plain Dealer* ran
a series of articles on A.A. featuring them upon its editorial page. A
rapid and successful growth ensued. This community has many active
groups totaling hundreds of alcoholic men and women. This activity
includes perhaps thousands of additional individuals—families, employers, and friends—who say they have been vitally touched and bene-
fited. Suppose several thousand alcoholics, most of them able and
energetic men and women coming from all walks of life, eventually
recover. Surely the effect upon this city would be potent.

There is another aspect of our activity which has often been over-
looked. Though no accurate census has been taken, it is probable that

* See appendix I—We invite correspondence.

90% of active A.A. members are now employed. Most of them reestablished themselves economically with no other help than we give each other. We believe we have demonstrated that when an individual commences to think straight and elects a sound spiritual basis for his life, he will presently find a way to maintain himself. This spiritual principle, which looks to many people like threadbare rationalization, seems to be practically proven by our employment record. The simple arithmetic of the situation tells the story.

One might elaborate for pages upon what has taken place in the past few years. Stories of spectacular recoveries, of intense spiritual experiences, of happy social contacts, of regained health, of hundreds who have returned to their churches, of families reunited, of seemingly impossible differences composed, of renewed business success; such narratives might be set down by scores. Nor should we fail to mention other hundreds who have quietly stopped drinking and resumed normal life. We could also tell of heartbreaking failures, of seeing those for whom we have formed great attachments continue to disintegrate before our eyes. Such is the warp and woof of A.A. everywhere.

APPENDIX II

569:1THE terms "spiritual experience" and "spiritual awakening" are used many times in this book which, upon careful reading, shows that the personality change sufficient to bring about recovery from alcoholism has manifested itself among us in many different forms.

2Yet it is true that our first printing gave many readers the impression that these personality changes, or religious experiences, must be in the nature of sudden and spectacular upheavals. 3Happily for everyone, this conclusion is erroneous.

4In the first few chapters a number of sudden revolutionary changes are described. 5Though it was not our intention to create such an impression, many alcoholics have nevertheless concluded that in order to recover they must acquire an immediate and overwhelming "God-consciousness" followed at once by a vast change in feeling and outlook.

6Among our rapidly growing membership of thousands of alcoholics such transformations, though frequent, are by no means the rule. 7Most of our experiences are what the psychologist William James calls the "educational variety" because they develop slowly over a period of time. 8Quite often friends of the newcomer are aware of the difference long before he is himself. 9He finally realizes that he has undergone a profound alteration in his reaction to life; that such a change could hardly have been brought about by himself alone. 10What often takes place in a few months could seldom have been accomplished by years of self discipline. 11With few exceptions our members find that they have tapped an unsuspected inner resource which they presently identify with their own conception of a Power greater than themselves.

570:1Most of us think this awareness of a Power greater than ourselves is the essence of spiritual experience. 2Our more religious members call it "God-consciousness."

3Most emphatically we wish to say that any alcoholic capable of honestly facing his problems in the light of our experience can recover provided he does not close his mind to all spiritual concepts. 4He can only be defeated bv an attitude of intolerance or belligerent denial.

5We find that no one need have difficulty with the spiritual side of the program. 6Willingness, honesty and open mindedness are the essentials of recovery. 7But these are indispensable.

Note: Herbert Spencer quotation is located at it's original position on Page 387 of this volume.

INDEXES

This is an index to the conceptual cross-references contained throughout *The Applied Alcoholic Anonymous*. Every reference has the third edition page and sentence number followed by the page on which this reference appears in this volume. This index will be a helpful guide for personal and group study.

This table shows where in this volume 3rd Edition text may be found.